Moving People in Ethiopia

EASTERN AFRICA SERIES

Women's Land Rights & Privatization in Eastern Africa
Edited by BIRGIT ENGLERT
& ELIZABETH DALEY

War & the Politics of Identity in Ethiopia
Making Enemies & Allies in the Horn of Africa
KJETIL TRONVOLL

Moving People in Ethiopia
Development, Displacement & the State
Edited by ALULA PANKHURST
& FRANÇOIS PIGUET

*Living Terraces in Ethiopia**
Konso Landscape, Culture & Development
ELIZABETH E. WATSON

*Eritrea**
A Dream Deferred
GAIM KIBREAB

* *forthcoming*

Moving People in Ethiopia
Development, Displacement & the State

Edited by
ALULA PANKHURST
&
FRANÇOIS PIGUET

James Currey

James Currey
www.jamescurrey.co.uk
is an imprint of Boydell & Brewer Ltd
PO Box 9, Woodbridge, Suffolk IP12 3DF, UK
www.boydell.co.uk
and of Boydell & Brewer Inc.
668 Mt Hope Avenue, Rochester, NY 14620, USA
www.boydellandbrewer.com

© Contributors 2009
First published 2009
1 2 3 4 5 13 12 11 10 09

British Library Cataloguing in Publication Data

Moving people in Ethiopia : development, displacement & the state. -- (Eastern Africa series)
1. Migration, Internal--Ethiopia.
I. Series II. Pankhurst, Alula, 1962- III. Piguet, Francois.
304.8'0963-dc22

ISBN 978-1-84701-613-3 (James Currey Hardcover)

Typeset in 9/10½pt Baskerville
by Avocet Typeset, Chilton, Aylesbury, Bucks
Printed and bound in Great Britain by
CPI Antony Rowe, Chippenham, Wiltshire

In memory of Professor Seyoum Gebre Selassie
& Dr Mekonnen Bishaw

Contents

Part III
DEVELOPMENT-INDUCED DISPLACEMENT
Dams, Irrigation Parks & Urban Relocation

Part IV
THE EXPERIENCE OF STATE-ORGANIZED RESETTLEMENT

Part V
THE DILEMMAS OF REFUGEES, RETURNEES & DISPLACED GROUPS

Part VI
CONCLUSION

Acknowledgements

This book is an edited volume that includes chapters by fourteen other authors whose important contributions we wish to acknowledge. In particular we wish to thank Drs David Turton and Chris de Wet who played a vital role in providing international and theoretical perspectives. Professor Michael Cernea kindly agreed to write a preface to the book and made useful comments on the editors' chapters.

We had to reduce the number of chapters in this book and wish to acknowledge the work of those whose papers were included in the first proceedings but not in the book, notably Abate Jigo, Abdullahi Haji, Abiy Hailu, Abraham Sewonet, Bereket Tarekegn, Bezaiet Dessalegn, Lionel Cliffe, Dechassa Lemessa, Dinku Lamessa, Laura Hammond, John Kilowoko, Tafesse Mesfin, and Roberta Tranquilli. The initial workshop was organized by the Ethiopian Society of Sociologists, Social Workers and Anthropologists (ESSSWA), and the United Nations Emergency Unit for Ethiopia (now the UN Organization for the Coordination of Humanitarian Affairs, OCHA). We wish to thank the leadership and staff of both these organizations, notably Drs Ayalew Gebre, Gebre Yntiso and Yeraswork Admassie from ESSSWA and Paul Hebert, Ulrich Tobias Muller, Dechassa Lemessa and Abraham Sewonet from UNOCHA (ex-UNEUE) and Dr Wolde-Selassie Abbute who has since joined UNICEF. We also wish to thank government institutions and individuals who took part, notably the Administration for Refugee and Returnee Affairs and the Food Security Bureaux of Amhara, Oromia and Tigray Regions. In particular, we would like to thank Abate Jijo and Shumiye Abuhay for their contributions. Professor Lionel Cliffe, Dr Chris de Wet and Dr Johan Helland provided useful comments during and at the end of the workshop, and we also wish to thank the numerous participants.

Several donor organizations and their representatives provided useful reports and discussed their views with us, notably the UK Department for International Development, Irish Aid, the European Union, USAID and the World Bank. We wish to thank Fisseha Merawi, Hiwot Mebrate, Kevin Kelly, Veronique Lorenzo, Jonathan McKee, Michelle Philips, Nuala O'Brien, Tewodros Yeshiwork and Tim Waites. A number of NGOs and international organizations also shared their findings with us, notably ICRC, IOM, PCI, UNHCR, UNICEF, WFP and WHO. In particular, we would like to thank Abdi Umer, Louise Aubin, Gideon Cohen, Jarso Mokku, John Kilowoko, Lalem Berhanu, Gerit Van Uffelen and Robert Zimmerman. Several NGOs and their staff shared their concerns, notably Christian Aid, Concern, LVIA, MSF-Holland, MSF-France and ZOA. We also wish to acknowledge the work carried out by the Forum for Social Studies and the encouragement of its leadership, notably Ato Dessalegn Rahmato, Professor Bahru Zewde and Dr Taye Assefa, and the team that carried out a comparative study including Drs Gebre Yntiso, Kassahun Berhanu and Assefa Tolera, and the students: Abdurouf Abdurahman, Ayke Asfaw, Ahmed Mohammed, Asfaw Qeno, Asfaw Tihune, Desalegn Workneh, Driba Dadi, Fitsum Yeshitela, Mellesse Madda, Misganaw Eticha and Solomon Debebe. We should also like to acknowledge the useful work of numerous other students who wrote MA theses, and of researchers, notably Laura Hammond and Bezaeit Dessalegn, on whose reports we have relied.

We should also like to thank the previous Director of the French Centre of Ethiopian Studies, Dr Gérard Prunier, and the current Director, Dr François-Xavier Fauvelle-Aymar, for their encouragement. Special thanks are due to Professor Hans Hurni of the Centre for Development and Environment at Institute of Geography of the University of Bern, and Kaspar Hurni for producing the map. We wish to express our gratitude to our families for their encouragement during the time we spent working on this book. Last, but not least, we gratefully acknowledge the support of the Christensen Fund that enabled this book to be published, and we wish to thank in particular Tadesse Wolde and Ken Wilson for their faith in our work.

Acronyms

AAMPO	Addis Ababa Master Plan Project Office
AAU	Addis Ababa University
ARD	AIDS-related dementia
APF	African Parks Foundation
ARRA	Administration for Refugees and Returnees Affairs
AU	African Union
AVA	Awash Valley Authority
CISP	The International Committee for the Development of Peoples (*Comitato Internazionale per lo Sviluppo dei Popoli*)
CRMFADWV	Commission for the Rehabilitation of Members of the Former Army and Disabled War Veterans
CPR	common property resources
DfID	Department for International Development
DID	development-induced displacement
DIDR	development-induced displacement and resettlement
DIDPs	development-induced displaced persons
DPPA	Disaster Preparedness and Prevention Agency
EC	European Commission
EPRDF	Ethiopian People's Revolutionary Democratic Front
EEPCO	Ethiopian Electric Power Corporation
ERHS	Ethiopian Highlands Reclamation Study
EPLF	Eritrean People's Liberation Front
ESSSWA	Ethiopian Society of Sociologists, Social Workers and Anthropologists
EU	European Union
FDRE	Federal Democratic Republic of Ethiopia
FSCB	Food Security Coordination Bureau
FSPCO	Food Security Programme Coordination Office
FAO	Food and Agriculture Organization
FSS	Forum for Social Studies
GTZ	Gesellschaft für Technische Zusammenarbeit (German technical cooperation)
GWL	ground water level
HVA	Handels Vereeniging Amsterdam
HTP	harmful traditional practices
IAG	Inter Africa Group
ICRC	International Committee of the Red Cross

IDPs	internally displaced persons
IDR	Institute of Development Research
IDS	Institute of Development Studies
IEG	Imperial Ethiopian Government
IGAD	Inter-Governmental Authority on Development
ILO	International Labour Organization
IOM	International Organization for Migration
IMF	International Monetary Fund
IRR	Impoverishment Risks and Reconstruction
LVIA	Lay Volunteers International Association
Masl	meters above sea level
MoA	Ministry of Agriculture
MoARD	Ministry of Agriculture and Rural Development
MoFED	Ministry of Finance and Economic Development
MoLSA	Ministry of Labour and Social Affairs
MoUDH	Ministry of Urban Development and Housing
MSF	Médecins sans Frontières (Doctors without Borders)
MWARC	Melka-Warar Agricultural Research Centre
NCFSE	New Coalition for Food Security in Ethiopia
OECD	Organization for Economic Cooperation and Development
OFSPCO	Oromia Food Security Programme Coordination Office
OLF	Oromo Liberation Front
ONLF	Ogaden National Liberation Front
OSSREA	Organization for Social Science Research in Eastern and Southern Africa
PA	Peasant Association
PAPs	project-affected persons
PASDEP	Plan for Accelerated and Sustained Development to End Poverty
PCI	Pastoral Communication Initiative
PMAC	Provisional Military Administrative Council
PMGE	Provisional Military Government of Ethiopia
PRA	participatory rural appraisal
PDRE	Peoples' Democratic Republic of Ethiopia
PRS	Poverty Reduction Strategy
PTSD	post-traumatic stress disorder
REST	Relief Society of Tigray
RRC	Relief and Rehabilitation Commission
RSO	Regional State of Oromia
SAP	Structural Adjustment Programme
SDPRP	Sustainable Development and Poverty Reduction Programme
SENPRP	Southern Ethiopia National Parks Rehabilitation Project
SNNPR	Southern Nations, Nationalities and Peoples' Region
TADE	Tendaho Agricultural Development Enterprise
TB	tuberculosis
TGE	Transitional Government of Ethiopia
TPLF	Tigray People's Liberation Front
UNDP	United Nations Development Programme
UNEUE	United Nations Emergency Unit for Ethiopia
UNHCR	United Nations High Commissioner for Refugees

UNICEF	United Nations Children's Fund
UNMEE	United Nations Mission in Ethiopia and Eritrea
UNOCHA	United Nations Organization for the Coordination of Humanitarian Assistance
UNCHS	United Nations Centre for Human Settlements (Habitat)
UNRISD	United Nations Research Institute for Social Development
USAID	United States Agency for International Development
WCD	World Commission on Dams
WFP	World Food Programme
WRDAE	Water Resource Development Authority of Ethiopipa
WHO	World Health Organization
ZOA	Vluchtelingenzorg / Refugee Care (Netherlands)

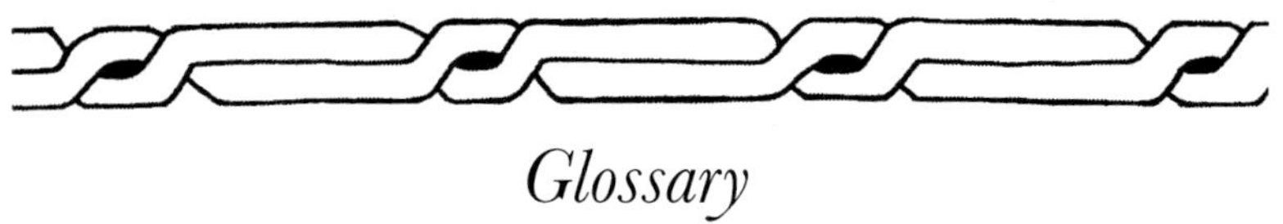

Glossary

All terms, unless otherwise indicated are Amharic.

Amicha	Affinal kin-based festive labour (Oromo)
Areke (*Areqe*)	Distilled alcoholic drink made from various local grains
Atmaki	Priest, involved in baptism
Balezar	Spirit mediums involved in imploring spirits, using incantations and medicinal herbs
Balinjera	Intimate friendship based on festive labour
Ballabat,	Landlord and/or clan leader
Ballo	A system of rotating cattle enclosures to obtain manured plots of land (Oromo)
Beati (*Bäati*)	Cave used during the civil war. It indicates abandoning civil life (Tigrigna)
Bego tetsi'ino	Well-intentioned coercion
Bel	Bond friends in South Omo (Hamar)
Beles (*Bäläs*)	Various *ficus*, including *vasta, carica*, etc.; fruits are regularly eaten and commercialized (Tigrigna)
Belg	Short rainy season between February and April mainly in the highlands
Birr	Ethiopian currency, 2.07 equivalent to US dollar in the mid-1980s, 7.25 in 1999, 8.6 in 2003, and about 10 in 2008.
Bisichu	Describes people who respond to life's problems with a great deal of irritability, intense gloom or severe anxiety
Buda	Evil eye; the possessed victim becomes ill, and may also succumb to shaking and incoherent vocalizations
bull'a	porridge made from *enset*
Chat (*khat, qat*) *catha edulis*	A plant that produces a mild narcotic intoxication when chewed and that grows and is consumed throughout the eastern Horn of Africa and in Yemen
Dabtara (däbtära)	Unordained member of the clergy, well versed in church learning; sometimes involved in healing and magical practices
Dabo (Däbo)	Large festive work parties organized for one day
Debri	House (Tigrigna)
Dega	One of the altitudinal agroecological zones between 2500 and > 3400 masl. with regional variations
Derg	Term for the Provisional Military Administrative Council (PMAC), which governed Ethiopia after the 1974 revolution

Duressa	Rich in terms of wealth according to previous land holdings, cattle size, number of wives, involvement in off-farm activities, etc. (Oromo)
Elfinna-qaso	Intimate friendship based on festive labour (Kambata)
Enset (Ensete ventricosum)	False banana tree
ferenj	Foreigner, particularly European
Fiqur	Bond friends in the northeast between Afar and Tigray highlanders (Tigrigna)
Ganda	Tray used for a coffee ceremony
Ganel gelach	Demons exorciser
Gebbar	Tenant-farmer paying the *gibir*, the main land tax
Gella	Dependent household with no land (Oromo)
Gereb	Customary institution for dispute settlement in the northeast between Afar and Tigray highlanders (Tigrigna)
Gesho (Rhamnus prinoides)	local plant used as alcohol fermentation agent
Gibri	Farm plot allocated to a household (called *Gibri*) can be full or half. Actual size of the *gibri* varies from one village to another depending on area available and population density (900 m2 to 2,500 m2) (Tigrigna)
Gidugelessa	Middle level in terms of wealth, according to previous land holdings, cattle holdings, number of wives, involvement in off-farm activities, etc. (Oromo)
Godo	Simple shelter literally meaning 'nest' (Oromo)
Gult	Lord's land rights, above all the right to collect taxes
Hadas	New (Tigrigna)
Hadra	Prayer ceremony organized among neighbours
Hash'o,	Mark made by the removal of a patch of bark (Tsamako)
Hidimo	Flat-roofed house (Tigrigna)
Hoko/Toro	Temporary mark made by banging pegs into tree trunk to indicate it has been booked for hanging a hive (Tsamako)
Ibd	Term used for people who wander naked in the streets and all forms of madness
Iddir	Funeral associations based on solidarity and mutual support to the mourning families
Injera	Pancake made mainly with *tef*, basic staple food in the Ethiopian diet
Iquy	Evil (Tigrigna)
Iqub	Rotating credit association (tontine)
Iyessa	Poor in terms of wealth according to previous land holdings, cattle holding, number of wives, involvement in off-farm activities, etc. (Oromo)
Kalazar	Also known as leishmaniasis, an illness spread by sandflies
Kayya	System of livestock-rearing for their use value (Oromo)
Kebele	Lowest tier of administrative divisions
Ketema	Garrison settlement and fortified town; currently a general term for town
Kiremt	Long rainy season between June and September

Kitta (qitta)	Circular pancake similar to bread
Kola (qolla)	Expression used for one of the altitudinal agroecological zones, the lowlands located below 1,500 metres, with an average annual precipitation of between 400 and 700 millimetres
Kristinna	Christening, and by extension godparent relationship
Likaso	Mark made by lopping which may be done before a tree is grown enough to support a bee hive (Tsamako)
Limmaano	Full-time supportive labour mostly for the disabled and needy (Oromo)
Mahber/Mehaber	Association of people with the same patron saint, meeting monthly on the saint's day in each others' houses in turn
Mana	House (Oromo)
Mangima	Bond friends between Gumuz and Highlanders in Metekel area (Gumuz)
Massa	Field, plot, about a quarter of a hectare
Meher	The long rainy season in parts of Ethiopia. *Kiremt* or *Meher* rains fall from June to September. Main growing season
Mefenakel	Literally meaning uprooting from normal life. *Indegena mefenakel* literally 'being uprooted again', by extension, refugee
Michu	Bond friends between Oromo, Gumuz, Shinasha, Agaw and Amhara (Oromo)
Mura	A generation-set among the Tsamako
Neftegna	Soldier-settlers of conquest period from the late 19th century.
Qaadi	Islamic judge in charge of application of Sharia law
Qocho	Staple food prepared with *enset*
Rist	System of hereditary land tenure
Sanga Midhani	Arrangement whereby grain is received in return for use of oxen (ploughing oxen/day for grain) (Oromo)
Sedqo	Customary conflict resolution mechanism between Somali and Amhara
Senbete	Association of people with the same patron saint, meeting monthly in a church compound and hosting the feast in turn
Siwa	Local beer (Tigrigna)
Tasa	Tin can used as measurement in the market place
Tebel	Holy water, believed to have healing properties
Tef (Eragrostis teff)	Highlands endemic cereal, the favourite Ethiopian grain used to bake *injera*
Tej	Mead, local fermented beverage made of honey, the consumption of which was associated in the past with noble status
Tella	Locally brewed beer usually made of barley and *gesho*
Tenkway	Sorcerers using spirit-invocation, divination, medicinal herbs, and animal sacrifices to cure clients
Tukul	Mud-plastered house with thatched roofing
Waari/maarfeja/toori	Supportive labour for the weak in the early hours of the morning before resettler-farmers go to their daily tasks (Oromo).
Wet	Staple spiced stew usually served with *injera*
Wenfel or *qaanja*	Pooling reciprocal labour
Wengele Werq	Register of tenure contracts in the church

Wereda	Administrative unit corresponding to the district level
Wetader sefer	Soldiers' area in a garrison town
Weyna dega	Middle altitudinal agroecological zone between 1600 to 2600 masl
Wofefe	People whose mood fluctuates suddenly
Woizero	Respectful title for women equivalent to Mrs
Wuqabi	Spirit which possesses people and requires exorcising
Yeafer iddir	Burial association
Yebetsira iddir	Association to construct houses together
Yeintil Korach	Uvula or tonsil cutters
Yekebt iddir	Local cattle insurance association
Yelimd awalaj	Midwives; traditional birth attendants
Yemedhanit awaki	Herbalist using traditional medicine
Yemote kedda	'Land of those who died and of deserters', which was redistributed
Yeqareza iddir	Association for transporting sick members to health centres
Yezimdina balinjera iddir	Funeral association of relatives and friends
Zar	Spirit-possession cult
Zelan	Nomad, derogatory term used to designate lowland pastoralists connoting normlessness

Notes on Contributors

Ayalew Gebre is Assistant Professor of Social Anthropology in the Department of Sociology and Social Anthropology, Addis Ababa University. He obtained his PhD in Development Studies from the Institute of Social Studies in the Netherlands. His thesis was published as *Pastoralism Under Pressure: Land Alienation and Pastoral Transformations among the Karrayu of Eastern Ethiopia, 1941 to the Present* (Shaker, 2001). He has carried out research on pastoralism, development, conflict management, civil society and HIV/AIDS.

Lewis Aptekar is Professor of Counselor Education at San Jose State University. He specialized in Clinical Psychology and has carried out research in Ethiopia on displaced people and in Kenya on street children, as well as in Colombia, Honduras, India, Swaziland and Zambia. His books include *Street Children of Cali* (Duke University Press, 1988) and *Environmental Disasters in Global Perspective* (Hall/Macmillan, 1994). He is President Elect of the Society for Cross-cultural Research.

Behailu Abebe obtained his PhD in 2005 from Queen Margaret University, with a thesis on 'War, Coping Mechanisms and Cultural Resources in Tigray, Ethiopia: Implications for NGO psychological programming'. He has written articles and chapters on his own and with colleagues on coping among war displaced people, street children and occupational minorities.

Micheal Cernea is Research Professor of Anthropology and International Affairs, George Washington University and Honorary Professor of Resettlement and Social Development of Hohai University. He has served for over two decades as the World Bank's Senior Sociologist and Senior Adviser for Social Policy and Sociology. He has authored, and edited and co-edited, numerous books on development and displacement, including *Putting People First: The Economics of Involuntary Resettlement* (World Bank, 1999*), Risks and Reconstruction: Experiences of Resettlers and Refugees* (World Bank, 2000), and *Can Compensation Prevent Impoverishment?* (Oxford University Press, 2008).

Chris de Wet is Professor of Anthropology at Rhodes University. He has worked on social-economic change in South Africa as well as resettlement issues internationally. His publications include *Moving Together, Drifting Apart. Resettlement Planning and Villagisation in a South African Homeland* (Witwatersrand University Press, 1995), *Transforming Settlement in Southern Africa* (Edinburgh University Press, 2001 and *Development-Induced Displacement: Problems, Policies and People.* (Berghahn Books, 2005).

Feleke Tadele is Country Representative of Oxfam-Canada, Ethiopia Program and has worked for the past fifteen years for several international NGOs. He obtained his MA degree in Social Anthropology in 1999 at Addis Ababa University. His thesis was published as *The Impacts of Urban Development on a Peasant Community in Ethiopia* (2006). He is currently completing PhD research in International Development at the University of Bath on migration. He has written articles and reports on internal displacement, migration, disaster management, development and gender.

Gebre Yntiso is Assistant Professor of Anthropology in the Department of Social Anthropology at Addis Ababa University. He obtained his PhD in Anthropology from the University of Florida with a thesis on resettlement. He has co-edited *Displacement Risks in Africa: Refugees, resettlers and their host population* (2005) and the *African Study Monographs, Supplementary Issue* No. 29 (2005). He has edited *Children At Risk: Insights from Researchers and Practitioners from Ethiopia* (2007). He has produced articles on migration and displacement, culture and development, food security, and inter-ethnic relations.

Getachew Kassa is a researcher at the Institute of Ethiopian Studies of Addis Ababa University. He obtained his PhD in Social Anthropology at the London School of Economics. His thesis was published as *Among the Pastoral Afar in Ethiopia, Tradition, Continuity and Socio-Economic Change* (International Books, 2001). He has authored numerous articles and book chapters relating to pastoralism, pastoral development and conflict resolution.

Kassahun Berhanu is Associate Professor of Political Science at Addis Ababa University. He obtained his PhD in political science from the Free University of Amsterdam. His thesis was published as *Returnees, Resettlement and Power Relations: the Making of a Political Constituency in Humera, Ethiopia.* (Free University Press, 2000). He has carried out research and authored articles and chapters on issues of governance and decentralization, refugees, resettlement, ethnic and social conflicts, democratization, electoral and constitutional processes, and the role of civil society organizations in socio-economic development. He is currently working as a guest researcher in the Nile Basin Research Program under the auspices of the University of Bergen, Norway.

Kassahun Kebede completed his MA thesis in Anthropology at Addis Ababa University in 2001 on the topic of 'Re-relocation and dislocation of communities by dam development projects: the case of Gilgel Gibe Dam (1962-2000) in Jimma Zone, Southwest Ethiopia'. He is currently working on his PhD at the Department of Anthropology, Maxwell School of Citizenship and Public Administration, Syracuse University on transnational migration among Ethiopian immigrants in the Washington metropolitan area.

Melesse Getu is Assistant Professor of Anthropology at Addis Ababa University, where he has served as Dean of the School of Social Work. His obtained his PhD in Anthropology from the University of Manchester in 2001. He wrote a thesis entitled 'A study of patterns of productive resource control among the Tsamako of Southwest Ethiopia'. He has authored several articles on the Tsamako and other issues related to pastoralism and development more widely, and is currently engaged in a five-year multidisciplinary research project in the area of public health.

Alula Pankhurst obtained his PhD from Manchester University in 1999. The book based on his thesis was published as *Resettlement and Famine in Ethiopia: the Villagers' Experience* (Manchester University Press, 2002). He has edited *Natural Resource*

Management in Ethiopia (Forum of Social Studies, 2001) and co-edited *Peripheral People: The Excluded Minorities of Ethiopia* (Hurst, 2003), *People Space and the State: Migration, Resettlement and Displacement in Ethiopia* (Ethiopian Society of Sociologists, Social Workers and Anthropologists, 2004) and *Grass-roots Justice in Ethiopia: The Contribution of Customary Dispute Resolution* (Centre Français d'Études Éthiopiennes, 2008).

François Piguet is a Lecturer at the Graduate Institute of International and Development Studies in Geneva, working within the Interdisciplinary Programme in Humanitarian Action. He has worked on social change among pastoralist societies and various topics linked with migration. His PhD thesis on economic history with a focus on sedentarization, survival strategies and the impact of food aid in the Horn of Africa was published as *Des nomades entre la ville et les sables: la sédentarisation dans la Corne de l'Afrique* (Karthala, 1998). He co-edited *People Space and the State: Migration, Resettlement and Displacement in Ethiopia* (Ethiopian Society of Sociologists, Social Workers and Anthropologists, 2004) and has authored articles related to internal migration, refugees and diasporas' business networks.

Taddesse Berisso is Associate Professor of Anthropology at the Institute of Ethiopian Studies of Addis Ababa University. He obtained his PhD thesis from Michigan State University in 1995. He wrote his thesis on 'Agricultural and rural development policies in Ethiopia: a case study of villagisation policy among the Guji-Oromo of Jam-Jam Awrajja'. He has published numerous articles on displacement, inter-ethnic relations, conflict, natural resources management and development issues.

David Turton is a Senior Research Fellow in the African Studies Centre at the University of Oxford, where he was formerly Reader in Forced Migration and Director of the Refugee Studies Centre. Before moving to Oxford he taught in the Department of Social Anthropology at the University of Manchester. His field research has been in southwestern Ethiopia, amongst the Mursi. His research interests have included warfare, ethnicity and the relationship between long-term ecological change and population movements, about which he has authored numerous articles.

Wolde-Selassie Abbute obtained his PhD from the University of Göttingen in Social Anthropology, Socio-economics of Rural Development and African Studies. His thesis was published as *Gumuz and Highland Resettlers: Differing Strategies of Livelihood and Ethnic Reaction in Metekel, Northwest Ethiopia* (Lit Verlag, 2004). He has authored articles on the human and environmental impact of resettlement which was also the subject of his MA thesis published by Addis Ababa University. He has worked for a number of UN agencies, international NGOs, and government organizations, and currently works for UNICEF.

Yisak Tafere completed his MA in Social Anthropology at Addis Ababa University in 2002 with a thesis entitled 'Socio-economic reintegration of ex-soldiers: a case of two cooperatives (one male and one female) in Addis Ababa'. He has authored several papers and articles relating to poverty, exclusion and reintegration, focusing on children and ex-soldiers. He has worked in the Wellbeing in Developing Countries project of the University of Bath as researcher and manager, and is currently working with the Young Lives Research Project as Lead Qualitative Researcher for Ethiopia.

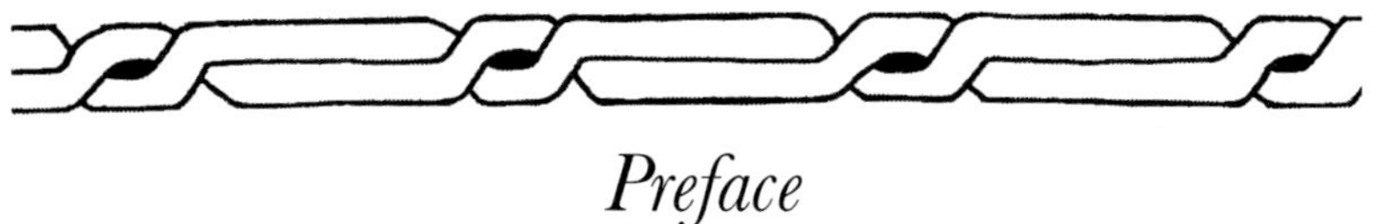

Preface

An Original Contribution
to Country-wide Displacement Analysis

MICHAEL M. CERNEA

Moving People in Ethiopia is the book long awaited by the international communities of researchers and practitioners working on forced resettlement processes and eager to understand and learn from Ethiopia's extraordinary experiences. It is also the book that, in my view, and rewardingly for the reader, fully meets head-on the unusual complexity of the many interwoven processes it examines historically, theoretically and empirically.

Resettlement processes in Ethiopia over the last 30-50 years have been so massive and frequent – or better said, so continuous – so nation-wide painful, so multi-causal and multi-form, that they secured for Ethiopia an unenviable special place in the history of the world's large-scale resettlements.

Ethiopia's unusual combination of displacement causes, types, magnitudes and outcomes has attracted international attention in many ways, ranging from the foreign donors' financial, technical or political assistance to the countless studies undertaken by social scientists, both Ethiopian and international. Yet, despite these innumerable studies, the intricate interwoven-ness of Ethiopia's population movements has proven hard to decipher plausibly and capture conceptually. It puzzled many scholars for many years, and it generated multiple contradictory and confusing interpretations. Controversies multiplied. The international social science literature on resettlement did embrace the valuable studies contributed by Ethiopian scholars themselves, primarily by Alula Pankhurst. But even the Ethiopian literature was incomplete and uneven in coverage, since it focused overwhelmingly on the major spatial population transfers related to drought and famine, with much less attention to other types of displacement, and also without attempting a comprehensive integration in some unitary conceptual or methodological approach. Thus, despite its rapid growth, the global resettlement literature has still been missing, until the publication of this, a comprehensive analysis of Ethiopia's experiences to date with displacement and resettlement (henceforth, D&R processes).

To place this volume in the context of the global resettlement literature, it must first be noted that the worldwide study of population displacement – caused by conflicts, disasters, and by development programmes – has vastly and rapidly expanded during the last two decades, surpassing several times the 'rate of growth' in prior decades in this domain. This has resulted in a new and growing body of empirical data, and also in a multiplication of policies on resettlement or in the codification of how-to-do guidelines and procedures. Some researchers regard the investigations in this domain as an emerging discipline or sub-discipline: the 'sociology of displacement' or the 'anthropology of displacement and resettlement'.

Nevertheless, despite this growth, only a very few books have been produced during this research explosion which deliberately attempted to examine simultaneously and comparatively major types of displacement within the same framework and use of the same concepts and analytical instruments. In line with this objective, *Moving People in Ethiopia,* under the guidance of Pankhurst and Piguet, is among the first two or three books in the world's literature which undertake the exacting task of encompassing all major types of population displacement and resettlement *at the level of an entire large country,* in a unitary manner. This is done, in this case, through the efforts of a group of researchers focusing empirically on different processes but putting together their findings with the aim of producing a well-informed synthesis about the substance, similarities and differences between the processes studied. This is certainly a daunting task. The result is a volume that will be enduring as a reference book on Ethiopia and as a significant enrichment of the worldwide literature on resettlement.

Several factors account for the worldwide growth of the resettlement research literature, mentioned above. Ethiopia's case should be considered vis-à-vis these factors as well. Among them are: the increasing magnitudes of the populations affected; the growing awareness of the disastrous effects of displacements and their political implications (although in the view of this writer, such awareness is still growing much too slowly); and the increasing opposition and organized resistance of the populations destructively affected by development-caused displacements.

On the magnitude of directly affected populations, the figures are nothing less than staggering. Researchers have calculated that in India alone, during the period 1949-2000, development programs have displaced over 60 million people (but resettled only a small fraction of them); in China, in a similar period (1950-2005), about 70 million people have been displaced. Every single year in the first decade of the twenty-first century, development programs forcibly uproot and displace from their houses and fields another cohort of populations conservatively estimated to total at least 15 million people, which is equivalent to between 150 and 200 millions for the decade. If the average period necessary for their relocation and livelihood restoration is estimated (conservatively as well[1]) to be only seven years, it means that the accumulated year-by-year cohorts of newly uprooted people represent at any point in time during this seven-year period over 105 million development-displaced people. The global figure of displacees is further compounded by the millions of people forcibly displaced every year by conflicts and wars,[2] and by the additional numbers of people displaced every year by natural disaster.

Within these horrible demographic proportions, the present book informs us that Ethiopia has had over 1.2 million people displaced over the last 30-35 years alone by its two waves of major state programs of population transfer. For the multiple other forced displacements, aggregate data are not yet available. Most displacements and resettlement processes took place during the Derg regime (started in 1974), but if the period we considered is 1950-2006, the number would be substantially larger. Furthermore, two outstanding factors must be considered beyond the size itself: first, *the diversity* of Ethiopia's D&R processes and second, *the extraordinary role the state has assumed* (under two different political regimes) in initiating national-scale campaigns for massive spatial population transfers.

The book's authors take collectively a holistic approach to forced displacements and cover all the main types of such displacements that have occurred in Ethiopia. At the same time, and to their credit, they do not ignore the fact that sometimes spontaneous (not forced) self-resettlement movements may also emerge from causes essentially similar to those of the forced resettlements and follow the same vectors.

For conflict- and war-related displacement, for instance, the book has rich material to explore, given the various wars and conflicts that have taken place in the Horn of Africa and also the direct Ethiopia-Eritrea war: all resulted in internally displaced persons and in refugees moving back and forth across borders. The book takes stock of such movements and of the many *sui-generis* population categories these conflicts have created: it focuses not only on the groups usually called 'internally displaced people' but also on the refugees, the returnees (whose relocation, given their numbers, is sometime an enormous problem), the demobilized soldiers and others. Ethiopia itself has been both a producer and a receiver of refugees and both a receiver and producer of returnees.

In sum, the conceptual apparatus employed in this book is remarkably diverse and refined to capture Ethiopia's specific situations.

For many of the types of displacement considered, the book reports findings from empirical analysis and also courageously engages in identifying not only outcomes that have already taken place but also likely trends for the future. One major conclusion emerges from this holistic analysis. In the past, resettlement in Ethiopia has been historically dominated by spatial population-transfer programs from the country's overcrowded highlands, which are chronically famine-prone, to the fertile and lower-density areas in the lowlands. This type of resettlement, in itself more radical than Tanzania's and Ethiopia's 'villagization' campaigns is far from having been uniform. It has itself caused conflicts between resettlers and hosts, and has generated some displacements among hosts as well.

In contrast, the book signals an important shift from this historical model. It states that Ethiopia has experienced in the current decade 'changing trends: notably development-induced displacement and its manifestations have become the most significant type of movement replacing earlier concerns with resettlement, refugees, returnees and demobilization'. Pankhurst and Piguet, as editors and synthesizers of the book's findings, also make another important observation: they note that the shift in the weight of development-caused displacement, compared with the previously predominant weight of environmentally triggered large population transfers, 'is beginning to be noticed by researchers, *but to date has not been sufficiently reflected in policy considerations… This requires greater attention to the right of displacees.*'

It is worth emphasizing that the book engages also in the important epistemological debate about the 'research divide' within and among the different research communities that separately study the displacements caused by the three major factors: conflict, disasters, and development. I have argued elsewhere myself that there are four very powerful reasons – empirical, theoretical, methodological, and political – for overcoming the research divide and excessive compartmentalization between the research communities engaged in studying the three types listed above. Focused and specialized research is obviously indispensable, but insularity in research is counterproductive. The book's opening theoretical chapter, contributed by David Turton – the British scholar who has the largest record of several decades of dedicated field research in Ethiopia – as well as the chapters contributed by Pankhurst and Piguet, take a similar stand in favor of bridging the divide, arguing for '*a unitary study of forced displacement*'. But the book goes far beyond a strictly theoretical argument. It undertakes a deliberate effort to overcome the research divide *in the book itself,* by analyzing and interpreting the findings and conclusions from research on various types on cases in Ethiopia.

For the book in its entirety, and particularly for the thinking developed in its Introduction and Conclusion, the unit of analysis is the country, rather than one or another individual case of displacement. The book displays a constant concern to highlight not just distinct types of displacement but how also these distinct types overlap, interact, and impact on each other in the country's social fabric. The studies constantly compare and contrast the different forms of displacement, stressing commonalities, differences, gray borders, instances when one type of displacement morphs into another type or takes on the characteristics of both types. This is a convincing demonstration in favor of bridging the divide.

An epistemic cause of the 'research divide' has been the fact that most individual studies of different instances of displacement were carried out and produced as scholarly reports disparate from one another. Disparate in this case means that these studies have been generated as stand-alone case studies, in different settings, at different points in time, and in different sectors, by individual researchers with little or no communication with each other. This definitely hampered comparison and synthesis, since the very units of analysis were unrelated. In contrast with that, the co-authors of the present volume have put an enormous emphasis on *contextualizing* each case study and on relating it comparatively to the other cases, always in the same country. The cognitive outcomes of this approach are obviously richer, and the book convincingly proves its point.

Certainly, within the broad mix of Ethiopia's displacement types, the single largest and most central process was the resettlement of over 1.2 million people under the population-transfer program from Ethiopia's highlands to its lowland areas. This process alone occurred in two phases: the first, during 1985-86 involving 192,000 households with about 600,000 people, and the second, during 2003-7 involving about 627,000 people. Controversies in interpreting this kind of population transfer have been abundant in the international literature, and will certainly continue. But it is gratifying to realize that this volume casts new interpretative light on this process, analysing its two phases, their causalities and their differences. The role of the state is central, and in the discussion of the two phases the perspective of '*seeing displacement as a State*', to use James Scott's expression, and the changes from one to the other, are amply documented and analysed. Alula Pankhurst, the author of the previous single most relevant book (1992) on the first phase of this process expands his analysis and brings it up to date, while also revising some of his own earlier analyses. This contribution of the volume is rich, and it is fair to say that the resettlement literature has gained through it an important building block.

Four distinct chapters of the volume each deal with one of four major types of development-induced displacement, following a sectoral approach. The studies refer to the construction of dams, to agricultural development projects and irrigation schemes as triggers of displacement, to the establishment of national parks, and to urban expansion. Each contributes significant, most interesting empirical findings and analysis. The integrative approach taken by the volume is obvious here too, in that several other chapters in turn also deal substantively with the theoretical issues, policy issues, or practical operational dimensions of development-caused displacement. These are the studies in the sections on theory and on the experience of state-organized resettlement.

The analytical contributions on development-related displacements (Kassahun Kebede, Ayalew Gebre, Getachew Kassa, Melesse Getu, Taddesse Berisso, Feleke Tadele, Gebre Yntiso and Wolde-Selassie Abbute) greatly add to what has been known previously about displacement in Ethiopia, regarding the major schemes of population transfers. In analysing the social impacts of such displacements, several authors use the Impoverishment, Risks and Reconstruction (IRR) model and highlight the paradox of impoverishment generation under projects which in fact are undertaken to reduce poverty. Through these and other chapters, the volume joins the ongoing and constantly expanding international debate about the unacceptability of impoverishing people and of creating new poverty while manifestly aiming for development.

Impoverishment under development programs diminishes the idea of development and the development's outcomes. The use of the impoverishment risks model enables the researchers to de-construct the syncretic process of impoverishment into its components and to highlight the mechanics of such processes by showing how the risks inflicted and not adequately counteracted victimize large segments of the country's citizenry. About this terrible social pathology – the unnecessary and unacceptable impoverishment through development-induced displacement – Chris de Wet's study asks his cutting, exasperated question: 'Why do thing often go so wrong in resettlement projects?' Writing from another part of the continent, Southern Africa, de Wet broadens the book's scope, corroborates its findings, and asks for the governments' recognition of complexities in displacement not just in policy discourse or in a set of partial 'inputs', but through a changed, altogether reformed way of organizing, financing and executing resettlement.

By revealing so forcefully the cluster of impoverishment risks, this volume opens a new chapter in the history of resettlement research in Ethiopia. Much will still have to be written and added to this chapter, as various development projects move to the front of the country's agenda. Much more research is needed and many findings will have to be publicly reported, no matter how distressing they are. New problem-solving solutions will have to be found in Ethiopia itself, with the help of social science researchers, to these daunting problems.

Certainly, the cumulative excellence of the present volume is rooted in the manner in which the research and analyses it reports were developed and brought together into a multifaceted yet unified book, meticulously constructed by its two editors. In contrast to many other volumes, this is not simply a happenstance collection of studies, but an integrated macro- and micro-research product resulting largely from the mutually complementary analyses of a group of researchers. Although from far away, I had the privilege of interacting with the group and witnessing the preliminary stages of the book's preparation. Well-known scholars have worked hand in hand with a number of young researchers in producing the building blocks of this endeavor. It is remarkable that within this book graduate students are joining, with their research findings, some of their professors and together they are presenting a forceful argument based on a broad spectrum of data, distilled through iterative debates and preliminary earlier presentations. The overall result is richer for that, more refined, better verified and interpreted more deeply. The data are squeezed of their meanings far beyond what appears visible at first sight.

I feel privileged to introduce this landmark volume to its expected international and national readership, confident that it will not only serve scholarly and learning interests but will also provide equipment for better policies and practical actions in a domain that is fraught with enormous complexity. Ethiopia's experiences have gained a new scholarly examination apt to inform fruitfully both the country itself and the international community.

Washington, DC

Notes

1. The condition of being economically displaced starts often even *before* the actual physical expulsion from the departing location. Their physical arrival at a different place should not be confused with 'the end of displacement', which is defined as relocation plus restoration of prior livelihood. The losses caused by the condemnation of land, house and assets, by expropriation and forced displacement, take a long time to be overcome. People who become worse-off remain impoverished for many long years until they can reconstitute their previous levels and reach the point where they would have been anyway 'without the project' which displaced them. This is why we see such a 7-year period as conservative, or more accurately as an underestimate. For large numbers of people, it takes much more than 7 years to reach at their relocation place a level of livelihood comparable to their pre-project level; achieving, on top of restoration, an 'improvement' takes even longer. A syndrome reported by many researchers studying the impoverishment risks inflicted on those displaced is that the actual impoverishment effects extend over an entire generation. Other researchers conclude that forced displacement and the loss of housing, land, means of production and access to common property resources, combined with sub-compensation levels and absence of investments and development-benefits sharing, jointly result in impoverishment effects over two generations.

2. Conflicts and wars result in waves of both internally displaced people and cross-border refugees, and these distressed population waves ebb and flow from one year to another. UNHCR indicated that at the end of 2002, the world's refugee population stood at approximately 10.6 million people (cf. UNHCR 2004, *2002 Statistical Yearbook*. UNHCR: Geneva).

Foreword

ALULA PANKHURST & FRANÇOIS PIGUET

> The aggregate analyses of recent social research glaringly reveal and factually document that new impoverishment is now taking place in Africa. This must be recognized as the biggest paradox, and the most unacceptable, in induced development: the fact that some development programs, although launched, financed, and designed to reduce poverty, end up causing more poverty to a segment of their populations. (Cernea 2005:240)

Development worldwide has increasingly involved population displacement. A recent estimate puts the global figure of annually displaced at 15 million people, adding up to about 280 to 300 million over 20 years. This represents a significant increase on the World Bank estimate in 1994 of 10 million displaced annually by public sector projects alone, or a total of 200 million people (Cernea 2008a:20). Ethiopia is no exception to this trend; population displacement, resulting from development as well as conflict, drought and conservation, has been on the increase since the 1960s. Ethiopia's pivotal position within the Horn of Africa and the internal dynamics between the central highlands and peripheral lowlands, as suggested in our introductory chapter, have been significant features in the country's historical and spatial social formation. Over the past fifty years the state through successive regimes has played a central role in developing the river valleys and lowlands, constructing dams, establishing conservation areas and organizing resettlement. The recent history of conflict in the Horn of Africa has also led to large-scale population movements of refugees, returnees, internally displaced groups and demobilized soldiers. The context of drought and food insecurity in the mid-1980s and again in the early 2000s added a further rationale and impetus for organizing state-led resettlement programmes. The increasing drive for development, involving the promotion of state and private agricultural investment in irrigated agriculture, expanding hydropower through the construction of dams, promoting tourism through establishing parks, and stimulating urban growth through increased investment, housing projects and expanding the road network, has also resulted in considerable displacement. Resettlement schemes for drought-affected people, refugees, returnees, pastoralists and demobilized soldiers as well as state and private investment projects have tended to converge in the river valleys and border lowlands, increasing pressure on resources and alienating the customary land and resource rights of local people, notably pastoralist groups, often leading to competition and sometimes resulting in unresolved conflict.

This book for the first time brings together studies of the different types of development, conflict and drought-induced displacement in Ethiopia, and analyses the conceptual, methodological and experiential similarities, overlaps and differences between the various forms of displacement. The issues were first raised at a workshop held in January 2003 organized by the Ethiopian Society of Sociologists, Social Workers and Anthropologists (ESSSWA) and the United Nations Emergency Unit for Ethiopia (UN-EUE) (now the Organization for the Coordination of Humanitarian Assistance - OCHA). At that time a new resettlement programme was being discussed as part of the development of a sustainable food-security strategy for Ethiopia. The editors were aware that much research had been carried out on this and related topics of displacement; however, there had been limited debate and dialogue between researchers, practitioners and policy-makers. Both editors had worked on the topic, on related aspects of these issues. Alula Pankhurst conducted research and wrote a book on the 1980s Ethiopian resettlement (Pankhurst 1992a) and from 1990 worked with Addis Ababa University colleagues, several of whom had carried out research on displacement issues; François Piguet published his research on pastoralism and food security in the Horn of Africa (Piguet 1998), and maintained his interest in pastoralism, displacement and refugees while working for the UN-EUE from 2001.

The workshop enabled researchers to present findings on a wide range of displacement issues including resettlement, and benefited from the participation of international scholars who had worked on forced migration issues, notably David Turton, who had been Director of the Refugee Studies Centre of Oxford University and presented a paper developing a common framework for the field of forced migration, Chris de Wet who had studied resettlement in South Africa and internationally and spoke about the reasons for the failure of resettlement projects worldwide, and Dr Lionel Cliffe who had advised the Oromia Region on Resettlement. The workshop also provided the opportunity to discuss and debate the papers with policy-makers and practitioners in government, UN and other international organizations and NGOs. The proceedings were published a year and a half later in July 2004 (Pankhurst and Piguet 2004a). This volume includes a selection of edited papers from the workshop proceedings, which have been revised and updated by the authors, taking into consideration changes and recent developments.

In the five years since the workshop took place there have been significant developments and changes in trends in the field of migration and displacement in Ethiopia and neighbouring countries, notably in relation to resettlement and development-induced displacement. A large-scale resettlement programme has been carried out already, involving over half a million people. The chapter by Pankhurst reviews the recent resettlement in comparison with the earlier phase in the 1980s. The high rate of growth and the drive for development through irrigation, dams, rural and urban investment and development have accelerated displacement trends. There have also been a considerable number of new studies, especially masters theses by students at Addis Ababa University. The editors review recent trends, developments, research and major issues regarding each of the types of displacement in the introductory and concluding chapters, and consider the similarities and differences between the various forms of displacement, their inter-relations and cumulative effects, particularly in the river valleys, lowlands and borderlands.

Outline of the book

In the introductory chapter the editors contextualize the issues in a broader historical and geographical framework within Ethiopia and the Horn of Africa. We argue for the need to understand the issues of migration and displacement in terms of highland – lowland dynamics and the role of the state. The chapter provides an overview of the consequences for pastoralists, the story of resettlement, various forms of development-induced displacement, and flows of forced migrants across and within the borders of Ethiopia. We conclude by highlighting the inter-related nature of different forms of migration concentrated in the lowlands and borderlands of Ethiopia tending to generate conflicts at local and regional levels.

THEORETICAL AND INTERNATIONAL PERSPECTIVES

Part II is composed of two chapters providing academic synthesis and international comparisons. The first, by David Turton, addresses the question of establishing a common framework for the study of forced migration. Cernea (1996a, 2000) had argued that there were empirical, theoretical, methodological and political reasons for bridging the research divide. Voutira and Harrell-Bond (2000:56) saw the need of 'arriving at a theoretical model of resettlement that applies to different situations of forced migration – those resulting from impoverishment, civil strife or "development" projects that uproot populations' as a 'major challenge' facing researchers. Turton takes up this issue, starting by noting that international attention has been focused on refugees and more recently internally displaced persons (IDPs). Even though they represent much larger numbers, less attention has gone to understanding those displaced by development projects such as parks, dams, or irrigation projects and by government-sponsored programmes using resettlement as a means of rural development and political control. He argues that a focus on the experiences of forced migrants and the challenges they face in re-establishing themselves in a new place reveals similarities between refugees and other forced resettlers on both empirical and conceptual levels. He refers to the analytical framework developed by Cernea (1997, 2000) on impoverishment risks and reconstruction (IRR), which considers eight inter-related impoverishment risks: landlessness, joblessness, homelessness, marginalization, increased morbidity and mortality, food insecurity, loss of access to common resources and services and social or community disarticulation. Conceptually, both categories have an ambiguous relationship to the nation state. Refugees in contradiction with the states they came from and seeking asylum elsewhere share similarities with forced resettlers displaced 'in the national interest' to make way for development projects. Many of the latter are economically and politically marginal minorities whose displacement is justified as required in the interest of the majority as represented by the state.

In his chapter seeking to explain the widespread failure of resettlement schemes worldwide, Chris de Wet starts by reviewing the few cases that have been hailed as successes. He critiques the conventional overly optimistic 'inadequate inputs' approaches which claim that resettlement can be made to work if the right economic and technical solutions are found. Instead he proposes an 'inherent complexity' approach suggesting that resettlement gives rise to a range of inter-related cultural, social, environmental, economic and institutional problems which together result in the likelihood of failure. de Wet complements the discussion of 'risks' proposed in the Cernea model (Cernea 2000) with the notion of 'threats'. He outlines how these threats operate at different levels from the individual and household to the community and project as an institutional process, which is linked to regional, national and even international levels. His conclusion echoes that of Robinson (2002) suggesting that 'forced relocation is more likely to be damaging to poor people's livelihood prospects than it is to improve them'.

Four of the case-study chapters in this book, those by Gebre, Wolde-Selassie, Kassahun and Feleke, make use of Cernea's IRR model to understand risks and reconstruction. Moreover, these create a bridge between development-induced displacements as they have been studied classically in relation to dams, agricultural projects, parks and urban expansion to consider resettlement programmes. As Cernea noted (2005:225): 'Taken together, they embody an important expansion in the analytical use of the IRR model beyond the category of development-displacements to the category of state programs for population territorial transfer and redistribution.'

DEVELOPMENT-INDUCED DISPLACEMENT

Though it is less visible and researched than many other forms of displacement, development-induced displacement has become an increasingly important phenomenon worldwide (Cernea 1996b), and particularly in Africa (Cernea 2005). In Ethiopia development-induced displacement until recently had not been the subject of much research, and in 2003 resettlement programmes were the main focus of the workshop and its proceedings. Five years later development-induced displacement has become a dominant concern, and can be expected to become even more significant with increasing national requirements for hydropower, irrigation, food security, cash crops and biofuel production. Part III of the book is composed of four chapters on different forms of development-induced displacement. The chapters relate to four major types resulting from: (i) hydro-power dams; (ii) irrigated agricultural schemes; (iii) the creation of parks; and (iv) urban expansion.

The first form of displacement relating to the effects of dams is addressed by Kassahun Kebede in his case study on the Gilgel Gibe Dam resulting in the resettlement of people living in the flooded area. The chapter uses Cernea's IRR framework to discuss the struggles of the resettlers to re-establish their livelihoods and social institutions and highlights the importance of settler participation in impoverishment-risk reversal. Kassahun considers differential adaptation depending on a number of factors including gender, age, wealth, and domestic cycle, and argues that social institutions play an important role in mediating risks.

The effects of recent dam construction in the Awash Valley for irrigation and the Beles and Omo-Gibe Valleys for hydropower have yet to be known. The potential effects of regulated flow and loss of alluvial soils and seasonal flooding required for flood-retreat irrigation in the Lower Omo and Lower Awash, and the question of water allocation in periods of drought and excessive rains, are potential causes for concern. There are ambitious plans by the Ministry of Water Resources and the Ethiopian Electric Power Corporation for further dams for irrigation for the production of cash crops, for hydropower for national consumption and export to neighbouring countries and for biofuels production stimulated by Western interests. These trends suggest that the issues relating to development-induced displacement are likely to become more prominent and that the need to reconcile national with local interests will become even more pertinent in the coming years.

The second and possibly the most prevalent form of displacement results from the es-

tablishment of dams for irrigated agriculture in the lowlands. The chapter by Getachew Kassa and Ayalew Gebre focuses on the Afar and Karrayu in the Awash Valley and the chapter by Melesse Getu on the Tsamako in the Wayto Valley. The authors point out that the introduction and expansion of irrigated mechanized farming and the setting aside of large areas of grazing land for national parks have had considerable socio-economic as well as political impacts on the agro-pastoralist subsistence economy.

In the Awash Valley the involvement and participation of the agro-pastoralist groups in the agricultural schemes is limited and has benefited mainly clan leaders and migrants from elsewhere. Land alienation reduced the resource base notably for grazing and pushed pastoralists into more marginal areas. In the Wayto Valley the irrigation affected the riverine bio-diversity as well as customary irrigation and gathering and hunting, and resulted in conflicts with migrants. The case studies raise common issues about land-tenure rights, restricted access to the best traditional irrigation and grazing areas, pressure on natural resources, effects on patterns of transhumance, impacts of in-migration on the environment and native people, and socio-economic change within agro-pastoral societies. The authors imply that both state-led and private investment in irrigated schemes have tended to be detrimental to the interests of local people living in marginal areas.

They conclude that the current process of decentralization requires a genuine devolution and consequently the active participation of local groups in the management of natural resources. Furthermore, the rights of agro-pastoral societies whose livelihoods are based on transhumance and irrigation need to be protected in a context of increasing economic and political pressure on resources and where the interests of investors may override those of remote and voiceless people. This may require the development of guidelines for resource sharing and resolving conflicts involving formal and customary institutions, in which government and other agencies could play mediating roles. There is thus a need to find a balance between protecting the rights and interests of marginalized groups of agro-pastoralists as defined in the Constitution, and promoting development in the national interest. This should involve negotiated resource sharing, as well as compensation and benefits in terms of infrastructure and service development for displaced and affected groups.

The third form of displacement has resulted from the creation of parks. This was discussed in the Karrayu case mentioned above in the chapter by Ayalew and Getachew and is the topic of the case study by Taddesse Berisso, on the displacement of Guji Oromo due to the creation of the Nech Sar National Park. Wildlife reserves and game parks have resulted in controversy between the interests of natural resource conservation and tourism, the needs of local populations and economic development worldwide and especially in Africa (Chatty and Colchester 2002). Taddesse shows that there has been very limited local participation let alone compensation in the planning and implementation of the resettlement programme, which did not adhere to international standards, had limited development funds and revealed a lack of concern for the rights of the local population.

Furthermore, in the Ethiopian context the ethnic federal structure and concessions to foreign investors have raised further issues. The Nech Sar park is located in the Southern Nations, Nationalities and Peoples Region (SNNPR) but on the borders with Oromia. Whereas the Kore people were resettled outside the park by the SNNPR authorities, most of the Guji-Oromo resisted resettlement in a situation of inter-regional state negotiations. The current context of national and international concerns over the rights of people and wildlife provides an opportunity to rethink national policy on parks, with a view to protecting the rights of local people, involving them in park management and tourism, questioning the wisdom of reliance on foreign investment for park management and agricultural development in the vicinity of parks, and reworking Federal and Regional responsibilities for park management.

The fourth form of displacement results from urban growth and the relocation of poor people from urban centres allocated for government housing and private investment to the suburbs, and the displacement of farmers in the peri-urban areas as cities expand. Feleke Tadele's case study in this book deals with the consequences for rural communities surrounding the capital, Addis Ababa. His chapter applies the processual model developed by Colson (1971) and Scudder (1993) and Cernea's impoverishment risks framework, and examines the consequences of dispossession, the risks of impoverishment for different types of household, and the various coping mechanisms pursued. Feleke argues for clear, consistent and fair policies and practices, respecting rights to compensation and minimizing the negative consequences of urban development projects. With increasing urbanization, a vigorous urban development policy, and the attraction of urban investment, these issues are likely to become increasingly prominent in the future.

RESETTLEMENT IN THE MID-1980s AND 2000s

Part IV consists of three chapters, two of which relate to resettlement in the mid-1980s and the third which considers the recent resettlement from 2003 and compares it with the earlier resettlement. The two chapters by Gebre Yntiso and Wolde-Selassie Abbute are based on their respective PhD fieldwork in the Pawe resettlement in the Beles Valley in the Metekel area. Both authors refer to the Impoverishment Risks and Reconstruction framework, with Wolde-Selassie's chapter focusing on the reconstruction aspects, and highlight the inducements and propaganda that persuaded settlers to move, and the lack of feasibility studies, proper planning and preparation. Gebre highlights the impacts on the 'hosts' as the 'hidden losers'. He also provides an important theoretical discussion of types of displacement, critiquing the simple voluntary-forced dichotomy and proposing a more sophisticated typology. He concluded that famine was the central concern, but that the government may have had additional aims. He notes a difference between the earlier and later settlers. The former volunteered, some out of desperation, others being famine migrants, already in shelters, viewing resettlement as temporary migration and attracted through deceptions and inducements, or because relatives had resettled. However, after mid-1985 resettlement became forced as peasants' hopes of obtaining crops rose with the coming of the rains and they no longer wanted to leave, whereas guidelines and quotas were imposed and sometimes abused to resettle people through corruption, favouritism, revenge and arbitrary round-ups from homes, market places, farms and relief centres.

Wolde-Selassie's chapter considers two phases in the resettlement process. The first was characterized by social disintegration of the previous institutions based notably on kinship, neighbourhood, friendship and religion, as well as burial, credit and work groups. Settlers who had lived in groups with a sense of belonging and community were mixed with strangers in large settlements, leading to social disarticulation, characterized by the break-up of families, resulting in particular difficulties for divorcees and widows. The lowland diet was unfamiliar and disliked, the climate was harsher, and diseases, notably malaria, took their toll. State control on production and exchange was imposed, and individual and group rights, notably of movement and religion, were curtailed. Relations with the local inhabitants, whose way of life had been seriously affected and whose resources had been expropriated by the settlements, were hostile, leading to serious clashes. The second phase was characterized by social rearticulation and livelihood reconstruction. Settlers re-established relationships both within the settlement and with neighbouring areas. Elders began to play an important role again; burial and religious associations and leaders re-emerged, assisting adaptation and providing a sense of optimism. With the withdrawal of collectivized production systems, smallholder production involving reciprocal and festive work groups and mutual help schemes was re-established. Trade and markets and entrepreneurial activities became important adaptive strategies. Wolde-Selassie argues that the re-established social institutions enhance access to livelihood resources, provide social security and safety nets, and facilitate local self-governance.

Gebre portrays a much bleaker picture of conditions in Metekel and considers the resettlement to be 'nothing but a failed project and a reminder of despair'. He describes the initial hardships, malnutrition, diseases and suffering of the settlers, especially in the first year, and the way in which the mechanized collectives and the massive Italian assistance failed, making the settlers more dependent and even poorer. Gebre also documents the abuse of the human rights of movement, religious observance, forming associations and engaging in social gatherings in the late 1980s. With the withdrawal of earlier massive Italian support in 1990, health and education services declined, mills and water pumps broke down and many settlers once again faced famine, notably when they were unable to pay for tractor services in 1995 and sought to re-establish ox-plough cultivation in unfavourable conditions. In the late 1990s differentiation occurred and his chapter also highlights ways in which the local population, the Gumuz, were excluded, dispossessed and displaced, losing their lands and the natural resources upon which they relied, notably the forests and the wild plants, game, fish and honey which were part of their livelihood. The Gumuz were also affected by diseases spreading from the settlements and a series of clashes had occurred by 1994. Gebre also notes the devastating effect on the environment with the clearing of the bush for cultivation and the cutting of trees for housing and fuel, resulting in considerable erosion and loss of soil fertility. He concludes that the Meketel resettlement caused livelihood deterioration, major health risks and lethal conflict over resources.

The chapter by Pankhurst reviews the recent trends in resettlement from 2003 to 2007 in comparison with the earlier resettlement of the 1980s, on the basis of recent studies. The need to find durable solutions to food insecurity, escaping aid dependence and addressing land shortage, is considered to explain the resurgence of resettlement as a key element of recent policy, despite awareness of the problems with the earlier resettlement. Similarities between the two phases include: the change in gear as a result of drought; basic concerns with food security as well as developing 'underutilized' lowlands; large-scale, state-led programmes with targets of numbers and a predetermined time-scale with limited consideration of direct costs and considerable indirect costs; government organization with scepticism from donors and NGOs and limited support; a campaign approach with limited time for planning and increases in numbers beyond earlier planning; a concentration in the lowlands and borderlands with high disease challenges; limited participation of settlers in the process; portrayal of resettlement in idealized terms with unrealistic promises; limited consultation with local people and opposition and lack of compensation over lost resources leading to tensions and conflict.

However, significant differences between the two periods include: an emphasis on voluntariness which was, however, constrained by drought conditions, social pressures and unfulfilled promises; land rights being guaranteed to settlers in their home areas for three years; inter-regional resettlement which did not completely avoid cultural and livelihood differences and resource conflict; more consideration, with some donor assistance, of planning, which was not always adhered to; prior visits to resettlement areas by community representatives; consultation of local communities who, however, often expressed opposition; better preparations of resettlement areas, although problems did arise in the provision of food, shelter, equipment and tools; better transport conditions; land and oxen provided on a household basis, though limited land availability, lack of clarity over whether the oxen were granted or loaned and livestock diseases present constraints; lack of the elements of control under the Derg resettlement; and more sustainable forms and limited levels of assistance, with large numbers of settlers becoming self-sufficient, although the ability of most of them to become rapidly self-reliant may have been overestimated, and longer-term issues of environmental sustainability and relations with local people remain unresolved.

Overall, most of the abuses, shortcomings and failures of the earlier resettlement were avoided. However, a range of problems re-emerged, in part as a result of the similarities in the state-led, large-scale relocation from the highlands to the lowlands in the context of food security with insufficient consideration of integration with people already living in the area. The pillars, principles and approaches set out in the New Coalition for Food Security document prepared jointly by government and donors provided an exemplary framework. However, the elements referring to a participatory, demand-driven, consultative, processual and community-managed design were in contrast to aspects of the programme which were pre-planned and state-led, and the ideals set out were not always adhered to.

The chapter also considers longer-term implications of resettlement based on the changing experiences of the 1980s resettlers, arguing that the longer-term implications are often unpredictable, depending on changeable political contexts. However, with time a greater material and social investment has taken place and, with the second generation born in the settlements becoming a majority, settlers' identities and sense of belonging have changed. Ultimately, though, the longer-term sustainability depends on establishing collaborative economic and social relations with local people.

The chapter further considers resettlement as a process in terms of three phases: (i) planning, costing, recruitment, site selection and preparation; (ii) relocation, transport and monitoring of infrastructure, services and assistance; and (iii) creating sustainable conditions for adaptation to lowland conditions, fostering positive relations with local people, preserving the environment and promoting self-reliance. Recommendations for improving current resettlement practice are put forward following this processual framework.

However, many of the problems with the current model of resettlement are arguably inherent and may be unavoidable. Pankhurst suggests that an alternative model that is more demand-driven, based on decision-making by the settlers, with the involvement of host communities, and aiming at joint development deserves to be considered. Such a model would seek to place resettlement within a broader migration framework that encourages linkages between the highlands and lowlands and promotes beneficial migration, while ensuring that the rights of people already living

in the lowlands are respected, that environmental concerns are addressed and that joint development between hosts and settlers is prioritized. This would imply a change of policy paradigm towards creating an enabling environment for enterprising migrants and simultaneously developing a regulatory framework that protects natural-resource rights and promotes sustainable usages and development.

REFUGEES, RETURNEES, DISPLACED GROUPS AND DEMOBILIZED SOLDIERS

Part V includes four chapters relating to refugees, returnees, displaced groups and demobilized soldiers. The different categories are often studied and treated in separate or different ways. However, they share some experiences, and the problems associated with settlement and resettlement. Many have experienced traumas of war, which may have left invisible scars, and from which they need time to recover. They may be isolated or neglected with limited recognition and assistance. By considering these categories within the same section, we would hope that the reader can see the parallels and that a better understanding of the common problems that they face can be developed.

The first chapter by Aptekar and Behailu is concerned with refugees from Eritrea who had Ethiopian origins, were expelled and ended up in a camp on the outskirts of Addis Ababa. The chapter focuses on the social and psychological effect of displacement. The authors consider moral dilemmas of humanitarian assistance, and discuss how their views and the coping styles of the displaced influenced their attempts to begin a mental health program during nearly two years of ethnographic fieldwork. The study considered the social marginalization of the people traumatized by war and sought to train some members to help others, and provide help with education, nursing and psychiatric care. This was seen as a form of empowerment, which, coupled with the people's spiritual traditions, helped them deal with their difficult life circumstances

The second chapter by Kassahun Berhanu, based on his PhD thesis, considers the case of refugee returnees from Sudan who were resettled in the lowlands of Tigray Region. The chapter presents a relative success story of this joint venture by UNHCR, the World Food Program (WFP) and the Ethiopian government. This resettlement was fairly small-scale, and by 1996 the resettled families had become self-sufficient and even started asset reconstitution. The chapter seeks to answer whether similar planned resettlement in other areas could bring a comparable situation of self-sufficiency of vulnerable groups, and what conditions are necessary to ensure sustainability of the initial success noted in such resettlement programmes.

The third chapter by Behailu Abebe, again based on his PhD research, discusses internal displacees who left the border area with Eritrea as a result of the war. The chapter describes the displacees' experiences of coping with war and internal displacement, in three phases. The first deals with the relatively prosperous conditions before the war, when the area had benefited from border exchanges between the new Eritrean state and landlocked Ethiopia. The second describes the trauma of the war situation, characterized by population displacement, two years of Eritrean occupation, expropriation, general impoverishment and uncertain conditions. The third phase deals with the aftermath of war. The author contrasts the experiences of people living in a town which was largely destroyed during the war and a rural village, as well as between two different villages. The chapter ends with a discussion of the impact of war on border villages in relation to changing identities.

In the final chapter Yisak Tafere considers demobilized soldiers and discusses a government initiative to support ex-soldiers to form cooperatives, and thereby facilitate their social and economic reintegration. The chapter contrasts the relative success of male cooperatives with the failure of women's cooperatives and discusses the reasons for this difference in terms of gender relations and their military background. Demobilization and reintegration programmes address broad issues of populations in transition. They may also contain valuable lessons for programmes that support the economic and social reintegration of other vulnerable groups, such as retrenched civil servants following political or economic adjustments, internally displaced persons, and refugees.

CONCLUDING REMARKS

In our concluding chapter we advocate a more holistic and inclusive approach to the study of various forms of forced migration within the same framework as spontaneous migration. Forms of migration that stimulate development can be promoted, while safeguarding the rights of people living in the areas to which migrants come and protecting the environment. This would require an approach that focuses on encouraging cooperation between settlers and hosts. In reviewing trends, the focus on resettlement seems to have receded. Likewise, issues surrounding refugees and returnees have become less salient with the repatriation of the major refugee populations in the post-conflict contexts. Instead, the various forms of development-induced displacement have become more significant with the encouragement of private investment and foreign capital in irrigated agriculture, bio-fuels, hydropower development, park management and urban growth. However, not much attention has been given to the rights of development-induced displacees, who are fragmented by the type of displacement and tend to be among the poorest with limited ability to resist eviction or obtain adequate compensation and little advocacy on their behalf.

The range of development initiatives often have cumulative effects, and the complex migration patterns and interactions tend to exacerbate tensions and result in conflicts and contested legitimacies over resource use. A better understanding of migration issues requires more consideration of dispute resolution and ways of promoting peace and cooperation at a local level. Moreover, appreciating and reconciling national and local interests has become all the more relevant and pressing in a context of increasing population, diminishing availability of land and natural resources, conflicting interests and the drive to ensure food security, promote export crops, and develop the country's irrigation, fuel and power potentials. These issues need to be considered in relation to highland-lowland dynamics, pressure on the river valleys and borderlands, the state's major development efforts and drive to attract foreign capital and the challenges and potentials of the current trend of greater decentralization.

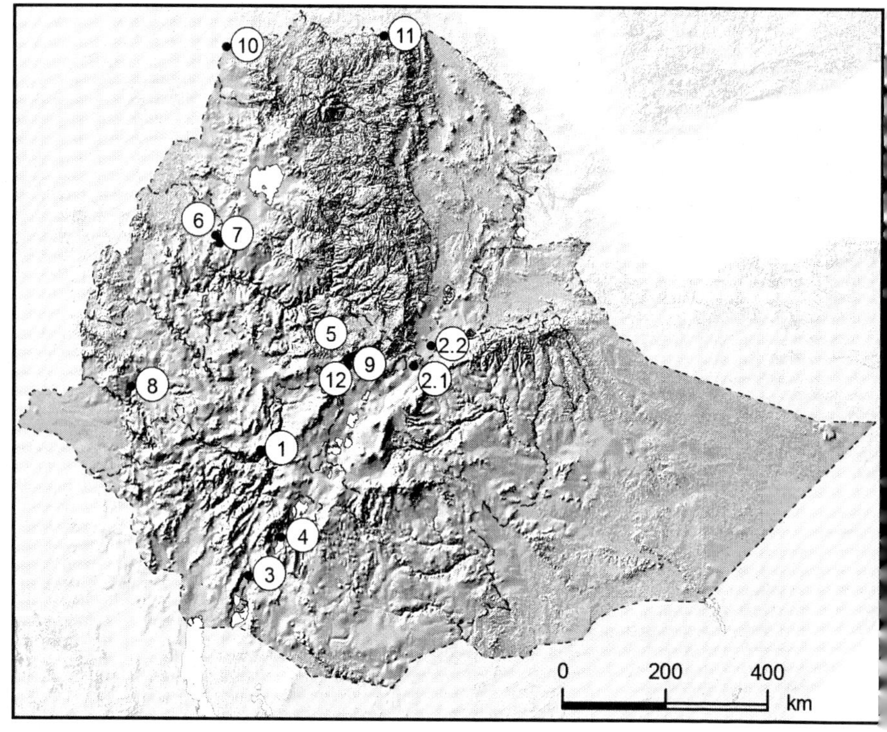

Numbers	Name of case study	Chapter
1	Gilgel Gibe (Oromia)	4
2.1	Metehara (Karrayu) (Oromia)	5
2.2	Amibara (Afar)	5
3	Wayto Valley (Tsamako) (SNNPR)	6
4	Nech Sar National Park (Guji) (SNNPR)	7
5	Addis Ababa (north eastern outskirts)	8
6	Metekel (Beni Shangul-Gumuz)	9
7	Metekel/Beles Valley (Beni Shangul-Gumuz)	10
8	Qeto (Wellega) (Oromia)	11
9	Kaliti (south eastern outskirts of Addis Ababa)	12
10	Humera (Tigray)	13
11	Zalanbesa (Tigray)	14
12	Addis Ababa (town centre)	15

Part I

INTRODUCTION

One

Migration, Resettlement & Displacement in Ethiopia

A Historical & Spatial Overview

FRANÇOIS PIGUET & ALULA PANKHURST

Migration between regions and states has been a constant feature of history. However, towards the end of the twentieth century, the importance and pace of migration increased dramatically with population dynamics, political and technological changes, and ease of transport and communications. Migration can thus be considered a paradigmatic condition of modern times (Castles and Miller 1993), raising crucial issues to do with rights and identities, in a context of the development of fortress mentalities seeking to restrict migration. Forced migration is becoming an increasingly important aspect or form of migration (Soguk 1999). However, the distinction between forced and voluntary migration is becoming more complex and problematic, the interlinkages between the two are becoming more significant, and the analytical validity of the dichotomy may be questioned (Van Heer 1998).

This introduction has the aim of setting the issues of migration, resettlement and displacement within a broader historical and geographical context within Ethiopia and the Horn of Africa. We suggest that the dynamics between highlands and lowlands and the involvement of the state are often crucially overlooked dimensions. At the same time, we draw attention to the international literature on the central issues linking debates within the Ethiopian context with global concerns. Further, we seek to highlight often little known and recent in-depth studies, mainly by Ethiopian anthropologists, providing valuable locally-grounded descriptions and analyses of specific contexts, which can help to build up an overall picture of complex and inter-related forms of migration.

This introduction consists of six sections. First, we begin by outlining highland-lowland dynamics in Ethiopia in terms of contrasts and inter-relations, complementarities and competition, and the role of state intervention. Second, we consider how lowland pastoralists are under pressure, with contrasting population dynamics, and changes in spatial movements and livelihood strategies. The third section provides an overview of state-organized resettlement in the last part of the twentieth century, from the late imperial period, through the first decade of Derg rule to the Emergency Phase in the mid-1980s. This is followed by a review of four types of development-induced displacement, resulting from agricultural development, the establishment of national parks, the construction of dams and urban expansion. The fifth section provides overviews regarding refugees, returnees, displaced people and demobilized soldiers. In conclusion, we consider the theme of complex and inter-related forms of migration concentrated in the lowlands and borderlands through state intervention, often generating tensions and conflicts at local and sometimes regional levels.

Highland-lowland dynamics

In order to understand the inter-related contexts of migration, displacement and settlement in Ethiopia we need first to consider highland-lowland dynamics in terms of both contrasts and inter-relations over space, time and social formations. Second, the complementarities and competition between highlands and lowlands provide crucial insights for appreciating the dynamics of population movements. Third, we must recognize the key role played by the state, the expansion of communications and agricultural policies and practices in enabling, facilitating, promoting, impeding or preventing self-initiated migration.

CONTRASTS AND INTERRELATIONS IN GEOGRAPHY, HISTORY AND SOCIETY

With high plateaux of over 2,000 metres in the central and northern part of the country, peaking at over 4,000 meters, contrasting with the greater part of the country composed of lowlands in the major Valleys, notably the Rift bisecting the country diagonally from northeast to southwest, and in the borderlands to the east, west and south, Ethiopian altitudinal contrasts are exceptional within the African context. What are the implications of this altitudinal distinction? How, then, can we characterize highland-lowland differences and relations? We argue that this often overlooked dichotomy and the ensuing interactions have been central to Ethiopian social formations offering opportunities and imposing constraints. In the following outline we argue that an understanding of these contrasts, complementarities and conflicts is a prerequisite to placing settlement, resettlement and displacement within the broader framework of migration patterns in Ethiopia.

Within an African context, Ethiopia is a relatively densely populated country.[1] Yet the population has been and remains concentrated in the highlands largely for geographical, historical and societal reasons, which can be considered under five inter-related headings: climate, technology, land tenure, population density and state formation. First, in climatic and environmental terms the highlands have benefited from more steady rainfall and the plateaux have been conducive to the development of agriculture (Mesfin 1991). In contrast, the lowlands are characterized by limited and more variable rainfall, shallow soils, and constraints on human settlements in terms of water availability and human and livestock diseases, notably malaria and trypanosomiasis respectively. Second, in the highlands ox-plough technology, going back to the first millennium BC, has led to intensification of production, continuous expansion of areas under cultivation, and denser population with implications for the social organization[2] of production and political structure (McCann 1995). In the lowlands, the use of hoes and shifting cultivation, or pastoralism associated with seasonal migration, have enabled livelihoods to be sustained within the existing environmental constraints leading to a sparse settlement. Third, the land-tenure system, which developed in much of the highlands along with plough agriculture, was based on kinship groupings allocating land-use rights to individuals (Hoben 1966). With increasing population, this has led to the gradual decrease of the size of plots[3] managed largely by household labour. In contrast, in the lowlands, communal tenure over large areas of land, with some collective regulation of access and limited individual rights, remained the norm in areas of pastoralism and agro-pastoralism. Fourth, a much higher population density developed in the highlands, due to the more conducive climate and rainfall along with the ox-plough technology in the North and Enset-based agriculture in the South (Dessalegn 2007). In the lowlands, in contrast, scarcity of water and rainfall, and lowland human and livestock diseases curbed population growth. Finally, the combination of the factors discussed above allowed for the development of surplus and state formation going back to the Axumite period from the early centuries AD (Phillipson 1998), and centralized social formations have been a key enduring feature of the political landscape (R. Pankhurst 1998). In the lowlands, with some notable exceptions, particularly in the east and especially the Afar sultanate (Piguet 1998), local groups remained relatively egalitarian and autonomous until the late nineteenth century, though local leaders often wielded power based on religion and control of labour.

Relations between highlands and lowlands go back to early government interest in resources from the lowlands, partly prompted by trade, notably in salt, gold, wild animal products, especially ivory, and most importantly slaves for domestic use and export (R. Pankhurst 1997). With the depletion of resources in closer proximity, the central government increased its sphere of influence over the surrounding lowlands largely through raiding expeditions. Over the centuries settlement of the highlands and escarpment areas expanded and the centre of state power shifted southwards.[4] Local highland groups became incorporated within the State system through a process of Abyssinianization, involving the spread of the *rist* system of hereditary land tenure, the adoption of the Amharic language and the expansion of the Orthodox Church (Donham 1986:10-11). However, a difference between the eastern and western borderlands arose in the Middle Ages, with the rise of Muslim principalities in the East and their dominance of trade relations with the coast. Recent discoveries of Muslim towns in Ifat in central Ethiopia with thick walls, numerous buildings and large mosques demonstrate a strong presence of Muslim settlements on the foothills of the highlands. (Fauvelle-Aymar *et al.* 2006). In contrast, interaction with the western and southern lowlands was characterized mainly by pillage, enslavement, and displacement of local groups who tended to retreat to more marginal areas (James 1986). The power of the central state was weakened in the sixteenth century by the invasion led from the eastern lowlands by Ahmed Ibn Ibrahim (known as Gragn, the left-handed), resulting in an expansion of Islam. Then the Oromo migrations from the southern lowlands and their settlement in the central and western highlands brought about further changes in the social configuration, resulting in three processes: resistance by powerful centralized kingdoms in the south; assimilation and incorporation of peasant communities often through clan-based adoption or intermarriage in the central areas; and marginalization or displacement mainly of shifting cultivators in the far west (Negaso 1984; James 1986; Mohammed 1990; Triulzi 1981).

In the late nineteenth century Emperor Menilek's conquests and the expansion of the state began a process of land alienation by *neftegna*, soldier-settlers, and the establishment of *ketema*, garrison settlements (Bahru 1991). In the highlands either the central state obtained tribute from local leaders, or the soldier-settlers extracted tribute and labour from *gebbar* 'tenants'. However, in the fringe peripheries inhabited largely by agro-pastoralists and pastoralists, local leaders were designated as *ballabat*, landlords,[5] and collected tax for the central state, but otherwise central influence and control was limited. Relations between the centre and the peripheries were divided into three types by Donham (1986: 37-43): (i) those areas, previously independent kingdoms, that were made directly tributary to the crown, (ii) those areas where the so-called *gebbar* system was established, where northern governors were appointed and local people made into near-serfs; and finally, (iii) those areas in the far peripheral lowlands inhabited by hunters, shifting cultivators and pastoralists.

In the course of the twentieth century the bureaucracy became more centralized and wide-reaching, and the economy more commercialized. The French-built railway to Djibouti expanded Red Sea trade and the British Nile steamer to Gambela opened up the Nile route which increased the volume and speed of trade and created incentives for the development of mainly coffee plantations and cotton production. The Italian occupation of the late 1930s left a road network that made highland areas more accessible. The commercialization of agriculture in the 1950s led to the development of private farms and foreign investment, notably in the Awash Valley for cotton and sugar production, resulting in the alienation of land from Afar and Karrayu pastoralists as noted by Ayalew Gebre and Getachew Kassa in Chapter 5 in this book. The development of towns and road networks in the Rift Valley provided a context for the sedentarization of sections of the pastoralist societies. Land shortage also led to spontaneous migration into the remaining less populated highlands, and, gradually, from the escarpment to the foothills of the lowland areas. From the late imperial period land shortage also led to the expansion of more intensive agriculture in the lowlands themselves, where resources, notably access to water, permitted settlement. Pastoralists, partly in response, began to turn to some agriculture, and sections of agro-pastoralist groups became more sedentary around key resources, notably rivers and water points, and began to exploit trading opportunities resulting in the emergence of small towns. A process of enclosures of communal lands, particularly by clan leaders or powerful and wealthy individuals, began to take place (Hogg 1997a).[6]

COMPLEMENTARITIES AND COMPETITION

Historical relations between the highlands and lowlands have been characterized by alternating periods of conflict and coexistence. Trade relations have been major linkages along the routes to the coast, the west and the south. Inter-relations between highland agriculturalists and lowland pastoralists have involved some complementarity, notably in exchanges of livestock for grain, particularly as a survival strategy in times of hardship. Pastoralists in some areas have grazed livestock on fields after the harvest in the highlands, and peasants in some areas have bond friends among pastoralist groups.[7] In some cases highlanders send cattle to bond friends in the lowlands as a form of entrustment and vice versa, taking advantage of seasonal differences in the rainfall patterns.[8] Occasionally joint institutions were established especially for conflict resolution, such as in the east between the Afar and Tigraway and the Somali and Amhara, and in the west between the Gumuz and the highlanders.[9] Intermarriage can also be a form of interlinkage and lowlanders may have a second wife from among highlanders.[10]

With gradually decreasing land availability peasants from the highlands have tended to migrate along the escarpments into lower areas in search of land. This involved both short-distance and seasonal migration and long-distance and permanent migration, the former sometimes becoming a step towards the latter (Wood 1977, 1982). Recurrent drought and rainfall scarcity and land and soil degradation, with decline in soil fertility resulting in food insecurity, were additional factors (Tesfaye 2007). Many of those who moved in the imperial period to become tenants of landlords gained access to land after the 1975 reform which transformed their land-use arrangements into recognized rights. From the late imperial period further migrants have often started as seasonal labourers at peak seasons of weeding and harvesting and coffee picking in the west or as employees, share-croppers or renting land under annual agreements with local landholders.[11] Migrants moving to the lowlands tend to maintain links with relatives in the highlands and are sometimes involved in seasonal migration and exchange of produce. In particular, differences in agricultural seasons, types of crops, production dynamics and livelihood systems create favourable conditions for exchange. Migrants through their networks may also sponsor or bring in relatives, resulting in a snowball effect or chain of migration (Assefa 1999; Tesfaye 2007).

The lowland economy is characterized by more land availability but less reliable rainfall[12] and limited crop diversity. Moreover, there are often cycles of 'boom' and 'bust' with good years followed by bad ones, so that there is scope for increasing production rapidly and cultivating cash crops in better years, but also a need to fall back on help from highland relatives in bad years. In the highlands, at least in the past, rainfall had generally been more reliable, but land-holding sizes have been decreasing, and grazing land in particular is limited, with communal pastures becoming eroded through expansion of cultivation and due to reafforestation projects during the Derg period (Yeraswork 2000). Highland peasants will therefore often send livestock for breeding or fattening with relatives or employed herders to the lowlands where they will stay with contacts among earlier migrants or bond friends. In recent decades climatic conditions in the highlands appear to have been changing for the worse, with an apparent shortening of cycles between droughts, and the short *belg* rains, where they exist, often coming late and running into the main *meher* rainy season. This has presented an important push factor for peasants seeking to cultivate areas in lower altitudes.

Conversely, among agro-pastoralists there has been the opposite tendency for some groups to seek better rain-fed higher areas and to become more involved in agriculture as a safeguard against years of drought. There has also been a perception of declining or less reliable rainfall patterns. Among some of the southern agro-pastoral groups there has been a gradual northward and upward drift, 'in search of cool ground' as the Mursi put it.[13] This convergence of two migratory tendencies from both the highlands and the lowlands has meant increased pressure from both directions on the intermediary escarpment zones in the east, the west and the south, generating conflicts over resource use.[14]

Highland self-initiated migrant settlers have often sought to establish relations with local individuals, groups and their leaders, sometimes involving informal tenancy, share-cropping, share-breeding or other resource-sharing arrangements. These relations are often intended primarily as economic strategies to gain access to land, but may be initiated or strengthened through social, cultural and religious ties, sometimes between groups or communities, but usually on an individual dyadic patron-client or bond-friendship basis, and occasionally, religion permitting, even through intermarriage (Assefa 1995; Berihun 1996; Piguet 2006). When conflicts arise, such ties can to some extent provide local protection and mitigate dangers of escalating the conflict, which may otherwise lead to loss of property or life, or even expulsions (Miyawaki 1996; Schlee 1990). However, when conflicts are less localized and involve larger groupings, such social and economic ties may not be sufficient to de-escalate tensions and avoid serious fighting, which can take on an 'ethnic' garb. Although there have been migratory tendencies from both the lowlands and the highlands, given higher and increasing densities in the highlands, the downward migratory movements and pressure have been more intense, fuelling the resentment of agro-pastoralist groups about incursions into territory they perceive as theirs, and alienation of land formerly used by them less intensively and/or seasonally.

The differences in modes of livelihood and social organization were reflected in diverging cultural values, notably a divide between the largely Christian highlands and the mainly Muslim lowlands. However, there were Muslim principalities in the highlands, and traders in towns and Christians settled in lowland urban areas. Each side also characterized the other in terms of derogatory stereotypes. Thus the highlanders looked down on the lowlanders for their nomadic way of life, summed up in the expression 'they follow the tails of their cattle', rather than subjugating the oxen for ploughing. They referred to the lowlanders as *zelan* with negative connotations of nomad or vagabond, without a stable home. Conversely, the pastoralists viewed a sedentary lifestyle as constraining and being tied to the land like slaves or dependants, instead of being able to move freely over wide expanses. Fears of the 'other' were also deep-seated. The lowlanders had experiences and memories of the brutalities of the slave raiding of highlanders, and conversely the custom of the emasculation of victims by some lowland groups created a strong sense of terror among the highlanders. The spread of rifles from the end of the nineteenth century and automatic weapons from the 1980s, especially with the fleeing Derg soldiers selling off weapons cheap in 1991, dramatically reduced the terms of exchange between weapons and livestock in the lowlands (Matsuda 1997) and created the means for escalated confrontations and exacerbated cycles of raiding and counter-raiding, making peaceful inter-relations more difficult to sustain.

THE ROLE OF STATE INTERVENTIONS

In the second half of the twentieth century the gradual but increasing pace of the development of state administration, communication networks and agricultural policies and projects has facilitated self-initiated migratory tendencies both indirectly and directly, in three major ways, even without taking account of the establishment of organized settlement schemes.

First, the expansion of state administration and services, and improvements in communications and transport, have created an environment more conducive to migration. This has meant that longer-distance migration has become much easier. Whereas expeditions of traders taking salt to the south and bringing back coffee and hides may have taken months until the mid-twentieth century, the existence of roads, trucks and bus services has meant that migrants could travel for seasonal labour to cash-cropping areas, and could move easily to settle in the forest areas notably in the southwest, involving both short-distance and long-distance migration (Wood 1977,

1982). Better communications and transport also facilitated the flow of information, so that migrants sharing their experience and knowledge of opportunities and conditions elsewhere were able to influence and sponsor relatives and other potential migrants in the areas they came from, thereby intensifying migratory flows.

Secondly, the commercialization of the economy and the promotion of private international and national investment created opportunities for wage labour mainly on a seasonal basis in cash crop areas, particularly in areas conducive to producing coffee in the south and southwest, cotton and sugar cane in the Rift Valley and the Awash Valley in the east, and sesame, beans and oil seeds in the north-western borderlands. Between the end of the Italian occupation and the 1974 revolution an estimated two million hectares were distributed by the government to individuals and groups in southern and western parts of the country. This also led to attention being given to infrastructure development, resulting in the displacement of pastoralist and agro-pastoralist groups.

Thirdly, and most importantly, the setting up of agricultural development projects and other state-sponsored schemes, either directly by the government or indirectly by facilitating international or private investment, had the effect of encouraging migrant labour into the lowlands. This resulted in the settlement of labourers and the development of urban centres, and the migration of traders catering to their needs. This was most clearly in evidence in the late imperial period in the Awash and Rift Valleys, as well as in the western lowlands, particularly in the northern parts around Humera and Metemma and to a lesser extent in the south-western area around the Gojeb and Omo valleys. These projects required and attracted labourers, some of whom settled in these areas. Moreover, they also involved the alienation of the best-watered lands along the river valleys, which were often dry-season grazing areas for pastoralists and key resources for shifting agriculturalists as noted in many studies.[15] Many nationalized schemes and state farms continued to attract labourers during the Derg period, and additional and new projects were set up more recently in most of the lowland areas as irrigation came to be seen as a major way of promoting agricultural development and food security. Most recently, the rapid expansion of private flower production encouraged by the state in the Rift Valley and areas in relative proximity to the capital city has also encouraged labour migration and involved some displacement.

Lowland pastoralists under pressure

In the arid and semi-arid rangelands of the Horn of Africa, given the limited rainfall, the most easily viable form of livelihood relies on transhumant pastoralism (Manger 1996, 2000). Increasingly pastoralists living in such environments have found themselves marginalized politically and excluded from the best watered resources by agricultural development projects, the establishment of parks and the settlement of farmers. Such processes often exacerbate the effects of drought and lead to conflicts and impoverishment. As a result, some of the poorest are forced to abandon pastoral livelihoods (Baxter and Hogg 1990; Baxter 1991). In part due to increasing pressures, some sections within pastoralist societies have become more sedentary, either in response to crises or to opportunities in rural as well as urban contexts. This has also led to enclosures, either by clan leaders or powerful and enterprising individuals involved in livestock fattening or agricultural ventures, often engaging migrant labourers on contractual bases.

CONSTRASTING POPULATION DYNAMICS IN THE LOWLANDS

Sedentarization and settlement of pastoralists have constrained mobility and generated two contrasting and sometimes contradictory population movements, as noted by Ayalew Gebre, Getachew Kassa and Melesse Getu in this book. On the one hand, pastoralists and agro-pastoralists have been forced to abandon riverbanks and flooded areas, restricting their access to water and wetlands, which were key pasture reserves for the dry season. Pastoralist groups have been limited to marginal grazing land, as their traditional rights over pastoral lands have often not been respected, despite constitutional guarantees.[16] On the other hand, agricultural labourers from the highlands have come to work in the irrigated schemes, particularly in the Awash Valley, and many others have settled in towns such as Dubti, Melka Werer and Metahara.

Development projects along rivers and in urban areas resulted in restrictions to the 'normal' pattern of pastoralist transhumance, and consequent concentration of livestock in marginal areas, resulting in overgrazing and environmental degradation. Today, none of the pastoralists subsist on the produce of their herds, and the grain they consume is either grown locally or purchased, as an increasing proportion of their income derives from the market and wage labour. In these semi-arid areas, intensive human activities have exacerbated agricultural encroachment on pastoral lands as well as deforestation and wood and charcoal processing, often resulting in conflicts over grazing areas and scarce water resources. At the same time, pastoralists have become more integrated within the market economy, and have sought to increase their herd sizes, placing further pressure on grazing lands and rendering themselves more prone to the effects of drought. Those who have lost their herds tend to become involved in low-skilled and low status activities as a survival strategy, and during difficult periods they rely more and more upon kinship and food aid (Piguet 1998). Furthermore, the influx of highlanders has modified the regional demographic balance and exacerbated population pressure.

CHANGES IN SPATIAL MOVEMENTS AND LIVELIHOOD STRATEGIES

Plans to settle pastoralists have faced numerous difficulties. Four main reasons for the failure of so many attempts can be cited. First, the logic of pastoral livelihood is predicated on seasonal migration, which is often the only environmentally sound strategy for making a living in the lowlands, given the unreliable rainfall patterns. Second, there is an unclear policy environment, and measures seem to be taken in haste on an *ad hoc* basis without much consideration of the social and longer-term environmental consequences. Third, there is a lack of appropriate planning, as most development focuses on crop production and neglects livestock and pastoral livelihoods. Fourth, there has been a lack of detailed feasibility studies and pastoralist settlers' participation. In this book Getachew comments on Afar 'absenteeism' and lack of interest in farming, leading the authorities to replace them by migrant workers, which resulted in conflict between Afar, wage labourers and settlement managers, and the interruption of projects. Restrictions on the amount of rangeland and subsequent pastoral movements have engendered conflicts between Afar and Issa in the east and the Argoba and Karrayu in the centre.

At the peak of crises pastoralists may move further away and for longer periods. With more intensive economic activities in the pastoral areas, the rights of pastoralists over the land they have been using have been eroded, and they have been increasingly squeezed out of the best lands. In the long term they are in danger of becoming further marginalized. As a result, some pastoralists are increasingly involved in seasonal migration in search of casual work and in rural-urban migration. Others have become more sedentary, in clan-based settlements, which sometimes result in heightened inter-lineage, clan or group conflicts due to land disputes. Thus many of the adverse effects on pastoral livelihoods have been supported either directly or indirectly by state interventions through development projects and settlement schemes (Hogg 1997a).

State-organized resettlement in the last part of the twentieth century

State-sponsored resettlement became increasingly important in the last third of the twentieth century, with some *ad hoc* initiatives started in the late imperial period and increasing interest in resettlement during the Derg regime, culminating in the massive Emergency Phase resettlement of over half a million people in 1985-6 (Dessalegn 2003).

THE LATE IMPERIAL PERIOD 1965-73

For a decade from the mid-1960s various localized resettlement initiatives were promoted by governors, missions and aid agencies. Resettlement became part of government planning from 1966, with the establishment of the Ministry of Land Reform and Administration and the Third Five-Year Development Plan produced in 1968, seen as a means of redistributing population and developing less populated areas (Wood 1985; Pankhurst 1992a; Dessalegn 2003).

Although reviews revealed that settlements run by individual peasants were relatively more successful than large-scale ones, both government and non-governmental agencies tended to promote high-cost, large-scale schemes. By the time of the 1974 Revolution some 10,000 households, representing less than 0.2 percent of rural households compared with over 5 percent of households which settled spontaneously, had been resettled at an estimated cost of $8 million, with some irrigated schemes costing 15,000 Ethiopian dollars per family (Wood 1985:92). Schemes included various kinds of settlers, and resettlement was seen as a remedy for all ills. The projects were set up with ambitious economic, social and political objectives: to deal with famine, provide land for the landless, increase agricultural production, introduce new technologies, establish cooperatives, remove urban unemployed, stop charcoal processing, settle pastoralists and shifting agriculturalists, form defences on the Somali border and rehabilitate repatriated refugees.

The results were generally poor, the schemes tended to fail, and most settlers left the projects. The government's own assessments suggested that the difficulties stemmed from inadequate planning of programmes, inappropriate settler selection, inadequate budgetary support, and inexperienced staff. However, the problems were more deep-rooted, resulting from questionable assumptions about available land and potential settlers' motivations. Moreover, a range of mistakes were committed at all stages, from the design through to the implementation of projects (Dessalegn 2003).

THE FIRST DECADE OF DERG RULE: 1974-83

After the Revolution, state land nationalization, the establishment of institutions[17] and the repeated incidence of drought resulted in an increase in the pace of resettlement. Within the ten years prior to the 1984 famine some 46,000 households comprising about 187,000 people were resettled in 88 sites in 11 administrative regions. However, reports highlighted high economic and social costs and reliance on state inputs. Among the major problems were poor planning and site selection and preparation, haphazard and poorly organized recruitment, and enforced cooperativization. Most large-scale schemes failed to become self-sufficient and collapsed, with high desertion rates and negative consequences for the environment and local populations in the settlement areas. On the eve of the 1984 famine, the Relief and Rehabilitation Commission (RRC) had concluded that such schemes were unworkable, and a new approach based on small-scale oxen-reliant projects was proposed. The resettlement programme was in crisis, providing minimal benefits at high cost and involving much damage and wastage of resources. The demographic impact was minimal or non-existent. Dessalegn (1988a:18) concluded:

> Resettlement failed to live up to its expectations. It had absolutely no impact on the unemployment problem in the urban areas, and did little to ease the agricultural or environmental crises facing the country. Indeed, there is reason to believe that the damage caused by resettlement far outweighs its benefits and the vast resources wasted on the various programmes would have been more profitably employed elsewhere.

THE EMERGENCY PHASE: 1985-86

The Emergency Phase of resettlement carried out by the Derg in the aftermath of the 1984 famine has been the subject of extensive research. Three doctoral theses in anthropology have been produced (Pankhurst 1989; Gebre 2001; Wolde-Selassie 2002), and several books and numerous articles have been published on the subject.[18] Over half a million people were moved in under a year and a half from October 1984 to January 1986, representing one of the most complex, ambitious and draconian measures ever attempted by the Ethiopian government.

Large-scale movements were initiated under the Derg regime and the authoritarian way of resettling people resulted in traumas and conflicts between newcomers and the host communities. The 1980s programmes resulted in failure due to misconceived plans and careless implementation. Analysts seeking to explain these 'failures' can be broadly divided into those who stress that the unfortunate outcomes were a result of the way in which the resettlement programme was formulated, and a second approach pointing to more fundamental misconceptions about the presuppositions – of abundant cultivable land not occupied or claimed – and about the considerable costs of the implementation. The resettlement programme was also linked with the villagization approach. The Derg administration intended to regroup dispersed small villages in rural areas so that it would be easier to provide social services and facilitate administration and control, and thus had no specific agricultural or food security objectives. The implementation modalities of both programmes were unplanned, non-participatory and hasty.

Why did the Derg move from a position of advocating a gradual approach to resettlement as a minor component of agricultural policy as outlined in the Ten-Year

Plan and advocated by the RRC, to a hastily increased pace regarded as a national imperative of the highest order, with direct involvement of the head of state and under the direction of the Workers' Party? Why did the government venture along the costly road of moving so many people at the very moment when the country was almost bankrupt and at the height of a famine when resources were most stretched? A major consideration seems to have been the value of resettlement as a symbol of hope in addressing the problem in lasting ways, and as proof of action in the face of the galling blow of famine and dependence on donors. Resettlement was portrayed as an assertion of independence in spite of external opposition. It was also viewed as a way of addressing the food-security crisis in a durable way through a dual strategy of relieving population pressure in the highlands, which were perceived as chronically drought-prone, over-populated and environmentally degraded, and, on the other hand, making lowland areas, which were perceived to be fertile, under-populated, and under-exploited, more productive. Resettlement was also seen as an opportunity to introduce social and economic change and pursue policies of socialist transformation through mechanization, villagization and cooperativization. It has also been suggested that the government assumed that during a time of famine it would be easier to persuade or force people to move, and also that the programme had the political motives of depopulating areas of support for the Tigray Peoples Liberation Front (TPLF) and creating garrison buffers against the Oromo Liberation Front (OLF) in the west (Clay and Holcomb 1986; Niggli 1986; Africa Watch 1991). At a regional or local level, too, other 'add-on' rationales were included by administrators and local leaders. A 'campaign mentality' took over, resulting in a logic of its own. Overzealous officials turned targets into quotas; resettlement was used to move people off areas designated for state forest expansion or development projects; and there were cases of Peasant Association leaders who coveted the land of others or rid themselves of opponents by sending them to resettlement areas.

The question of the extent of involuntary versus voluntary resettlement has been, and remains, controversial. All the more so since willingness to resettle is complex and socially embedded, given the way in which individual decision-making is linked to that of spouse, family, other kin, peer and community pressures. The process is also politically embedded, given the ways in which national and regional political and media pressures, as well as local-level politics, influence decision-making. Moreover, there is a continuum between being forced at gun-point and enthusiastic voluntary participation, with a wide range from voluntary to coerced motivations in between (Gebre 2002a, 2004). Although in times of crisis, particularly of famine, a much larger number of people may be seen to express a 'willingness' to resettle, in many ways, of course, this is not a genuine willingness but one prompted by desperation and lack of choice (Pankhurst 1992a; Gebre 2002a). Those who had already left their villages for famine shelters had generally exhausted their assets, and had abandoned their land to others, so that they no longer had any real choice. They had 'surrendered to the state' and no longer had much say in whether they were resettled or not. There were cases in the 1984-5 famine when the camps became 'rat traps', where famished families went seeking food and found themselves encouraged or forced to resettle under the threat of food aid being withdrawn.

Most studies have focused on the abuse of human rights and the numerous injustices of the involuntary resettlement. However, what needs explaining is the voluntary end of the spectrum which has tended to be overlooked in highlighting the coercions and impositions. A significant proportion of those who joined the resettlement 'voluntarily' in 1985 tended to be the younger generation, generally men, in search of better opportunities. Many of these saw little prospect of gaining access to sufficient land to become independent producers in a context in which diminishing landholdings were controlled by the older generation. The idea of starting a new life in the 'far west' thus had a certain appeal. Despite some land redistributions, the limited options for access to land by the younger generation therefore no doubt contributed to their 'willingness' to resettle, and can be considered an underlying structural factor.

Whatever the overt and covert motives of the state, regional and district administrators, local leaders and the strategies of households and individual settlers, the overall verdict is that the experiment was a clear disaster. Politically, resettlement was unpopular, enforced, and driven by cadres often opposed to the more pragmatic and cautious approaches suggested by technical experts. It resulted in power abuses and serious conflict between settlers and local people, fuelling opposition to the government. The donor boycott of resettlement and the consequent strained relations with Western countries represented severe political costs of the government's decision to go ahead with a programme that involved heavy-handed measures and abuses.[19] In terms of human rights, for the settlers, the process involved coercion and serious infringements of personal choice, loss of freedom of movement and of religious practice in an attempt to instil a communist ideology, and alienation of household labour for collective purposes. For the 'host' communities, it involved coerced labour in preparing shelters, houses, and food for the settlers on arrival, forced expropriation of land and other key resources without consultation let alone compensation, displacement, marginalization and consequent enforced changes in livelihood. The resource conflicts fuelled grievances and led to the settlers being unwelcome, and the settlements were at times attacked.

Economically, the programme poached personnel and diverted food, funds, services, aid and other resources from ministries and existing programmes and projects, and thereby further aggravated the mounting crisis in the country. Settlements absorbed resources without showing signs of becoming self-sufficient. Settlers faced imposed mechanized collectivization which went against the deeply engrained sense of autonomy of peasant households using oxen. For the hosts, the loss of resources, notably land, forests exploited for coffee and honey production and access to rivers, was strongly resented. The settlements did, however, result in more market interaction, with the settlers initially purchasing grain and livestock from local people and later producing mainly cereals for sale in local markets.

Socially, the programme resulted in considerable suffering for the settlers, due to high morbidity and mortality, particularly during the transport and the initial phase, as well as family separation, disintegration of institutions (Wolde-Selassie 2002), impoverishment, and difficulties in adaptation. The lowland diseases, notably malaria and trypanosomiasis, presented new threats and challenges. The mixing of people from different areas, ethnicities, and religions heightened tensions and social conflict. For the 'host' population, the immigration of large numbers of settlers with different values and ways of life represented a threat.

Culturally, for the settlers the changes in environment in the hot lowlands and the more monotonous maize- and sorghum-based diet involved a reduced quality of life, and the memory of lost cherished homelands and burial grounds affected their senses of identity and wellbeing. For local people dispossession of sites of cultural importance such as sacred forests and burial grounds aggravated their grievances. In terms of the environment, the programme led to massive deforestation to build shelters, houses and facilities, and environmental degradation as a result of land clearing and intensive settlement. Serious conflicts arose between settlers and local people over resources that the latter had used and considered as belonging to them and for which they had local management institutions which were being undermined.

At the time of the overthrow of the Derg in 1991, the vast majority of settlers remaining in resettlement areas voted with their feet and went back to their former homelands. On their return they generally found that their land had been redistributed, and many of those who did not have strong social networks joined the ranks of the landless, rural poor or urban destitute, having, in their view, wasted seven years of their lives and returning home impoverished and often marginalized (Pankhurst 1991, 2001a, 2001b, 2001c; Erlichman 2000). This even led some of these to go back to the resettlement sites they had left. However, minorities of settlers remained in the resettlement areas, many of whom have become established, and some of whom have prospered, in part due to the easing of population pressure with the departure of the majority of the settlers and the redistribution of the land they were using. The younger generation born in the settlements seems to have developed a new sense of belonging, centred more on local identity rather than on their parents' homeland, though their future is uncertain in a context of ethnic federalism where they are minorities that can be considered unwelcome (Pankhurst 2002a). The resurgence of resettlement since 2000 and a comparison with the earlier phase in the 1980s are the subject of the chapter by Pankhurst in this book.

Development-induced displacement

Development-induced displacement, though less visible and researched than many other forms of displacement, particularly those involving refugees crossing international borders, has become an increasingly important phenomenon worldwide (Cernea 1996b). In terms of frequency, size and dire consequences, development-induced displacement has been acknowledged as the most important contributor to forced migration (Hansen and Oliver-Smith 1982; McDowell 1996). Cernea (2000:11) notes:

> During the last two decades of the previous century the magnitude of forced population displacements caused by development programmes was on the order of 10 million people each year, or some 200 million people globally during that period.

However, internally displaced groups are less visible than refugees crossing international boundaries, receive less support, and have not been studied to the same extent. In Ethiopia, too, the issue has received limited attention to date. Over the past few decades an increasing number of local communities have faced the consequences of the establishment of infrastructure such as hydro-electric dams, the extension of agricultural development schemes and the establishment of national parks, all of which are considered to be in the national interest, but compete with these communities for land and access to resources. In some cases these development projects have marginalized local populations, excluding them from areas in which they have lived and relocating them or forcing them to look for land in marginal areas. Around urban centres as well, rural communities have faced similar pressure, as the interests of urban elites have been given more weight than those of the surrounding peasantry.

Four major types of development-induced displacement are common as a result of: (i) construction of dams, (ii) agricultural development projects, (iii) establishment of national parks and (iv) urban expansion.

CONSTRUCTION OF DAMS

The building of dams has been one of the best studied types of displacement in Africa, notably with the pioneering work of Colson and Scudder who have followed the Gwembe who were displaced as a result of the building of the Kariba dam over several decades (Colson 1971; Scudder 1993, Scudder and Colson 1982), as well as work on displacement resulting from the building of the Volta and Aswan dams (Fernea and Kennedy 1966).

In Ethiopia the displacement effects of dams have not been the subject of much research, and the case study of the Gilgel Gibe Dam by Kassahun Kebede presented in this book is one of the first of its kind. It can be expected, however, that dams for irrigation to promote food security and the production of cash crops for local consumption and export, notably of cotton and sugar cane, which is being produced as a bio-fuel, as well as dams for hydropower will be further promoted with likely displacement effects in the future. The issues of the differential impact of displacement and of compensation rights and options therefore deserve greater consideration.

AGRICULTURAL DEVELOPMENT

Agricultural development projects led to displacement in several areas during the imperial period. The establishment of the Chilalo Agricultural Development Unit in Arsi resulted in some displacement of peasants who moved to Bale. However, much more significant were the development ventures in the Awash Valley where the large-scale cotton and sugar plantations had severe repercussions on the pastoralists living in the area, notably the Afar and Karrayu, restricting their access to dry-season grazing areas. Some displacement also resulted from private investment in the Rift Valley and in the western lowlands. During the Derg period state farms, some of which took over nationalized private farms, resulted in further displacement. In the southwest, a notable case is the Ethio-Korean cotton farm in the lower Omo which alienated land that the agro-pastoralist Dassanech had been using for flood-retreat cultivation. Some private and later state farms in the Gibe and Gojeb Valleys, and the Wushwush tea plantation, established in 1981, also displaced local people and encouraged the settlement of migrants. Private investment in agriculture has been promoted since the overthrow of the Derg and is having some detrimental effects on livelihoods in the river valleys. However, where traditional rights over land are recognized and forms of compensation and resource-sharing are negotiated, this can lead to more favourable outcomes, as some recent cases from the Awash Valley suggest. The restriction of pastoralists' access to resources vital to their survival becomes an issue of resource security, which is related not only to pastoral livelihoods, but also to the environment (Mohammed Salih 1999). The disruption of traditional patterns of pastoralism has led to overgrazing, soil salinization and declining fertility.

Changes in the pastoral environment have resulted in a lack of confidence and trust between pastoral communities, immigrant groups and the administration. Pastoralists often expressed animosity towards the government and were suspicious of outside interventions, which they assume are intended only to take away their land behind empty promises of compensation. Competition over scarce resources and disputes over land rights developed into confrontation and outright conflicts often leading to violent clashes. The encroachment into grazing land and the expansion of irrigation schemes have also rendered the pastoral economy vulnerable to recurrent drought and famine since the 1970s. Irrigation schemes and natural reserves are denying pastoralists access to flooded grazing areas and watering points or riverbanks, reducing the most productive grazing areas – up to 60 percent for the Karrayu (Ayalew Gebre, 2001).

The three case studies of the effects of irrigation schemes raise common issues about land tenure rights, restricted access to the best traditional lands and grazing areas, pressure on natural resources, the effects on patterns of transhumance, the impact of in-migrants, notably on the environment, and socio-economic change within pastoralist societies. In regions where people with low and uncertain incomes are critically dependent on natural resources, customary tenure rules had been the main ways of providing security of land tenure and food security. The authors imply that both state control of land tenure and private investment have tended to be detrimental to the interests of local people living in marginal lands.

CREATION OF NATIONAL PARKS

An additional constraint on pastoralist and agro-pastoralist livelihoods came from the establishment of national parks in important grazing areas, notably the Awash Park in the east and Nech Sar Park in the south which are discussed in this book, as well as the Omo and Mago Parks in the southwest, and the Senkele Swayne's Hartebeest sanctuary in the Arsi lowlands (Zerihun 2007).[20] Displacement effects on local people in the Bale and Simien National Parks seem to have been limited, though tensions with local people over resource use are still a serious concern. The prevalent mistaken view that there is a necessary contradiction between wildlife, herding and seasonal agriculture is based on the assumption that these areas were 'virgin wildernesses' whereas such ecologies have in fact been shaped by centuries of interaction between livestock and wildlife.[21] The view therefore that people living in these areas with their herds have to be excluded not only affects the viability of the livelihoods of many pastoralist groups but is also to the detriment of the parks. As cattle are excluded, the current ecology will be altered since the grasses and bushes that the presence of the cattle controlled will expand, affecting the ruminant wildlife and the predators that depend on it. In other African countries a more enlightened approach to park management, which involves local people gaining benefits, has become more common.[22] Such insights were discussed at a workshop on participatory wildlife management in Addis Ababa in 1995.[23] However, this enlightened thinking does not yet seem to have taken root in Ethiopia. Exclusions, resettlement and conflicts with groups that are prevented from using areas over which they consider that they have traditional rights, have continued and may well escalate.

URBAN EXPANSION

Displacement as a result of urban expansion and 'slum clearance' has been increasing rapidly worldwide, and is becoming a significant phenomenon particularly in the large cities of the developing world (Cernea 1993). In Ethiopia the urban population remains a small but rapidly expanding minority, currently representing less than a fifth of the total population, but projected to grow at a much faster rate than rural areas. The current urban growth rate is estimated at 7 percent, and urban expansion both in the large cities and in smaller towns, especially road-side towns, is a predictable process, which will increase rapidly. However, the question of the effects of urban expansion and the resulting displacement of peasants from the surrounding areas has not been a topic of much research. The case study presented in this book by Feleke is one of very few such studies of urban displacement. Some further work has been done on the displaced as a result of 'slum clearance', notably masters theses by Nebiyu (2000) and Fitsum (2006) on those displaced from the area where the Sheraton Hotel was built in Addis Ababa. Given the rapid growth of towns, particularly the medium-sized and smaller towns, with the current decentralization, the questions of conflicts between urban and rural interests, the differential effects of displacement, and the need for formulating and implementing compensation options are likely to become more salient issues in the foreseeable future.

Refugees, returnees, internally displaced people and demobilized soldiers

The different categories considered in this section – refugees, returnees, internally displaced and demobilized soldiers – are often studied and treated in separate or different ways. However, they share some experiences, including the problems associated with settlement and resettlement. Many have experienced traumas of war, which may have left invisible scars, from which they need time to recover. They may be isolated or neglected, with limited recognition and assistance. By considering these categories together, we would hope that the parallels become apparent and that a better understanding of the common problems they face can be developed.

Africa[24] and in particular the Horn,[25] has been one of the world's main producers of refugees, largely as a result of the civil and inter-state wars that have ravaged the continent over several decades. Refugees have either settled 'spontaneously' or been placed in settlements, usually in border areas. The relative advantages and disadvantages of planned versus spontaneous settlement have long been debated.[26] Worldwide and within Africa, the question of repatriation of refugees has also become increasingly significant, especially given the UNHCR's concerns about 'protracted case loads'.[27] As with refugees, whether repatriation is spontaneous or organized, the different experiences of returnees who are resettled in state-sponsored settlements or return to their home areas on their own has been a subject of research and debate (Black and Khoser 1999; Long and Oxfeld 2004).

Ethiopia has been both a producer and a receiver of refugees over the past few decades. Refugees from Ethiopia at various stages of conflicts have sought asylum in Sudan, Somalia and Kenya (Mekuria 1988). Conversely Ethiopia has been a host in the east to Somali refugees and in the west to Nilotic refugees from Southern Sudan. All the countries of the Horn have experienced significant refugee flows in both directions, resulting from a range of conflicts and wars, often compounded by famine. At times refugee influxes have involved several hundred thousand people. The sudden mass influxes[28] often resulted in the hasty establishment of camps along the border, which soon became important trading centres. In the mid-1990s repatriation programmes were conducted from Sudan to Ethiopia and from Ethiopia to Somalia. The 1998-2000 Ethiopia-Eritrean war generated new flows of refugees, deportees and displacees on both sides;[29] the complex effects on them are described in two chapters in this book. The first by Aptekar and Behailu considers the consequences of displacement on mental health and the survival struggles of displacees who ended up in a camp on the outskirts of Addis Ababa; the second by Behailu concerns the effects of the displacement of people in camps in Tigray on the border with Eritrea and their attempts to rebuild their lives, which is the subject of his PhD thesis (Behailu 2005).

The Horn of Africa continues to be affected by considerable and long-standing refugee problems linked with regional conflicts.[30] The scale and complexity of the refugee problem in the Horn has been compounded by three factors. First, while armed conflict and human rights violations have been the primary cause of the mass displacements, environmental and economic factors have also contributed to the problems. Second, the conventional categorizations employed by UNHCR are often not appropriate or relevant in the cultural and socio-economic context of the Horn of Africa. This factor has been especially true of the large proportion of refugees who come from pastoralist backgrounds. Third, many of the groups of refugees and returnees straddle both sides of the borders, such as in the east the Somali and Afar, internally displaced since 1998, in the south the Borana, Gabra and Garri,[31] and in the west the Nuer, Anywaa and Uduk. Many of these groups are pastoralists who have often moved back and forth to take advantage of seasonal pasture variations, to exploit trade opportunities and even for pilgrimages to ritual sites.[32] UNHCR's main recent concern has been to find lasting solutions for people who have lived in exile for many years, focusing on the region's two largest refugee populations: the Somalis in Ethiopia and the Eritreans in Sudan.[33]

The following three points deserve to be stressed in terms of our central theme of state intervention in a context of highland-lowland dynamics. First, refugees, returnees and demobilized soldiers have tended to concentrate and be placed in settlements in the lowlands in the borderlands, many of which are also areas where both spontaneous and state-organized resettlement was undertaken in the past, and is still being undertaken; these same lowlands are areas where pastoralists, agro-pastoralists or shifting cultivators have been making a living and where they are being marginalized by population influxes. Second, international and inter-state politics in the region have affected the fate of groups of people in such a way that there have been movements of refugees and returnees back and forth from the neighbouring countries, mainly Sudan, Kenya and Somalia. Some groups such as the Uduk have crossed the border back and forth several times (James 1996). Third, the concentration of large settlements in areas of the lowlands where the population had traditionally been rather sparse, has created pressure on the local environment, notably on water and wood. This has often resulted in conflicts, notably over resources, with groups previously living in the area. However, the relationship between refugees, the environment and development is complex, and studies have questioned the assumption that refugees necessarily have a negative impact or are the only actors involved, and highlight the dangers of blaming the victims (Black 1998) This pressure has also led to some urbanization and social and cultural change, with both positive and negative consequences and differential effects in terms of wealth, gender, and occupation (Abraham 1995; Bizuayehu 2004).

There is a growing recognition that there are similarities between refugees and other internally displaced groups (Cernea and McDowell 2000; Robinson 2002). If we take a broader view, the settlement of refugees has many parallels with the resettlement of returnees, demobilized soldiers and other displaced groups. Moreover, many of these categories have been affected by state interventions, or are viewed in similar ways by the state (Turton 2002a). Furthermore, the connections between refugees and migrants in global terms and the parallels between different kinds of migration are also becoming more recognized worldwide (Zolberg and Benda (2001).

REFUGEES

Refugees in Ethiopia have been concentrated mainly in the border areas in all directions in the lowlands, in the east, south and southwest, and more recently in the north, although urban refugee populations have been on the increase. Almost all ethnic groups have been divided by the establishment of Ethiopia's international borders, and large population groups used to cross the border from one side or the other following unrest, clashes and wars. In the south, Borana, Gabra and Garri refugees were repatriated in the late 1980s and especially after 1991, but due to clashes in Kenya more than 2,600 Borana came back to Ethiopia as refugees (UNHCR, *Statistical Yearbook* 2007). In the east, in the Somali region, the largest influxes of Somali, most of whom were settled in large-scale settlements where they remained for over a decade, were repatriated between 2004 and 2007, though it is unclear how the more recent conflict will affect returnee reintegration and further refugee flows. Likewise, in the west, with the peace agreement in South Sudan the refugees who have been in camps for protracted periods are now on their way to being resettled. Falge (1997) considers the adaptations of the Nuer in camps in the Gambella area, James (1996) those of the Uduk who crossed the border several times, and Blain (2003) the impact of refugee settlements on the environment. Recent refugee flows have been related to the war with Eritrea, where refugees, deportees and displaced persons were placed in camps both near the border areas in Tigray and in Addis Ababa and other main towns. In this book Behailu considers the complexities of decision-making and the strategies of people living in a war environment in the border areas. The plight of those living in camps, who are among the most marginalized and neglected of the urban poor, and their social and economic adaptations in the face of adversity are considered by Dinku (2004) and Aptekar and Behailu in this book.

RETURNEES

Repatriation to and from Ethiopia has involved significant population flows. This occurred on a large scale from Sudan, Somalia and Kenya after the overthrow of the Derg in 1991. The extent to which individuals and groups repatriate of their own volition and how much encouragement, incentives or pressure are involved have been a subject of debate. On return, two different approaches have often been offered to returnees: going back to their home areas with a grant or joining settlement schemes. Whereas we know very little about the reintegration of the former, the resettlement of repatriated returnees in schemes in the eastern lowlands area of Tigray especially around Humera has been the subject of two PhD theses, one by Kassahun presented in his chapter in this book and the other by Hammond (2004) in which she explains how the returnees create a sense of 'home' by giving meaning to a an unfamiliar space and creating a sense of community. It is noteworthy that these returnee-resettlement schemes are in areas with a long history of migration and settlement. Not only are they areas where commercial farming had been promoted during the imperial era in the 1960s and where seasonal wage-labour migration and spontaneous migration to the area had developed, but the western lowlands have also been an area of resettlement under the Derg and where demobilized soldiers have been resettled (Mulugeta 2000). The repatriation of Garri and Borana returnees from Somalia and Kenya in the Borana area of Southern Ethiopia was complicated by the prior relationships between the groups, migration trends, conflicts over resources and limited awareness of these issues by the implementing agencies (Getachew 1996a; Bassi 1997). However, the departure of the refugees has left a mixed legacy including environmental consequences, infrastructure development, altered livelihood patterns, increased urbanization, and socio-cultural change (Bizuayehu 2004).

INTERNALLY DISPLACED PEOPLE

The question of internally displaced persons or groups has tended to receive limited attention, notably in comparison to refugees, returnees and resettlers, as well as development-induced displacees resulting from the creation of parks and dams, who tend to be more visible and whom the state has more of an interest in resettling. The problem of the internally displaced has therefore been the subject of limited research. Even in terms of numbers and categories less is known about the internally displaced.[34] They have been among the poorest in both rural and urban areas, often have lost access to land or other resources, and are involved in the informal sector or remain reliant on charity or assistance. Their survival strategies in Addis Ababa have been studied by Ephrem (1998).

DEMOBILIZED SOLDIERS

After 1991, demobilization became an important issue for the liberation groups that had overthrown the Derg. Like returnees, the demobilized soldiers were given two different options. For the most part they were given grants and returned to their home areas, or they were moved to urban areas. Little is known about those who returned to their home areas. However, some of the Tigrayan demobilized soldiers were resettled in agricultural settlements in the western lowlands, and their differential adaptations in an agricultural settlement scheme and the challenges they faced in reintegrating into civilian life have been considered by Mulugeta (2000). Some of the former soldiers who opted to remain in urban areas have tried to make use of their skills to form cooperatives. In this book Yisak provides a case study of the differences between more successful male cooperatives and failed female ones.

Convergences and contradictions in migration phenomena

The processes resulting in displacement discussed in this chapter seem at first sight to be rather different and unconnected, including war and refuge, internal conflict, repatriation, famine and resettlement, exclusion from areas assigned to development projects, dams and parks, and displacement due to urban expansion. However, there are sound reasons for treating the phenomena within a common framework. including spatial patterns and concentrations, political involvement and direction of the state, the marginalized status of displacees relocated in the national interest, their experience of displacement and struggles to re-establish their livelihoods and communities, and the cumulative potentially conflictual effects.

The various types of migration ranging from the areas of convergence of 'spontaneous' migration between the highlands and lowlands to the different forms of displacements at the coercive end of the continuum are interrelated in complex ways; in combination they have incremental effects. Moreover, the central dimensions with which this chapter has been concerned – the highland-lowland factor and the pervasive role of the state – are crucial to understanding this complexity.

In spatial terms the lowlands are where most large-scale settlements and agricultural development and investment projects and parks are located in the larger river valleys, notably the Awash and Omo-Gibe, and especially in the border areas, closer to refugee and returnee flows. Thus we find in the lowland border areas, particularly in the west, resettlement projects, former state farms and more recent agricultural investment projects, settlements of refugees, returnees and demobilized soldiers within the same space, competing with local people whose access to resources is often constrained by these developments.

From a state perspective the establishment of large-scale projects is seen as a means of achieving notable and tangible results and transformations in cost-effective ways, attracting donor and investor support, and using the opportunity to develop neglected and under-serviced areas assumed to have a high underutilized potential. However, as Turton points out in this book, both the refugee and the forced resettler have an ambiguous relationship with the nation state. Refugees, in contradiction with the states they came from and seeking asylum across borders, share similarities with forced resettlers, displaced in the national interest to make way for dams, parks, development projects, irrigation schemes, investment projects, etc. Many of the latter are economically and politically marginal minorities whose displacement is justified as required in the interest of the majority as represented by the state.

The experience of displacees is shared and often follows similar patterns of forced migration or dislocation involving loss of resources and social capital, and disruption or disintegration of social networks resulting in a range of forms of impoverishment as discussed in the risks model developed by Cernea (1996b, 2000). There are also similarities in the phases required for the gradual rebuilding of a sense of place, community and identity in a new setting through the re-establishment of social relations and institutions.

Due to the complex migration patterns and interactions, the various types of settlement reviewed in this book have tended to result in serious conflicts and contested legitimacies, notably over resource use, between indigenous peoples, spontaneous settlers from different periods, state-organized settlers during the Derg and currently, various waves of refugees and returnees, displaced groups and demobilized soldiers. The concentration of settlement in the lowlands through state intervention is a potential source of tension and conflict, notably over scarce natural resources, and there is growing evidence of a nexus between migration, environment and conflict (Tesfaye 2007).

Several reasons suggest that these trends will increase in the near future. These include decreasing land availability in the highlands, with household plot sizes reaching a viability threshold, the national need for increasing agricultural production for food self-sufficiency and for export, the desire to make use of the river potential, perceived as wasted, through irrigation and harnessing the hydropower potential to reduce dependence on oil imports and to export electricity to neighbouring countries. Unless the implications in terms of migratory trends and their consequences are understood and taken into consideration, further and even escalating conflict is not unlikely in the areas of convergence between highlands and lowlands, in the large river valleys and in the lowland border areas.

Notes

1. The current density of 70 persons per square kilometre is higher than most areas in sub-Saharan Africa, except for Burundi and Rwanda, (World population data sheet, *Population Reference Bureau*, Washington DC, 2007).

2. The difference between ox and hoe cultivation was central to the distinction made by Goody (1976) between Eurasian and African systems.

3. In much of the highlands average land-holdings per household are below one hectare and in some areas the average is nearing a practically unviable half hectare.

4. From Aksum to Lalibela to Gondar, Ankober and Addis Ababa (R. Pankhurst 1998).

5. Referred to as *Okal* in the Afar and Somali areas.

6. For the Borana see Helland (1997); for the Somali Ahmed (1997), and Hogg (1997b); for the Afar see Ali (1997) and Getachew (2001).

7. Bond friends in the northeast between Afar and Tigray highlanders refer to each other as *fiqur* (Assefa 1995:73-6); in the west among Oromo, Gumuz, Shinasha, Agaw and Amhara they are referred to as *michu* and play an important role in conflict resolution (Wolde-Selassie 2002:273); in the south among agro-pastoralists in South Omo they are referred to as *bel*, and are particularly important in times of hardship (Lydall and Strecker 1979). On the role of bond-friendship in dispute resolution see Pankhurst and Getachew (2008).

8. The Tigray highlanders send cattle to Afar bond friends around January when there is limited pasture in the highlands but rains in the lowlands. The Afar use the milk and butter, but rarely the oxen for ploughing, and have been given barley or wheat flour; however, more recently a payment of ten *birr* was collected by the *kebele* association. Conversely during the *kiremt* rainy season from July to September the Afar send their cattle to their *fiqur* in the highlands. The highlanders would likewise use the milk and plough with the oxen, and receive some money, which was set at ten *birr* per month (Assefa 1995:76-80).

9. Such as the *Gereb* institution between the Afar and Tigray (Assefa 1995:87-99), the *Sedqo* between the Somalis and Amhara (Tibebe 1994), and the *Mangima* between the Gumuz and the highlanders (Wolde-Selassie 2002:247-69).

10. This may be a deliberate strategy to provide a base in towns or settlements and access to resources. The children born of such marriages can become intermediaries, with access to schooling and proficiency in both languages and cultures (Piguet 2006:155-175).

11. Tesfaye (2007:69) found the most frequent strategies to be employment as a farmer in a local's house, becoming a sharecropper, or renting land from local people.

12. Webb and von Braun (1994: table 2.2) show regional differences in seasonal rainfall variations.

13. This expression, recorded by David Turton among the Mursi, was used as the title of the book edited by Allen (1996).

14. For the eastern escarpment, see Ahmed (2007, 1994); for the west (Berihun 1996) and for the southwest (Sutcliffe 1992).

15. See Flood (1976), Harbeson (1978); Ali (1997); Ayalew (2001); Buli (2001); and Getachew (2001).

16. The 1995 FDRE Constitution, article 40 number 5 states: 'Ethiopian pastoralists have the right to free land for grazing and cultivation as well as the right not to be displaced from their own lands'. Article 43 states: 'Rural development projects should serve not only the national needs but should also benefit the existing population in project areas' (p. 73). However, the constitutional land rights of pastoralist societies have not yet been put into practice.

17. The Relief and Rehabilitation Commission was established after the 1973 famine, and a Settlement Authority was set up in 1976 within the Ministry of Agriculture which was renamed Ministry of Agriculture and Settlement. The Settlement Authority was merged with the Awash Valley Authority and the Relief and Rehabilitation Commission in 1979.

18. These include Agneta *et al.* (1993); Alemneh (1990); Clay and Holcomb (1986); Dieci and Viezzoli (1992a); Eshetu and Teshome (1988); Gebre (2001, 2002, 2003); Dessalegn (1988a, 2003); Kloos (1990); Pankhurst (1990, 1992a, 1994a, 1998, 2002a); Prunier (1994); Sivini (1986);

JAMES EARL CARTER LIBRARY
GA. SOUTHWESTERN UNIVERSITY
AMERICUS GA 31709

and Wolde-Selassie (1997, 2000, 2002).
19. The mounting tensions with donors, notably over the expulsion of *Médecins sans Frontières* for criticizing forced resettlement, had an impact on donor attitudes not just regarding resettlement but also concerning the provision of aid to the country in general.
20. See Turton (2002b) on the predicament of the Mursi 'sandwiched' between the Mago and Omo parks.
21. The ecological argument about people and their animals shaping the environment in the parks and the consequent case for integrating people and parks is clearly made in Homewood and Rodgers (1986); Hobbs and Huenneke (1992) and Pimbert and Pretty (1995).
22. Such an approach recognizes that the interaction between people, their livestock and wildlife has created the current environment, accepts that local communities have rights to the resources, sees them as the custodians of the wildlife, involves them in park management as guides and guards, and shares the benefits of income from tourism with them so that there are incentives for them to protect the wildlife.
23. The Proceedings were produced by the short-lived Ministry of Natural Resources Development and Environmental Protection and FARM Africa (1995).
24. For overviews of African refugees see Gaim Kibreab (1985) and Adelman and Sorenson (1994). In 2005, UNHCR estimates the number of refugee in Africa at 2,571,500. (www.unhcr.org/statistics). UNHCR data include estimates of numbers of 'persons of concern' who fall under the mandate (refugees, asylum seekers, refugees returning home and internally displaced people).
25. Five countries of the Horn (Eritrea, Ethiopia, Djibouti, Somalia and Sudan) account for 30% of Africa's total population of refugees, asylum seekers and internally displaced persons (772,000 out of 2,571,500) (www.unhcr.org/statistics). In the last five years, the number of African refugees registered by the UNHCR has drastically decreased. However, IDPs do not benefit from UNHCR protection and in four years the ongoing Darfur crisis has generated over two million IDPs hosted in shelter camps and a further 230,000 refugees over the border in neighbouring Chad (www.reliefweb.int, source Oxfam Canada, April 2007).
26. See for instance Harrel-Bond (1986) and Kuhlman (1994b).
27. An estimated 3.5 million refugees were repatriated between 1971 and 1990 in Africa (Rogge 1994:16-7). In 1998 alone UNHCR estimated that 3.5 million of the 22.5 million refugees and internally displaced persons worldwide returned (Long and Oxfeld 2004:1).
28. For instance, in 1988 within a couple of weeks more than 300,000 Somali refugees entered Ethiopia fleeing Hargeisa and other main cities of Somaliland bombed by the Somali national army and air force.
29. Some 67,000 people were alleged to have been expelled from Ethiopia, and around 39,000 people from Eritrea. At the beginning of 2000 more than 350,000 Ethiopians had been displaced in the border areas (Tekeste and Tronvoll 2000:47-8).
30. See Zolberg *et al.* (1989), particularly chapter 4, for the historical background. In 1992 a year after Mengistu Haile Mariam and Siyad Barre were ousted from power in Ethiopia and Somalia respectively, there were 1,784,700 refugees in the Horn of Africa and among them 431,800 in Ethiopia (UNHCR *Statistical Yearbook* 2001 and 2005). According to UNHCR in 2005 there were some 772,000 refugees from the Horn of Africa and Ethiopia was hosting around 100,800 refugees, mainly from Somalia and Sudan.
31. For two versions explaining the complexity of events and inter-ethnic relations surrounding refugee and returnee movements in the south see Getachew (1996c) and Bassi (1997).
32. See Schlee (1990) on the ritual journeys of the Gabbra who cross the border from Kenya to Ethiopia on their pilgrimage routes.
33. UNHCR 'Kofi Annan's view of the world's refugees' quoted in *The Reporter*, 18 February 2004.
34. Over two million people were estimated to have been displaced in 2001, including refugee returnees, demobilized soldiers, settlers leaving resettlement areas and groups displaced due to conflict. Of these, 300,000 people were displaced as a result of internal conflicts and over 250,000 were returnees from resettlement areas (Pankhurst 2001c).

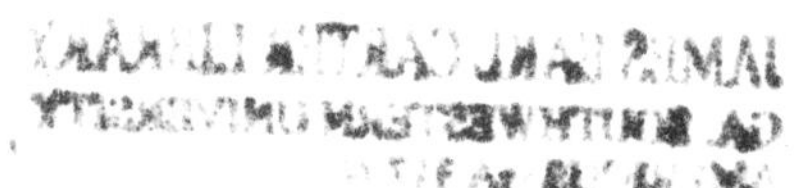

Part II

THEORETICAL & INTERNATIONAL PERSPECTIVES

Two

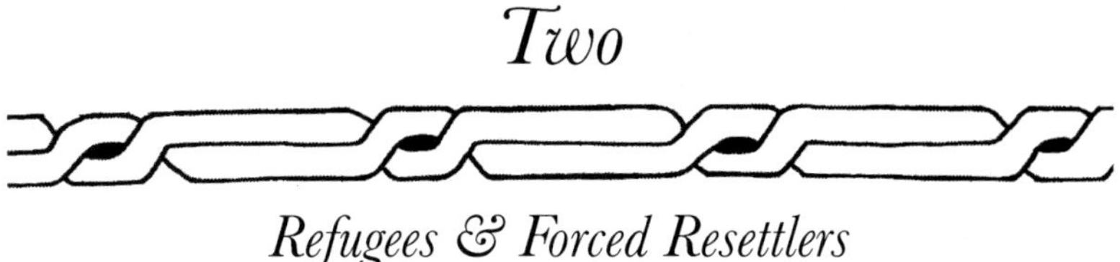

Refugees & Forced Resettlers

Towards a Unitary Study of Forced Displacement

DAVID TURTON

There has been a growing tendency, over the past few years, in both academic and policy circles, for refugees to be mentioned alongside 'other forced migrants', almost as though these were interchangeable categories. This is consistent with another noticeable development within the refugee studies field – the growing use of the term 'forced migration' to describe the scope of its interests and activities.[1] Consider, for example, the Refugee Studies Centre, in Oxford, with its Summer School and its masters degree, both in 'Forced Migration', and its periodical publication, *Forced Migration Review*, which developed from the earlier publication, *Refugee Participation Network Newsletter*. Consider also the professional association of the refugee studies community, which has given itself the name 'International Association for the Study of Forced Migration'. And consider the recently established research and teaching programmes at the University of the Witwatersrand in Johannesburg and at the American University in Cairo, which have called themselves 'Forced Migration Studies' and 'Refugee and Forced Migration Studies' respectively. Consider, finally, three recent publications by leading scholars of, respectively, international relations, law and international migration: Gil Loescher (2000), Anne Bayefski and Joan Fitzpatrick (eds.) (2000), and Susan Martin (2000). Each of these publications can be seen as falling squarely within the field of refugee studies and yet each uses the term 'forced migration' or 'forced displacement' to describe its subject matter.

It is at first surprising, then, that these same scholars show so little interest in the substantial literature on certainly the most numerous[2] and arguably the most 'forced' of all forced migrants, those displaced by development projects. According to Michael Cernea, formerly Senior Adviser on Social Policy at the World Bank and architect of the Bank's policy on involuntary resettlement, the lack of interest is mutual.

(T)he literature on 'refugees' coexists side by side with a literature on 'oustees' or

> on 'development-caused involuntary displacement'. There is little communication and mutual enrichment between them. Concepts and propositions are not interlinked, and empirical findings are rarely compared and integrated. For instance, most of the writings on refugees omit oustee groups from the typology of displaced populations. In turn, research on oustees forgoes the opportunity of doing comparative analysis by studying refugees. As a result, the chance for more in-depth treatment is being missed. (1996a: 294)

I shall begin this chapter by asking who the 'other forced migrants', so often referred to in the same breath as refugees, actually are and why they do not include those whom I shall refer to as 'forced resettlers'. I use this latter term to refer to people who have not only been forced to move because of a development project but who have also been allocated a specific area in which to resettle and been provided with at least a minimum of resources and services in order to re-establish themselves. Forced resettlement may also be called 'development-induced displacement and resettlement' (DIDR), while those forced to move by development projects may be called 'oustees', 'development-induced displaced persons' (DIDPs), 'project affected persons' (PAPs), 'development refugees' and 'resettlement refugees'. I prefer 'forced resettlers' because this term can also be used of those who are resettled by government-sponsored programmes which use resettlement as a technique of rural development and political control (as they were used in Tanzania, Ethiopia and South Africa in the recent past). It also avoids both the term 'refugee', which has a specific definition in international law, and such acronyms as 'PAPs' and 'DIDPs' which have an objectifying, depersonalizing and, ultimately, dehumanizing effect. Secondly, I shall discuss some of the empirical and conceptual similarities between refugees and forced resettlers. Finally, I shall suggest that the main obstacle to what Cernea calls the 'bridging of the research divide' (1996a) between these different populations of forced migrants is an over-reliance on *ad hoc* distinctions which have important political and policy implications but which result in categories which are ill-suited both to comparison, and to the observation, description and analysis of empirical data.

Who are these 'other forced migrants'?

They are, of course, 'internally displaced persons'. Usually referred to as 'IDPs', these are people who, because of the circumstances causing them to move (in practice, military conflict and violence), would have been considered worthy of international protection, under existing interpretations of international law and of the mandate of the UNHCR, if their move had taken them across an international border.[3] This is made abundantly clear by the three publications by Loescher, Bayefski and Fitzpatrick and Martin, just referred to.

Loescher's call for a 'comprehensive approach' to forced migration focuses exclusively on refugees ('people who have fled from and are unable to return to their own country because of persecution and violence') and the internally displaced ('people who have been uprooted because of persecution and violence but who remain in their own countries') (Loescher 2000: 190). He mentions 'people who have been uprooted by development projects', but only to point out that they are amongst the 'millions' of forced migrants 'who are outside UNHCR concern' *(ibid.*: 191). He includes a section on 'the growing problem of internal displacement', in which he notes that

'A new comprehensive international regime for forced migrants will necessarily have to place internally displaced persons [as defined above] at the centre of its concern'. And he calls attention to the need to strengthen the international human rights regime, so that the international community can better 'monitor developments in human rights issues and intercede on behalf of forced migrants' (ibid.: 210). It is here that one might reasonably have expected some reference to be made to the rights of forcibly resettled people, but it is clear that Loescher's sights remain firmly fixed on those who have been forced to move by conflict.

The lack of any reference to human rights issues affecting forced resettlers is even more glaringly apparent in the book edited by Bayefski and Fitzpatrick, the entire purpose of which is to discuss the human rights of forcibly displaced populations. The book does include, however, a chapter on the internally displaced (to which I shall return). Finally, Martin defines forced migrants, 'For the purpose of this paper', in the same way as Loescher, namely, as 'persons who flee or are obliged to leave their homes or places of habitual residence because of events threatening their lives or safety' (Martin 2000: 3). Also like Loescher, she makes only passing reference to forced resettlers, although she does note that they could become of concern to the international community if their governments were unable or unwilling to provide them with protection and assistance (*ibid.*: 6).

The interest of refugee studies scholars in the internally displaced has been fuelled, if not inspired, by the growing concern of the international community with the 'IDP problem', a concern that is motivated not only by humanitarian considerations but also by the political objective of preventing and 'containing' refugee flows. Be that as it may, and the 'real world' being what it is, it cannot be denied that there are strong practical reasons for maintaining a clear distinction between refugees and the internally displaced on the one hand, and forced resettlers on the other. The key point here is that both refugees and the internally displaced are unable or unwilling to avail themselves of the protection of their governments, while forced resettlers have been deliberately moved by their own governments in the name of 'eminent domain' law, which allows private property to be expropriated for the sake of a wider public good. Forced resettlers, therefore, expect to be compensated for the land and property they have lost and it remains the responsibility of the government that moved them to provide them with protection and assistance

> Development-induced displaced persons (DIDPs) generally remain in their country of origin and their legal protection should theoretically be guaranteed by the government. In terms of the international state system, the government is responsible for ensuring that the rights of people under its jurisdiction are respected… the complexities of DIDR [development-induced displacement and resettlement] result specifically because the government that is responsible for the displacement is also responsible for ensuring the protection of DIDPs. (Barutciski 2000: 2)

There are also strong practical grounds for maintaining a clear distinction between refugees and the internally displaced, because of the different statuses of these two categories of forced migrants in international law. Refugee protection, for which there exists a strong body of legally binding norms and principles, 'is essentially about promoting asylum in foreign countries', while the protection of the internally displaced, for which there are no legally binding norms and principles, 'is basically about humanitarian intervention in troubled countries' (Barutciski 2000). There is, of course, much debate about how to address the needs of the internally displaced, given that there is no single international organization with a mandate to protect and assist them. But what is generally agreed is that it is important not to risk 'diluting' the protection currently afforded to refugees under international law by extending the term (as would be perfectly meaningful in everyday speech) to other forced migrants who do not qualify for the same level of protection – to speak, for example, of 'internal' and 'external' refugees.

Refugees and forced resettlers: tracing the connections

But, just because there are practical advantages in distinguishing sub-classes within a class of empirically related phenomena, does this mean that academic research dealing with the sub-classes so distinguished should proceed as though on parallel tracks? One person who definitely thinks not is Michael Cernea (1996a: 294). He first argued in favour of more integration of the literature on forced resettlers and 'internal refugees' in an article published in the *Journal of Refugee Studies* in 1990 ('Internal refugee flows and development-induced population displacement') and he was still arguing the case ten years later in *Risks and Reconstruction: Experiences of Resettlers and Refugees* (Cernea and McDowell 2000). In this book he repeats the summary he gave in his 1996 chapter of the benefits to be gained from ' bridging the research divide':

> This potential for gain is fourfold. *Empirically*, the two bodies of research could enrich each other by comparing their factual findings. *Theoretically*, they could broaden their conceptualizations by exploring links and similarities between their sets of variables. *Methodologically*, they could sharpen their inquiry by borrowing and exchanging research techniques. And *politically*, they could influence the public arena more strongly by mutually reinforcing their policy advocacy and operational recommendations. (*ibid.*: 17, emphasis in the original)

The reasoning is persuasive but, judging by the way the term 'forced migration' continues to be used by the refugee studies community, it has fallen largely on deaf ears. Before attempting to explain why this should be so, it is worth mentioning briefly some points of similarity and difference between those forced migrants who fall within the category of 'refugees' and those who fall within the category of 'forced resettlers'. I shall approach this question, first, by focusing on the *experiences* of forced migrants and on the challenges they face in re-establishing themselves in a new place. Here I shall rely mainly on Cernea himself, and on an unpublished essay by Elizabeth Colson, 'Coping in Adversity' (1991), which is a rare example of an attempt to achieve precisely the kind of 'bridging' between two bodies of 'research literature' that Cernea has been calling for. Second, I shall move from the empirical to the conceptual level and suggest that the figure of the refugee and the figure of the forced resettler can both be seen as revealing underlying contradictions in the ideology of the nation-state as the dominant political organizing principle of the modern world.

The definitions and labels used to separate subsets of forced migrants are based on the causes of flight, or the 'imputed motives' (Colson 1991: 6) of those who flee, and on the prevailing norms and principles of international law. They are not based on the experiences of forced migrants after they have left home. Both Colson and Cernea emphasize the 'commonalities of experience…among the uprooted, however they are set in motion' (*ibid.*: 1). Colson focuses on the psychological stress caused by the experience of being forcibly displaced. She notes that, while all migrants are liable to increased levels of stress, this is compounded for *forced* migrants by bereavement at the loss of their homes and anger and resentment towards the agents and institutions which forced them to move. This is likely to lead, for both refugees and forced resettlers, to a loss of trust in society generally and to the expression of opposition and antagonism towards the administrative authorities, and towards the staff of humanitarian organizations, who continue to have power over their lives. For refugees, this is seen most obviously in a critical and resentful attitude towards camp personnel, as reported, for example, in Harrell-Bond's account of Ugandan refugees in Sudanese camps (1986) and in Malkki's account of Hutu refugees in Mishamo refugee settlement in Tanzania, who regularly described themselves as the 'slaves' of the Tanzanian authorities (1995a: 120).

Unlike most refugees, forced resettlers (I refer here specifically to those displaced by infrastructural projects) have no choice about leaving their homes and cannot entertain the slightest hope of returning to them. Also unlike refugees, of course, it is theoretically possible for their move to be planned well in advance. The authorities can therefore take steps to ensure that the disruptive impact of the move is minimized and that the standard of living of the resettlers is improved, or at least maintained. In practice, however, this hardly ever happens: those displaced by development projects are not only (like refugees), typically, amongst the poorest and politically most marginal members of a society but they are also likely to become even more impoverished as a result of the move. Forced resettlers, therefore, may end up 'as alienated from their governments as the refugees who have fled their countries' (Colson 1999: 15). Based initially on her study of the forced displacement of the Gwembe Tonga, of Zambia, by the Kariba Dam in 1957-58, Colson has attempted, in conjunction with Thayer Scudder, to demarcate phases in the *process* of forced displacement, which will also be found to apply to refugee populations. First ,there is a stage of denial ('this cannot happen to us'), when 'the possibility of removal is too stressful to acknowledge' (Scudder and Colson 1982: 271). After the move has taken place, there is likely to be a phase during which people will cling to old certainties and take no risks, even if this prevents them from taking advantage of new economic opportunities.

> Following removal, the majority of relocatees, including refugees, can be expected to follow a conservative strategy. They cope with the stress of removal by clinging to the familiar and changing no more than is necessary. (*ibid.*: 272)

Here we may see a clear illustration of the difference which force, or the relative lack of choice in deciding whether, when and where to move, makes to the behaviour of migrants. The greater the area of choice available to them, even though they may be escaping from difficult or even life-threatening, circumstances, the more likely they are to show high levels of innovation and adaptation in taking advantage of the opportunities offered by their new environment (Turton 1996).

The fact that forced resettlement, unlike the flight of refugees, can be planned in advance, and the fact that it is an inescapable consequence of economic development have provided both the motive and the opportunity for social scientists to study its long-term consequences. This research, much of it carried out by social anthropologists, has produced a huge amount of detailed information that has been used in efforts to promote improvements in the design and implementation of resettlement projects. Cernea, who has been at the forefront of these efforts, has presented what he calls an 'impoverishment, risks and reconstruction model' of forced resettlement, which is intended to act as a guide to the actions needed if the potentially impoverishing effects of forced resettlement are to be avoided or minimized. Two of these effects are particularly relevant to the comparison of forced resettlers with refugees: landlessness and loss of 'social capital'.[4] According to Cernea, empirical evidence shows that loss of land 'is the principal form of decapitalization and pauperization' of forced resettlers (2000: 23) and that 'Settling displaced people back on cultivable land…is the heart of the matter in reconstructing livelihoods' (*ibid.*: 35). Loss of *social* capital refers to the disruption and disintegration of the informal social support networks, which are vital to economic survival in communities where individuals and households are vulnerable to short-term and unpredictable fluctuations in income. Both of these potentially impoverishing effects of forced migration clearly apply to those forced to move by conflict, whether across international borders or not, at least as much as they do to those forced to move by development projects.

On an empirical level, then, it is clear that refugees and forced resettlers 'confront strikingly similar social and economic problems' (Cernea 2000: 17). But it is also possible to trace a connection between them at the conceptual level, by considering their relationship to the nation-state, or to what Malkki (1992) has called 'the national order of things'.[5] The refugee, as a person who is unable or unwilling to obtain the protection of his or her own government, makes visible a contradiction between citizenship, as the universal source of all individual rights, and nationhood as an identity ascribed at birth and entailing a sentimental attachment to a specific community and territory.

> (…) the twentieth century became the century of refugees, not because it was extraordinary in forcing people to flee, but because of the division of the globe into nation-states in which states were assigned the role of protectors of rights, but also that of exclusive protectors of their own citizens. When the globe was totally divided into states, those fleeing persecution in one state had nowhere to go but to another state, and required the permission of the other state to enter it. (Adelman 1999: 9)

The figure of the refugee exposes a contradiction in the idea of the nation-state, as both a culturally homogeneous political community and the universal principle of political organization. The refugee is 'out of place' in a conceptual as well as an empirical sense. He or she is an anomaly produced by the universalization of the nation-state as a principle of political organization.

The forced resettler, as a person displaced 'in the national interest' to make way for a development project, makes visible a contradiction between the nation-state as, on the one hand, the ultimate source of legitimate political control and the principal agent of development in a given territory and, on the other, a community of equal citizens. The main objective of a project involving forced resettlement is, of course, to benefit a much wider population than that of the displaced themselves. And the key characteristic of this wider population is that it shares with the displaced population membership of the same nation-state. Co-membership of the nation-state, therefore, makes legally and morally legitimate a situation in which, as Cernea has put it, 'some people enjoy the gains of development, while others bear its pains' (2000: 12). But who are these 'others' who are also fellow-citizens? In what sense are they 'other'? Is it just that they are 'not us' or is it, more fundamentally, that they are 'not *like* us', that they have a different, and systematically inferior, relationship to the sources of state power?

The empirical evidence suggests the latter answer is correct. In case after case of forced resettlement, we see the state exercising its right to expropriate private property for public use against a relatively impoverished and powerless group of its own citizens, with typically disastrous consequences for their economic, physical, psychological and social well-being.[6] In many cases, the displaced people are members of an indigenous minority who are forced out of their home territory or part of it. They are economically and politically marginal to the nation-state within which they were incorporated in the process of nation-building, and their forced displacement can be seen as a continuation of that same process. Writing about the contribution of forced resettlers to the 'greater common good' in India, Arundhati Roy notes that well over half of those due to be displaced by the Sardar Sarovar Dam on the Narmada River belong to ethnic minorities which make up only 8 percent of the Indian population as a whole. She comments:

> This opens up a whole new dimension to the story. The ethnic 'otherness' of their victims takes some of the pressure off the Nation Builders. It's like having an expense account. Someone else pays the bills. People from another country. Another world. India's poorest people are subsidizing the lifestyles of her richest… (1999: 18-19)

In other words, forced resettlement is a 'price worth paying' for the good of the nation, provided somebody else pays it, where 'somebody else' refers to fellow citizens whose relationship to the state is different from, and inferior to, our own. It follows that, when affected populations form themselves into campaigning organizations to resist resettlement, they are challenging not just a particular project, or the development policy of a particular state, but the idea that underpins the state's claim to sovereign power over its territory: that it is a 'nation'-state, a national community of equal citizens. They are challenging, in other words, the legitimacy of state power. On this basis, the forced resettler has an equal claim, along with the refugee, to being considered the 'Achilles heel' of the nation-state system (Adelman 1999: 93). Both categories of forced migrants expose underlying contradictions in the ideology of the nation-state.

There is no doubt that the empirical and conceptual connections that can be traced between refugees and forced resettlers support Cernea's call for more interchange of ideas and findings between researchers focusing on these two categories of forced migrants. Although Cernea himself considers that trends in this direction are 'getting stronger and gaining ground' (2000: 17), he does not give the evidence to support this claim and one can therefore be forgiven for remaining sceptical about it. But, in any event, his basic contention – that communication and cross-reference between these two bodies of literature has been notable by its absence – remains valid and, in the light of the above discussion, requires explanation.

An explanation

Cernea's principal motive for wishing to see a more effective dialogue between researchers focusing on refugees and those focusing on forced resettlers is that this would improve the quality of research, theoretically and methodologically, in both areas and thereby help to improve policy. Specifically, it would help to recognize, and then prevent or minimize, the risks of impoverishment that are faced by both categories of forced migrants. Paradoxically, however, there are good reasons to believe that it is precisely the close relationship between the academic field of refugee studies and the world of policy and practice that has worked *against* the interchange of ideas and findings between these two areas of research. According to Cernea, 'The key policy objective in resettlement is restoring the income-generating capacity of resettlers' (1996a: 314), while refugee protection, in the words of Barutciski, quoted earlier, 'is essentially about promoting asylum in foreign countries'.

> While conceptual models that emphasize the reconstruction of livelihoods are appropriate for DIDR situations which may or may not involve abuse on the part of local authorities, they are not necessarily appropriate for refugee emergencies that are by definition situations in which the victims' human rights are violated...it would be overly ambitious to believe or insist that emergency refugee assistance is intended to restore the livelihoods of victims of persecution or conflict to levels before their flight'. (Barutciski 2000: 2)

There was a time, of course, when such an objective was not seen as 'overly ambitious' but as part of a desirable progression from 'relief to development'. That was during what has been called the 'asylum phase' (Crisp 2000) in the history of the post-war international refugee regime (from the 1960s to the 1980s), when the integration of refugees in the country of first asylum (usually in the developing world) was seen, along with voluntary repatriation, as the most viable and feasible 'durable solution'. Thus, during the 1960s and '70s agricultural settlement schemes for refugees were set up with the help of the UNHCR in several African countries, the aim being to help refugees re-establish themselves in a new country and to become self-sufficient.

> Between 1961 and 1978, approximately 60 rural settlements have been installed, most of them in Burundi, Uganda and Tanzania... In the 1990s, nearly a quarter of all refugees in sub-Saharan Africa were estimated to be living in 140 organized settlements, most in the eastern and southern regions... Planned land resettlements have long been considered the best means for promoting refugee self-sufficiency and local integration. (Lassailly-Jacob 2000: 112)

It is here, in the planning of agricultural settlement schemes for refugees, that research on forced resettlement has, potentially, the greatest practical relevance to refugee policy (Gaim Kibreab 2000: 324-331). But this policy has significantly changed since the 1980s, to one which focuses on prevention and containment in countries and regions of origin, and on early repatriation, rather than on the reconstruction of refugee livelihoods in countries of asylum.

> The days are past when many rural refugees could be assisted toward achieving self-sufficiency in exile. Going into exile now means hiding among locals or surviving in transit camps, where the living conditions are so poor that few wish to stay on. (Lassailly-Jacob 2000: 123)

There is consequently little incentive for policy-oriented research in refugee studies to concern itself with the findings of the equally policy-oriented research on forced resettlers.

But there is another, more fundamental, way in which 'the dominance of policy concerns in refugee studies' (Black 2001: 67) can be seen as working against the integration of research findings on different populations of forced migrants. I am referring here to the *intellectual* dependence of refugee studies on categories and labels which are the product of political and policy concerns rather than of scientific ones. The scientific point of distinguishing subsets within a class of related phenomena is to encourage and facilitate comparison between those subsets, in order to throw light on the wider class, and to aid (in the sense of make more acute) the observation, description and analysis of empirical data. These objectives are interdependent, since there must be a constant readiness to revise and sharpen abstract categories in the light of empirical observation. The trouble with the categories used within refugee studies is that, being dictated by political and policy concerns rather than scientific ones, they actually discourage comparison within the broader category of forced migration and are not amenable to revision in the light of empirical evidence.

Consider the term 'refugee' itself. This, of course, is a legal category, based on the 1951 *Convention Relating to the Status of Refugees*, which was itself heavily based on the 'strategic political objectives' of the Western powers at that particular historical moment. (Hathaway 1991, quoted in Chimni 2000: 14). Hathaway distinguishes 'five essential elements' in the Convention definition, of which the first is 'alienage': the claimant for refugee status must be outside his or her country of origin. But, as Hathaway points out, the exclusion of 'internal refugees' from the Convention definition was not 'so much a matter of conceptual principle, as it was a reflection of the limited reach of international law' (1991, quoted in Chimni 2000: 401). He quotes Shacknove's argument that 'alienage is an unnecessary condition for establishing refugee status. It...is a subject of a broader category: the physical access of the international community to the uprooted person' (Shacknove 1985: 277) and concludes that

> ...the physical presence of the unprotected person outside her country of origin is not a constitutive element of her refugeehood, but is rather a practical condition precedent to placing her within the effective scope of international protection'. (Hathaway 1991 quoted in Chimni 2000: 401)

The key criterion, then, that distinguishes refugees, as the term is used in the language of refugee studies, from 'other forced migrants' is not based on 'conceptual principle' and is not a 'constitutive element' of refugeehood. It follows that the term does not distinguish a 'subset' of forced migrants that can be meaningfully compared to other subsets. As Malkki has put it, the term is not 'a label for a special, generalisable "kind" or "type" of person or situation' but 'a descriptive rubric that includes within it a world of socio-economic statuses, personal histories, and psychological or spiritual situations' (1995b: 496).

The 'IDP' category is even more hazy and imprecise. The internally displaced are defined, in the 'Guiding Principles on Internal Displacement' of the UN Office for the Coordination of Humanitarian Affairs (OCHA), as

> persons or groups of persons who have been forced or obliged to flee or to leave their homes or places of habitual residence, in particular as a result of or in order to avoid the effects of armed conflict, situations of generalised violence, violations of human rights or natural disasters, and who have not crossed an internationally recognized State border. (quoted in Chimni 2000: 242)

The 'essential' purpose of the definition is to 'help identify persons who should be of concern to the international community because they are basically in refugee-like situations within their own countries' (Cohen 1996, quoted by Chimni 2000: 407). The inclusion of people who have fled their homes because of 'natural disasters' (itself a highly ambiguous and imprecise concept) is intended to cater for cases where governments 'respond to such disasters by discriminating against or neglecting certain groups on political or ethnic grounds or by violating their human rights in other ways' (Cohen 2000: 82).

A first point to make here is that, on these grounds, it would be logical and understandable to prefer the term 'internal refugees' to 'internally displaced persons'. This would both recognize the 'refugee-like' situation of the people being referred to and make clear the distinction between them and forced resettlers, who are also displaced within their own countries but who are not in a 'refugee-like' situation. As noted earlier, however, the logic which dictates the use of 'IDP' rather than 'internal refugee' is a practical, not a conceptual, one: it has to do with a concern not to undermine the protection available to refugees under the 1951 Convention, which makes 'alienage' an 'essential element' (Hathaway 1991, quoted in Chimni, 2000: 15) of the legal definition of a refugee.

Secondly, the form of words used to justify the inclusion of those displaced by 'natural disasters' could easily be used to extend the definition to many if not most of today's forced resettlers, even though they are not mentioned in the formal definition. Indeed, principle 6.2(c) states that all human beings have a right to be protected from 'arbitrary displacement', including cases of 'large-scale development projects, which are not justified by compelling and overriding public interests' (quoted in Chimni 2000: 427.) But this ignores the main issue in forced resettlement, which is not simply that people should be protected from 'arbitrary displacement' but that, however compelling the public interest reasons for displacing them, there remains an obligation on governments to protect their political, social and economic rights (Pettersson 2002). In principle, then, the definition is extendable to a huge variety of different situations, groups and individuals and is too vague (note such qualifiers as 'in particular', 'essentially' and 'basically') and inclusive to serve as a meaningful analytical category for comparative purposes.

For the same reason, the categories 'refugee' and 'IDP' are also unhelpful when it comes to the observation, description and analysis of empirical data – of the world as it actually is. It happens that the then Head of UNHCR's Evaluation and Policy Analysis Unit, Jeff Crisp, speaking at the biennial meeting of the International Association for the Study of Forced Migration in 2001, lamented the fact that UNHCR staff 'seem to know less and less about the people and communities we work with' (Crisp 2001: 9). He gives a number of *ad hoc* explanations for this: security problems, which keep UNHCR staff away from rural areas where refugees are mainly found, increased paperwork which ties staff to their computers, and rapid staff turnover 'in remote locations'. He also complains that researchers in refugee studies are spending too much time in libraries and not enough in the field. By way of illustration, he mentions having met several postgraduate students in the recent past who wanted to write dissertations about the international community's responsibilities towards the internally displaced, but none who wanted to investigate the situation of the internally displaced 'on the ground' (*ibid.*). This call for more in-depth empirical research in refugee studies is greatly to be welcomed. It also goes to the heart of the matter I have been discussing in this chapter, because it puts the focus on the *experiences* of refugees and 'other forced migrants', rather than on the causes of their flight or their status in international law. But the argument I have presented here suggests that the explanation for this lack of knowledge of the everyday lives and preoccupations of refugees 'and other forced migrants', goes deeper than mere lack of time and/or interest amongst UNHCR staff and academics respectively.

Empirical research, as opposed to mere random observation, cannot proceed except in the light of general propositions which, among other things, identify the phenomena to be investigated and group them into meaningful general categories. These categories must, in turn, be open to refinement and revision in the light of particular observation. This condition cannot be met, however, by categories which are designed to meet the needs of practical politics and humanitarian assistance rather than of scientific enquiry. The category distinctions which I have discussed in this chapter are rightly and tenaciously upheld by academics, policy-makers and activists alike, on the grounds that they are vital, given the current 'reach' of international law, for the protection and assistance of refugees. The trouble is, they would not stand up to the close scrutiny which would inevitably result from the kind of field-based, empirical research that Crisp is calling for (Allen and Turton 1996: 5-9). If taken seriously, therefore, such research could lead to a wholesale questioning of the unexamined assumptions upon which the current international regime of refugee protection and humanitarian assistance – and possibly much else – is based. I do not wish to rule out the possibility that it is precisely because he wishes to see this sort of questioning take place that Crisp has called for more 'extensive field-based research' in refugee studies (Crisp 2001: 9).

Conclusion

I take it for granted that it is through the questioning of taken-for-granted assumptions that academic research can make its most valuable contribution to the general improvement of the human condition. But, of course, when knowledge has potentially radical and disturbing consequences for established thought and practice, ignorance may be considered bliss. This presents a fourfold challenge to all those involved in the study of forced migration and in the design and implementation of policies intended to improve the situation of forced migrants. First, we need to adopt a unitary and inclusive approach to the definition of the field. Second, we need to encourage research which is aimed at understanding the situation of forced migrants at the local level, irrespective of the causes of their flight. Third, we need to recognize that such research will, inevitably and rightly, call into question the adequacy and usefulness of existing generalizations, assumptions and categories. And fourth, we need to recognize that it is by the questioning of taken-for-granted assumptions and categories that academic research can have its most beneficial impact on policy and practice.

Notes

This chapter began life as a paper for the Refugee Studies Centre's International Summer School in Forced Migration, with the title 'Refugees and "other forced migrants"'. Longer versions have been published as a UNHCR Working Paper in the series 'New Issues in Refugee Research' (No. 94, 2003) and in C. de Wet (ed.) *Development-Induced Displacement: Problems, Policies and People*, New York and Oxford: Berghahn Books, 2006.

1. For a discussion of the logical and other difficulties raised by the term 'forced migration' see Turton (2005).
2. Based on a study of projects involving involuntary resettlement which were assisted by the World Bank between 1986 and 1993, it has been estimated that about 10 million people per year were displaced during the 1990s as a result of dam construction, urban clearance and road-building alone (Cernea 1996a: 300). More recently, Cernea has estimated that 'during the last two decades of the previous century, the magnitude of forced population displacements caused by development programmes was some 200 million people globally…' (2000: 11) and 'rises to about 280-300 million over 20 years, or 15 million people annually (2008b: 20).
3. I shall refer to them as 'the internally displaced' and use the acronym 'IDP' only in inverted commas.
4. The others are 'joblessness', 'homelessness', 'marginalization', 'food insecurity', 'increased morbidity' and 'loss of access to common property resources' (Cernea 2000: 20).
5. The argument that follows is set out at greater length in Turton (2002a).
6. In a recent paper, Chris de Wet (2001) has considered why this should be so and whether such results are avoidable. He argues that 'the resettlement components of development projects display a very high failure rate… because of the inherent complexity of what is involved when we try to combine moving people with improving their conditions'.

Three

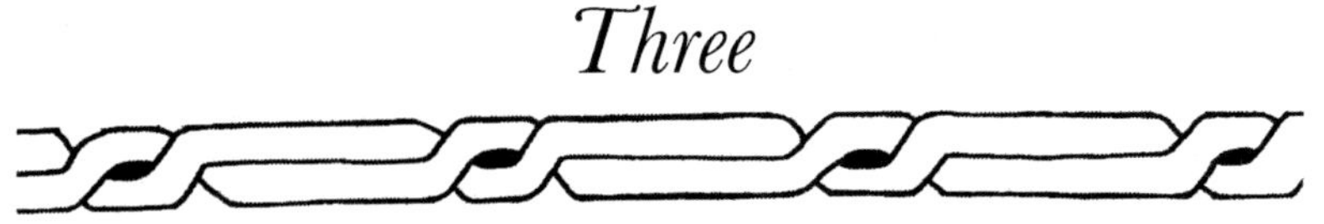

Why Do Things Often Go Wrong in Resettlement Projects?

CHRIS DE WET

Introductory remarks

WHY SUCH A NEGATIVE TITLE?

This chapter develops a framework to explain why it is that things so often turn out badly for the resettled people and host populations affected by the resettlement. It is not necessarily the case that resettlement will always turn out badly for the affected people. But if we are to do something constructive about it, we have to start with the reality that on the whole the news is not good, and that cases where resettled people are better-off, or even better-off in some ways, for having been resettled, seem rather few and far between. Why not start with the good news?

Cases that could be termed either successful, or partly so, include: the Egyptian side of the Aswan Dam resettlement; aspects of the Kainji Dam resettlement in Nigeria; the Rican Arenal Hydroelectric project in Costa Rica; the Urra 1 project in Colombia; and, of course, resettlement arising out of the Shuikou and Xiaolangdi Dams in China. The two Latin American cases were still at a relatively early stage at the time of the reports that suggested that they were successful (Partridge 1993; de Castro Illera and Egre 2000). Aswan's positive trajectory after ten years of looking like failing seems to relate to very case-specific circumstances (Fernea and Fernea 1991; Fernea 1998). With Kainji, agricultural success resulted from the dam, but, seemingly, more as serendipity than because of anything the project did. People took the initiative and used small petrol-powered pumps to irrigate the area above the water level of the dam, as well as using the draw-down area for livestock grazing (Roder 1994: 57).

What about the Chinese cases? The Shuikuo and Xiaolangdi cases have shown a significant degree of settler participation, a substantial increase in household incomes, better housing and services, a high degree of flexibility in actual implementation, and, apparently, a high degree of settler satisfaction (Picciotto *et al.* 2002; Travers and Kimura 1993). Without detracting from these successes, we need to ask how representative and sustainable they are. A number of cases have not been remotely as successful elsewhere in China and have also taken place after the critical resettlement policy reforms of the 1980s; economic changes resulting from globalization and the move to a market economy in China, coupled with difficulties in finding land or jobs to replace land lost to resettlement, are seemingly making it increasingly difficult for China's undoubtedly progressive resettlement policy to be implemented in practice, and for livelihoods to be guaranteed for resettlers (Meikle and Zhu 2000).

We also need to ask how replicable the Chinese experience is in poorer, and administratively weaker, countries which do not have a long history of resettlement. I would therefore be inclined to say: let's look and see what China did right, and see what we can learn from it? However, China clearly is something of a special case, and it may not be able to sustain its successes to the same degree in the future. So, that brings us back to the sad fact that the overwhelming majority of cases of resettlement worldwide, including in Africa, have not been successful.

Two views as to why things so often go wrong in resettlement

Why does resettlement so often go wrong, and end up leaving the resettled people (and often others as well) economically, socially and psychologically worse-off than before? There seem to be two broad approaches to answering this question, which one might call the 'Inadequate Inputs' and the 'Inherent Complexities' approaches respectively. These different 'diagnoses' have implications for how we should go about attempting to improve resettlement outcomes.

The 'Inadequate Inputs' approach is largely associated with the initiatives and policies of the World Bank. This approach argues that resettlement goes wrong, principally because of a lack of the proper inputs: national legal frameworks and policies, political will, funding, pre-resettlement surveys, planning, consultation, careful implementation and monitoring. Lack of these inputs are what gives rise to what Michael Cernea has conceptualized as the following eight principal 'impoverishment risks': landlessness; joblessness; homelessness; marginalization; food insecurity; increased morbidity; loss of access to common property resources; and community disarticulation (Cernea 2000: 20 and 22 ff).

This approach is however, basically optimistic in tenor, as Cernea argues that 'the general risk pattern inherent in displacement can be controlled through a policy response that mandates and finances integrated problem resolution' (ibid.: 34). Proper policy, political will and provision (particularly funding) can overcome the problem of inadequacy of inputs, and the impoverishment risks can then be turned into opportunities for reconstruction, such that resettlement becomes resettlement with development, leaving the resettled people better-off than before (*ibid.*: 35 ff).

The approach is broadly economic (Koenig 2001) and technical in character. Most of the impoverishment risks relate to economic resources, with Cernea emphasizing the importance of the risk to people's livelihoods, and the centrality of reconstructing livelihoods (Cernea 2000: 35). The key problems confronting resettlement are seen as essentially operationalizable, as problems that can be dealt with through the reform of policy and procedures, and the provision of the necessary resources. The complexity of the resettlement process can thus, in principle, be mastered and turned to good effect.

In contrast to this is an approach which I have found myself moving towards, as a result of trying to synthesize some of the writings on resettlement. I call it the

'Inherent Complexity' approach. I argue that, because of the nature of involuntary resettlement, it is characterized by a complexity which gives rise to a range of problems that are more difficult to deal with, and involve more than providing the kind of inputs mentioned above.

'Risks', or 'threats'?

Cernea has used the idea of '*risks*' in conceptualizing his perspective on the problems confronting attempts at successful resettlement. Others have wondered whether this is in fact the most appropriate term to convey the kinds of problems to which Cernea is referring. Let us briefly consider this terminological issue, as it has implications for the way in which I shall present my arguments in this chapter.

Cernea defines 'risk' as follows:

> We use the sociological concept of risk to indicate the *possibility* that a certain course of action will trigger injurious effects – losses and destruction (after Giddens 1990)...Risks are often directly perceptible, and also measurable through science (Adams1998), as they are an objective reality. The cultural construction of a risk – be it a social or a natural risk – could emphasize or de-emphasize (belittle) its seriousness, or could also ignore it, but this does not change the objective nature of risks (Stallings 1995)...Consonant with most of the current risk literature, risk may be defined as the possibility embedded in a certain course of social action to trigger adverse effects. (Cernea 2000: 19, and footnote 5)

For Cernea, risks thus have an objective nature, independently of how they are subjectively understood.

Dwivedi, writing in the context of the damming of the Narmada River in India, feels that 'risk' is not the appropriate term for what Cernea wants to convey. He argues that

> The meaning implied in the term 'risk' in [Cernea's] model is 'danger'. Drawn from sociological contributions ... on the pervasive nature of ' risks' in modern society and life... the model is almost synonymous with certainty. For a warning model it is only prudent to draw attention to the certainty of adverse displacement effects. (Dwivedi 1999: 46)

Dwivedi thus seems to be arguing that what Cernea calls 'risks' are in fact more like predictions, i.e. that if specific counter-actions are not taken, there is a very high certainty that landlessness, joblessness, etc. *will* occur. He argues that it is necessary to maintain the conceptual distinction between certainty and risk, as risk, which he defines as the 'subjective probability calculations of actors' (1999: 46), is about the *uncertainty* of outcomes. It seems to me that it is precisely because the outcome is uncertain that people take a gamble, a risk, whereas Cernea seems to be arguing that, unless we take appropriate preventative action, it is effectively certain that the negative condition related to the risk (e.g. landlessness) will be realized.

'Furthermore.' argues Dwivedi, 'to use risk and certainty synonymously is to ignore a critical phase in displacement impact; affected people spend a period of time under conditions of "uncertainty", without adequate information on the nature of impact and the resettlement entitlements, if any.' He then develops his own position, arguing that he understands risk as 'the subjective [probability] calculations of different groups of people embedded differentially in political-economic and environmental conditions…[and that] the calculations of losses and gains are influenced by cultural norms of acceptance and [by] legal frameworks of assigning compensation' (Dwivedi 1999: 47). For Dwivedi, risk is thus subjective, although embedded in and informed by contexts and conditions which have an existence independent of the subjectively calculating and risk-taking individual or group.

I fully agree with Cernea that there appear to be objective conditions and tendencies, seemingly inherent in the nature of resettlement, which, if not countered, lead to negative outcomes for many of the resettled people. I also agree with Dwivedi that it is important to maintain the distinction between certainty and uncertainty, and between objective conditions and subjective calculations and initiatives – even if the latter are influenced by people's reading of the former, and may impact back upon the former. 'Risk' seems best suited to deal with the dimensions of uncertainty, and of the subjective; so we need another term to accommodate the realm of (greater) certainty and the (more) objective, that relates to the (very real) kinds of problems that Cernea is dealing with.

I would suggest that the term '*threats*' might serve our purpose, defined as 'an indication of imminent harm, danger or pain; a person or thing that is regarded as dangerous or likely to inflict pain or misery' (Collins English Dictionary, 1982: 1513). 'Threats' thus refer to a negative condition, which has a high likelihood of occurring. I therefore suggest that we distinguish between 'threats' and 'risks' in relation to resettlement.

The 'Inherent Complexity' approach to why things so often go wrong

Having cleared some of the ground, let me now outline the 'Inherent Complexity' approach to why resettlement so often goes wrong. This is an exploratory exposition, and by no means a final formulation. I shall try to identify what I consider to be some of the main characteristics of involuntary resettlement, and show how they generate a complexity around resettlement, which gives rise to the threats which, while not necessarily all equally threatening in all instances, seem to me to be all but inherent in the process of resettlement as such. These threats seem to operate at different levels of comprehensiveness or incorporation, and I shall suggest a schema for analyzing threats in this way. Where we locate threats and their source will have implications for how we go about attempting to deal with them. I refer to African cases in my exposition, but cannot go into any great detail.

WHAT ARE THE MAIN CHARACTERISTICS OF INVOLUNTARY RESETTLEMENT?

(i) *Involuntary resettlement involves imposed spatial change, in the sense that it involves people having to move from one settlement and area to another.* This has cultural, social, political and economic implications. Particularly in small-scale rural settings – but also in urban working-class settings (Western 1981; Whisson 1976, for Cape Town, where 'Coloured' communities were relocated because of the Group Areas Act, during the apartheid era) – relationships have a strong territorial component, and are in this sense to a considerable degree spatially based. The spatial change thus requires people to develop new sets of relationships. Depending on the scope of the spatial change, and the speed and degree of participation with which it takes place, people may experience serious social disruption, or 'dislocation', in Cernea's terms. In some of the more extreme cases, the Sudanese Nubians were moved about 800 kilometres from their original homes, and away from the banks of the Nile River (Fahim 1973: 43), while in the case of the Akosombo Dam on the Volta River, the formation of Lake Volta started more than a year ahead of the originally planned date, which put tremendous pressure on the planning and preparation of resettlement (Lumsden 1973: 119).

(ii) *Spatial change usually involves a change in the patterns of people's access to resources.* Typically, resettlement and the agricultural plans accompanying it in rural cases involve a change in land use and often land tenure. In the case of a number of villagization schemes in South Africa, and elsewhere in Africa (de Wet 1995: 26-38), people have often found themselves with less arable and/or grazing land, as well as further from resources such as water and wood. Most of the time, compensation for lost lands or other resources has been inadequate, and/or late in being paid (e.g. Nangbeto Dam in Togo; World Bank 1998b: 8ff; Manantali in Mali; Grimm 1991:136).

(iii) *Resettled people usually find themselves in larger, and more heterogeneous, settlements than previously.* Thus, in the cases of the Aswan Dam and the Volta River Project, people found themselves in settlements from ten to thirty times larger than they had been accustomed to (Fahim 1981: 55-57; Butcher 1970: 89). Not only have new settlements been larger, but also more ethnically diverse. This tends to give rise to problems around the competition for resources and the negotiation of political leadership within new settlements. While such tensions are usually most acute in the early years after resettlement, easing off with time, in some cases, such as some new settlements in the Volta situation (Diaw and Schmidt-Kallert 1990:120) twenty-five years on, divisions have persisted, and even worsened. The day-to-day handling of cultural diversity in new settlements remains a sensitive issue, with new procedures having to be worked out for such sensitive matters as how to conduct funerals. Christians and Muslims were unable to sustain combined burial societies in the Qeto resettlement area in Wellega in Ethiopia after they had been moved there with the massive drought/politically related resettlement of the mid-1980s (Pankhurst 1992a: 185-92). Tensions and even conflict have characterized many new settlements.

(iv) *Resettlement involves people in wider structures.* They are drawn into the structure of the resettlement scheme and its administration, as well as the development project of which the resettlement project is part. They are also drawn into provincial/regional-type administrative and political structures, and economic marketing networks, into which the resettlement scheme becomes incorporated. (see Thiele 1985, 1986 for the *ujamaa* villages in Tanzania; Pankhurst 1992a for Ethiopia). People are also brought into the domain of national- and international-level structures. This is because resettlement-inducing development projects are usually part of national-level development-cum-political/ideological programmes (as in the Aswan Dam and the Akosombo Dam in Egypt and Ghana respectively: Fahim 1981: 15; Lumsden 1973:117), which bring the affected people under the influence of the relevant government department. Projects are often funded by international banks or aid agencies, which then also exercise their influence upon the resettlement area and its people.

(v) *Resettlement involves accelerated socio-economic change.* Development-induced displacement and resettlement, as a planned intervention by an outside agency (e.g. a government agency, or a private development company) powerful enough to foist its will upon the 'receiving' community, takes place largely in terms of the agenda and timetable, which will artificially speed up and telescope the ongoing processes of change at local level. Certain physical changes, such as the new land-use plan and the actual relocation, have to take place within the agency's project cycle. DIDR also speeds up the process of local communities' increasing involvement with, and often dependence upon, their wider political and economic setting. The fact that DIDR often results in diminished access to agricultural land, or disrupts local means of livelihood, makes resettled people more dependent upon cash sources of income, driving them outwards to the regional or national labour market. The changed balance between subsistence and cash sources of income tends to lead to changes in patterns of consumption, and to a more urban-oriented focus (de Wet 1995: Ch 4). The project also involves new types of leadership, geared to the new type of community (e.g. agricultural scheme, party cell, bulwark against guerrillas, as in the socialistically-oriented settlements in Tanzania in the 1970s and in Ethiopia in the 1980s; Hyden 1980; Pankhurst 1992a) that the outsiders wish to establish via the resettlement scheme, and again speeds up involvement in the wider political and administrative structures of which these new types of communities are seen as part.

Such accelerated change usually impacts negatively upon the capacity of – already disrupted – communities to control their own socio-economic situation, and the terms of their interaction with their wider context. Their diminished capacity to influence the terms of that wider interaction in turn further serves to accelerate the process of social change.

The combination of the above factors of resettlement tends to lessen people's material wellbeing, limit their choices and control over their circumstances, and increase the presence of social tension and conflict within new settlements. The involuntary nature of both the resettlement and the conditions under which they are resettled, the frequent loss of resources, the incorporation into wider, more powerful, more directive and more remote structures, and the dislocation involved, as well as the accelerated fashion in which it all happens, serve to limit the choices open to people and, accordingly, the degree of control they have over, and the degree of harmony in, their day-to-day circumstances.

THE RESETTLEMENT PROJECT AS A PROBLEMATIC INSTITUTIONAL PROCESS

A number of factors at the level of the resettlement project as an institutional process combine, usually in such a way that the goals of the resettlement component of the overall project are not realized, resettlement with development does not happen, and people are left socio-economically worse-off than before.

(i) Alan Rew (Rew *et al.* 2000) has coined the term 'policy practice' to suggest that policy and its implementation should not be seen as two separate phases, but as part of one process. He suggests that policy is significantly transformed in the process of implementation. This is because policy outcomes reflect problems inherent in the institutional process of resettlement and rehabilitation. Policy is usually a negotiated outcome that has to accommodate the concerns of various interest groups. It is implemented in a context characterized by poor communication and coordination between the various agencies, by work pressure, and by capacity and resource shortages – which allows considerable discretion to local-level resettlement officials, who cut corners and develop their own operational routines in order to cope with the demands of their situation. Resettlement policy thus effectively becomes what local-level officials make of it on the ground.

(ii) The above situation seems to be a direct outcome of the fact that countries or regions needing infrastructure projects are faced by a number of mutually reinforcing critical shortages. They usually lack the very things needed to make resettlement work, such as money, staff, skills and, critically, time, since lack of the other resources tends to result in resettlement planning. This is made worse by the fact that, with the exception of countries like Brazil, China and India, the lessons learned and the skills acquired are not usually transferable across projects. Projects such as Kariba (Zambia); Nangbeto (Togo) and Volta (Ghana) were firsts for those countries, and each country accordingly has to build up its resettlement administrative structures and experience pretty much from scratch. Expert missions or 'helicopter anthropology' cannot close that gap, as there is no substitute for the local development of institutional capacity.

(iii) Development projects are about infrastructure and about generating revenue from that infrastructure. As a result, in some cases, resettlement is seen as an external cost, as a hassle that has to be accommodated if the overall project is to go ahead. Thus, an official on the Volta River Project referred to the 80,000 people who would have to move to make way for the project, as 'the fly in the ointment' (quoted in Chambers 1970). Officials seconded to resettlement do not necessarily have the social training, and accordingly are unlikely to have either the social understanding or the commitment, necessary to make resettlement work. Resettlement accordingly often has to make do with an allocation of less than 10 percent of the overall project budget (Scudder 1997:688-9). Resettlement is thus treated as a subordinate consideration, a necessary cost, in situations where it is seen as economically rational to allocate as few resources as possible to resettlement.

(iv) Given that resettlement projects in Africa have often been part of wider political agendas and programmes (see below), and have been conducted in the context of critical shortages and by officials and technicians who have seen infrastructure provision as a key to economic progress, it is not surprising that many resettlement projects have been characterized by inadequate consultation and participation. This has been the case for resettlement arising out of dams, drought relief, political programmes and villagization. While actual participation has varied across schemes, and while officials have listened to what affected people had to say, by and large resettlement schemes have been planned and implemented on behalf of and for, rather than by and with, the affected people. The interests and concerns of the planners and implementers accordingly influence the way the resettlement component develops much more strongly than do those of the affected people.

(v) Following from this, resettlement is usually not deliberately planned as a development exercise, intended to leave the resettled people better-off.

(iv) The result of the above factors is that, by default, resettlement becomes reduced to relocation. For project officials, the priority becomes to get people out of the area where the infrastructure is to be placed, to have an effect and to make sure that they are relocated to the new resettlement area, or wherever else they are to go. Once resettlement has taken place, the development of those new areas often goes largely by the board, with the resettled people being left to find ways of generating their own livelihoods in the new context. The predictable result is impoverishment.

Aspects of the resettlement process potentially not amenable to rational planning and procedures

Resettlement processes do not seem to be readily amenable to the essentially rational approach preferred by officials, and which seems to characterize the Inadequate Inputs approach discussed earlier. If certain issues are beyond the reach of rational planning, then that has implications for the way in which we should go about resettlement.

(i) Large-scale infrastructure projects, such as dams, irrigation schemes, or highways, are often seen by the authorities as part of national, and even nationalistic, projects. Such projects have to fit in with essentially political objectives and timeframes, regardless of whether these are compatible with sound planning, financing and implementation. Resettlement thus has to adjust to 'national priorities', with predictably negative results.

(ii) The combination of externally imposed spatial change, new resource access and accelerated socio-economic change gives rise to developments that cannot always be anticipated or planned for.

(iii) A whole range of things, of different orders, happen all at once. Cernea (2000: 31) argues that the impoverishment risks he identifies hit affected people all at once, and that they 'must deal with these risks virtually simultaneously, as a patterned situation, not just one at a time. The result is a crisis.' The same problem confronts those implementing resettlement; they must handle all at once a host of legal, administrative, institutional, financial and personnel demands, as well as having to deal with the people to be resettled. The result, for both affected people and officials, is *ad hoc* crisis management rather than rational procedure, with unanticipated and unintended outcomes.

(iv) DIDR embodies conflicting timeframes, which further work against the likelihood of a rational approach. Firstly, the timeframes of the infrastructure and of the social aspects of the overall project are often out of synch, and pulling in different directions, which tends to lead to resettlement being rushed. Secondly, the timeframes for change held by the project, and by the affected people, are often also at odds, which makes for conflict, which further messes up time lines and other aspects of resettlement planning.

(v) DIDR involves competing visions of the nature and the process of development. Outsider government and development agencies usually have a very different view of *what constitutes development*, who are the key constituencies and how to go about achieving development, from that of people at the local level, who tend to have a much more localized, territorially-based view of the issues and who may feel themselves deeply threatened by outsider perspectives. They would also tend to see the *process of development* very differently, particularly the role and importance of dialogue and negotiation, and how that relates to matters such as autonomy and self-respect. They may respond to these differences with resistance, as a means of keeping the dialogue going and of keeping their vision of development in the public eye.

(vi) Actors' responses feed back into the way a resettlement project develops. The affected people, or those implementing resettlement, or those being resettled, respond to the situations in which they find themselves (e.g. by resisting, by changing plans, by changing allocations of resources). These actions feed back into the way things unfold, and often cannot be predicted or planned for.

In combination, these factors reinforce each other, making the resettlement process even less amenable to a rational, technical approach.

Some ethical conundrums

While ethical issues are also not readily amenable to strictly rational considerations, I wish to discuss them as an issue in their own right, so as to draw attention to their central role in any development undertaking. Given space constraints, I merely list some of the more difficult questions, which I have called 'conundrums' precisely because there is no clear rational way of resolving them.

(i) Is it acceptable to impose a culturally specific view of development upon other people?

(ii) Can we argue that, if there is no other way, some should suffer for the greater good?

(iii) What are we to do if negotiation does not get to a stage where the parties agree on a course of action? Should any party have the power to impose or to veto a project? Can we decide how much negotiation is 'enough'?

(iv) How are we to decide between the rights of various parties or interest groups? Should the fact that some have to move or suffer disadvantage for the benefit of others, give them a kind of 'extra vote'? Surely a number of different parties are suffering in different ways?

(v) What are we to do when there appears to be a conflict between fairness and equality of treatment of different categories of affected people?

(vi) How are we to evaluate cultural loss/damage for purposes of compensation? Distasteful as cost benefit analysis may be, is there any realistic alternative?

(vii) Is compulsion ever acceptable? If so, under what conditions?

Ethical issues add to the complexity of resettlement because of the human rights issues involved and particularly in light of the fact that the resettlement is of an involuntary nature. Policy-makers need clarity in terms of issues such as criteria for making decisions and allocating resources – and the kinds of openness that respecting other people and taking ethical issues seriously require.

The 'Inherent Complexity' position thus argues that there is a complexity in resettlement which arises from the interrelatedness of cultural, social, environmental, economic, institutional and political issues – all of which is taking place in the context of imposed spatial change. Interlinked and mutually influencing transformations take place simultaneously, as ongoing processes of change interface with changes initiated by the imposition from outside of a development project and the resultant resettlement to which it gives rise. Understanding this complexity, and attempting to come to terms with it, seems to require a more comprehensive and open-ended approach than the predominantly economic and technical perspective which characterizes the 'Inadequate Inputs' approach and Cernea's analysis of impoverishment risks.

Levels at which threats operate in resettlement

I submit that the complexities sketched above give rise to a number of threats within the resettlement process. While this suggests some kind of causality, I do not propose here to try and map out a set of mechanical, one-to-one-type causal correspondences between particular kinds of complexity and particular threats – not least because its very integration is what characterizes and powers the kind of complexity I have been trying to get across. The resulting threats would, however, seem to operate at various levels of comprehensiveness and incorporation, and I would here like to develop the outlines of a framework for understanding how this works.

THE INDIVIDUAL/HOUSEHOLD LEVEL

Most of Cernea's risks, with the exception of social disarticulation, would seem to operate at this level, as would risks suggested by other authors, such as psychological marginalization (Fernandes 2000: 212), loss of access to services (Mathur 1998: 70), loss of access to schooling (Mahapatra 1998: 218), as well as aspects of loss of civil/human rights (Downing 1996). This relates to the threat of the loss of natural, economic and human capital.

THE COMMUNITY LEVEL.

a) Here we find Cernea's 'social disarticulation', which relates to the disruption of "the existing social fabric... patterns of social organization and interpersonal ties… kinship groups …informal networks… local voluntary organizations...", i.e. to "social capital" (Cernea 2000: 30).

b) Linked to social disarticulation, there is what one might similarly term the threat of 'cultural disarticulation', or what Downing calls "disruption of the spatial-temporal order" or " social geometry" (1996: 33-34). This would include threats to the cultural integrity and autonomy of a group.

c) Economic impoverishment can take place at a collective, community level, as in the loss or lessening of access to communal property resources, to community services, or to schooling.

d) Different sections of the resettled group, such as rich and poor, young and old, men and women, healthy and ill, will experience the threats inherent in resettlement with differential intensities, and correspondingly be more or less likely to succumb to them.

e) Resettlement fundamentally alters the institutional context in which people find themselves (McDowell 2002: 183). Rapid change poses the threat of institutional instability, as new local-level institutions struggle to establish themselves in relation to their new setting and wider context. This in turn negatively affects their ability to negotiate access to resources.

f) Linked to this is what one might call the threat of 'political disarticulation'. Koenig (2001: 17) suggests that 'involuntary resettlement is also impoverishing because it takes away political power, most dramatically the power to decide about where and how to live.' Groups find themselves displaced, with less political autonomy and rights, less command of the resources in their area, and being more tightly controlled by wider political and administrative structures. They lose resources and autonomy because they did not have the socio-political 'capital' to take an effective stand against the intruding outsiders. The conjunction of territorial, economic, administrative and political change leads to crises of leadership, which may result in factionalism and intra-community conflict. The interaction between resettlers and the local host community is a fault line along which such conflict often crystallizes, as between the Gumuz hosts and their highland neighbours in the Metekel region of Ethiopia (Wolde-Selassie Abbute 2002).

g) The cumulative result of the interaction of the above factors holds the threat of a sense of fatalism and dependency developing in resettled communities. This would characterize situations where settlements have not been able to achieve what Scudder (1993) calls the stage of economic development and social formation.

THE LEVEL OF THE RESETTLEMENT PROJECT AS INSTITUTIONAL PROCESS

a) At this level threats come into play which relate to issues raised above in the discussion on Project Logic, viz. policy practice; mutually reinforcing critical shortages; resettlement being seen as an external cost; and as a result, the very real threat of resettlement becoming reduced to relocation, with any plans for resettlement as development effectively falling by the wayside.

b) The fact that the resettlement component of a development project often runs out of time in relation to the other aspects of the project, coupled with the coordination problems arising out of 'Project Logic', gives rise to the threats of the resettlement component being unable to meet its goals, and accordingly of Cernea's impoverishment 'risks' becoming actualized.

c) Limited participation by resettlers raises the real possibility of the way they see the threats and opportunities with which resettlement confronts them not being taken into account, with the threat of planning and subsequent action being not only inappropriate but actively damaging to the welfare of the resettlers.

d) Not seeing the resettlement project, with all its different constituencies, as an integrated whole, carries the threat of the risks facing parties other than the resettlers not being taken into account – which raises the spectre of even further alienation of local resettlement officials, who are already overworked and short on capacity and resources, and of the local-level institutional process becoming increasingly unworkable.

THE NATIONAL/REGIONAL LEVEL

a) The absence of proper legal and policy frameworks at national level, as well as of sufficient political will, commitment, fiscal restraint, and functional coordination between the various agencies responsible for different aspects of resettlement, creates the threats of resettlement projects not being properly planned, funded or implemented, of the rights and wishes of the affected people not being respected, and of socio-economic failure.

b) Where the wider context within which a resettlement scheme finds itself is characterized by political and economic weakness and instability, this creates the threat, not only that the scheme will not become effectively integrated, but that the wider context will function in a way which is actively disabling for the scheme, leading to its social and economic decline.

c) The same state that initiates and enforces resettlement is also the author and supposed upholder of the laws that are supposed to offer protection to people billed for resettlement. The state is both player and referee, and there is thus the real threat of affected people having little, if any, effective recourse to the law to protect themselves against the state.

THE INTERNATIONAL LEVEL

a) The fact that international law does not appear to provide effective protection for DIDR resettlers, together with the fact that the resettlement guidelines of funding agencies such as the World Bank are not always observed or properly policed, and that a number of financing institutions in the private sector are seemingly happy to lend money without worrying too much about the niceties of resettlement, all raise the threat of resettlers effectively having no protection when they are the victims of unjust laws and action on the part of their national government.

b) There is no free lunch, and aid and assistance, whether from funding agencies or from NGOs and activists, raises the threat of resettlers, who need outside help in their struggles concerning resettlement, becoming vehicles or puppets for other groups to advance their agendas, yet again having their autonomy further eroded.

Policy implications and challenges

Policy and 'post-modernism' do not usually sit well together, in the sense that policy requires clarity of criteria for making evaluations and decisions, and clearly mapped-out procedures, rather than accounts of complexity, of the kind anthropologists regard as the measure of their worth.

If there is a complexity inherent in resettlement, that does in fact give rise to threats and consequences on the way. If we are to come up with a policy approach that is able to counter those threats, it is going to have to be able to deal with that complexity. The challenge is to find a creative way of accommodating complexity within the requirements of effective policy.

This appeal to complexity is in no way an attempt to do away with existing policy initiatives or with Cernea's risks and reconstruction approach. Unless we deal with the risks/threats that Cernea has identified and explored, there will be no successful resettlement. And unless we secure the proper 'inputs', such as national-level legal frameworks and policies, political will, funding, pre-resettlement surveys, planning, participation, careful implementation and monitoring, we shall not be able to turn those risks/threats into reconstruction opportunities. Where Cernea and I see things differently, is that, whereas I understand him to believe that getting the above inputs right can overcome the complexities in resettlement, I do not believe that this is sufficient. As I have tried to show, however necessary 'adequate inputs' are, there are complexities in resettlement that cannot be dealt with in this manner; and that this is not simply a matter of getting better legal frameworks, policies, funding, planning, etc. Dealing with complexity requires us to start from open-endedness and flexibility, rather than from the boundedness of framework and procedure. Trade-offs will have to be negotiated and lessons learned on an ongoing basis, project by project. Policy reform is a process.

I would like to outline three broad and interrelated ways in which to try and build in that open-endedness and flexibility.[1] To ensure genuine participation and improve project outcomes, policy reform requires:

A DEMOCRATIC PARTICIPATORY APPROACH TO PROJECT PLANNING AND IMPLEMENTATION, INVOLVING:

- authentic participation which involves the ability to influence decisions;
- decision-making criteria which move away from the purely economic to more dialogic, consensual considerations;
- recognition of resistance as a legitimate form of expression in the dialogue about development options;
- re-examination of the criteria allowing the state to relocate people and appropriate property;
- development of skills necessary for all parties to engage in open-ended negotiation as equal parties; and
- free flow of information at all stages of a development project which may cause resettlement.

A WIDE RANGE OF RESETTLEMENT AND COMPENSATION OPTIONS, INVOLVING:

- approaches designed to open out choices, allowing people to mix and match options to their needs;
- appropriate and just forms and levels of compensation determined in genuine consultation with affected people;
- options that will not increase economic differentiation, while yet encouraging the rich to invest in the resettlement area.

A FLEXIBLE, LEARNING-ORIENTED APPROACH TO RESETTLEMENT PROJECTS, INVOLVING:

- projects designed so as to be able to adapt as unexpected developments occur, and in response to ongoing input by affected parties;
- the necessary range of skills in the implementation team, as well as sufficient funding, to allow for flexibility.

These considerations should be informed by the suggestion of the World Commission on Dams (2000a: 206) suggestion that 'an approach based on "recognition of rights" and "assessment of risks"[2] be developed as a tool for future planning and decision-making'.

The challenge is thus to develop policy that enables a genuinely more participatory and open-ended approach to planning and decision-making which is better able to accommodate the complexity inherent in resettlement. I cannot see any other way to do so. This may in turn increase the risks for planners, implementers and funders, all of whom might wish to draw clear boundaries and time lines around projects. But the case material repeatedly shows us that this is false economy. An unrealistically constrained process generates problems, resistance and unanticipated outcomes of its own, usually in a very costly manner. Genuine open-ended participatory planning brings people on board, identifies real problems and practicable solutions, makes for realistic budgeting and plans, enhances local capacity and leadership, and reduces conflict (Koenig 2001).

In the end, it comes down to a question of respect: respect for the people we presume to put through resettlement for the 'greater good', and respect for the complexity of what such resettlement involves. That critical shortage, which results in a lot of the necessary detail being overlooked, is why things so often go wrong in resettlement projects. How are we to translate the more general issue of respect into the specifics of policy and planning? That is the challenge, and policy reform is a risky business. Trying to find ways of developing criteria and procedures that allow us to keep open people's choices and to cater for complexity in the process, for as long as possible, seems a good place to start.

Notes

1. This approach is taken from the project that I coordinated from 1998 to 2002 for the Refugee Studies Centre at the University of Oxford, on Improving Outcomes in Development-Induced Displacement and Resettlement Projects. While I collated the final report, most of the actual suggestions came from my fellow project members and I here present the recommendations in a short bullet-point style.
2. 'Risks' as used here by the WCD would seem to incorporate both Dwivedi's sense of risk, as well as that of Cernea, which I would label as 'threats'.

Part III

DEVELOPMENT-INDUCED DISPLACEMENT
Dams, Irrigation Parks & Urban Relocation

Four

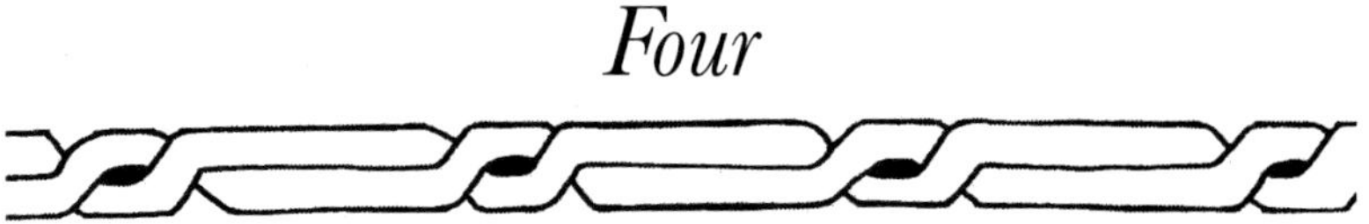

Social Dimensions of Development-Induced Resettlement

The Case of the Gilgel Gibe Hydro-electric Dam

KASSAHUN KEBEDE

Introduction

The numbers of people affected by Development-Induced Displacement (DID) have been rising steadily, and Dam-Induced Displacement is an important part of this, with effects that have long been studied, particularly in Africa with the Kariba Dam (Colson 1971; Scudder 1996; Cernea 2000). In Ethiopia people are internally displaced regularly for various reasons but the literature has been dominated by studies dealing with resettlement and villagization. The first major dam-induced displacement in Ethiopia resulted from the construction of the Gilgel Gibe dam. The project was conceived during the late imperial period, after the Koka dam built in the late 1950s (S. Pankhurst 1958) was found to be insufficient to meet the country's growing electricity needs and was closed down. However, only a reconnaissance report had been produced by the time of the revolution in 1974. During the Derg period several feasibility studies were undertaken and construction and relocation of some 10,000 people began in 1985 but was interrupted and only resumed in 1996 after the EPRDF took power. The EPRDF government, with the support of the World Bank, embarked on the Gilgel Gibe Project (GGP), the second largest Bank-supported resettlement operation in Africa at that time. The dam was expected to generate 180 MW per year, thereby increasing Ethiopia's annual power generation capacity to 640 GW. Up to the year 2000 about 6,000 people had been displaced, excluding those removed during the Derg regime. The benefit accruing to the nation was publicized with widespread media coverage and official visits to the dam construction, but with little attention paid to the resettlement villages.

This chapter reviews the project's history and examines its social performance in relation to government attempts to reconstruct the resettlers' livelihoods. It documents the resilience of the resettlers in countering the ensuing impoverishment risks, in relation to the Impoverishment Risk and Reconstruction (IRR) model developed by Cernea and the Sustainable Livelihoods Framework (Scoones 1998).

Theoretical outline of DID studies

The traditional critique of anthropology as immune to development has faded away (Robertson 1984) and development-induced displacement (DID) has become an area to which social anthropology has contributed (Cernea 1988) However, the pace of progress towards formulating a coherent theoretical framework guiding research and action has been slow, despite increasing empirical data (Pankhurst 1992a).

Two approaches have been dominant. The Scudder-Colson model (1982) which considers stages in adjustment to displacement takes a long-term view and suggests that successful rehabilitation cannot be judged in the short term and may need considering for two generations. Despite its limitations, the model may be helpful in spontaneous population resettlement analysis (Scudder 1985). It may also be that 'Whether resettlers stave off or descend into abject poverty may depend on the social characteristics and resource endowments of the areas into which they were moved' (Sharp and Spiegel 1985:134).

Cernea's Impoverishment Risks and Reconstructions (IRR) model marked a shift from the stages-ridden archetype to packages of risks in DID thinking (Cernea 1997, 2000). This model is empirically corroborated and serves predictive, diagnostic, problem-resolution and research functions. Cernea further split the cumulative impact into its pervasive components – eight major impoverishment risks, namely landlessness, joblessness, homelessness, loss of common property, marginalization, increased morbidity and mortality and social disarticulation. Cognizant of the differences from one project to another, the model allows for the addition of further risks and notes that 'the variables are interlinked and influence each other, some play a primary role and others a derivative role in either impoverishment or reconstruction' (Cernea 2000: 19). However, the terms of participation, negotiated forms of compensation and ways of reversing social risks through community institutions do not seem to have been elaborated sufficiently (Dwivedi 2002; Kassahun 2001). The model does not specify the time needed for displaced communities to regain their normal tempo, which can lead planners to advocate early withdrawal after the blueprinted risks have been generally addressed.

The IRR model: the urge for a theoretical synergy

Cernea (1997:1583) noted that, 'despite all the recent expansion in research, there is much that we still do not know about resettlement, especially about the behavioral response of various populations and subgroups, and about their own initiatives for coping and reconstruction'. At this juncture a theoretical synergy is required to explain resettlers' initiatives, i.e., the role of the people in coping with displacement as a response to foreseen risks. The Sustainable Livelihood Approach developed beyond the concern for DID may fill the gap (Scoones 1998). The presentation of livelihood strategies and the attention their framework renders to societal institutions make it ideal for the topic under study. McDowell (2002) calls for such a theoretical blend and the need to ascertain how people respond to the risk of processes of impoverishment, and the role of institutions, associations and other forms of relationships in mediating their access to and control over the resources necessary to rebuild livelihoods. This chapter therefore raises the following questions linked to the Sustainable Livelihood thesis. What is the status of basic resources and institutions for sustainable re-establishment? To what extent did the project involve communities' in risk management? What are the risk-reversal attempts in terms of infrastructure ? What are the social and cultural relations/proximity between the resettlers and the hosts?

The Gilgel Gibe dam: history and process of displacement

The idea of the project dates back to the imperial period, with a reconnaissance report produced in 1973. During the Derg era feasibility studies were carried out by Yugoslav, Chinese, Korean and Italian teams.

Interviews and discussions were held with the local communities and registrations undertaken. This interest prompted elders to state: 'we were sure that the land had got gold in it'. During 1982 construction of the dam resumed, followed by the relocation of more than 100 households. During the 1984/85 villagization, about 1,964 households within the boundary of the dam were villagized on the escarpments overlooking the reservoir area. However, the progress of the dam was thwarted by government instability and devillagization, with a return to the previous settlements at the time of the final collapse of the Derg in 1991.

The World Bank enabled the construction of the dam's surface reservoir of 48 square kilometers with a 26,000 hectares buffer zone. The total cost of construction was estimated at $US281.88 million, excluding tax and, importantly, the money needed for the rehabilitation of the displaced. The economic return rate was estimated to be 11.7 million percent (World Bank 1997).

Proposal for resettlement

No mention was made regarding those people resettled during the Derg era in the new project document. The second phase of re-relocation began in 1999 and the social costs were to be taken into consideration.[1] It was stated that (a) consultations had taken place with each one of the affected households and stakeholders; (b) the selected site was not only large enough to provide land for the project-affected population but also its soils were similar to that cultivated by the people previously; (c) the rate of compensation was considered reasonable and every household had received a visit; (d) the new houses would be built by the occupants themselves, following local tradition, but with building materials supplied by the project; (e) the Regional State of Oromia (RSO) would transform the resettlement action plan in a way that would enhance the livelihoods of the people.

A year later the executing RSO agency was replaced by the Ethiopian Electric Power Corporation (EEPCO), as many of the above points were largely neglected during the implementation process.

BEFORE THE MOVE: HOW THE PROCEDURE WAS CONDUCTED

House-to-house registration was carried out without coming to a final decision regarding the number of people to be displaced. Hence, there were attempts to escape or hide from the enumerators. A number of households reportedly disguised or underestimated their holdings, scared that the plan was to increase tax rather than to displace them. Following registration, payments were made for immovable assets. Those who refused to join the resettlement village received compensation for their houses and immovable assets, excluding the land which is government-owned. As informants indicated, another flaw was that they were rarely consulted as to what should be eligible for compensation and at what price. Communally owned assets were outside the purview of compensation and settlement was biased towards perennial crops. Under-compensation became evident and some reported that they received only 30 *birr* for a granary. Some posed critical questions, such as how many years are enough for a coffee seedling to bear fruit?

The total amount of money allocated to households was on average US $4,600, which was very low for a dam generating 180 MW based on international standards. The project therefore suffered from what Cernea (1999) aptly described as compensation mostly taking the form of a willing buyer and seller neglecting consumer surplus.

VISITS TO THEIR HOMES AND THE MOVE

In accordance with the promises, some people paid symbolic visits to the selected Resettlement Villages. The project summary document also noted:, 'every household visited their homes' (World Bank 1997). However, resistance and opposition in several villages disfigured the visit. The main source of resentment was the alien nature of the land , its inadequacy for their subsistence activities and the marshy character of the site. Some households changed their minds about being willing to be resettled, pointing out to officials that the land was very marshy and unsuitable for house building, but their views fell on deaf ears.

Ultimately the move was imposed. Informants recalled living in tents during the preparations and most of their belongings were left behind. They characterize the move as a death and at the time the fieldwork was over there was one household which was still refusing to join the Villages.

THE RESETTLEMENT SITE

The site is located in Jimma zone, Qersa district (RSO), in a former government military training ground. The district is between 1700 and 2300 meters above sea level, but the Resettlement Villages are at the bottom between 1700 and 1750 masl, typically referred to as the Gilgel Gibe plains comprising virtually flat land, located along the middle reaches of the river, and characterized by clay and dominantly swampy vertisols. This land is waterlogged during the rainy season and cracks when the rain tapers off (MoA 1989).

The Resettlers

The people studied are mostly Oromo agro-pastoralists and their subsistence relies on rain-fed agriculture and livestock-rearing. Several types of cereals (maize, *tef*, sorghum), tubers (potatoes) and perennial crops like coffee, *chat* and banana are planted. Livestock-rearing is strongly tied to their livelihoods as a source of traction power, diet, cash and restoring soil fertility. Harvests are modest, and land is abandoned or left fallow when the soil is overworked, as noted by feasibility study documents (ENEL 1982). Many were unfamiliar with the inorganic fertilizer the project supplied.

The settlement pattern was fairly dispersed, though there were mutual help associations. for welfare (*Abba Jigga*) consisting of 3-5 neighbouring villages of up to 200 households each of which, among other things, arranged marriages, pooled money and administered sanctions. Other associations were for cattle-rearing (*Abba Ulee*), with turn-taking in herding and mutual assistance in the case of the death of cattle.

The reconstruction and re-establishment process

The reconstruction processes can be considered following the impoverishment risks described by Cernea.

LANDLESSNESS: NEW LAND, IS IT ENOUGH?

During 1985 land was allotted communally in the spirit of collectivization. Following the fall of the Derg in particular those unable to migrate to town parceled out the land with the average holding being exceptionally below 0.5 hectares. Thus round-one evictees are still struggling with landlessness after two decades.

In the second phase of displacement, the attempt to mitigate the risks also involved compensation in the form of land. However, according to a study made by the MoA (1989) the resettlement land was waterlogged and suffered from poor drainage, and was subject to frost. The impacts of the above points were clear within the span of two years. The variety of crops grown shrank mainly to *tef*, maize and finger millet. The use of modern fertilizer in place of the traditional technique of restoring soil fertility through cattle enclosures took precedence, due to the thin layer of topsoil. In several instances waterlogging in maize fields as well as frost and crop diseases reduced harvests.

The project 'awarded' every household 2.5 hectares of land but glossed over equity issues, thus creating stress for large households. Farmland was confused with land for other purposes. The 2.5 hectares of land was to include the homestead, the farm and grazing land. This reduced the total land for farming and made fallow unthinkable, clearly resulting in soil impoverishment. Only married people were considered eligible for compensation, and young bachelors remained landless or were obliged to migrate. Some households were forced to convert private grazing areas into farmland, resulting in frequent clashes with the project people as the resettlers often encroached on land reserved for planting trees for communal use.

Loss of common property resources (CPR)

The losses of CPR are what are often undervalued in resettlement activities elsewhere. At the Gilgel Gibe project relocatees mourned the loss of communal property resources in both phases (the 1985 and the 1999 displacements). Forest, grazing lands and sand extraction sites were the most notable resources forgone. Grazing lands were the most significant in a society where livestock-rearing plays a significant part in subsistence. In the villages the allocation of half a hectare for grazing indicates how little significance was accorded to dependence on cattle.

The cattle economy involves networks of economic relations externally and internally. The tradition of cattle entrustment allows middle and poor sections of the community to work as caretakers for livestock owners from neighbouring towns and rural villages where the plantation of perennial crops (mainly coffee) creates land shortage. The caretakers secure traction power, milk products, and dung to fertilize their land and enjoy equal rights in the sale of the offspring.

With the commencement of resettlement, the entrusters pooled their cattle owing to the inadequacy of pasture in the relocation area and more significantly to keep their cattle within the limits of close supervision. Consequently, 27 percent of the relocatees became oxenless and 21 percent remained with only one ox when deciding to move, thus exacerbating the traction power deficiency. The loss of income for women due to the loss of revenue from the sale of livestock products is rarely considered and not easily quantifiable. Even those who decided to go to the resettlement villages left their cattle behind, sometimes driving them back and forth, as pasture in the villages was scarce, particularly since the host community members were also grazing their animals on the land. For instance, in one of the villages the total communal and private grazing land amounted to 227 hectares. Thereafter the total number of cattle increased to more than 2,000 excluding those of the resettlers, which obviously doubled the size of the herd resulting in a ratio of 0.1 hectare per animal (Nazif 1999).

The loss of forest and income from the sale of sand for construction purposes affected the community, particularly the off-farm-based and migrants. Planners never mentioned the sale of charcoal as well as sand as being basic components of a subsistence strategy described as 'illegal' activity. Such sectors are often overlooked in DID planning. However, Forsbrooke (1962) had argued that: 'a sizable proportion of village subsistence in Africa comes not from agriculture or pastoralism but from full utilization of the surrounding bush and forest.'

JOBLESSNESS

Before the move the relocatees participated in various livelihood activities related to the abundance of CPR. Such diverse livelihood portfolios were practised to overcome the unreliability and uncertainty of depending on a single strategy. Hence, besides farming and cattle-rearing, charcoal, firewood and sand selling, petty trade and daily labour were among the activities identified. Most of these became impossible due to the resource-poor nature of the locations selected for the resettlement villages. In particular, ferrying people across the river on market days was no longer an option.

The involvement of the affected population in the construction of the dam was extremely limited, since migrants obtained many of the skilled jobs and the resettlement villages were up to 30 km from where the intensive work was taking place. The project also made no attempt to enhance the prospects for commercializing local products. Nor were vocational training or income-generating activities planned.

FOOD INSECURITY

Food insecurity remains a critical risk to overcome in many resettlement undertakings. It results from loss or breakdown of livelihood activities and resources that directly or indirectly contribute to the diet. The unplanned displacement in 1985 was followed by food shortage and dependence on food aid for two years. The provision of aid was interrupted as the government was unable to administer it and many households fled to their previous villages or towns in search of jobs and alms. It was also a source of ridicule to be forced to depend on hand-outs in comparison with the self-reliant host communities. The diminishing availability of land led to inability to meet the annual food requirements resulting in food deficiency up to the present in comparison with the local population.

The recent displacement attempted to overcome the problem by helping the settlers with land preparation, seed and other inputs such as fertilizer. According to project officials, productivity doubled if not tripled in the pilot village. However, this was misleading as some households still depended on income from their previous homes. The increase in productivity was also the result of the use of fertilizer provided by the project, which will wither away when the project pulls out.[2]

Food deficiency was observed especially for off-farm-based households, and those suffering from waterlogging. As a result, some of them had to enter into mortgages or grain indebtedness with their share-croppers. Some also reported that they managed to overcome the food deficit with bought grain.

With the withdrawal of assistance, the issue at stake will be food requirements due to the decline in productivity, reduction in the diversity of produce and the loss of perennial crops. This will result in a lack of capacity to purchase inputs and other consumption items currently covered by grain sales. As one woman put it:

> This land grows only maize, finger millet and *tef*, no potato, no cabbage, no pepper, tobacco etc. Maize is used as a means of transaction in order to purchase items we used to sell. You know maize is like 'kerosene', as we sell it to pay for the grain mill and to buy other things which we used to sell.

One of the key food-security concerns is that the soil is not suitable for growing *enset*, which has long been a staple and an emergency food item during the hunger gap between annual cereal crops. The crop served as a shield during the 1984/85 famine, which overwhelmed the country.

HOMELESSNESS: 'WE BECAME LIKE YOU'

Of all the risks identified by the resettlement literature, house restoration is seen as the most easily soluble.[3] Homelessness is still a lingering risk for those expelled in the first round, particularly among the elderly. The host communities under compulsory mobilization built them shelters, but what they call *godo* (nest) rather than a proper house (*mana*). Three months after their displacement they were forced to move for villagization. The fall of the Derg again forced them to return to the original relocation quarter, making the whole thing a traumatic experience.

In the second phase the project constructed corrugated-iron-roofed houses for those who decided to come to the resettlement villages, despite the initial statement that 'the people were expected to build their house following the local building tradition but with building materials supported by the project' (World Bank 1997: 11). The tradition was opposed, resulting in technical and social engineering flaws. The iron-roofed houses were highly appreciated and the glittering iron symbolized a successful resettlement venture. The previous house size was retained so that some obtained a house the size of a warehouse while others received a kitchen-sized one. The relocatees dislike the fact that the houses have small verandas allowing storms to penetrate windows and doors, resulting in water trickling in. The waterlogged nature of the land makes the house damp. A post-resettlement study undertaken jointly by Jimma Zone Agricultural and Health Departments recommended the removal of 30 households to a more elevated place. Problems commonly mentioned included the lack of enough space for gardens, weak doors and windows, and internal divisions not made according to their wishes.

Some of the resettlers who obtained better compensation spent the money making improvements to the houses extending verandas to control surface run-off. In spite of this, there is growing concern about the durability of the houses because of the marshy foundation and the lack of additional construction materials. Lack of euphorbias, used as windbreaks, in conjunction with the close proximity between houses with small compounds, further fueled resettlers' resentment, and raises questions about the meaning of house restoration.

Increased morbidity and mortality

The change of environment due to the unexpected relocation and the accompanying erosion of resilience precipitated high morbidity and mortality in the first phase of resettlement in 1985, which was expressed by an informant as follows: 'People perished like animals unable to adapt to the change of environment.' No attempt was made to curb the risks, notably of malaria. Some viewed themselves as abandoned in the wilderness. One informant recalled:

> I lost five of my children and later my wife due to hunger and malaria. I am 'buried' below my neck and do not feel mentally well. Death has visited every member of our people. When we hear what is being done for those displaced by the present government we say we are really cursed with a bad fate.

In the 1999 relocation the project attempted to avoid the problem. Water taps were installed, though no training was offered regarding proper maintenance. The endeavour to build latrines was found incompatible with people's priorities. The project also built a 'beautiful' health post; however, a year after the relocation the clinic remained empty, due to disagreements between the project and the zonal health department, which felt that the project was supposed to provide the necessary logistics and manpower to run the clinic which was beyond the department's annual plan and capacity. Project officials consider it to be the responsibility of the department to take over and run the clinic with the basic logistics and staff. People suffering from malaria and common waterborne diseases were obliged to resort to expensive treatment at a private health post. One woman remarked 'I take my child to the private clinic so long as the compensation money is in my hand. For the sake of Allah, when do you think these people will start giving us services?' Furthermore, given the population of more than 5,000 people excluding the hosts, the adequacy of a single health post may be questioned. Project officials argue that the people did not have a health post in their previous settlement; however, this matter did not receive attention, in the light of the anticipated relocation.[4]

Marginalization

The marginalization processes began in the imperial period when the land was condemned to becoming a reservoir area. The uncertainties held back attempts to carry out normal livelihood activities and led to lack of attention from the government.

The subsequent villagization and devillagization processes affected most of the affected population. Those displaced during 1985 found themselves in economically inferior positions. Their reduced land holdings forced them to work for others. For the resettlers of 1999 further threats related to production constraints. The initial high agricultural productivity resulting from the use of fertilizers could not be sustained, as the peasants could not afford the cost following the withdrawal of project assistance.

Dependence on the market increased, due to the limited type of crops that could be grown, the breakdown of cattle entrustment and the reduction in off-farm income-generating options. Income from milk products which was a hedge against food shortage was threatened by constraints on pasture and livestock production.

However, it is premature to assess the social dimension of marginalization due to economic decline. Established relations with the hosts and ethnic and religious similarity may reduce such threats. The mosque built for the resettlers by the project symbolized their improved religious position but there was competition for private mosques in their respective villages.

SOCIAL DISARTICULATION

Cernea (1985) suggests that DID submerges the social system of the community, resulting in unravelling or 'social impoverishment' (Downing 1996). Those displaced during the Derg period were dumped on the hosts' land with no integration. They were seen as burdens by the hosts, who were forced by the government to plough the resettlers' land. Informants remember that it took them years to become members of the larger welfare associations of the hosts and that they were unable to form their own associations. Most of the locals did not even attend their funerals and they remember that the first marriage between the host and the resettlers took place seven years after relocation. A decade and a half after resettlement they are still stigmatized as *sefari* (resettler), connoting rootlessness.

However, proximity with the host community in terms of religion and ethnicity coupled with frequent visits and contacts at market places with their relatives minimized the social stress. But nostalgia for the land of their ancestors and separation from kin were felt keenly. Moreover, the relocation within the settlements broke up neighbourhood and kinship ties, despite resettlers' attempts to make adjustments by exchanging houses to be closer to former neighbours.

The institutional unravelling affected the *Abba Jigga* and *Abba Ulee* associations even though they were recreated after relocation. These institutions were incapacitated and were unable to discharge their customary roles due to changing relations and a significant reduction in the number of members.

Individuals who obtained land in spite of their previous dependence and non-membership in the associations are often accused of failing to be rule-bound. These individuals also tried to redefine their status. Disputes at *Abba Jigga* meetings were common, and the elders referred to the village as an ox and a bull tied together, pointing the finger at dependants. This has undermined the *Abba Jigga* in handling internal affairs. As one elder commented: 'Villagers rush to take their case to the police rather than to elders as usual, making us people who fail to abide by the judgment of the elders in front of the hosts. We are guests, yet everybody behaves wildly in the new settings as we have no customs.'

The *Abba Ulee* was also in a phase of dissolution as rearing cattle privately was valued in order to make the maximum use of the scarce grazing land. Some individuals withdrew from the association without prior notification as the tradition dictates, even allying with the hosts who had better pasture holdings. This has implications for inter-household cooperation and resource degradation.

Ridicule among the settlers was common seemingly due to the increased social scale minimizing the social space. Moreover, the building of homesteads close to one another without euphorbia as fencing aggravated tensions. The resettlers dropped traditional group prayers (*hadra*) or performed them secretly in order not to be labelled non-Islamic. An old person explained: 'If you are holding a *hadra* a neighbour may suddenly knock on your door since there is nothing to stop him/her. Soon it is known around the villages. What can you do since most of them behave like "fanatics"?' Such religious differences were intensifying, leading to clashes in the mosque due to differences in the components of the prayers.

POLITICAL DISEMPOWERMENT[5]

A challenging but less considered problem is that of political disempowerment. Where resettlers should fit in the administrative structures poses daunting problems. Furthermore, conflict of interest between the host and the resettler related to resource tenure exacerbates the problem. Initially rapid integration of the resettlers with the hosts was advocated, and meetings were called. The agenda related to where to fit the relocatees, i.e., whether they should be allowed to form an independent peasant association or whether they should be integrated with that of the hosts. The district administration advocated incorporating the relocatees, which the hosts wanted, but the resettlers seemed more in favour of their own administration, arguing that they had been given such promises, and if incorporated there would be marginalized minorities whose voices would be unheard. One of them made the following case: 'if cattle of the host are missing or stolen we are the first to be suspected and imprisoned. But if we set up our own PA no one has the right to do so. An independent PA means self-reliance and we can exempt our poor members from government obligations, whereas the hosts will attempt to control the communal grazing land.' Both the hosts and the district administration were against an independent PA for the resettlers. The hosts argued that they could not afford to lose land for a second time, referring to the contested grazing land along the river. One of them said that, if the resettlers were allowed to form their own independent PA, they would never be allowed to water their cattle, let alone graze the land.

The district administration decided against the settlers, aware of the potential repercussions in terms of resource conflict, on the grounds that the resettlers' arguments were less convincing and that they had no mandate to establish a new PA in the region and could be fairly represented in the existing PA administration. They also pointed out that the hosts had already made a considerable sacrifice in giving up land for the resettlers. Consequently, the resettler villages were divided among the six host PAs, leading to some conflict of interest among the relocatees themselves in a bid to choose PAs with better resources.

The decision was in line with the hosts' interest, and the resettlers felt defeated and were not fully convinced that they would not suffer discrimination. In a bid to avoid conflict between the hosts and relocatees, boundary stones were erected around disputed farm plots and unusually there were two boundaries within a single PA.

Differential impacts and adaptations

In much DID research the impoverishment of resettlers is treated uniformly. However, it is important to consider differential impacts rather than assuming automatic wholesale impoverishment (Pankhurst 1992a). In this study the effects of the domestic cycle, gender and age are considered.

THE DOMESTIC CYCLE AND DISPLACEMENT EXPERIENCE

The domestic cycle was a crucial factor in relation to resources in the resettlement villages. The provision of 2.5 hectares regardless of household composition has affected households with large families detrimentally. It has created stress for families, often resulting in intra- and inter-generational tensions as well as conflict between husband and wife, particularly in polygamous households.

GENDER: 'HERE YOU SIT LIKE YOUR HANDS ARE TIED TOGETHER'

Gender issues are often neglected in displacement especially in relation to compensation and job creation. In the case of the Gilgel Gibe project only men and female-headed households were eligible to collect compensation payments, which resulted in the growing dependence of women on men. Perennial crops, already converted into household cash, used to be the source of money to finance household expenses. They will now take years to mature. In addition, annual crops like tobacco, pepper, *enset* and other vegetables, which helped generate income, are no longer grown in the villages.

The return from *kayya* cattle markedly affects poorer women in relation to the dwindling amount of cash from the sale of dairy products. Fuelwood can no longer be a source of income and also has to be collected from further away. There were complaints from women about the lack of opportunities for income generation, as expressed in the saying 'here you sit like your hands are tied'. Some poor women complained that they were not helped by the community and exempted from labour and money contributions, as had previously been the case. According to one woman, 'Now everybody tends to say help yourself if you can.' Nevertheless, women praise the resettlement for the access it created to grain mills and water points.

Age

Age was found to be an important variable in relation to vulnerability to and/or taking risk. In most cases the impacts of the projects are age-specific.

THE ELDERLY: 'WE ARE LIKE A LAMP INSIDE A JAR'

The attitude of the elderly towards resettlement was generally very negative. Grieving-for-the-lost-home syndrome was a lingering pain even among those resettled in 1985. As one man put it: 'We are like a lamp inside a jar.' He explained this as representing their sense of being knowledgeable people living in an alien land, always seen as guests and ignored by the natives. There were similar reactions during the 1999 resettlement. The elderly were not even ready to use the compensation money and mostly went back on reverential visits to their previous settlements that had not yet been inundated. For them the social pain and stress was made worse with the widening rift between them and the young. The elderly blame the implementation of the project after so many years on the sinful deeds of the younger generation. Conversely, the young challenge them, saying that the displacement has nothing to do with them, and some criticize the elders for mixing indigenous religious concepts with Islam. However, underlying all other motives the pressure on the part of the young to get a share of the land and to form their own families was at the heart of the contradictions.

THE YOUNG: 'WE DO NOT HAVE COMPENSATION FOR WHAT IS UNDER WATER'

The young are greatly affected by the resettlement process. Many are pessimistic, having been given virtually no opportunities for employment or resources in the foreseeable future. Underemployment of the young was a common observation, as their present agricultural activities and the resources to hand are far from being enough to enable them to secure sufficient income. Many asked for compensation but the reported response was 'we do not have compensation for what is under water.' One young person said that their previous sources of income were just like 'butter dropped in a fire', meaning they were impossible to claim. As another youth recalled:

> I started selling sand when I was rearing cattle. I never bothered my parents to buy me clothes, provide me with an ox or even finance my marriage. All I own now was bought with the money obtained from the sand selling. I almost missed the registration while working on the sand. Recently, I sold the radio I bought from the sand sales. For me the project is like a blow to my core source of earning subsistence.

CHILDREN

Resettlement is often associated with malnutrition, school drop-outs and high death rates affecting children. Mahapatra (1999) suggested that dropping out of school should be included as a risk of relocation. The 1985 eviction involved the above problems, and in particular reported high infant mortality. However, the 1999 resettlement was different and school enrolment increased. This may be related to the role of project officials in creating awareness and pressure to send children to school. However, the increased number of students put pressure on the host schools; children had to share places, and drop-out cases were reported associated with low quality of education and teacher absenteeism. Disruption of Quranic schools was also noted.

Wealth as a factor of differentiation

People can be divided in relation to land holding into those having formal legal titles to land and those with no recognizable legal right or claim, and who were dependent on the former communal property resources.

THE *GELLA*: LANDLESS AND DEPENDENT HOUSEHOLDS

The *Gella* are those households with a migrant status which mostly joined the valley from adjacent areas, mainly from *enset*-dependent communities, working originally as daily labourers because of land shortage. They gradually annex themselves to rich households, taking wives locally with whom they usually form close economic ties. The rich households mostly exempt themselves from strenuous agricultural activities, which involve making shifting cattle enclosures throughout the year to manure their plots of land, and make use of the *gella*, who are not allowed to be members of either the PA or of traditional associations; even if they marry locally and have children, they are often treated as dependent families.

During the displacements the dependants were denied compensation or assistance, as entitlement to such benefits was used as the sole criterion for legal land ownership. Many of the *gella* then migrated to adjacent places but few of them succeeded in re-establishing themselves. With the assistance of their employers, some were able to register as independent families or as dependants of those households which decided not to join the villages. As a result, a few dependants obtained land and found it hard to believe the change in their previous deplorable status. One person referred to them as being 'just like a germinating seed'. However, most such households obtained no financial compensation and were not entitled to plant perennial crops. Their economic ties withered. Consequently, most of them were oxenless and decided to hand over their land to the rich and assume their previous dependent status. Nevertheless, the attempts of some exceptions to improve themselves are notable, as the following case shows:

> Abba Temam aged 35 was a dependent householder at the previous site. He registered as an independent household despite his employer's resistance. He then moved to the resettlement where he obtained land and other benefits equivalent to those of his employer. He also secured employment, though short-lived, from the project which helped him to buy an ox, which he pairs with that of his neighbour. He also established a close relationship with some of the hosts and sharecropped land from one of them, who supplied seed, fertilizer and labour. He says displacement is a reincarnation, as he has improved himself, but he has reservations about the future of households like his if the project does not continue helping them in regard to fertilizer until they re-establish themselves.

Among the resettled, those with legal land titles were classified into three groups: rich (*duressa*), middle-level (*gidugelessa)* and poor (*Iyessa)* according to previous land holdings, number of cattle, number of wives, involvement in off-farm activities, etc. The rich were mostly polygamous, owning up to 10 hectares of land, entrusting their cattle to the poor, and administering dependent household members, and were rarely engaged in off-farm activities. During displacement, therefore, they obtained better compensation and many opted to resettle by themselves, mostly in town. Those who came to the villages were disadvantaged by having large livestock herds and sold their cattle to cope with the diminished pasture and reduced land holdings. They also lost labour as dependants either migrated or achieved an equal amount of land. This often resulted in stormy relations and antagonism with others, in particular former dependants, with the rich trying to maintain the continuity of previous subordinate relations. Those in the middle category were also affected in terms of land, and the poor also claimed to be suffering declining living standards. Many gave back their *kayya* cattle, and the loss of common property resources affected them as there were no safety-net provisions from the project. However, not all the poor were disadvantaged and some even took advantage of opportunities, as the following case illustrates.

> Mohamed Amin was 28, married with two children. He was an orphan and it was his father's brother who brought him up. He used to subsist on half a hectare of land belonging to his late father. He had no ox prior to displacement. Fortunately his holdings fell outside the coverage of the project and he sold the land for nine 900 *birr*, which together with the little money he obtained as compensation enabled him to buy a pair of oxen. He fattened the oxen, sold them and, together with some money from the sale of maize from the previous year's harvest, was able to buy four oxen. For him relocation was more of an opportunity than a threat, due to his risk-taking efforts.

Adaptation dynamics

Adaptation to the risks and stresses of resettlement has become an important area of study addressed by the IRR model and the Sustainable Livelihoods Approach. In the Gilgel Gibe project agricultural intensification/extensification, livelihood diversification, migration and socio-cultural rearticulation were key responses.

AGRICULTURAL INTENSIFICATION/EXTENSIFICATION

In order to cope with economic decline and uncertainty due to the poor nature of the soil, the resettlers tried to intensify and extensify their agricultural activities by exploring the opportunities created. This involved developing relations with the hosts in terms of the exchange of land as the resettlers' land was suitable for *tef* while that of the hosts was ideal for maize. However, in the exchange the resettlers had to complement the host with money or inputs like fertilizer since maize fields are more highly valued. Sharecropping arrangements were also strengthened. Members of the hosts who lacked traction power, inputs and labour used the opportunity to sharecrop out land to the resettlers, often on the arrangement of a one-third share of the harvest, with the owner of the land providing labour during the harvest. The provision of fertilizer and compensation money to the resettlers enhanced their bargaining power. One informant remarked: 'Almost all of the resettlers, poor and rich, sharecropped land from the hosts. However, no one is sure that this land will grow maize.' Links were also maintained and reinforced with those living close to their former land. They took shelter with them when ploughing their previous land and/or provided them with oxen, fertilizer and other contributions to make use of this land to the extent possible until the flooding. There were householders who employed tractors on the previous site to make the maximum use possible, as the following case of a rich household illustrates.

> Abba Macha owned 5 hectares of farmland previously. When deciding to come to the resettlement village he received 8,000 *birr* as compensation, with which he bought three oxen and fertilizer, which he used intensively on land in the previous site by leaving some family members behind. He sharecropped land from two resettlers and a host. He believes that he can get a good harvest this year but is pessimistic since the dam will take over his previous farm land.

LIVELIHOOD DIVERSIFICATION

The resettlers also made notable efforts to diversify and to cope with temporary adversity and seek sustainable alternatives. As a result, the portfolio of livelihood activities identified encompasses both agricultural and non-agricultural activities. The latter include tailoring services, shops, grain mills, wholesale grain trade, and importantly renting out oxen, seemingly the domain of the rich. In contrast, involvement in labour-exchange parties, working as daily labourers, and taking *kayya* cattle entrustment were predominantly strategies of the poor.

One of the visible livelihood alternatives was renting out oxen for grain. Some of the resettlers bought oxen with the compensation money to rent out to the resettlers themselves and to people from the previous site, as well as to the hosts. Oxen became the scarcest resource due to the return of their *kayya* cattle, which created an opportunity for rich households to buy more oxen to obtain grain. Nevertheless, it created competition, resulting in conflicts over the bidding for oxen.

For the poor, the attempts to absorb the shock involved reinstating their previous livelihood activities, mainly working as daily labourers and selling their labour to labour-deficient households. The buyer pays 2 *birr* per day per individual working in his fields. Sometimes up to three individuals from the same household would enter into such contracts to generate income for the household. There were instances in which a wife sold her labour to her husband to generate money for household expenses. The following is an example of a poor household striving to make ends meet:

> Tadu is a young man in his late twenties. For him farming was like a sideline activity at the previous site. What he obtained from the sale of sand, charcoal and *kayya* cattle entrusted to him by his uncle were his principal sources of income. When deciding to move, his uncle took all the cattle but he succeeded in pleading with him to keep two cows. He bought an ox with the compensation money but the animal died from trypanosomiasis. Now, besides farming, he works as a daily labourer for the host community earning 5-8 *birr* a day.

MIGRATION

Those who refused to be resettled by the project mostly migrated to nearby towns, mainly Asendabo. Migration as a facet of adapting to economic decline was observed mainly among households with large families, newly married couples and unmarried young men. The teenagers who married after the registration did not obtain land in the resettlement villages. Their fate was to work on the previous land, chiefly engaged in off-farm activities.

In the villages there were also absentee resettlers who still resided in the previous sites. Some of these households had already handed over their resettlement land to other family members and were farming their previous fields. These were an asset for those whose land happened to be adjacent to those who were not displaced, as they could take shelter with them when they were working in the locality. The young men and off-farm-based households returned to the previous sites to engage in off-farm activities, especially to sell sand, firewood, etc. Some even commuted using public transport and there were instances in which individuals working in sand retailing managed to buy a bicycle to reduce travel costs.

SOCIO-CULTURAL REARTICULATION

The adaptations were not wholly economic but also comprised social rearticulation, although these were interlinked. Hence, to cope with the risk ensuing from displacements, forging social ties with the hosts and among themselves was crucial. Following relocation they re-established the institutions of *Abba Jigga* and *Abba Ulee* based on religious proximity and in response to the vital need for institutions. However, reduced membership, lack of cohesion and diminishing resource tenure limited the success of institutional revitalization. Nonetheless, social capital was retained by some villagers who maintained inter-household cooperation and exchanged farm and household utensils.

In relations with the hosts some households had already established marital arrangements, paying regular visits, chewing *chat* and organizing prayer sessions together. This even went to the extent of the hosts and the resettlers building a mosque together. In one case a resettler gave his daughter to a host and another managed to obtain a wife for the host from the previous site. Coincidentally, both of them were sharecropping on land from the host partners. Thus it seems that marriage arrangements served as a vehicle for cementing social linkages and resource sharing.

Conclusion

In a bid to generate electric power human settlements are constantly being converted into water masses. The losers in such ventures whose land is flooded are exposed to potential destitution. However, the outcry on the part of researchers and those affected has resulted in limited moves to improve the lives of people often labelled as refugees of development.

The displacees of the Gilgel Gibe project paid huge costs, though they benefited to a certain extent. In fact, they were the first dam-induced displacees in Ethiopia to be rehabilitated. Nonetheless, for half a century the project was flourishing on paper, beaming signals of displacement and causing a state of uncertainty in their lives. Those displaced during the Derg had to suffer untold economic and social problems, and in 1999 were affected once again.

The 1999 displacement plan showered displacees with arrays of promises. In a bid to screen out 'ineligible' people three rounds of registration were carried out. The outcome was registration apathy and underestimation of assets by the displacees, who feared that it was a move related to tax increases, and failed to participate fully at each stage as to specifically what should be compensated at what price.

At first sight it might seem that the relocatees responded well to impoverishment risks. However, the risks on the ground were quite different. In relation to land, all households received equal amounta of land regardless of household size, composition and ability to plough. This was particularly insensitive to the expectations of young people coming of age. Observations and secondary data revealed that sites selected for resettlement were areas of inferior quality and not the promised fertile land, which led to constraints in reconstruction efforts. Ironically, too, the social planning was faulty. Housing arrangements ignored the previous settlement patterns and increased social scale, which affected harmonious relations. Furthermore, political disempowerment was unmitigated in the rehabilitation process. In general, risk management at the project level attempted to respond more to the blueprinted risks than to how the risks manifested themselves on the ground, with little attempt to explore people's readiness to help themselves.

Rather than wholesale impoverishment, a certain level of opportunity-threat was apparent. Factors like wealth, household size and composition, age, gender, the resource endowments of the arrival site, the amount of compensation obtained, etc. were the major sources of differentiation. Coping responses such as agricultural intensification/extensification, livelihood diversification and migration reflected such factors, whether the endeavours were in response to opportunities or threats. The process also included commendable social rearticulation, which involved institutional revitalization, making housing arrangements to be closer to their families, and organizing social ties with the host and resource-sharing facilitated by similar social backgrounds.

Notes

The French Center for Ethiopian Studies in Addis Ababa supported fieldwork for the study, carried out in two phases of three months as part of MA thesis research in 2001 using qualitative methods of data collection.

1. World Bank Operational Directive on Involuntary Resettlement.
2. Similar studies in West Africa indicated that the initial success in productivity was unsustainable with the erosion of incomes to purchase inputs, due to the infertile nature of the soil (McMillan *et al.* 1998).
3. Better shelter conditions are one of the relatively easy aspects to achieve improvements in resettlement livelihoods (Cernea 2000). Ferradas (1995) comments that sociologists value a house built in the urban style surrounded by roses. McAndrew (1995) underlines the fact that peasants value houses, gardens and surroundings rather than buildings constructed by projects in the urban style. This study argues for better roofing, given the ecology in which the houses are situated rather than symbolic galvanization of roofs.
4. Cernea argues that reconstruction efforts tend to compare the previous living standards of the community before the move with what the project has done. Existing services should not be a point for comparison, since these places were doomed and had been denied development opportunities for many years.
5. I called this the risk of political disempowerment following Dwivedi (2002) (though he used the term in a different context) for lack of a better word to explain how resettlers remain a minority in the new circumstances. In this case in a bid to control resources conflict between the relocatees and the hosts, they were distributed among the existing peasant associations, though the relocatees insisted on forming their own local administration, anticipating disadvantaged minority status.

Five

The Effects of Development Projects on the Karrayu & Afar in the mid-Awash Valley

AYALEW GEBRE & GETACHEW KASSA

Background: general conditions of pastoralists

In Ethiopia nomadic pastoralists constitute about 5 million people (Fecadu 1990) living in the dry lowlands and relatively arid climatic zones.[1] Mainly transhumant, they belong to some 29 linguistic groups classified as Cushitic, Nilotic and Omotic. The area they occupy covers slightly less than 50 percent (500,000 km^2) of the country and encircles the central highlands and border areas of neighbouring countries (UNDP/RRC 1984).

Mainstream thinking holds that parts of Ethiopia inhabited by population groups whose economic mainstay is livestock husbandry are geographically, environmentally and economically marginal. However, these areas occupied by pastoralists are believed to be endowed with unexploited natural resources. Oil and gas are said to be in relative abundance in most lowland areas, notably the Ogaden (Yacob 1995). The lowlands are further characterized by plains watered by perennial rivers; the Blue Nile, Tekeze, Omo and Wabeshebelle Rivers and the Baro Akobo and Ganale-Juba-Dawa systems meander through the pastoral lands of Ethiopia before they cross the country's frontiers in almost all directions (*ibid*). Thus, the pastoral areas, by and large, lend themselves to large-scale agricultural development and are therefore attractive to outsiders.

For a long time, there was no comprehensive and integrated policy ensuring a sustainable livelihood for people in pastoral areas in Ethiopia. In the late 1950s, the Ministry of Agriculture initiated rangeland development projects aimed at harnessing pastoral resources. Such moves were, however, driven mainly by the interest to get access to the resources allegedly held by the pastoralists (Fecadu 1990; Coppock 1994). Even when pastoral, as opposed to livestock, development was thought worthy of being seriously considered, the attempts were propelled by the need to procure products for regional and world markets, to satisfy the consumption requirements of urban dwellers and to facilitate integration and assimilation of the pastoralists into the mainstream mode of life characterized by the market economy.

With the progressive decline in environmental security in the highlands, peasants and agro-pastoralists from the highlands often migrate to land in lower altitudes to make up for the losses sustained in their traditional niches. The state is also making increasing claims on pastoral land for various development purposes. This represents a threat to pastoral groups, as Dietz (1996: 35) notes:

> The tragedy of pastoralism in many parts of the world today is that the survival niches nature supplied to pastoralists have also been discovered by cultivators, gold diggers and fishermen and have become opportunity niches or, even worse, have been privatised as speculation zones … or as forbidden game reserves.

These circumstances result in tense and sometimes openly hostile relations among the protagonists, The concrete manifestations of misfortunes that have befallen agro-pastoralists in Ethiopia include massive displacements, removal of large tracts of prime grazing land to make way for irrigated agricultural schemes, parks, game reserves, plantations, closures for conservation projects and resettlement programmes, considered in this chapter in relation to the Awash Valley.

Development of large-scale commercial farms in the Awash Basin

The Awash Valley covers an area of approximately 70,000 km^2, accounting for 6 percent of the total area of the country (Bondestam 1974). During the imperial period, the Awash Valley Authority (AVA), a large state organization instituted in January 1962, was entrusted with the task of exploiting the natural resources of the area. Under the auspices of the AVA many concession farms, the Awash National Park, the Koka Dam and the hydroelectric plant were constructed (Ayalew 1995; Seyoum 1995). Thus, the Awash Valley became one of the most coveted regions in the country.

The AVA granted and administered concessions for irrigated agriculture and conducted feasibility studies and prepared projects for plantation agriculture. However, some of the large-scale commercial agricultural enterprises were already in existence when the AVA launched its activities.[2]

Settlement as development policy, past and present

Since the 1960s Ethiopian governments have held that pastoralists such as the Afar and Karrayu own vast and surplus unutilized land which could be allocated for irrigated agriculture. Moreover, pastoralists were viewed as possessing a large number of animals, which could benefit the national export income if their stock management and local breeds were improved. The various regimes insisted on policies that aimed at transforming mobile pastoralists into 'law-abiding', modernized and productive citizens. Accordingly, they tried to coerce pastoral groups like the Afar and the Karrayu to stay in 'tribal areas' and to settle in sedentary agropastoral villages. They created and enforced bordering administrative territories which interfered with tribal grazing areas, peasant and/or pastoral associations and other territorial administrative units. Pastoralists failing to respect government rules were severely punished. These measures were imposed on the communities without any assessment of the rationales for pastoralists keeping large herds and their need for mobility. The planners failed to understand the climatic and ecological conditions of areas used by pastoralists, the efficiencies of their land-use practices, their livestock ownership and use rights, herd management, lending, distribution and resource-sharing practices, as well as the history of inter- and intra-ethnic relationships of peaceful and violent resource use and sharing.

Government officials have often justified the settlement of pastoralists in restricted areas on the grounds of their obtaining protection from raiders and better access to education, human and animal health care, clean water, markets and food aid. Thus, the development of pastoral communities and their attainment of a higher standard of living were viewed as only attainable in settlements. However, studies on pastoral sedentarization show that past attempts to engage pastoralists in settlement programmes and alienation of their lands for other uses have often been disappointing.. Sedentarization often fails to result in a higher standard of living for settled herders, or in environmental conservation, food security and an increased contribution of pastoralists to the national economy.

Hogg has argued that the introduction of irrigated farming and settlement farming schemes in the pastoral areas was highly biased in favor of wealthy stock owners, since such schemes could not be sustained without heavy government and donor capital subsidies and imported technologies and expertise.

> Vast sums of money have been expended over the last forty years on development in the areas over which pastoralists graze their herds and flocks yet, nevertheless, most pastoralists are worse off than they have ever been and pastoral productivity is lower than it has ever been. (Hogg 1997a: 10)

(A) The Karrayu and the Metehara Sugar Estate

The Karrayu who inhabit the Metehara Plain and Mount Fentale area are Oromo-speaking transhumant pastoralists. Apart from livestock herding, the Karrayu have also started practising both rain-fed and irrigated agriculture since the early 1980s, mainly as a response to the expropriation of their pastoral land and the subsequent weakening of pastoral livelihoods.

Until the early 1950s, the Karrayu were the dominant land users of what is called the Fentale district and the Metehara plain. After this period, however, several large-scale plantations, mostly managed by foreign agribusiness in joint ventures with the state, were set up in the area. The Dutch firm Handels Vereeniging Amsterdam (HVA) established the Wonji Shoa and Metehara Sugar estate in the Upper Valley. Likewise, the Awash National Park was legally established by the state in 1969 located between Metehara and Awash Station, and enclosed 80,000 hectares of dry and wet season grazing, formerly used by the Karrayu and the Afar. This entailed serious consequences, depriving them of access to grazing land, which they used at critical periods. The establishment of the irrigation schemes and the Awash National Park changed the traditional transhumance patterns and has significantly altered the land rights of the pastoralists and their land tenure system.

COMMERCIAL FARMS AND THE PASTORALISTS' PREDICAMENT

The increase in the number of development projects and the area of land they covered seems to demonstrate that such agricultural schemes are unqualified successes both from the point of view of foreign capital during the imperial period and in the eyes of the government during the military era and at present. However, the adverse outcomes of such development ventures for the pastoralists' livelihoods tend to be ignored.

LOSS OF PRIME DRY-SEASON GRAZING

Traditionally, the Afar and Karrayu used grazing areas particularly along the Awash river, which were eventually found to be highly suitable for irrigated agriculture. Of special importance to pastoralism were the resources on the flood plains which, to a large extent, were taken over by the concession farms. The major consequence was the alienation of grazing lands formerly used by the pastoralists as dry-season retreats and the subsequent disappearance of previously thick vegetation cover browsed by goats and camels.

The grazing land lost to irrigated agriculture on the state farms and conservation area amounts to 90,100 hectares. The total area of land traditionally used by the Karrayu was estimated by Jacobs and Schloeder (1993) to be 150,113 hectares. Therefore, the net land area currently used by the pastoralists stands at 60,013 hectares, a reduction of 60 percent. The problem has been compounded by the fact that these areas constitute the very grazing land estimated to have ten times the carrying capacity of dry land pastures (Lane *et al.* 1993). Thus, much more serious than the loss in terms of area is the quality of the grazing resources taken over for irrigation purposes.

Another grave consequence has been the disruption of the Karrayu seasonal patterns of mobility. Prior to the introduction of irrigation agriculture the movement of people and their herds followed a regular pattern. Karrayu herders seldom moved beyond 50 km from their usual places of residence. When they lost large tracts of their dry season grazing, their mobility was curtailed and the pattern became distorted and irregular.

Furthermore, planning is still under way to develop additional tracts of land for agro-industrial purposes, whereas no compensatory measures have been considered in return for the expropriated holdings. In July 1997 the Metahara Sugar Estate attempted to encroach further into land used by the Karrayu. The plan did not materialize due to fierce resistance by the agro-pastoralists.

DEPRIVATION OF ACCESS TO WATER SOURCES

The Awash River is crucial for the Afar and the Karrayu who, together with their animals, rely heavily on it during the long dry season, which stretches from mid-December to early June. Subsequent to the introduction of irrigated agriculture in parts of the valley, pastoralists were not only deprived of their dry season grazing land, but were also denied access to almost all the major watering points on the Awash, leaving them desperate and vulnerable. Access to permanent water sources along the Awash River became completely impossible once the Metehara Sugar Estate expanded northwards across the river as well as into the southwestern section of the Awash National Park. Similarly the Afar have lost access to many of their waterpoints in Amibara.

In short, since the Afar and the Karrayu rely heavily on land and other resources for their subsistence, land and water alienation as a direct consequence of deliberate government policy interventions has impaired their livelihood security as pastoralists. The denial of their access to resources vital to their survival has become an issue of resource security, which is related to both pastoral sustenance and to the environment (Mohammed Salih 1999).

DISPLACEMENT OF THE PASTORALISTS

Another consequence of the expansion of agricultural estates and concessions in the Afar and Karrayu areas has been the eviction of the pastoralists from their ancestral lands. The displacement dates back to the early 1960s when private farming enterprises were introduced. The intensity of the displacement sharply increased over the last three decades as the socialist regime adopted a policy of state farm expansion. Exact figures of the displaced are not available. However, according to Karrayu elders and releases from the AVA, several thousands are believed to have been forced to move to the drier interior. During the imperial period and after, the Metehara Sugar Estate and the Awash National Park are remembered by the locals as notoriously responsible for the great displacements that took place. The plight of displaced Karrayu has been disregarded; few or no measures have been taken to compensate them. This is in contrast to the Afar of the Middle Awash Valley who were at least compensated in the form of settlement programmes and the provision of irrigated pasture. Such a failure to give due attention to the problem elicited intense mistrust and resentment from the Karrayu.

The eviction and displacement of the group from their villages forced them to take up new settlements in marginal, less fertile areas, with ever-shrinking resources, that gradually plunged them deeper into a spiral of reduced productivity and increasing impoverishment. Furthermore, part of the eviction crisis is the destruction of sacred funeral and ritual sites. The Karrayu ritual leaders interviewed[3] expressed their indignation about this. Land for the pastoralists is not only a grazing and browsing resource vital to their livelihood, but also constitutes an aspect of their cultural and ritual life. In relation to this Bradbury *et al.* (1995:21) state that, 'Pastoralists cannot sustain their livelihoods or their culture without land. …The loss of sites with cultural or spiritual significance is just as important as natural resources with economic value.'

INTENSIFICATION OF INTER-ETHNIC CONFLICTS

The displacements also affected the relationship of the Karrayu with other agro-pastoral groups in the region. When the Karrayu were driven away by private and state agricultural enterprises, they moved northwards and westwards in the direction of the Afar and the Argoba who are their historical enemies. Thus, competition over scarce resources and disputes over land rights developed into confrontations and outright conflicts, often leading to clashes with casualties on both sides, as illustrated in the following case of tension and conflict between the Karrayu and Afar.

THE CASE OF CONFLICT BETWEEN THE KARRAYU AND AFAR

The tribal section of the Afar known as the Debne are the northern neighbours of the Karrayu. One of the major factors contributing to the conflict is the continuing decline of the resource base for livestock brought about by the expansion of commercial farms. There is also the migration of other groups (the Ittu[4] and the Weima[5] Afar) into the Karrayu and the Debne Afar territories.

The area was traditionally inhabited by the Debne Afar and the Karrayu to the north and south of Mount Fentale respectively. The Weima Afar were consistently pushed further from their traditional habitat by the Issa Somali and kept moving into the Debne Afar territory. Other Afar groups were also evicted from their settlements by the expanding Melka Sadi and Melka Warer concession farms and migrated under pressure into the area of the Debne Afar. In addition, the Awara Melka mechanized state farm at Sabure had expropriated a large amount of grazing land from the Debne-controlled territory. Squeezed from all sides into a much narrower and more marginal area, the Debne Afar would have liked to shift further east to the Alleideghi Plain with abundant pasture. However, their migration was prohibited by the presence of Issa Somali enemies. The only alternative was for them to push further south into the traditional migration areas of the Karrayu. This brought the Debne Afar into conflict with the Karrayu. As a result, the dry-season grazing areas and the banks of the Kessem River, which were already densely stocked and settled, have become sites of confrontation between the Karrayu and the Debne Afar. Increasing inter-ethnic clashes due to dwindling grazing resources have also contributed to the degradation of the environment, as the concentration of displaced herding populations in limited areas will further aggravate the problem of overgrazing and contribute to the reduction of ground cover reduction by vegetation trampling and erosion by water and wind.

The Karrayu have become victims of land expropriation by a number of commercial farms and of overcrowding due to the arrival and settling in their territory of other groups, mainly the Ittu and Somali. As a result, the Karrayu have sometimes crossed over into the territory of the Debne Afar. The conflict was most intense over the Gebaba Plain between the great and little Fentales to which they resorted when forced out of the Arole rangelands by the Argoba, their western neighbours. Dry-season grazing areas inside the Awash National Park boundaries are also locations of frequent clashes between the Afar and the Karrayu, as these migration areas border closely on the territory of Debne and Weima Afar. The Karrayu often send out scouting parties before they graze their livestock there and water them at the Dinkuku Pond.The two wet seasons of 2000 and 2001 were marked by an absence of rain and the herders suffered badly from drought and lost cattle, while some of the highly nutritive seasonal grasses lay unused, since both groups hesitated to use these pasture lands for mutual fear of attack.

EXACERBATED VULNERABILITY TO DROUGHT

The encroachment into Karrayu grazing land and the expansion of irrigated schemes have also rendered their pastoral economy susceptible to recurrent drought and famine. Studies have established a close connection between the expansion of development and conservation programmes in the Awash Valley and the recurrence of drought and famines (Bondestam 1974; Harbeson and Teffera-Worq 1974; Kloos 1982; MacDonald 1991; Ali 1992; Gamaledin 1987, 1993; Lane *et al.* 1993; Muderis 1998). The Karrayu area has been hit by recurrent droughts over the past decades.[6] It was estimated that in the 1984-6 drought the Karrayu and Ittu lost 20 percent of their cattle, 7 percent of their camels, and 25 percent of their sheep and goats (Tibebe 1997). A much larger number of livestock and human lives are believed to have been claimed by the 1980-1 drought, which is still remembered as the most devastating.,

Among 60 selected households average losses were 11 cattle, 1 camel, 20 small stock, and 0.5 persons per household during the drought of 1973-4, and 27 cattle, 2 camels, 40 smallstock, and 1 person per household during 1980-1. A comparison of the effects of the three droughts reveals that the 1980-1 drought was 2.1 and 5.7 times more severe than the 1973-4 and 1984-6 droughts respectively. This period also coincides with the proliferation of small-scale irrigated agriculture and the consequent process of sedentarization or 'depastoralization' (Dietz, 1993). Compared with the 'rich' and 'medium-sized' stockowners, it is the poor and very poor households which lost much of their animal wealth in these droughts. The wealthy and medium-sized households are able to forge various forms of grazing alliances and stock associations both within and outside their tribal boundaries, enabling them to exploit alternative grazing areas in times of adversity.

Drought has contributed to depressing the animal population. However, the drought and the accompanying famines of the 1970s and 1980s were not entirely the result of rain failure and poor resource management. Rather, development-induced dispossession/displacement was evidently responsible for aggravating the drought problem as it was accompanied by diminishing natural resources and high environmental degradation. Access to flooded grazing areas is crucial for the Karrayu pastoralists to survive and exploit areas into which they move during the wet seasons. When a sizeable area close to the river is made unavailable for dry-season grazing, a much larger area far away from the flood plains is rendered almost useless. The Karrayu have thus been marginalized and exposed to frequent drought and famine by the deliberate conversion of their pastoral commons into private and state property over the last fifty years.

EFFECTS ON THE ECOLOGY AND RESOURCE-USE PATTERNS

The loss of population-sustaining dry-season resources has had a serious impact on the traditional resource-use patterns of the pastoralists. Thus, the dispossession set off a chain of events when the displaced herdsmen and their families, camps and stocks were forced to limit their movements to within the confines of marginal areas. In turn, the curtailment of their mobility led to heavy human and livestock concentrations in a narrow area with the result that overgrazing and resource depletion inevitably followed.

Lying at the heart of the environmental crisis in the Afar and Karrayu areas are the changes forcefully brought about in the ownership of land by the dominant state and other powerful interest groups.[7] In general, the land-use policies and tenure legislation[8] of the state encourage, if not explicitly stipulate, the expropriation of traditional pastoral resources in the interests of the wider society. In effect, this has nullified the role of customary institutions, which governed the traditional resource-management system. In land-based economies like pastoralism, when land changes hands, so does power. Hence, herders lose the traditional power they used to exercise in administering their local affairs including subsistence rights. In essence, 'these two distinctive forms of disempowerment contribute significantly to people's political and economic impoverishment' (Mohammed Salih 1999: 13).

Traditionally, the Karrayu followed the rain across their lands and the waters of the Awash River and the resources nearby, leaving an area before its resources were exhausted and returning only when it had recovered. Now, confined to smaller areas, following the elimination of crucial dry-season pasture along the banks of the river, they have no alternative but to abandon the traditional rotation strategies and graze off what is left until drought or over-use makes for environmental deterioration. A number of social and political barriers also prevent them from access to and sharing the resources of their neighbouring groups.

Such changes in the ownership of land by way of deliberate government interventions and the accompanying land expropriation and concentration in the hands of state-owned enterprises and private investors significantly contributed to the concentration of the herding population in smaller areas (Monbiot 1994; Mohammed Salih 1999). This in turn exacerbated overgrazing increasing livestock numbers within reduced grazing land, forcing herders to degrade their environment (ibid.). The problem is thus aggravated by curtailment of mobility, a fundamental pastoral adaptive strategy, both in time and space, brought about by the compression of the environmental space; this has contributed to fierce competition over relatively scarce resources and intensive pressure on the rangeland.

(B) The Afar and the Amibara irrigation agriculture and settler farm schemes

The Afar population (circa 1.2 million, CSA 1998) is predominantly pastoral and agro-pastoral. They rely on a system where extensive livestock-raising is the principal form of subsistence. The Afar way of life has undergone significant changes, setting in motion new dynamics both at the economic and the socio-cultural levels. Chief among the factors causing such change is the encroachment of irrigated development projects.

The Amibara Malka Saddi irrigated agriculture scheme was implemented by the Awash Valley Authority (AVA), and affected the Afar living in relation with the Awash river and its flood-fed lands. The interests of the pastoralists and the large-scale farm scheme centred on the same narrow strips of flood-fed banks or flood plains. The commercial investors and the state agencies were primarily interested in the high-potential flood-fed dry-season grazing land reserves, which could be easily irrigated. These lands were used by the Afar communities as dry-season grazing lands, farming places of agro-pastoralist minority groups, water access points, family settlements, holy places and graveyards. Since the creation of irrigated farms, the issue of land tenure and land-use rights in the Amibara area had been a matter of dispute between the state and agro-pastoral communities.

COMPOSITION OF AFAR SETTLERS IN THE AMIBARA AND HALLE-DEBBI SETTLER FARM SCHEMES

The Amibara and Halle-Debbi settler farms were established in 1967 and 1971, and were meant to compensate the Afar Debne and Weima clans respectively. At the start the Amibara settler farm had 97 hectares of land, while the land developed in Amibara was 30 hectares. The Amibara settler farm was located adjacent to the Malka Warar Agriculture Research Center and was virtually surrounded by the Middle Awash Agricultural Development Enterprise farms.

In the first year the Amibara settlement consisted of 72 Afar households. The AVA employees assisted by clan leaders recruited the settler households in Amibara and Halle-Debbi. The settlers were selected on the basis of physical fitness and relations with the clan heads. Moreover, as Abdulhamid (1989) argued, the Amibara settlement farm scheme was composed of neither developments-displaced nor marginalized pastoralists, destitute herders or drop-outs. Rather, the first batch of pioneer settler families had family livestock and sufficient means to cover their subsistence needs when they were settled. The clan leaders manipulated the procedures set by the AVA and recruited their close kin and members of their families. The Halle-Debbi settlement centre came under the Amibara settlement scheme but was intended for Weima clans; it extends to about 426 ha. of land with about 1,500 settlers.

The size of farm allocated to each settler farmer was between 0.2 to 0.5 ha and 2.5 ha during the Derg. As an incentive each settler received a monthly stipend of foodstuffs, equivalent to 30 *birr*. The settler farmers were expected to perform all the farm work, assisted by AVA employees who were expected to train them. Accordingly Afar settler families were given training for a year and the AVA selected those who could settle (Abdulhamid 1989: 101).

Each settler Afar was expected to grow cotton and maize. The operating cost of the farms was covered by the AVA. The cotton was sold by the AVA to the irrigated farm schemes. The annual stipend paid by the AVA to settler Afar farmers was calculated on the basis of the income obtained from the land after all the expenses spent on the operation of the farm had been deducted.[9] As a result of high international cotton prices the settlers in Amibara settlement farm obtained quite substantial incomes, attracting pastoralists to apply to be settled in increasing numbers (Abdulhamid 1989: 101).

The pastoralists maintained their livestock on the side, amongst family and kin living away from the settler farm in the pastoral areas. The settler Afar families were not willing to engage themselves as full-time settled agriculturists and abandon their pastoral way of life and their family herds (ibid.). They often employed farm labourers, especially highlanders, to carry out cultivation and associated farming activities on their farm plots. Thus, the settlement objectives as stated by the AVA were not achieved; since the Afar settler farmers continued their pastoral production away from the settlement areas.

PASTORAL SETTLEMENT DURING THE DERG ERA

The Amibara settler farm continued to operate after the fall of the imperial government in 1974. The rationales behind the continuation of the settlement programmes and the creation of new settlements were the following: to continue production in the nationalized commercial farms which were not converted into state farms; to maintain the workers in these farms in employment; and to accommodate the marginalized and famine and war-displaced Afar pastoralists (Abdulahamid 1989: 102). During the crisis years of drought, instability and famine of the 1970s,[10] the Derg insisted on the implementation of settlement programmes and promoted state-run mechanized agriculture to tackle the food shortages that were affecting the country and to increase export earnings through expansion of irrigated farming. This policy was in line with the Derg regime's socialist development programmes that emphasized collectivization and villagization. The government insisted on implementing settlement programmes as a national economic policy to transform the pastoralists and their 'backward economy'. The 1975 land proclamation that nationalized all lands stated that 'the government would take the responsibility to improve grazing lands, to dig wells and to settle nomadic peoples' (ibid.). In 1975 the Derg nationalized all privately owned commercial farms. Part of the nationalized irrigated farms was allocated for settling pastoralists in farming settlements.

The roles of AVA and RRC in settling Afar in farm settlements

Besides setting aside land, the government allocated substantial capital and manpower for settlement projects, under the responsibility of the AVA with supervision by the Ministry of Agriculture. Soon the role of the AVA was taken over by the Relief and Rehabilitation Commission (RRC) responsible for settlement and resettlement (Abdulhamid 1989: 103). The policy of government agencies had been to settle the pastoralists on mechanized farms supplemented with maize production, animal husbandry, dairy farming and irrigated pasture development. The government allocated funds for running the settler farms, which the farm managers used to purchase capital goods, other material inputs and labour. The settler farms obtained subsidized services (land grading, levelling, etc.) from state farms in the area. The output, in particular cotton, was sold to state purchasing agencies at fixed prices.

The settlement farms in the Amibara area continued to exist and expand in terms of size and number of settlers. In addition, other settlement farms were launched through the transfer of part of the nationalized irrigated farms of the Amibara Malka Saddi farm scheme and farms previously owned by clan heads and individual investors. The numbers of settlers increased as many Afar herders hit by drought and conflict were ready to settle. However, the farms faced problems as the cultivation of settlers' plots could not be undertaken without the use of tractors and irrigation water, and soon the Amibara and Halle-Debbi settler farms were non-operational, due to shortages of subsidies. In both settlements a few Afar households continued to cultivate vegetables and maize, in their small plots using their own resources. The livestock/dairy-farming programme intended for the settler Afar also ceased to exist after 1987-8 mainly due to the outbreak of livestock epidemics and for financial reasons. As to the provision of irrigated pastures, the pilot projects started before the 1980s were not realized until 2002 due to mismanagement and financial shortages.

Factors behind the failures of the settlement scheme

Development workers and researchers attribute the failures to either one or a combination of the following reasons:

1. There was no clear policy on how to settle pastoralists and the settler farms were established too quickly. The Amibara settlement farm was implemented primarily not as a tool to promote the transformation of the pastoral Afar but to mitigate the resistance by development-displaced Afar clans to the AVA and the Amibara Malka Saddi Farm scheme.[11] Thus, the settlement farm in Amibara was formed to appease the displaced Afar clans rather than to promote the development of pastoralists.

2. The settler farm programme in Afar areas was based on inappropriate planning insisting on crop production and failing to give due attention to the livestock production on which the pastoral economy is based.

3. The schemes were not implemented on the basis of detailed feasibility studies with full participation of the Afar settlers. Moreover, the use of mechanized means

and wage labourers in the operation of the farms and the failure of the AVA and RRC to promote settler herders' integration into the settlement farming activities provided disincentives to pastoralist settlers remaining full-time in the settlement farms. This resulted in absenteeism from their settlements and farm plots, as settler Afar farmers did not want to lose contact with their family herds and families and kin living away from the settler farms, and also led to a lack of interest in the farming activities, apart from the income (Getachew 1997, 2000; Abdulhamid 1989; Ali 1992).

4. The AVA and RRC failed to provide the Afar settler farmers with training in agricultural and machine-operation skills, and instead employed migrant farm labourers (Abdulhamid 1989). The understanding had been that the pastoralist settlers would pick up farming skills and knowledge while working side by side with the migrant highland farm labourers.[12] But soon conflict started to occur between the settler Afar farmers and the wage labourers and settlement managers, thus disrupting the operation of the settlement farms.

5.. The increased use of waged workers in the settler farms, the settlers' low level of participation, and the payment of stipends to absentee settler pastoralists, made the farms like a welfare programme or charity organization (Abdulhamid 1989).

6. Instead of focusing on the production of food crops that strengthen the food security of the Afar settlers, the settlement farm gave more emphasis to the production of cotton and other cash crops.

7. The handing over of the scheme from the AVA to the RRC, which was involved in relief with little experience in development activities, was also seen as a contributing factor, and the pastoralists became accustomed to relief supplies after the 1973-4 drought.

8. The settlers' farms were making losses and were run with government subsidies when the economic support and other public investments provided by the AVA, the RRC and the MWARC were insufficient to keep the Afar settlers on their settlement farms.

9. The settlement was heavily dependent upon external/state inputs, expertise, advice and technology and was unable to become sustainable and transform the Afar on a long-term basis. Thus, the Afar settlers were not interested in engaging themselves fully in the operation and management of their farms and invested very little time and resources since they considered such things to be the duty of the AVA/RRC and the government.

Major effects of irrigation farm schemes

Although the Amibara settlement farm project failed to achieve its main goals, it has introduced changes that have affected the economic base, land rights, the environment and cultural and social relations both negatively and positively. It resulted in a new type of land use and ownership, new farming techniques, new crops, and the presence of non-Afar settlers.

Perhaps the most important adverse consequence of these developments for the Afar has been the alienation of the dry-season pastures and clan lands upon which they were heavily dependent for their livelihood. These changes in land use and tenure have been further compounded by recurrent drought since the 1970s, leading to increased pressure on the remaining clan lands. This intensified inter- and intra-ethnic conflicts over remaining resources and led to violent confrontations between the displaced pastoral Afar clans and other parties involved in agricultural development, in particular the authorities of the irrigation farms and the settlement farm projects.

Debne and Weima Afar clans are currently afraid to take their stock to their traditional wet-season pasture sites in the Alleideghi Plain and the southwestern part of the Awash National Park. The alienation of land for irrigation farming in the flood plains of Amibara has exacerbated conflicts over pastoral resources. The Afar were forced to move into territories belonging to their neighbours during the dry seasons and years of prolonged drought. In such periods confrontations with the Issa, Karrayu, Amhara, Argoba and Ittu became inevitable and frequent. Such conflicts over resources also occurred between Afar clans. This happened whenever a certain clan moved into land which customarily belonged to another clan without any prior arrangement and permission (Getachew 1997, 2000, 2001, 2003).

As has been shown in many pastoralist development contexts in other African countries, settlement schemes are mostly biased and often benefit the rich minorities rather than the average and poor pastoralists and agro-pastoralists. Accordingly, in the context of Amibara the main beneficiaries were the clan heads and wealthy stock owners.

The settlement schemes and conflicts and insecurity restricted the mobility of pastoralists and their herds, resulting in serious consequences for the productivity of pastoralist herds, increased health hazards affecting both livestock and people, resource degradation, scarcity and conflicts over inter- and intra Afar resource use. In extreme cases, malnutrition and human and livestock morbidity and mortality increased due to the scarcity of fodder and water, and the increased incidence of diseases due to the overcrowding of people and livestock.

Conclusion

Planned development interventions in the pastoral areas of Ethiopia started in the late 1950s to develop the agricultural potential of the lowlands. The Third Five-Year Development Plan (1968-73) envisioned the expansion of commercial agriculture in the Awash Valley area and the imperial government embarked on making land grants to concessionaires. Individuals, transnational corporations and other concessionaire syndicates became involved in irrigated agricultural schemes that took little notice of the needs and problems of pastoralists. Pastoral land was further allocated for national parks designed to promote the tourist industry.

The Derg military regime continued a policy of alienation of lands that were not intensively cultivated as state domain and appropriated such lands for state-owned commercial farms and forced settlement schemes. The consequence was the same: eviction of the pastoralists from their land. Such actions were almost always taken with little or no alternative arrangements made for the sustenance of the displaced.

Ethiopian governments have thus insisted that pastoral land be regarded as primarily state land, thus in effect abrogating all customary pastoral land rights. The premise held is that the land occupied by herding populations is not permanently settled and legally possessed. In the words of Salzman and Galaty (1990: 19) 'It is thus not surprising that governments often feel pastureland to represent a national resource much more so than the privately developed agrarian regions'. The state maintains that it has the right to utilize such land in the best interest of the nation. This explains why drastic changes in the legal status of pastoral land are evident in the areas where governments have shown a particular development interest.

What can be learnt from the settlement programmes attempted is that any project that does not actively involve the people and that is not based on the real needs of the pastoralists is doomed to failure. Settling Afar on irrigated farm settlements is not an option for the vast majority of the population. Afar pastoralism has evolved in response to hostile environmental conditions and the fragility of the local ecosystem, which renders other modes of existence impracticable, since they may disturb the environment's delicate equilibrium. The emphasis on promoting large-scale mechanized agriculture, with its inappropriate farming technologies, and settling pastoralists in farming schemes will undermine local pastoral and agro-pastoral production systems. These forms of interventions in fragile eco systems like those of the Afar can typically lead to rapid overgrazing, soil salinization, resource scarcity and conflicts over the use of resources.

Such irrigated schemes may be justifiable and well motivated. The state may also have to reconcile contending demands from various population groups. Matters which need to be thus addressed may refer to the promotion of entrepreneurial interests, the pursuit of national food self-sufficiency, improving the country's export potential, and the resettlement of people from congested areas because of the increased population/land ratio. Therefore, the heart of the controversy does not lie in the intention behind state-sponsored utilization of pastoral land for other purposes, when this is deemed necessary. Rather, what has become contentious is that, as experience shows, such measures are taken without involving the pastoralists in the process or without at least paying adequate attention to their circumstances. On the contrary, previous and present practice indicates a notable failure to acknowledge the long-standing rights that herding people possess over their ancestral land by virtue of inhabiting it for a number of generations. The denial of access to critical environmental resources will, in effect, mean a gross reduction in the survival chances of pastoral households. Hence, it has to be a matter of concern for the state, as it already is for the victims, that one section of the population should not be at the receiving end of the consequences brought about by measures adopted in the interest of other population groups.

If, however, the resource entitlements and ownership rights of the pastoralists are ignored, conflicts of interest are sure to arise. Moreover, denial of access to a survival niche on which their very existence as a people depends, also raises a fundamental question. The demand for resource security and entitlement becomes a justifiable human rights concern in view of the fact that the source of subsistence for the pastoralists is basically the land appropriated by the state (Dietz, 1996; Dietz and Mohammed Salih, 1997).

An official argument commonly upheld by state authorities pertains to the propriety of developing rangelands for the attainment of wider national goals such as in the sectors of irrigation agriculture, wildlife conservation, game ranching and tourism. In such a situation, a real dilemma arises about reconciling two widely differing forms of land use. Handling the dilemma may call for working out acceptable and adequate compensation arrangements, taking the predicament of the losers into due consideration.

Pastoral groups have been the subject of pressure not from state administrations alone. Other protagonists have been land-hungry peasants in neighbouring territories. Competition over farmland arises where pastoral areas contain agricultural potential, and farming groups, due to growing population pressures in their region, become desperate for cultivable land. The ensuing incursions into agriculturally suitable grazing lands continue to take firm hold, with herding inhabitants being pushed out further into the margins, as the state mediates land rights and access in favour of crop-based agriculture. Thus, in the midst of consistent pro-farmer or anti-pastoralist bias, herding groups will at the end of the day become the losers in the competition. A major determinant in the process is the general tendency in the mindset of government policy-makers to associate agriculture with development and pastoralism with primitivism.

It is thus clear that contending demands come to the fore from the state and different population groups in connection with the ever scarcer land resources. This does not mean that governments must desist from introducing remedial measures involving pastoral land as part of possible solutions. However, it does mean that measures need to be exercised with the utmost caution and that formulas need to be worked out in a fair and equitable fashion to meet the needs of the various stakeholders involved.

Obviously, a reversal of the land alienation process in the sense of restitution is belated and politically impractical. Nevertheless, the present view and practice denying pastoralists legal rights to the resources on which they survive remain an issue for debate and policy initiatives. In this regard, ensuring a secure access for herding communities to a measure of their environmental resources with the right to control or manage them presents itself as a highly rational option. At the centre of the debate is the fact that populations in marginal areas directly depend on a stable access to natural resources. This means that the question of resource tenure should necessarily head the development agenda in national initiatives in pastoral policy. The treatment of resource-tenure issues in policy agendas may constitute a first step in the process of 'de-marginalizing' nomadic populations. A policy drive that addresses this major pastoral interest, on the principle of equity with other communities, might be regarded as a pastoralist-friendly one. Such a policy should be geared towards laying down the legal and institutional frameworks vital for establishing secure pastoral resource tenure.

To ensure a stable resource tenure would require, first and foremost, the creation of a system whereby the present arbitrary and unlawful seizure of land can be controlled and prevented. A mechanism also needs to be worked out to introduce alternative land-use strategies that will facilitate and guarantee the continuance of pastoral practices. This can be accomplished through the legal and physical demarcation of land-use zones,[13] whereby the separation of pastoral grazing areas from other lands allocated for non-pastoral purposes can be managed. By so doing, the vulnerability of pastoralists to a growing external demand for land will also be minimized. However, there may still be cases in which the state will have to move into the territorial domain designated for the traditional livestock sector. When such action is necessitated by wider public interests, an appropriate system of compensation for the land lost needs to be put in place and duly implemented.

Notes

1. The lowlands or *kola* are located below 1,500 metres, with an average annual precipitation of between 400 and 700 millimetres.

2. For example, the Dutch firm Handels Vereeniging Amsterdam (HVA) in the Upper Valley and the British firm Mitchell Cotts of the Tendaho Plantation Share Company (TPSC) in the Lower Plains were established in the late 1950s.
3. Interviews with Bula Hawas, Bulga Arboye and Fentale Senbetu, ritual leaders (*Qallu*) of the Basso Tribal section of the Karrayu, 23 July, 22 August, and 8 October, 1997.
4. The Ittu are predominantly agro-pastoralists inhabiting the highlands of West Harrerghe, mainly Habro District. Most Ittu inside the Karrayu territory migrated there over the last forty years, particularly since the mid-1970s, as a result of the droughts of 1973/74 and 1984/85 and the recurrent inter-ethnic clashes with the Issa Somali.
5. Weima are the second biggest federations of Afar clans inhabiting the northwest rangelands in the Middle Awash.
6. The first severe one took place from 1972 to 1974, the second from 1980 to 1981, the third from 1984 to 1986, and the fourth in 1989-90.
7. In the context of the Karrayu, these other powerful groups or institutions are made up of the landlord classes, transnational companies such as the Dutch firm HVA and other concession farms during the imperial period and, since the Revolution in 1974, state farms.
8. The land tenure policies which have been in place in most African countries since independence are also known by the generic name 'project tenure policies', which bestow on the state unlimited power to evict the pastoralists from their ancestral land in favour of state-owned enterprises and private and foreign investors (Mohammed Salih 1999).
9. Almost the entire operations as well as the costs of the settlement programme were borne not by the Afar, but by the AVA, and later by the RRC and the Agricultural Research Centre until 1987. The participation of the Afar was limited to collecting income from the AVA. Consequently, Afar households learnt very little about agriculture and other associated production skills from the settler farming scheme.
10. The early years of the Derg era were characterized by crisis: serious droughts and famine and instability were common. Several thousands of Afar lost their herds due to the drought of 1973-74 and conflicts with neighbouring Issa Somalis, highland farmers and irrigated farms. These Afar families were forced to leave their home areas and move to small towns and irrigated farm schemes to seek famine relief and security from enemy raids.
11. Primarily they failed to involve the majority of the displaced population. The amount of cultivable land available, i.e., which was not occupied by the irrigation scheme, and the capital invested were insufficient to accommodate the largescale and radical transformation of the local pastoral households into sedentary farmers and ranchers. The tracts of land given to the displaced Afar households in the form of compensation proved far below what the Afar clans of Amibara district had lost to the Amibara Malka Saddi irrigated farm. Moreover, the projects and settlement farm schemes led to an increased concentration of livestock and human population in Amibara district, leading to overstocking and further environmental degradation.
12. As shown in Abdulhamid's 1998 paper (Table 4), there was on average nearly one farm hand employed for every settler herder family in 1982.
13. In the 1950s, British Somaliland set up a physical demarcation between agriculture and grazing land-use zones called the Meter.

Six

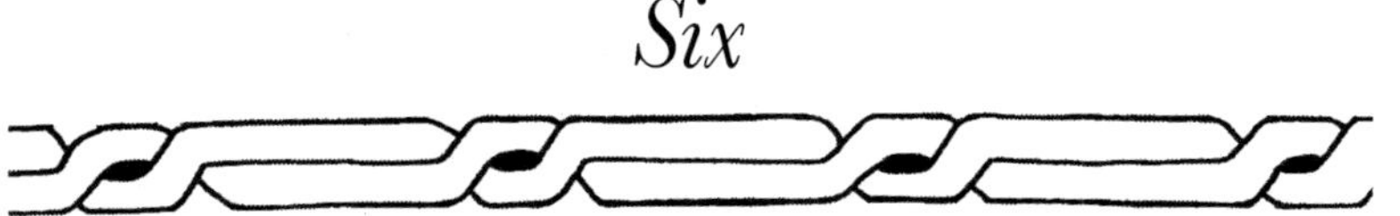

The Effects of Investment on the Livelihoods of the Tsamako in the Wayto Valley

MELESSE GETU

Following the assurance problem approach (Bromley and Cernea 1989), the present chapter argues that, in a region where people are 'critically dependent on natural resources with low and uncertain incomes', customary tenure rules are efficient and provide security of tenure. Neither the present legally enforceable state rights over natural resources, nor the private system proposed by the World Bank, are viable options as far as the future of agro-pastoralist societies are concerned. Given the limitations of legally enforceable rights to natural resources, and the historically foreign origin of the 'freehold system', it seems that the values and worth of customary tenure rules should be reconsidered with the objective of, if not codifying them as law, at least giving them formal recognition, as stated in the 1995 Constitution.

The investment policy supports large-scale farmers having a presumed capacity to make the country self-sufficient not only in terms of food production, but also by creating jobs and increasing foreign earnings, a process which may be at the expense of smallholder producers and against the constitutional rights of pastoralist societies,[1] as evidence from this case study shows. In the Wayto Valley the presence of commercial farms has resulted in land alienation and an influx of migrants, exacerbating deforestation. The investment project has seriously affected the small-scale irrigated and flood-retreat cultivation of several local communities, the use of pesticides has endangered honey production, and the presence of migrants involved in charcoal processing has reduced the savannah woodlands and the wild animals that inhabit them, affecting the ability of indigenous groups to engage in hunting and gathering. Large-scale farming has increased pressure on natural resources, notably trees, pasture, wildlife and water, adversely affecting local resource-use regulation mechanisms and collective action. These problems suggest that the rights of agro-pastoralist communities assuring their livelihoods have been neglected.

Introduction to the Tsamako and the Wayto Valley

Located almost at the southernmost end of the Rift Valley, Tsamako territory in the Southern Peoples' Regional State is a semi-arid lowland area. The main rainy season is from March through May and the small rainy season in September and October.

The area is estimated to receive about 600 mm of rainfall per annum; however, there is considerable variability in the rainfall patterns, and consequently annual flood levels vary. Most of the Tsamako territory is lowland, covered with grass, thorny bushes and trees, mainly acacia.

According to national censuses the Tsamako were estimated to number about 10,300 in 1984 and 9,500 in 1994. They speak a dialect of the Werizoid language which belongs to the lowland East Cushitic category (Bender 1971). Their genealogies suggest that they might have lived in the present territory for at least 350 years. As far as living memory can tell, they have almost always been sedentary, although the young people usually move back and forth with livestock during the dry seasons.

The Tsamako are dependent on agriculture, with varieties of sorghum and maize as staple crops, on animal husbandry and honey production and on the collection of wild food, incense and other gathered products that they sell at local markets. Crop husbandry and livestock-raising are inseparably linked, one supplementing the other although they are not free from competition for labour and other resources. Livestock, particularly cattle, are the main means of wealth accumulation and the principal standby in times of crop failure or general crises. The livestock economy is partly made indispensable because of the precarious nature of grain production. Pastoralism continues to shape the ideological orientation of the Tsamako, although grain production has been the mainstay of the economy, as manifested in the dietary composition.

Until the late 1970s, which saw the construction of the only all-weather road linking the Tsamako country to the south and the west, the area was virtually isolated from administrative centres. Two elementary schools and a health post were set up in the 1980s and an additional school was established in1995. A clinic has been run by the Norwegian Missionary Church since the mid-1980s. Otherwise the Tsamako and their neighbours have been left to their own devices. In one sense, this provides an opportunity to appreciate how local people's own systems work with little external intervention. In another, it is evidence of how such groups are marginalized by central policies and institutions.

THE WAYTO VALLEY

The Wayto Valley is an area of savannah woodland which forms part of the Chew Bahir basin in the southern Rift Valley on the Ethiopian-Kenyan border.

Rainfall is erratic and unevenly distributed. Five production systems co-exist in the Valley, namely, crop cultivation, herding, agro-fishery, honey production and hunting and gathering. Cultivation cannot be reliably sustained in the Valley on the local rainfall, and is thus traditionally based on flood recession and irrigated agriculture. The Valley was, and the western part still is, the home of a wide range of wild animals, most of which are on the verge of extinction due to the establishment of commercial farms and related developments.

Ethnic groups which have been exploiting resources to the west of the Wayto River were the Banna, the Birale, the Hor, the Maale and the Tsamako. Part of this Valley to the east of the River has been accessible to the Borana, the Gewada and the Konso.

MEANS OF ESTABLISHING RIGHTS OF ACCESS TO TREES

Big standing trees, suitable for hanging beehives, display a set of marks denoting the fact that they are controlled by someone. Trees are often branded with one or a combination of three types of marks which are devised for establishing primary user rights. The first, *hash'o*, is made by the removal of a patch of bark about 10 cm by 10 cm square. This easily detectable mark is usually made during the later stages of growth and, though it may gradually shrink, remains on the tree throughout its life. The second *hoko/toro*, is a temporary mark made by banging pegs into the trunk to indicate that it has been booked for a honey barrel. The third is by lopping (*likaso)*, which may be done before a tree is grown enough to take a barrel. A man who marks a tree should do it with a witness and also show neighbours and friends in case someone challenges his claim. Marks may need to be remade from time to time so that they remain clearly visible. Once a honey barrel has been hoisted up a tree the need to maintain the marks ceases.

The first person who makes any one of the three marks secures his primary user rights over that tree which also includes the right to cut branches for fence construction. The right-holder has the right to transfer it to other individuals or groups at will. A right-holding unit can be either a household or an individual. The right-holder can also grant temporary or secondary user rights. Primary user rights are transferred from generation to generation through the prevalent form of property transmission from the father to his eldest son and thereby to his younger sons.

Secondary user right-holders hold the right of use for a certain period of time. Members of the same generation-set and neighbours are most likely to offer secondary tree use rights to one another. Secondary rights can only be obtained from individuals who made the first tree mark and consequently hold effective control. A secondary user right-holder can lose his rights at any moment when the primary user right-holder revokes his rights.

RIGHTS TO FELL TREES

Individuals have public responsibility to protect and conserve trees and to use them. This public responsibility is expressed by communities as represented by the council of elders. There are a number of compelling reasons for the public to keep an eye on standing trees. Every resident is prohibited from cutting big standing trees of any species and fruit-producing trees of all sizes. Even when people cleared woodland for cultivation, they were expected to retain such trees.

A man's place of residence and thereby his territorial affiliation, combined with active participation in the affairs of a territorial unit, determines his rights of access to a range of jointly managed productive resources such as arable land, pasture, trees and other savannah woodland resources. Although such rights and entitlements to land, trees and savannah woodlands are secured by affiliation to a given territory, primary user rights over such resources can only be established by the investment of labour in the resource. The most important factors which mediate rights in such resources are, therefore, place of residence or territorial affiliation and labour investment.

Conventional wisdom about common property resources

Those who write against the notion of the 'tragedy of the commons' (Bruce *et al.* 1993b) and critiques of property rights and environment management advocate a shift of natural resource control from the state to rural communities whose means of livelihood depend directly upon these resources (Chambers 1993). Advocates of 'community-based' approaches argue that a centralized control of natural resources by the state has not only caused serious threats to rural people's security of tenure but has also led to the 'degradation' of natural resources (Bromley 1992; Ostrom 1990; Yeraswork 1995). Many authors write in a similar vein against the assumed inevitability of private property (Berkes and Favar 1989), and the presumed superiority of 'world-ordering' of scientific knowledge over 'indigenous' knowledge and community perspectives (Chambers 1983; Scoones *et al.* 1996). The call for such 'bottom-up' approaches fits well with conventional anthropological narratives maintaining that the customary property rights systems of 'traditional' communities are in harmony with the environment (Berkes and Favar 1989; Bruce *et al.* 1993a).

Another approach to the study of property rights is the concept of 'entitlement' conceived by Amartya Sen (1981: 49):

> There can be ambiguities in the specification of entitlements…in pre-capitalist formulations there can be a good deal of vagueness on property rights and related matters. In many cases the appropriate characterization is in the form of 'fuzzy' sets and related structures.

The 'entitlement approach' devised by Sen for the analysis of poverty and famine focuses on the 'legal ownership of commodities' to the neglect of other weaker forms of claims over resources, such as rights of access. This approach is criticized for failing to 'consider contexts where property rights are exercised institutionally rather than individually' and taking entitlement generation as 'given' and therefore neglecting the 'political economy of entitlement generation' (Devereux 1996).

Following these criticisms, Devereux's (1993, 1996) proposition offers some useful insights for the analysis of property rights in natural resources in Africa. Firstly, common property rights in natural resources in Africa are mostly 'held by multiple individuals and institutions' and the allocation of 'rights occurs according to institutional rules that first screen applicants (eligibility rules) and then prioritize their claims (queuing rules)' (Devereux 1996: 1). Secondly, there is a need to make a distinction between legally enforceable state control and informal community control over natural resources. Thirdly, there are conflicts over resource rights at different levels, such as conflicts between the state and communities and between households within a community.

The pessimistic view of some economists about common property resources has been criticized because it failed to account for the central roles played by the social institutions taken as given. Recently the new institutional economics gave a fresh impetus to the study of the commons. The new paradigm has emerged from mainly theoretical research into the problems of collective action, which appreciates customary management systems. This approach identifies a range of conditions under which the management of the commons might succeed. The decline of some of the commons is associated with external intervention, notably increasing population pressure and technological change.

The role of rules, norms and customs in enhancing mutual assurance between co-users of common pool resources and encouraging cooperation has been highlighted, particularly by collective action theory (Ostrom 1990). A range of community attributes are associated with the performance of user-groups in the management of the commons, the most important of which are group size, residence of group members and group heterogeneity.

The gist of the argument is related to the general propositions that there are resources 'managed with communal sanctions' (Galaty 1994) rather than 'open to all' or 'free-for-all'. Following Ostrom and Schlager (1996), customary property regimes as evolved, implemented, monitored and enforced by the people themselves may be considered more 'cost-effective' and sensitive towards the environment than has been acknowledged by the conventional wisdom of the systemic approach. This argument is related to interrelated propositions: (a) there are no unregulated or 'open-access' productive resources; (b) competition for them among social actors and the strategy for establishing rights of control over productive resources are geared towards the productive capacity of the resource and not the resource *per se*; and (c) the customary systems of property rights and natural resource regulations are cost-effective because they are more flexible than the legally enforceable state ones.

Faulty international scenarios and biased national policies

In Ethiopia 'unoccupied', fertile and 'underutilized' lands are terms used to refer to high-potential valleys and river basins in pastoralist areas. In practice these are dry-season grazing and/or flood-retreat cultivation areas for most agro-pastoralist societies.

The 'notions of development' and narratives about pastoral societies at national and regional levels reflect pastoral policies in particular and development philosophy at national level in general. Such policy narratives and public opinions stress the agricultural bias and misperception of pastoralist societies as 'backward'. Misunderstandings and conscious policies of marginalization based on simplistic assumptions were, and still are, pervasive. The stereotype of pastoralists managing livestock according to 'irrational economic principles' which are technically 'stagnant' and 'backward' is in part the result of the influences of earlier publications on pastoralist societies, like 'the cattle complex' and 'the tragedy of the commons'. Although such views and models were more popular outside than within anthropological circles, the legacy of such premises and their influence in shaping the opinions of policy-makers and administrators were considerable and still persist. The 'tragedy of the commons' model continues to influence policy-makers in Africa and scientists in the West. Following these faulty international scenarios, national development policies in Ethiopia have been urban-biased in relation to rural areas and peasant-biased in relation to pastoralists.

Because of the limited understanding of these societies, misconceptions were pervasive. Agro-pastoral societies were often perceived as people who are always 'on the move', lacking permanent addresses and having a different orientation to 'modernity' often defined in relation to an 'urban way of life'. Statements like 'follower of the tails of cattle' were, and still are, the dominant representations of peripheral agro-pastoralists by the centre. Such misrepresentations and cynicism stem from the officials who persist in confusing the practice of seasonable transhumance with 'aimless wandering'. Agro-pastoralists inhabit the peripheries of the country and are perceived as being '*zelan*', 'normless'.

Even in some academic circles, agro-pastoralists are presumed to subsist on livestock rather than on agricultural produce and to be less dependent on arable land; their customary land and land-based resource tenures are therefore presumably less complex. Such misrepresentations prevail despite ethnographic evidence suggesting that many subsist mainly on agricultural rather than pastoral produce.

Until recently, most of them practised crop cultivation based on hand-hoe tillage as opposed to an ox-plough system. Apart from acquiring grain from their neighbours through trade, these societies have practised crop cultivation for many centuries. Even those ethnic groups, for example the Borana, who have been characterized in the past as largely subsisting on pastoral products and therefore labelled as 'pure pastoralists' were no longer able to subsist on a purely pastoral diet (Helland 1996, 1997). In spite of the evidence, the myth of 'pastoralists' and 'pastoralism' as a 'backward' and 'archaic way of life' prevails in Ethiopia.

Development and investment policies

The history of development policies towards pastoralists in Ethiopia shows that at best they were neglected and at worst their lands were alienated for commercial cropping since the imperial time. Although almost all rural areas of the country remain poorly developed and effectively isolated from towns and urban centres, the pastoral lowland areas were, and most of them still are, by far the most marginalized areas. Development policy documents both past and present contain very little about pastoral areas. Comparing the situation of highland peasants with that of the lowland pastoralists during the Derg era, Fecadu (1990: 205) contends:

> In the highlands, the state has established an extensive administrative superstructure and has a greater hold of every citizen. The state has built and provided physical and social infrastructure, thereby enabling the citizens to play a greater role in the national life. In contrast to the central highlands, the peripheral lowlands suffered a paucity of infrastructure and social services and hence isolation from the center and from each other in every sense of the term, which limits their participation in national development.

The present EPRDF (five-year) development plan is rural-led, but has very little to say about pastoral societies. In this regard Hogg (1997a: vii-viii) wrote:

> In terms of current development policies the government has embarked on an ambitious agricultural-led five-year development plan which is intended to make Ethiopia self-sufficient in food. This plan is concentrated in the highlands. So far as the pastoral areas are concerned, apart from the development of irrigation agriculture, there is little new planned... The future of pastoral areas is uncertain.

The remoteness and lack of infrastructure have meant that the actual imposition of state polices and control was limited, and local institutions continued to exist and to exert control over and manage a wide range of productive resources. Thus until the early 1990s relationships and reactions of the Tsamako to the centre were largely confined to taxation paid in kind and later in cash.

Despite radical policy shifts following government changes, there were basic similarities in the content of these policies. Since imperial times such policies saw large-scale farming as the main avenue to increase agricultural production to feed the growing population and generate foreign-exchange earnings. The March 1990 mixed economic policy of the Derg is similar to that of the 1992 investment policy of the EPRDF government. Gavian and Gemechu (1994: 147) noted:

> Two major pieces of legislation provide the basis for large agricultural investments. As part of its package of economic reform, the TGE [Transitional Government of Ethiopia] laid down its investment policy 1992 in Council of Representatives Proclamation No. 15. In the following year the government repealed the previous Mengistu legislation pertaining to agricultural investments, incorporating most of those earlier provisions with Proc. 15 to derive a new agricultural investment code (Proc.120).

As stated in the investment code, the main objectives are to stimulate economic growth, to improve the level of technical know-how and to 'activate, protect, develop, enrich and utilize the natural resources of the country' (Council of Representatives 1992). Furthermore, a set of incentives should be given to those who want to invest in agriculture, including improved access to credit and hard currency; exemption from duties and taxes on imported capital goods, equipment and the like; and a three- to eight-year exemption from income taxes, depending on the region and area of investment. The rationales for encouraging large-scale farmers rather than small-holder producers are that large-scale farmers (a) have a presumed capacity to make the country self-sufficient in food production, (b) create jobs and (c) increase foreign-exchange earnings.

It seems that this has been done without giving consideration to their greater likelihood of overexploiting the environment linked to short-term leases and interests. Thus, although some economies of scale may accrue to large-scale mechanized farmers, there seems no evidence that they are more efficient producers than small-holder producers.

Large-scale investors are required to obtain investment certificates issued by the Investment Office of Ethiopia. Investors are expected to meet a set of criteria including relating their project proposal to environmental protection and showing the impact on natural resources. They must prove that the proposed site is free from other holders by producing written approval from the *kebele* council. In short, revised Proclamation 120 requires protection of the rights and interests of the local population. Given these policy environments, what were the official views of the commercial farms?

The opinions and attitudes of the administration and agricultural extension workers at zone and *wereda* levels alike seemed to have been shaped by these unfounded assumptions and prejudices about pastoralism. It is quite difficult to trace the origin of these stereotypes and prejudices. Nevertheless, the socialist-oriented military regime, backed up by its urban-biased development policy, seemed to have given a fresh impetus to these persistent public opinions and prejudices. Pastoralism as a way of life in Ethiopia has, therefore, been considered not only as simple or less sophisticated than the highland peasant way of life but also as categorically of lower status. Fecadu (1990: 205-6) wrote:

> Until recently, most policy makers displayed limited knowledge about pastoralists and their habitat. There are various misconceptions about the mobility and lack of crop cultivation of pastoral nomads. The widely held assumption is that the pastoralist lacks knowledge of crop production and that he does not farm and does not want to settle down in one place…It is often assumed that the pastoral nomad is devoid of any rationality concerning outsiders, that he attacks them without good cause. Lastly, there is the notion that the pastoral nomadic area is suitable for crop cultivation and, if and when it is so used, the pastoral nomadic group will not be affected. Hence, approaches to the development of the pastoralists often seek to settle them and to use their unused land as much as possible.

Pastoralist land use and resource management were assumed to be 'irrational' and therefore should be replaced by agriculture and other forms of resource management. These assumptions justified the tacit acceptance of the land lease policy – originally formulated by the Federal government – by the Southern Peoples' Regional State. The overall effects of such public attitudes, opinions and, above all, policy environments were considerable.

The high-potential grazing savannah woodlands of pastoralist and agro-pastoral ethnic groups in the south-western part of Ethiopia were considered as 'open access resources' and presumed therefore to be 'waste no man's land'. Little attempt has been made to distinguish between common property regimes and non-property regimes. Failure to make such a distinction has meant that any piece of land outside the category of a household plot was considered to be an open access resource. Given the poorly developed infrastructure in a woodland area, the region was often not easily accessible to local administrators and employees of the Ministry of Agriculture regional offices. Many administrators, including agricultural experts, paid only short visits to these semi-arid areas. Most visits were confined to locations accessible by vehicle. Many administrators mentioned the difficulty of staying longer than a couple of hours in these areas because of the hot weather. Administrators and even agricultural extensionists who were supposed to know better, had very little direct exposure to the values and life-styles of the indigenous people.

These situations seem to have led many local administrators to favour large-scale commercial farmers who have managed, in their eyes, 'to convert the desert into an oasis'.

The Birale commercial farm

In early 1990 the Derg regime leased out 4,000 hectares of high-potential land used for multiple agro-pastoralist purposes to private investors for thirty years. The farm known as Birale Agricultural Development Private Limited Company came into existence soon after the issuance of the last regime's mixed economic policy. The government rents this land out to private investors at roughly 130,000 *birr* a year. This farm, held by a couple of private investors, produces mainly cotton and some tropical fruits primarily for the international and domestic markets respectively. During the 1995/96 and the 1996/97 harvest years it produced 26,000 and 40,000 quintals of cotton respectively.

Technically the farm was estimated to be able to produce more than 30 quintals of cotton per hectare. It is worth noting that it is a mechanized irrigated farm, along with the application of chemicals such as pesticides. The use of such methods is not without certain costs that people who live in and around the valley have to pay.

As already mentioned, up to 1990 today's commercial farms used to be places where people from six ethnic groups practised some form of flood-recession and small-scale irrigated agriculture and livestock dry-season grazing. The local people's form of irrigated agriculture was exclusively gravity-flow from the Wayto River. They were able to divert water from the river and cultivate many varieties of maize and sorghum using local means and labour. For instance, in 1980, according to the Halcrow feasibility study, there were two water diverting points from the river. The total area of the irrigated cultivation fed with water from these diversion points was estimated to be 50 hectares. According to this report the yield of these subsistence farms amounted to 5-10 quintals per hectare.

> Thus for the local people both flood recession and irrigated crop cultivation used to serve, next to cattle, as an insurance scheme or standby at times when the rain-fed often drought-prone agriculture fails. A generation-set called *mura* guided and supervised by the members of the senior generation-set used to measure and re-distribute such land on behalf of the community. (Melesse 1995)

OFF-FARM EFFECTS OF THE COMMERCIAL FARM

What does the history of large-scale mechanized commercial farming in Ethiopia tell us? As Bruce *et al.* (1993a:28) point out, large-scale commercial farming in Ethiopia has many faces: 'It has often been credited with opening up "unutilized land" for cultivation, providing off-season employment to peasants, and making some contributions to the country's export drive; it has also been faulted for land grabbing and for large-scale eviction of peasants from the land.' Since the 1960s large-scale farms have changed their form and content along with changes in government, and so do not lend themselves to generalizations. However, they seem to have shared one thing in common, i.e. their interest in profit maximization. The Ethiopian experience has shown that large-scale commercial farmers or investors, as they are often called, have a short-term interest in profit maximization. Dessalegn (1994:15) summarizes the role of large-scale commercial farmers as follows:

> The experience of the country since the 1960s... has not been a salutary one: large scale investors were solely concerned with high and rapid rates of return on their investment, showed very little interest in investing in the land and in resource and environmental protection, and siphoned the agricultural surplus out of the rural areas. The 'external' investor, in brief, simply mined the land. In contrast, the peasant entrepreneur (the 'internal' investor) will have a long-term interest in investing on the land and enhancing its productivity, given tenure security and security of land transactions.

The years shortly after the establishment of the commercial farms witnessed an influx of migrants, some of whom ended up settling in the area. They cut wood and constructed houses for residence and running small businesses, whilst others are engaged in charcoal production. The immigrants have different cultural and religious backgrounds and they speak different languages. They therefore do not form a cohesive social group with shared values capable of showing an interest in preserving the local natural resources. Many immigrants interviewed stated that they had neither aspired to settle in the area on a permanent basis nor were they interested in integrating with the Tsamako. Members of the migrant community are not therefore under any obligation to abide by the social rules of the host community. They expected neither rewards for observance nor punishments for transgressing the rules of the local people.

The land alienation and other developments associated with it have resulted in some of the following unintended consequences. First, because of the loss of land, small–scale irrigated and flood-retreat cultivation is no longer possible for not only many communities among the Tsamako but also other communities inhabiting the lower river bank such as the Arbore (Hor), Birale and Konso ethnic groups. Secondly, informants spoke of the decline of honey production in association with the aerial spraying of pesticides by the commercial farms. Thirdly, the loss of savannah woodlands has resulted in the disappearance of many species of wild animals and trees which, in turn, has led to the termination of the practice of hunting and gathering in these areas.

Apart from these short-term effects, the commercial farms have also incurred some long-term negative consequences including increasing pressure on renewable natural resources such as trees, pasture, wildlife and water, and the weakening of the regulation mechanisms of local resource use as a result of an influx of people such as daily labourers who end up cutting trees indiscriminately for charcoal production. Furthermore, the effect of such an influx on the health status of the Tsamako needs to be mentioned with regard to spreading various communicable diseases and finally HIV/AIDS.

A more worrying trend is the fact that collective actions, rights and obligations are slowly disappearing. Local communities had previously had the power to prevent access by outsiders and to establish restrictions on felling trees. Those people who breached the rules were warned, beaten, and fined beer and/or smallstock. The most severe of all the punishments such a violator has to face is social boycott. All of these rules were enforced not by a specialized third-party enforcement agent but by the local people themselves. Such local enforcement mechanisms are no longer effective among new settlement areas in and around the Valley.

It seems likely that local people's access to grazing and irrigable lands will be increasingly restricted and that the commercial farms will be given more and more priority. This is reflected by the perceptions of many administrators and development agents which seemed to have been shaped by the old unfounded prejudices against agro-pastoralists. The lack of an avenue for the local people to communicate their side of the land alienation story and the language rift between local administrators and the local people are knotty problems. The lack of a mechanism for proper compensation is another. It seems that land issues in the Wayto Valley are only going to get increasingly problematic. It will undoubtedly become even more difficult to reconcile the different needs and interests of commercial farmers and the many agro-pastoral ethnic groups whose resource base is in one way or another related to the flow of the Wayto River downstream. Last but not least is the fact that the modern farming system, which is characterized by the use of chemicals, might cause irreversible resource degradation in the area.

The land alienation has far-reaching repercussions, and because of its especially political nature, it seems to be very difficult to remedy. Customary coping strategies of moving between ecological areas of the Valley are being undermined by the degeneration of the diversity of natural resources in the area. More and more people among both the Tsamako and some of their neighbours are being obliged to exploit marginal lands. Under such circumstances it seems unlikely that these groups will consider environmental conservation a priority, given the lack of long- or medium-term employment opportunities outside the rural sector. This has a wide range of repercussions not only for the livelihoods of the inhabitants but also for the well-being of the environment at large. It should be noted that the root of the problem lies in the land nationalization policy of the Derg and the lease system, both of which remain a mystery to most of the groups living in and around the Valley.

Local institutional mechanisms of regulating and managing resources are being eroded by external threats, notably population immigration. The establishment of the commercial farms and the demand for casual labour encouraged migration from the highlands (Welayta and Konso) to the lowlands, the net result of which has been encroachment on pastoral land and/or multiple use of savannah woodlands (Melesse 2000). Both commercial farmers and migrants compete with the indigenous people for resources. Contradictory resource uses since the 1990s gave rise to the present mosaic of natural resource use in the Valley which is at best absurd and at worst absent. The competition for resource use in the Valley led to an outburst of violence in 1995, when 18 people were killed from both parties. The friction born of competition for natural resources led to the emergence of buffer zones within which contested use rights are often dominated by the more powerful commercial farmers, who have not only policy support but also the money to garner support at various levels of the administration.

Conclusion

Competition for natural-resource use rights and the debates over the legitimacy of competing property claims are likely to continue to create tensions and violence between groups of resource users in and around the Wayto Valley. The priorities of local groups are markedly different from the interests of the elite both at regional and national levels.

The constitutional land rights of pastoralist societies have not yet been translated into practice; moreover there is no space where the predicament of such groups can be addressed.[2] The Tsamako are unable to articulate their problems for a number of reasons. One of the most practical limits placed on those Tsamako who expressed their wish to take their case before the court is the difficulty of access to the formal legal system. They do not have the resources necessary to pursue their cases through the appropriate legal channels. Most importantly, their lack of knowledge of legal rights and remedies is the basic hurdle they face at the moment.

In a situation where basic education is difficult, people are not aware of their constitutional rights in general and land rights in particular. Furthermore, in a region where only a few people have a working knowledge of the official language of the regional state and can read and write, those wishing to seek the enforcement of constitutional land and other resource rights are not likely to be successful in the foreseeable future.

Envisaging an important problem, the environment policy document of Ethiopia states: 'Given the need to harmonize potentially conflicting state and community or private commercial sectoral demands on natural resources and the environment, the institutional responsibility for undertaking land use planning at the federal and regional levels should not be within a single line ministry but in an agency which is impartial to all' (FDRE 1997: 36). Most importantly, the masterpiece of the policy is the decentralization of resource conservation strategic planning and the management of natural resources with the active participation of smallholder producers. In order to initiate decentralization one needs to acknowledge local resource management practices and vest the authority of local-level decision-making about resources in customary institutions and local groups. Needless to say, devolution of power is the guiding principle of the present government. It is one thing for the government to legislate devolution of power but quite another to implement this legislation, and something else again to recognize and empower local institutions. Thus, there is ample evidence to suggest that the role of the state needs to be reserved to addressing the regulation of conflicting rights over high-potential key resources in and around river basins that have been a point of struggle and competition among different interest groups in the region. There is a need therefore for the state to go beyond lip-service with regard to protecting communities' rights and ensuring that the short-term interests of investors are not prioritized over the longer-term rights of local people. Finally, the lack of an operational governmental natural-resource-management strategy is one of the major problems needing urgent attention.

Notes

1. Article 40 (The Right to Property) N0. 5 of the new Constitution of Ethiopia, promulgated in 1995, states: 'Ethiopian pastoralists have the right to free land for grazing and cultivation as well as the right not to be displaced from their own lands' (EDRE 1995: 73).
2. Article 43 (The Right to Development) No. 2 of the Constitution states: 'Nationals have the right to participate in national development and, in particular, to be consulted with respect to policies and projects affecting their community' (FDRE 1995: 101). As explicitly stated in the Constitution, the stated intention of the government is that rural development projects should not only serve national needs but also benefit the existing population in project areas.

Seven

Planning Resettlement in Ethiopia

The Experience of the Guji Oromo
& the Nech Sar National Park

TADDESSE BERISSO

Background

This chapter is a case study of how resettlement was planned in Ethiopia in relation to the Guji-Oromo of the Nech Sar National Park. In 1994 the Federal government signed an agreement with the European Union for a project to rehabilitate three National Parks in Southern Ethiopia: Nech Sar, Mago and Omo, in order to (a) improve the long-term security and integrity of the country's wildlife resources and protected areas; (b) optimize benefits from the exploitation of natural resources by way of sustainable development and management initiatives; and (c) improve the long-term wellbeing of the local people through their participation in these initiatives.

The Southern Ethiopia National Parks Rehabilitation Project (SENPRP) was a five-year project, originally envisaged in two phases. A two-year preliminary phase was to pave the way for substantial assistance by the European Union to rehabilitate the parks as protected areas with emphasis on development for tourism. Implementation of the main phase of the project was to depend on a number of preconditions to be fulfilled on the Ethiopian side, among them: (a) the finalization of a wildlife conservation policy, which the Federal government should formally adopt and promulgate; (b) the early gazetting of the three project National Parks; and (c) the resettlement of the people living in and around the parks.

Nech Sar National Park and the Guji-Oromo

Nech Sar is 500 km south of Addis Ababa. According to official reports, it covers 514 km^2 of protected area. The park has been under development since the late 1960s. Although not yet gazetted, it has been operating as a *de facto* national park since then. The park was proposed primarily for the prolific wildlife of the Nech Sar plains where some 38 species of mammals and 190 species of birds have been recorded.

Some 500 Guji families (approximately 3,500 people) live inside the park in five villages. They are pastoralists who depend predominantly on cattle herding. Some of them cultivate maize, sorghum, *enset,* coffee, banana, sugar cane, *gesho* and cotton, irrigated by water from the Sermule river. The park is also used for honey production and collection. The Guji have been living in and around the park for centuries. They are part of the greater Guji-Oromo group who were probably cut off from the main population during the Oromo expansion of the sixteenth century. In 1982, the Guji were forcefully evicted from the Nech Sar Park by the military regime. Houses were burned, property was destroyed and families suffered from hunger, but they gradually returned to the park, the land they believe belongs to them.

About 550 Kore/Amaro families (approximately 3,850 people) also live in the north-eastern part of the park, between the Hitu and Sermule rivers. The Kore came to the park from the larger community of Koyera neighbouring the park, whose number is approximately 1550 families (about 10,850 people). They are farmers who were organized into five Peasant Associations (PAs). The Kore cultivate a total of 220 ha. of maize, sorghum, and *tef* irrigated by water from the Sermule river. A few Kore are also traders engaged in trade in food, beverages and *chat*. This study concentrates on the Guji-Oromo.

Concerns about the proposed resettlement

In 1996 the Guji who were to be resettled, the Oromia local government and some international NGOs and scholars were concerned about how the resettlement would be implemented. Some planned steps were not clear, in particular the adherence of the proposed resettlement to international guidelines (namely, World Bank and OECD policies on involuntary and 'development-induced' displacement), the involvement of local communities in the project process and the rights of the inhabitants of the area. There was therefore a fear that the project might spend a large proportion of the €16 million given to the project, and end up with neither a managed nor a sustainable wildlife park.

To investigate the situation, fieldwork was conducted in the Nech Sar National Park in November 1996. A review of available project documents, reports, minutes and publications at local level was carried out. Discussions, observations and interviews were conducted with Guji about the proposed resettlement, their role in the design, and their views and attitudes with regard to the project. Part of the answers were tape-recorded and photographs showing Guji socio-economic life were taken. Formal and informal discussions were conducted with the park warden, Guji leaders and the authorities at *wereda* and zonal offices.

Research findings

PROSPECTIVE RESETTLERS' PARTICIPATION IN THE PROJECT

In theory at least, the Contractor's Proposal (1994) fully accepts the need to involve resettlers in the project from the start and consequently to ascertain their views and attitudes. It aims to achieve this by means of 'Participatory Rural Appraisal' (PRA), a method which the contractors claimed would allow the participation of local communities in the project design. The proposal, for instance, states, 'without their support, successful project implementation is very doubtful ... active involvement at the very beginning of project conception is essential and will require much time and sensitivity'. It also promises that all parties must meet and discuss all aspects of the programme, i.e., everyone must be fully aware of what is proposed (Solomon 1996:5).

Unfortunately, however, not much has been done in practice to involve prospective resettlers in project planning. Discussions with Guji informants reveal that the project's socio-economic consultant depended primarily on a questionnaire to collect the socio-economic data needed for planning the resettlement. The questionnaire was completed by local young people employed for this purpose. This method did not, however, initiate debate and discussion within the local communities. The sociologist consultant did not use PRA techniques, despite the emphasis placed on this method in the contractor's technical proposal. During his 30 days of fieldwork in the Nech Sar area, he spent only one week with the Guji, and even this short stay was not spent with the community, but with a Guji family whose head was employed as a scout by the National Park.

Thus, the inappropriate method employed by the project consultant and the insufficient time spent in the field with the Guji did not allow community participation in any real sense. The research was conducted without participation, although even the proposal emphasized its importance. Consequently, the local communities to be resettled did not get the chance to express their views and concerns about the project in general and the resettlement in particular.

The consultant's claim that local people participated was apparently also based on a workshop held at Arba Minch from 15 to 17 May 1996, at which the people to be moved were represented by elders and village leaders in the case of the Guji and by Peasant Association officials in the case of the Kore. However, these elders cannot be said to represent all groups. Prospective women resettlers were not invited to the workshop and consequently had no chance to express their views about the project, to present their options for resettlement, and to contribute to the project's design. Moreover, some Guji individuals, especially the young people, claimed that they knew nothing about the proposed resettlement. They were ignorant of plans for the park and more importantly how they would be affected by the proposed resettlement. This is in conflict with the consultant's own suggestion that every one must be fully aware of what was proposed. Genuine community participation in project design and implementation requires much time, patience, openness for discussions and criticism, and negotiations. A one-off meeting with community representatives under the pressure of the administration would not ensure genuine community participation. Consequently, the Guji cannot be said to have been genuinely involved in planning the proposed resettlement, despite the fact that they would be directly affected. The project was thus not built upon local knowledge and has not recognized the interests and rights of local people. This implies a top-down approach, in which local communities are required only to implement decisions that have been made elsewhere.

PROPOSED RESETTLEMENT IN RELATION TO INTERNATIONAL STANDARDS

In relation to international standards, the proposed resettlement presents several weaknesses.

1) Alternatives to resettlement. Other options were not fully considered before the decision to resettle was made. The World Bank's policy states as its first requirement that, whenever feasible, involuntary resettlement must be avoided or minimized and alternative development solutions must be explored. However, alternatives to displacement and resettlement have not been fully considered. At the meeting held in Arba Minch, project consultants and government officials presented an 'either/or' alternative from which the community representatives had to choose: either the resettlement of the communities, or the total disintegration of the Park and its use for only human settlement and activities. In spite of pressure put on them to choose resettlement, the Guji representatives at the meeting chose neither option. Rather, they came up with an alternative, which was not considered by the officials who were predetermined to resettle them. According to the minutes of the workshop, the alternative presented by the Guji suggests that they continue to live in the park, where their ancestors have lived for centuries. From the Guji perspective, the park is large enough to accommodate both wildlife and human settlement. The Guji live in harmony with the wild animals and the environment in the park. There are no poaching problems nor abuse of the forests, and the Guji requested a clear demarcation of the park territory. Furthermore, they made demands to be involved in the park's administration, and share the benefits from its income.

Ignoring this Guji alternative, the officials who attended the meeting distorted the issue and reported that 'the Guji have voluntarily accepted resettlement'. Guji informants, however, clearly argue that they in no way accepted the proposed resettlement. Rather, they asked the officials to give them time to discuss the matter with their community and visit the suggested site before making any decision.[1] In any case, the option of leaving the existing residents in the park and finding ways of making it worth their while to collaborate with, and contribute to, the project objectives was not seriously considered.

Furthermore, the consultant's document mentioned that 'there must be general acceptance of the programme by the people to be resettled. Forcible resettlement will not be contemplated.' However, the Guji representatives argue that the administration wanted to resettle them without their consent and against their will. The proposed resettlement is therefore forced and must be treated in accordance with the World Bank's standards on involuntary resettlements.

2) Participation of women and host communities. The participation of women and representatives of the host communities was not ensured in the three-day meeting held in Arba Minch on the basis of which the resettlement was planned. The absence of women representatives is in conflict with the World Bank's Guidelines which state that community participation in planning and implementing resettlement is essential and should include women. The Guidelines note:

> Since the women are to a great extent responsible for making the natural resource base productive (with their knowledge, skills and labour), and thereby contribute significantly to the well being of their families, communities and national economies, planning for relocation should consider their preferences and should address their specific needs and constraints. (World Bank 2007, 1998)

Besides, representatives of the host communities, who, according to the World Bank Guidelines, should be involved in the planning process and assist in overcoming possible adverse socio-environmental consequences for the resettlement, were not invited at all.
3) Involvement of settlers in site selection. Prospective resettlers or their representatives were not involved in the site selection. The resettlement site was suggested by the sociolo-

gist consultant. More than 95 percent of the Guji informants interviewed in Nech Sar had no idea of the suggested site. Besides this, the Oromia Regional Government, where the suggested site of Tore is located, had not agreed on the resettlement of Guji on this site.[2] Moreover, it is unclear why, despite the availability of ecologically similar and sparsely populated areas around the park, there was a need to move the Guji over 160 km to another Region.[3]

4) Development funds. The project has limited development funds. According to the World Bank's Guidelines, all involuntary resettlements should be conceived and executed as development programmes, providing sufficient investment resources and opportunities for resettlers to share in the project benefits.

In the case of Nech Sar, the Contractor's documents indicate that a little over 5 million *birr* (almost US$58,000) was allocated for the resettlement of the Guji and Kore communities. The stated amount is presumed to be used for transportation, construction of new houses, access roads, schools, clean water, clinics, veterinary inputs and, also for eight months' food aid rations. The fund would come mainly from the Regional government, but there are three basic problems with this proposal:

(i) The amount allocated is not enough to cover compensation for resettlers' property, let alone the expenses of the infrastructure and social services mentioned. Prospective resettlers possess large amounts of perennial plants like coffee trees, *enset, gesho*, orange trees for which they demand compensation if resettled.

(ii) Governments sometimes make promises, which they do not keep. The empty promises made by the previous regime to provide communities with basic social services in the forced resettlement and villagization are still fresh in the minds of prospective resettlers. It is one thing to make promises on paper and quite another to implement them in practice. The project is in no position to give guarantees that even the limited budget earmarked for this operation will be provided and used for what was intended. In addition, leaving the responsibility for implementing the project to a regional government that seems to be dominated by ethnic groups currently in conflict with the Guji who are to be resettled, will only increase suspicions.

(iii) The park may not attract many visitors, and thus it is unlikely to be financially self-sufficient, let alone to generate net benefits which could be used to secure the cooperation of local communities. Nech Sar's highest income from visitors was 42,181 *birr* in 1998 (US$4,770) and this amount would not even meet the need to maintain the park itself. In addition, if the administration goes ahead with the proposed resettlement of the Guji in Tore this will be too far away to involve them in the park's administration and subsequently to benefit from its income. In other words, the resettlement will alienate the Guji from the park so that their chances of fruitful cooperation with the project in the future will be substantially reduced. In short, there is no guarantee that the prospective resettlers will gain tangible benefits.

RIGHTS OF LOCAL COMMUNITIES IN RELATION TO ETHIOPIA'S WILDLIFE LAW

The legal consultant of the project has drafted wildlife legislation. The draft law technically recognizes that the only way to conserve wildlife will be to bring in and involve the local communities. There is an emphasis on community participation, with communities having rights of access to resources and rights to participate in decision-making, including boundary decisions. However, the legislation is still a draft policy that has not yet been promulgated.

Thus, resettling people from Nech Sar in the absence of any adequate wildlife law and gazetting of the park, is troubling. It is like putting the cart before the horse and a violation of the human rights of the communities to be resettled.

Discussion with the Zonal Office about the Project Plan and its implementation

The zonal and *wereda* officials in Arba Minch and Awassa believe that Nech Sar cannot be a viable National Park while there are people living there or using land within its boundaries. They justify their point of view on the grounds that, with an area of only 514 km^2, Nech Sar Park cannot accommodate both human settlement and wildlife. According to them, it is not proper to keep wild animals and people together, and the people living in and using the park are so backward that they need to be provided with basic social services like schools, clinics, clean water, etc. outside the Park.

These justifications, which were considered by officials to be basic reasons for resettling the Guji-Oromo communities from Nech Sar, are less convincing from our knowledge about the park. Although Nech Sar is a small park in comparison with the Omo and Mago National Parks, its size has been underestimated for reasons which are unclear. The park has gradually and steadily increased in size and its current actual size is between 550 and 700 km^2. According to Guji informants and from observation, the pressure on the land is highly exaggerated.

The second justification is a reflection of the officials' view about conservation. Both *wereda* and zonal officials as well as the project consultants hold 'protectionist' views that presume that local people are 'obstacles to conservation' who need to be excluded from 'protected areas'. This is a discredited view that has lost importance in many parts of the world, particularly in Africa. The total exclusion of human activity from protected areas is not desirable, since the flora and fauna co-evolved with humans. In addition, the Guji way of life does not exert much pressure on the park. They have lived in tune with nature, and hence in harmony with both wildlife and its habitat. In spite of this fact, the authorities failed to involve them in natural-resources protection, conservation and sustainable utilization. The general approach was top-down, with the government as the sole official guardian of natural resources.

Regarding the third justification, if there is a real concern to develop communities living in and around the park, social and infrastructural services could be more easily, effectively, humanely and cheaply provided to the people right in their natural habitat, as has been suggested by the Guji. Indeed, as tax-paying citizens, the Guji have a legitimate right to be provided with all necessary social and infrastructural services, which they are totally denied in the park.

While the above are explicit justifications given by the local and zonal officials of the SNNPR to move the Guji-Oromo out of the Nech Sar National Park, the underlying implicit reason seems to be political. The Guji are part of the Oromo people who, according to these officials, live outside Oromia Regional State, and are yet administered under Oromia. The big fear of the officials is that Oromia may clam the park some day on the grounds that Oromo live there. The attempt to move the Guji to Tore seems to be a means of overcoming this fear.

Recent developments

In February 2004 a contract was signed between the Federal Government of Ethiopia (in collaboration with the Southern Nations, Nationalities and People's Regional State) and the African Parks Foundation (APF). The APF has agreed with the government to take responsibility for the management, development and funding of the Nech Sar Park for 25 years. It is a condition of the contract that no people be present in the park. The Park will soon have electric fencing; rhino and elephant will be 're-introduced'; beautiful accommodation will be built and tourists will be driven around a 'pristine' environment devoid of people.

Consequently in February 2004, about 1020 Kore family household heads (approximately 7140 people) who used to live in and around the park were resettled. Local government officials and the park administration have exerted great pressure on the Guji-Oromo to resettle them outside the park, in spite of their continued appeals requesting their rights to stay in the park to be respected. However, on 25 November 2004 it was reported that 463 Guji-Oromo houses in the park were burned down to force them out of the park (see Lynch 2005; Thompson 2005). Following this incident about 60 Guji family heads of household were forcibly relocated from the park and resettled with the Kore. The remaining Guji-Oromo population (about 5000 individuals) was pushed into a small corner of the park in preparation for resettling them sooner or later. Here they are denied access to the natural resources they previously used and this has threatened their livelihood alternatives and exposed them to further poverty.

Summary and concluding remarks

The Southern Ethiopia National Parks Rehabilitation Project (SENPRP) was proposed, on paper at least, to conserve and rehabilitate wildlife parks by involving local communities in participating in all aspects of the project from the very beginning. However, there was limited involvement of the communities in designing the project, due to the inappropriate methods used by the socio-economic consultant. Women were excluded from attending the workshop held in Arba Minch and from presenting their concerns about the project; some people, particularly the youth, were not informed about the project at all; and officials at the meeting did not consider the views of the community representatives on alternatives to resettlement.

In addition to this, the project contractor and consultants seem to have very little knowledge about the international standards for involuntary resettlement, and consequently the project fails to fulfill some of the basic guidelines of the World Bank. Alternatives to displacement and resettlement were not fully considered before the decision on resettlement was made; the participation of women and representatives of host communities in designing the project was not ensured; the prospective resettlers were not involved in the selection of resettlement sites; and insufficient development funds were allocated. Even the limited funds were to be managed by the regional government which is not trusted by the prospective resettlers.

Moreover, the preservationist attitude of the project consultant and the zonal government officials, which is in favour of the exclusion of communities from the Park, goes against the interests of the local people. Since there is no national park and wildlife law in the country at present, there is nothing in place that could protect the rights of the communities. The project thus seems to fail to put the interests and well-being of the communities at the centre of its activities.

In the past, the importance of involving local people in the conservation of wildlife was largely ignored in Ethiopia. The economic benefits that accrue from wildlife resource development were not directed towards integrated development nor were any management roles given to the local communities. Instead, people were often considered as 'obstacles to conservation' and were forced to resettle by being completely denied any customary rights to their land. As a result, efforts and achievements regarding the goal of conservation were largely a failure. When the previous government fell in 1991 many of the parks, including Nech Sar, were overrun by settlers, infrastructures were destroyed and wildlife killed. However, the people who have lived harmoniously with their ecology and thus with the wild animals and their habitat, were portrayed as the main threat to the animals (Mesfin 1995: 3).

Currently too, failing to draw lessons from past experience, the authorities of the Nech Sar Park and local officials of the SNNPR are exerting great pressure on the Guji to settle them outside the park. This is not only against the basic rights and interests of the Guji, but is also against initiatives to conserve the natural resources of the park. In poverty-stricken areas like rural Ethiopia, it is very unlikely that the application of a 'protectionist' approach, based on restrictive and exclusive state law enforcement of wildlife management, can achieve any reasonable success in natural-resource conservation. This is simply because people will, in one way or another, be forced to use those resources so long as they are poor and have no better alternative means of livelihood. The conservation strategy should therefore follow the principles of community participation. The local community should be willing and fully involved in the conservation plan.

As Turton (1995; 25) notes:

> The reasons for turning away from a 'preservationist' approach are as much biological and economic as they are moral and political. Firstly, since virtually all existing eco-systems are functions of human use and disturbance, artificially to exclude such disturbance runs the risk of reducing bio-diversity rather than preserving it. Secondly, not only are the technical and logistical costs of attempting to exclude human activity from protected areas very high but such efforts are also certain to fail. They alienate the local population from conservation objectives and thus require an ever-increasing and, in the long run, unsustainable level of investment in policing activity.

Conventional approaches based on a centralized management authority have now given way to more decentralized and participatory approaches in which the return of financial and other benefits to local communities is seen as the key to stimulating both communal and individual responsibility for, and investment in, more sustainable natural-resource management.

Thus, all plans for resettling the Guji from Nech Sar Park should be dropped. They should remain in the park and utilize its resources. Intensive investment from the park's income should be used to increase the productivity of their land and new income-generating possibilities should be considered. This would help to intensify and improve the Guji economy and increase their living standards, which in turn would reduce pressure on the park. If the activities undertaken by the Guji happen to be incompatible with the management and conservation objectives, then alternative income-generating activities that need investment would have to be discussed with them. These may include: fishing, handicraft activities, modern bee keeping, eco-tourism, etc. However, in such cases market linkages and availability of other infrastructure should be considered.

The investments are not going to be solely or primarily directed at Guji communities living in the Park just for the sake of their economic development, but for the sake of the protection of the Park through eliciting their support. Such support will come by ensuring that the Guji do not become economically or socially worse-off because of their support for conservation of the Park but are, in fact, at least economically and socially, better-off than before.

It is also important to redefine the park boundaries and zones to differentiate core protection areas from those where controlled multiple use involving the local people can be allowed. Then the managing parties (i.e., the park authorities and the local communities) must agree on how the resources in the park are used and how responsibilities/roles are shared in managing them. Co-management and benefit/revenue-sharing agreements need to be brokered. Mutual understanding, information sharing and situation analysis would be the first step to be undertaken to conserve the Park's resources. Currently there is an understanding that conservation will never win if it sacrifices basic human rights to pursue a narrow green agenda and/or if it sides with the rich (moneyed) against the poor. Conservation practitioners are thus expected to work with previously, potentially or currently marginalized people living in and around parks to achieve socially just and ecologically sustainable conservation.

Notes

1. In the view of my Guji informants, the distortion of what they said by those who led the meeting is ridiculous and immoral and, if the Guji claim is correct, unethical This could have been verified only by analysing the recording, to which I was denied access despite repeated requests.
2. Minutes of the meeting held in Arba Minch, 1996: 41-42.
3. Tore is located in Oromia Region some 160 km away from Nech Sar across Lake Abaya. According to the Resettlement strategy set up by the Federal government in the 1990s, Resettlement movements are supposed to be intra-regional. This case constitutes an exception, as it is planned to move long-term settled Guji-Oromo communities from the SNNPR into Oromia Region.

Eight

Urban Development & Displacement of Rural Communities around Addis Ababa

FELEKE TADELE

Introduction

Internally Displaced People (IDPs) are among the least studied categories of people in the world and, hence, there are no internationally agreed operational definitions for them (Hampton 1988). The working definition that was used by the Brookings Institution and the Global IDP survey describes them as 'persons or groups of persons who have been forced to flee or to leave their homes or places of habitual residence as a result of, or in order to avoid, in particular, the effects of armed conflict, situations of generalized violence, violations of human rights or natural or human-made disasters, and who have not crossed an internationally recognized state border'. Some scholars (McDowell 1996; Sorensen 1998) argue that this definition does not give the necessary emphasis to people displaced by development projects. We can, therefore, adapt the operational definition for 'development-induced displaced people' as 'persons or groups of persons who are forced to leave their lands or homes or their possessions as a result of a development process that undermines, excludes or ignores their full participation in development and puts their livelihoods in danger without protection, in a given national territory'.

The number of IDPs is increasing with about 10 million people worldwide entering the cycle of forced displacement and relocation on an annual basis, mostly due to development projects for urban and transport infrastructure and dam construction. Of these, urban development projects reportedly cause the displacement of some 6 million people every year (Cernea 1995). As the demands of the urbanizing population increase, notably in Africa and Asia, the need for infrastructure development will grow enormously and displacement is likely to occur on a massive scale (World Bank 1995 quoted in McDowell 1996). Despite this, the attention given to improving the lives of the displaced seems limited at micro, macro and global levels.

In Ethiopia, since the overthrow of the socialist government in 1991, large numbers of people have been displaced due to the promotion of privatization and the conversion of rural agricultural fields to urban land. Since most private investment has so far concentrated around the main urban centres, the problem of displacement is becoming a primary concern. In the case of Addis Ababa City, through the launching of the Urban Land-Lease Regulation No. 3 of 1994, investments in development infrastructures have been growing annually through the conversion of over 200 hectares of agricultural and forest land to urban land use (Beeker, 1997). As a result, 14 Peasant Associations (PAs) with a total population of 6,000 households (30,000 individuals) face the effects of the urban expansion and the negative consequences of dispossession.

Although the city administration considers that its land-lease allocation system boosts the market value and proper exploitation of urban land, most of its projects are not in accordance with international and national policies and the norms set by agencies like the UN, the World Bank and the Environmental Protection Authority (IDS 1997). Rural people affected by urban projects are also not actively involved in the assessment, feasibility studies, planning and implementation process. Rather, urban development projects have tended to give more attention to local and foreign investors than to the urban poor and peasants who live in the vicinity of the city.

Even if the Addis Ababa Region Administration has arranged cash compensation payments for some of the displaced people, there is little consultation and the compensation seems inadequate. As a result, most displaced families can be exposed to further social and economic impoverishment. If the expansion of urban areas and industrial complexes continues in the same way, a large number of displaced people will soon face enormous problems. Therefore, research that assesses both the negative consequences and the net benefits/dividends of urban 'development' projects can play an important role in filling the existing knowledge gap and in influencing the policies that cause displacement.

OBJECTIVES AND METHODOLOGY

This chapter focuses on the consequences of urban development for a peasant community in the vicinity of Addis Ababa, in particular the consequences of the project for the lives of people evicted from or dispossessed of their rural lands and houses. The study seeks to contribute to the advancement of theoretical models to better understand the impact of urban development on rural populations and to formulate policies and programme strategies to minimize the negative effects on local people.

Fieldwork was conducted at Yeka Taffo PA, on the eastern outskirts of the town, where the Regional Administration had already begun action to evict farmers to create residential real estate by leasing land along the Kotebe route. Fieldwork between August and October 1998 involved community and institutional meetings, discussions and observations using a combination of qualitative and quantitative methods. Secondary data were gathered mainly from the reports of the Real Estate Village Development Project, the Urban Planning Institute, the Addis Ababa Regional Administration Offices and the Yeka Taffo PA's office.

The relevant literature largely focuses on the construction of big dams and its effects on rural people. Two dominant models have emerged to explain the theoretical underpinning of development-induced displacement. Scudder and Colson's five stages of a successful resettlement cycle[1] and Cernea's impoverishment risks analysis model[2] are used for the theoretical argument of this study.

The chapter concentrates on three critical issues related to Scudder's and Colson's model. (i) Do communities act in common organic ways at all cycles of the displacement process? (ii) Do individuals and households in a community accept, react or resist displacement situations by adopting different strategies? (iii) Is the process of people's impoverishment determined only by the responses of the displaced people or is it determined by other actors who deal with the planning and management of development projects such as the press, the government, non-government organizations and other relevant institutions?

In the context of the framework of Cernea's approach, the study focuses on (a) the different ways in which sources of livelihood are lost or threatened by development-induced displacement; (b) the importance of the economic and social impoverishment variables and the need for considering additional variables; and (c) analysis of the dynamic nature of displacement and identification of factors that contribute to individuals who gain and lose from the displacement process.

Addis Ababa: from a small settlement to a metropolitan city

The capital acquired its present name Addis Ababa in 1886 from Menelik's wife, Queen Taytu, who used to descend from the settlement at the top of Entoto mountain to enjoy hot springs in the Filwuha area. Soon, a centrally located palace encircled by encampments of the different military officials and ruling élites characterized the structure and lay-out of early Addis Ababa. Land was allocated according to military ranks and the hierarchies in feudal aristocratic structures. The military leaders and their entourages were allotted large tracts of land around the royal palace, followed by palace workers, the clergy, the foreign legations and then the tenants and servants (Birkie Yami 1997).

The first urban land-tenure edict was issued on 27 October 1907. It transformed the temporary possession of land into permanent occupation (R. Pankhurst 1968) and Addis Ababa municipality, responsible for urban land settlement, was established after a couple of years. During the Italian occupation in 1936-41 plans with defined functions and ethnically segregated zones were prepared. The Addis Ababa plan of 1936 established segregation between European and native train stations, bus stations, and residential areas (Tuffa 1995). Even though this plan remained in effect for only about five years, it has left its mark on the present city landscape. Economically active neighbourhood locations like Piazza, Merkato and Kassanchis were founded during this period.

After the Italian occupation, Emperor Haile Selassie commissioned architect Patrick Abercrombie to prepare a city plan intended to guide the development of the city for three decades, but it lacked detailed implementation procedures and tools. The city officials ignored the plan and large areas of urban land were allocated as rewards for the services and support rendered by the nobility. According to the land survey in 196l, for instance, 58 percent of the total urban land was held by 1768 landowners, 12 percent by the Orthodox Church, 9 percent by the royal family and 12.7 percent was given to government departments and foreign embassies. Only 7.4 percent of the urban land was held by about 25,000 ordinary people (Berhanu 1989).

A small-scale site clearing and resettlement programme was undertaken in the 1940s when the imperial government was intending to construct modern buildings and educational premises in Arat Kilo and moved the inhabitants to resettle in the Tekle Haimanot area. Large churches like Tekle Haimanot and the grand Mosque in Merkato have become attractive business centres, as well as sites for the poor to build squatter settlements (Feleke 1994).

After the 1974 Revolution, Addis Ababa experienced significant spatial expansion.

The promotion of housing cooperatives and the construction of state-owned apartments and villas activated the exploitation of urban land and improved the structure of the settlements. The socio-spatial and administrative organization of the city was then structured at three levels, which now consist of five *Ketenas* (Zones), 28 *Keftegnas/Woredas* (Districts) and 285 *Kebeles*. However, this administrative structure had little influence on shaping the settlements of the city.

After the fall of the Derg government in 1991, a land-lease system was introduced following the issuance of the national lease system, in accordance with Proclamation no. 107 of 1993. Until 1996, there were no major changes in the urban settlement since construction was limited to the completion of previously approved housing units (Birkie Yami 1997). However, the spectacular buildings of the Sheraton Hotel can be cited as a major undertaking that involved moving hundreds of people from Filwuha to the Kotebe periphery (Nebiyu 2000). All these city-clearing measures seem to relocate not only the poor people but also the urban problems from one corner to another.

In relation to its population size, Addis Ababa has shown tremendous growth and has become forty times larger than a century ago. As its expands in both population size and spatial coverage, the municipality officials continuously convert peasant farm and grazing lands in the surrounding areas for urban use. In this respect, the total numbers of peasant associations to be affected are reportedly 14, with a total of 6000 households (about 30,000 people).

YEKA TAFFO: A RURAL COMMUNITY UNDER THREAT

Yeka Taffo is one of the eight PAs of the Kotebe urban development scheme area, which is situated in the north-eastern part of the capital. The total population of Yeka Taffo is estimated to be 1,115. Women account for 15 percent of the total of 231 household heads. 95 percent of the total population are Oromo and the rest are Amhara. There are strong social networks and inter-marriages between the two ethnic groups. Most of the inhabitants of Yeka Taffo are Orthodox Christians.

Land, livestock, housing and other household assets are considered to be the main indicators for measuring wealth. Out of the total of 231 households, 30 are ranked as rich. The rich own 5-10 hectares of farm and grazing land, a pair of oxen, cows, sheep and pack animals such as donkeys and horses. Their houses are also built of corrugated iron-sheets. The middle-level households number 66, of whch six are female-headed. These households own 3-5 hectares of land, an ox, a cow, sheep but no pack animals. Their houses are *tukuls* with modest mud plastering and thatched roofs. The majority, 135 households, fall into the poor category. They occupy less than 3 hectares of land, own a cow and a small number of sheep and chickens. They do not have oxen or pack animals. Their houses are *tukuls* but are not well built. Almost 84 percent of the female-headed households fall into the poor category.

Common property resources include water, grazing land, roads and forests used for firewood and construction. However, except for water and roads, the community has lost the other common resources over the last thirty years. The main crops grown include wheat, *tef*, lentils, chickpeas, and occasionally horse beans. There is no cash-crop production. Livestock are the main sources of household investment. Both men and women attend the weekly market to trade. While men are mostly engaged in grain and livestock trade, women trade smallstock, livestock products (butter, cheese and dung cakes), chickens and eggs. Women also sell firewood, dry grass, and vegetables (mostly cabbages and onions). Many women earn some cash by selling local alcoholic brews such as *Tella* and *Areke*. There is no permanent migration trend to other areas, although a few people migrate to Addis Ababa and the neighbouring districts for marriage, education or employment. Men plough, build houses and fences, weed, harvest, thresh and perform social duties. Boys are involved in farm work, wood and water collection, childcare and crafts. Similarly, girls assist their mothers in domestic work such as childcare, milking, brewing, and fetching water and wood as well as petty trading. Most of the farm and domestic activities are done by household members but there are still work-sharing practices often during weeding, harvesting and social feasts. Such social practices are strongly linked with mutual-aid associations like *dabo* work groups, *Iddir* funeral associations and *Iqub* rotating credit associations.

The Real Estate Development Project

A national private company, established by a hardworking entrepreneur, whose rights are guaranteed by Ethiopian civil and business codes, implements the development project. Official activities began in August 1997. The project's overall objective is to promote real estate development in accordance with the government's economic policy. The immediate objective is to construct dwelling units that can be made available for rent and to enable tenants to own a house through mortgages payable within 30 years. Housing construction is sub-divided into four phases over 7-10 years, at the end of which the company is to create a new 'village' that caters for 25,000 residents with their own electricity, water supply, roads, parking, recreational facilities and social catering. As part of its strategy, the project has secured sufficient land by dealing with the government. Its official document, however, does not explicitly indicate anything about this deal or relationships with peasants.

In accordance with its proposal, the project estimated that it requires a total of 2,400,000 square metres of land. The total capital of the project is reported to be 4,442,875,460 *birr* (US$445 m.). Of this, the first phase of the project, enabling the construction of 6,250 housing units, requires a capital of 1,116,809,600*birr* (US$112 m.). The sources of finance are reported to be national private companies and loans from Ethiopian banks.

The project's relationship with the Yaka Taffo peasants began when the government took the land from the local people and the company started actual site-clearing. The project was proactive in the implementation of cash compensation for the dispossessed. Unlike other real estate development projects, it dealt with the city administration to effect a one-time cash compensation for the project-affected people instead of installation-based payments. The project pursued this on the grounds that the dispossessed peasants needed to be able to avoid the risks of market fluctuations and speculation. The project has also facilitated the introduction of a banking system for the peasants by bringing the bankers of Abyssinia Bank to their doorsteps and lobbying for the bank to introduce a monthly interest-rate payment for the peasants who deposit their cash compensation. The initiative of the Abyssinia Bank was warmly welcomed by the dispossessed peasants who feel their cash is being securely managed.

Land-use policy, planning and implementation practices

In order to understand how the urban development process has affected rural households, it is important to discuss the relevant land-use policies, implementation mechanisms and the corresponding urban management structures, as well as the survey and research methods used for town planning purposes.

LAND-USE POLICIES

Up to 1975, six landlords owned the land in Yeka Taffo. Most of the peasants were their tenants. Land taxes were therefore collected by these landlords and the peasants' land security and tenure depended upon the will of the individual landlords. The proclamation of the 1975 Rural Land Reform ended the existing feudal-tenant relationships and land was distributed to all households in the Peasant Association.

A villagization programme took place in 1988 and moved households to settle in one part of the village. This led to material and labour losses since most people had to build new houses and abandon their permanent plants such as eucalyptus trees. After the change of government in 1991 and until the real estate development project came to the area in 1996, most peasants had been returning to their old villages.

According to the regionalization policy of the Transitional Government and the restructuring of regional authorities since 1992, Yeka Taffo was incorporated within the Addis Ababa Regional Administration. The launching of the urban land-lease policy can be said to have been detrimental to peasants like those in Yeka Taffo, since the Urban Land-Lease Regulation No. 3 of 1994 encourages investment in development infrastructures through the conversion of agricultural and forest land to urban land use with only cash for compensation. As a result, a substantial number of the local people consider this policy a serious obstacle that threatens their livelihoods. As one of our informants, Wordefa, stated: 'a the lease policy is like honey for the "chosen people" (meaning the investors) and poison for unfortunate poor people like us.'

URBAN MANAGEMENT STRUCTURE AND ADMINISTRATION

Until the Addis Ababa Municipality was established in 1909, responsibility for the city's administration rested totally on the local chiefs. Accordingly, the chiefs of different urban settlements had the responsibility of administration, security and justice in their designated areas (Birkie 1992). In addition to the local chiefs, the imperial palace officials were charged with different sectors of responsibility for administering the city (R. Pankhurst 1987). The first decree that identified the role of city mayors was enacted in 1942 under Decree No. 1 of 1942 (IGE 1942). This decree spelt out the role of the city council, which was supposed to deliberate and advise on matters related to the prosperity of the city, the wealth of the inhabitants and the fixing of municipal taxes. Subsequently, the imperial government issued a Proclamation in 1945 to provide control over the municipalities and townships and stipulate their relationships with other government departments. Thus it stated that the municipality of Addis Abba should be supervised by councillors composed of representatives of ministries and resident members who own immovable properties. (IGE 1945). In 1954, the Addis Ababa municipality was accorded chartered status (IGE 1954). However, the proclamation failed to recognize the fact that urban developments are meant not only for urban property owners but also for the rest of the residents (Akale 1997).

A revolutionary departure in urban management was introduced in 1975 when the government enacted Proclamation No. 47/1975, according to which, urban land was nationalized and became government property. No compensation was proposed and no one was allowed to hold land as private property. The proclamation also provided for the establishment of Urban Dwellers' Cooperatives, later named associations. However, there was no provision for linking these associations with the main organization and functions of the urban administrations (PMGE 1975). In addition, the issuance of the Urban Dwellers' Association Consolidation and Municipalities Proclamation (PMGE 1976) established the different hierarchies of sub-local governments and brought the administration of municipalities under these central associations. According to this arrangement, the City Mayor of Addis Ababa was accountable to the congress and the standing committee, which was formed through 'election'.

Since the defeat of the socialist government in 1991, there have been a series of re-organizations of the larger units, which are now called *Weredas*. At the same time, the Municipality was replaced by the Addis Ababa Administrative Region called Region 14. From 1997 to 2002, the status of Addis Ababa was changed and its administration came under a Council, which was accountable to the Federal government. In November 2002, the Addis Ababa Regional Administration was restructured with the establishment of a transitional administrative body composed of individuals appointed through the different political organs of the Ethiopian People's Revolutionary Democratic Front (EPRDF). According to the new administrative structure, Addis Ababa would have 184 *Kebeles* and 10 district municipalities, each comprising 250,000-300,000 people.

URBAN PLANNING METHODOLOGIES AND APPROACHES

The first national body was founded by the imperial government under the Municipalities Department in the Ministry of the Interior, in 1963. (Birkie 1997). The department was active until the establishment of the Ministry of Urban Development and Housing (MUDH) in 1974 (Mathewos 1997). Under the auspices of this Ministry, the National Urban Planning Institute was established by proclamation in 1987 to lead and coordinate master plan studies for all urban centres in the country (PDRE, Proclamation No.317 of 1987). The Addis Ababa Master Plan Project Office (AAMPPO) was instituted through Ethiopian-Italian technical cooperation within the MUDH in 1984. The master plan was based on a three-level planning approach: the Regional Development Scheme, the Metropolitan Development Scheme and the Urban Development Scheme.

The Regional Development Scheme aimed to make Addis Ababa self-sufficient in food and other basic items supplied from Shewa and Arsi. In order to create balanced relationships among the existing urban areas within the region, the scheme suggested the reduction of in-migrations to Addis Ababa by boosting economic development opportunities at the growth-pole-centres of the planning region. In line with this scheme, it was expected to attain a population limit of 3 million for Addis Ababa by the end of 2004 (Mathewos 1997). However, this scheme was not able to achieve the expected outcome as the population growth had already reached 3 million by the beginning of 2002.

The Metropolitan Development Scheme was to include areas more directly linked to Addis Ababa's urban system and areas which hold a strategic value for the purposes of city development, such as the expansion areas, reserved areas, green belts and specialized agriculture (AAMPPO 1984). This scheme was also found to be less practical (Mathewos 1997).

The Urban Development Scheme focused on the main urban expansion areas, based on the previous two schemes for Addis Ababa including Kotebe (with 7 PAs in addition to Yeka Taffo), Keranio, Kotari and Akaki-Kaliti. This plan addresses the spatial organization of urban functions (AAMPPO 1984). However, it does not consider implications for the livelihoods of the rural people.

According to the master plan schemes, housing developments had taken place in the eastern, western and southern parts of the city. A number of hotels and small-scale industries were also constructed and were considered as major achievements of the implementation of the master plan during 1986-91. All these constructions had, however, taken place by displacing hundreds of farmers, even without paying cash compensation on the grounds that land is the sole property of the government.

After the fall of the socialist regime in 1991, the urban development master plan was the only one accepted by the Addis Ababa City Council. Accordingly, activities got under way to conduct detailed planning studies for the Kotebe district that encompasses Yeka Taffo and 7 other PAs. The implementation of large-scale projects like the Special Housing Project, the Ring Road Project and the Kotebe Diplomatic Residential Area have caused the demolition of a large number of housing units, the displacement of farmers and the creation of small urban 'enclaves' adjacent to the poor peasants. The planning approaches for the Kotebe district had followed an 'expropriation' approach instead of an income and social re-establishment model to support dispossessed peasants. The expropriation model permitted only the option of paying cash compensation for land or assets lost by urban expansion rather than extending multiple forms of support for the re-establishment of rural livelihoods.

The planners have adopted only financial cost-benefit analysis to compensate for the negative social and economic consequences of urban projects for the lives of the rural population. Moreover, they lack indicators and participatory development methodologies in analyzing the effects of urban expansion on the various cross-sections of rural communities. The survey methodologies that are being pursued to involve the farmers have been limited to their consultation during formal surveys and the administration of questionnaires.

The Real Estate Village Development Project and rural livelihoods

INITIAL PROJECT IDENTIFICATION AND RECRUITMENT STAGE

The project idea of the real estate development project came from an Ethiopian investor, who had the idea of addressing the shortage of urban dwellings for the middle- and upper-income groups through a mortgage lasting thirty years. Although this project idea was developed during the socialist regime, the project made its first application in January 1996 for getting lease land following the regulation of the Region 14 Administration in 1994. The initial six months of the project period, January to

August 1996, were dedicated to site selection and planning. The project did not consult the Yeka Taffo people and only relied on the opinion survey it gathered from its leaseholders. Towards the end of August 1996, it was permitted to officially undertake real estate development in the Yeka Taffo Peasant Association and surrounding areas.

SITE PREPARATION AND TRANSITION STAGE

In November 1996, the Addis Ababa Administration circulated an official letter to its subsidiary bodies and, through the Wereda Office, to the Yeka Taffo PA's Office giving orders to clear and prepare land for the Real Estate Development Project. Since no consultation had been undertaken with either the Yeka Taffo officials or the people, the decision led to panic among the inhabitants. They were outraged when they heard of the decision made behind their backs. They started to talk about their concerns, in peer groups and in social gatherings and agreed to demonstrate their protest in a rally. The local officials tried to show their sympathy with the people by explaining their reaction to the Member of Parliament who represented their *Wereda*. In turn, the parliamentarian reported their concern to the zonal level of administration and to the President of the Addis Ababa Region. Within a month, a meeting was organized to hear the inhabitants' concerns . The local people were very keen to meet the President and discuss their problems. This created an opportunity to air their dissatisfaction. They told the President ironically: 'A person raises a dog to bark for him, not to bark back at him,' and they used this statement to suggest that the President himself coming from an Oromo family should protect the rights of the Oromo peasants. The local people consider the land to be their own 'territorial land' and the manifestation of their identity. However, they were told that the land belonged to the public according to the regional government land policy, and they could only negotiate about the amount of compensation for the harvest and the properties they might lose.

Once the local people understood the lack of any viable choice, some of them began to adjust by developing bargaining mottos: 'Leaving land without compensation is equivalent to losing one's sight', and 'If someone is forced to become a slave, he has no option other than being sold for a good price'. Nonetheless, the people of Yeka Taffo continued to show their resistance by sharing their concerns in neighbourhood gatherings and *Iddirs*. They held a demonstration at the project construction site, and barricaded the passage of trucks and boycotted the unloading of construction materials. These demonstrations were effective in sending the message to the government and the project that no construction work would begin prior to the settlement of cash compensation.

Subsequently, a local committee consisting of officials and elders was set up to set the rate of compensation for people who lost their land and properties. At this juncture, unlike most lease-holders, the project management took the initiative to resolve its misunderstandings with the displaced people, since it believed that good relations with the displaced people would lead to the 'peaceful implementation' of its project.

Finally, the project agreed to pay the monetary compensation at market values. It also promised that it would consider the promotion of 'modern agriculture' and 'alternative employment opportunities' to enable the displaced households to re-build sustainable livelihoods. Although these promises initially convinced some peasants, failure to put them into practice can gradually backfire on the project and threaten its future stability.

Implementation of construction work and the risks of impoverishment

EXPERIENCING LANDLESSNESS

Since the peasants in Yeka Taffo were not entirely uprooted from the localities they had known for ages, the risks of impoverishment are not as severe as for the people affected by resettlement programmes elsewhere in Ethiopia and Africa (Pankhurst 1992a; Colson 1971). However, the issue of land ownership and insecurity of tenure is still the main factor contributing to the impoverishment of the Yeka Taffo peasants.

The city administration made a unilateral decision to lease a total of 2,400,000 square meters of rural land by evicting 172 households. All those evicted are now left with their backyard plots alone and have lost their farming and grazing land, ranging from one to over ten hectares per family. As a result of the decision, peasants have now become landless and have stopped farming. They are seriously insecure with the potential threat of a second wave of displacement. In order to minimize the problem that arises from landlessness, on the one hand, and to 'ensure a peaceful transition' for the project, on the other, the project agreed to pay cash-for-land compensation to all the evicted peasants.

It took the responsibility of paying this compensation itself to avoid the risk of delays, and guaranteed the payment of compensation to the appropriate persons. Three categories were used to determine the classification of the compensation: the poor, who own less than 3 hectares, the middle-level peasants, who own 3-5 hectares, and the rich, who possess 6-10 hectares. The project has made an additional rate of payment of 25 percent for the poor. On the other hand, this arrangement excluded the payment of compensation for the rich farmers owning over 10 hectares, for their extra land. In order to get round this criterion, some rich farmers used the tactic of sharing their extra land with their senior 'sons' and appealing on their behalf. After the payment of the cash compensation, no further organized action was taken by government officials, the project or other NGOs to enable landless peasants to cope with their future lives. As a result, most households were forced to pursue their own strategies.

All our informants agreed that they had greater amounts of cash than before. They started to withdraw money from the Abyssinia Bank, where their cash compensation was deposited. However, most of the peasants are uncertain about their future and do not have specific plans about what to do with the money; they were dependent on their cash deposits and withdrew cash whenever they needed to buy food or basic consumer goods or prepare social feasts such as weddings and funerals. An increasing number of dispossessed people also started to spend their money on non-productive items: on drinking, smoking, gambling and eating out in hotels. That is why almost all the informants agreed that, despite the immediate cash benefit, it would have been better to secure non-cash support and alternative land that could have been used throughout their lifetimes and been transferred to their children.

Individual families started to devise their own strategies for rebuilding their livelihoods. Some families which gained a lot from the compensation payment even attempted to change their status from being landless peasants. Some have been able to increase their livestock by buying smallstock and draught animals as well as by contracting land from other peasants and close kin nearby. A few households bought grain mills and started transport businesses by buying second-hand vehicles.

EXPERIENCING UNEMPLOYMENT

According to the farmers joblessness is defined as the loss of regular farming activities, or as not being active in farm work. Most elderly farmers over 50 became jobless when their land was taken over, except for daily jobs in the construction project of the real estate development project. However, wage labour does not facilitate the creation of additional assets through savings, so that they are insecure about their future.

Another contribution to make up for land losses was the establishment of the Real Estate Basic Construction Skills Training Centre, which admits young people with a literacy background, to acquire formal and practical training in masonry, carpentry and painting. The centre conducted training for 285 boys and girls, in two shifts for three months and, upon graduation, the project assigned the trainees to its construction work. The trainees received a monthly payment of 150 *birr* as pocket money. Discussion with them revealed that they welcomed the establishment of the centre and supported the potential employment opportunities created by the project for the coming decade. However, they are concerned about the possibility of getting employment opportunities after the construction work is completed.

FOOD INSECURITY

Household food security can be seen as a matter of productivity, availability, assets and entitlement to food. The first three factors are key to determining the food security of displaced households in Yeka Taffo. People used to produce wheat, *tef*, chickpeas and horse beans. In most cases, they did not buy additional grain to satisfy the needs of their staple diet. Apart from the landless households, most produced enough food to feed their family for an average of nine months per year. During the three months of the rainy season, women play a significant productive role in filling the food gap by way of augmenting their family's income through the sale of firewood, dung, dairy products and smallstock.

After displacement, landlessness has affected the capacity of displaced families to either produce food for their sustenance or to earn cash. Thus cash compensation by itself cannot become an alternative means to enable households to buy or rent enough land. Even if some peasants have tried to contract land from their neighbours and relatives, the amount of land that can be contracted does not exceed a *massa*, which is a quarter of a hectare. Extreme shortage of farmland is therefore seriously threatening their food security.

Nevertheless, there is no significant change in relation to the access to food at household level. The displaced households spend the majority of their wage earnings and compensation on buying food from peasants in neighbouring villages or from the nearby markets. Most households have increased their stock by buying livestock with the compensation money. They often sell the dairy products to satisfy their need for food essentials, and the animals if they are facing a crisis. Some households have also found it profitable to undertake sheep breeding as a means of getting additional income. However, the shortage of grazing land threatens livestock raising.

To sum up, except for the production of food, access to food has not shown a significant change for most displaced households. The threat to food security could become critical if they lost their wage earnings and the shortage of grazing land increased in the future. Given the fear of losing their employment with the project and the lack of support to improve livestock management, it is likely that most households will face food insecurity in the future. This indicates the need for supporting them with alternative off-farm activities and improving livestock and crop productivity.

SOCIAL DISARTICULATION

Lassailly-Jacob (quoted by McDowell 1996: 188) used the breakdown of social structure, social networks and belief systems as variables for measuring social disarticulation during forced displacement. These seem relevant variables for measuring the social disarticulation aspect of the effects of displacement in Yeka Taffo. Since the regional authorities have not resettled people outside their areas of origin, 'traditional' social associations were not threatened. Mutual self-help associations like *Iddir, Iqub* and *Mehaber* have continued to play their original roles. These associations were not officially recognized or encouraged to participate in the planning and implementation of the project. However, they have remained the main informal forums for exchanging ideas and discussing problems caused by displacement.

Since most of the inhabitants are followers of Orthodox Christianity, they attend church services on Sundays and festivals. However, the church has not played a significant role in dealing with the displacement situation. The place of worship and the residence of a diviner were demolished by the construction project. However, he was paid cash compensation for both, and was also given support to construct a new place of worship adjacent to his residence. His followers are happy about the special attention given by the project to reconstructing the worshipping site.

A serious concern that has been emerging following the landlessness and the engagement of the young people in wage earning is deviancy and emotional instability among the youth. Crowds of young people were observed around the newly established local taverns and the main gate of the project construction site. Indeed, such types of behaviour were also witnessed in other displacement situations such as those described by Colson (1991) and Lassailly-Jacob (1996). They could serve as a breeding ground for crime and prostitution in the near future.

HOMELESSNESS

To prevent the risk of removing people from their shelters, each homeless household was compensated with 250 sq. meters of homestead land and 9,000 *birr* (US$1400) to enable them to construct new dwellings. As a result, 27 households started construction work in the Real Estate Project colony. The displaced families are expected to meet the standard and quality of construction set by the municipality. As these standards are very new to them and do not fit their life-style in the rural settings, over 20 households have left their new houses to live with their old neighbours and relatives. The majority of the local people have the intention of selling their new houses, when completed, as a worthy capital investment, since they are not comfortable living in the project colony with rich and middle-class urban people.

MARGINALIZATION

Economic marginalization often overlaps with landlessness, joblessness and homelessness (Cernea 1996b). In Yeka Taffo, the condition of the landless young and adult households improved after the operationalization of the project since they got employment in the project construction work. In contrast, elderly people who perviously had land are the ones who have 'lost' their economic resources and become marginalized due to landlessness and limited access to the employment opportunities created by the project.

ACCESS TO COMMON RESOURCES

Since Yeka Taffo was already a settled community before the project was launched, the types of common resources that were available were grazing land and water resources (a river and two springs). The project site claimed a portion of the already existing grazing land when it evicted households. It is therefore interesting to observe that, after the cash compensation was paid, while the number of livestock and the demand for cattle fodder are increasing, the supply of grazing land is decreasing. This calls for either the diversification of cattle feed or the intensification of grazing lands in the future.

THE SEARCH FOR SUSTAINABLE LIVELIHOODS

The municipality is primarily concerned with how rural lands are expropriated to supply the real estate project with land. In the view of the project management, once dispossessed household heads get cash compensation and young members of the community are offered wage employment, they can easily reconstruct their past lives and even change their lives positively. The responsibility of searching for sustainable livelihoods has rested on the shoulders of individual rural households. It would therefore be interesting to examine the different strategies and coping mechanisms pursued by individual households to reconstruct their lives.

Cernea indicated the importance of re-establishing households' assets after displacement. However, he did not dwell on the impact that development projects have on 'migration'. He also indicated how his risk assessment models can be used to promote positive outcomes, but he did not consider systematically how households achieve sustainable livelihoods. Four elements of livelihood can be considered: agricultural intensification, crop-livestock integration, livelihood diversification and migration as developed by the Sustainable Livelihood Programme of the Institute of Development Studies at the University of Sussex (McDowell and De Haan 1997).

Agricultural intensification. In Yeka Taffo, most peasants have not used 'modern' innovations either in pre- or post-harvest agricultural production. Peasants depend on rain-fed agriculture to grow *tef*, sorghum, barley, chickpeas and lentils. Women grow cabbages and onions in their backyards. Most peasants use traditional farming implements such as ox-ploughs, sickles and axes, with family and group labour. Men thresh with sticks and livestock on earthen floors polished with cow dung, tossing grain in the air using pitchforks. Women use a circular flat tray made of dry grass to separate grains from husks. They do not have alternative energy sources, so that they depend on wood and dung cakes for cooking. All theses processes suggest that the dispossessed have few means of intensifying their agricultural production.

The Ministry of Agriculture has introduced chemical fertiliser to the area since the 1970s. However, the escalation of fertilizer prices and the lack of subsidies have hampered its application since the economic reform programme that devalued the currency and cut fertilizer subsidies in 1993. The Sasakawa Global 2000 Agricultural Extension Project, initiated in 1996, selected ten 'model' peasants in Yeka Taffo to benefit from access to a credit scheme for improved varieties of seed, chemical fertilizer and pesticides. According to these peasants, the agricultural inputs have almost doubled their yields in wheat production. However, given the small size of their plots of land, the net income gained from the sale of their harvest could not offset the fertilizer debt. After peasants had been dispossessed from their lands, no systematic measures were introduced to help those affected intensify their agricultural production. The expansion of urban development projects therefore puts them under the threat of further displacement. No dispossessed household was observed taking initiatives to intensify agricultural production. Most dispossessed households argue that, in the absence of land tenure security and the presence of continuous threat of conversion of agricultural fields, intensifying one's agriculture is a non-profitable option.

Livelihood diversification. Even prior to the project period, the common means of livelihood diversification for most rural households has been livestock production. All the dispossessed households which were paid compensation have started to replenish their assets through the purchase of livestock. They bought oxen for traction and to be fattened for sale. They also bought cows to sell their butter and cheese. Most of the female-headed households have also bought sheep and chickens to raise them for sale and augment their low income. However, the reduction in communal and individual grazing land and the absence of alternative feed are becoming potential threats for livestock raising. Other important types of off-farm activities are selling livestock (often sheep), livestock products (butter and cheese), chicken and eggs, firewood, grass, dung cakes, and clay pots. Women are also increasingly engaging in distilling *areqei* and producing *tej* – local alcoholic beverages.

In addition to this, dispossessed families started to contract out their oxen in exchange for crops. Young men and women have also obtained employment opportunities to work as daily labourers, masons, carpenters and guards in the project construction sites. The daily wage ranges from 6 to 12 *birr* (US$ 1-2), which is equivalent to the rates paid in other parts of Addis Ababa. In the short term, this employment opportunity is found to be the best means of livelihood diversification since it helps the young people to generate a monthly wage ranging from 180 to 360 *birr* (US$ 28 to 56) to assist their parents.

Migration. The field survey indicated that all the current inhabitants were born in Yeka Taffo and only 9 percent of their parents came from the Shewa and Arsi Oromo areas. The inhabitants have close social ties and exchange family visits among the neighbouring villages. Permanent out-migration was not common even before the project period. Since the village is close to the capital, peasants often earn income by selling their products in the city markets. After the project, the inability to engage in agriculture left most dispossessed households with the option of earning a livelihood through wage labour. This has caused the present landless people to remain in touch with Yeka Taffo. On the other hand, the availability of temporary employment opportunities in Yeka Taffo is attracting in-migration of daily labourers from the central part of the city. This may not be a threat for the time being. However, the project should take measures to protect the employment needs of the dispossessed

In the absence of the present employment opportunities, and perhaps when the real estate project has completed its construction work, the dispossessed peasants feel that there is likely to be much out-migration since their ability to achieve a sustainable livelihood in Yeka Taffo will be limited. Most of the young peasants who were attending skill training in masonry and carpentry were pessimistic about the possibility of getting employment elsewhere, given the number of unemployed skilled workers.

Concluding remarks

The urban land-lease policy is not very friendly to rural households in general and the poor landholders in particular. The policy has not taken into account the lives of rural peasants living in the vicinity of Addis Ababa. As a result, the implementation of the policy has resulted in the marginalization of the rural settled peasant communities. The City Council and its different departments do not seem to have constructed an institution that deals with dispossessed rural people who are affected by the expansion of the city boundary to facilitate the restoration of their livelihood.

The urban planning methodologies that are being pursued by the planners of the city council and the National Urban Planning Institute lack social engineering skills. Even the methodologies being used by the social and economic team of the planning unit are limited to the administration of a questionnaire crafted for the extraction of information that serves to calculate 'compensation'. The NGO community seems to have little knowledge about the scale of the problem of displacement caused by urban development projects. This has prevented them from using the opportunity to cooperate with the city council and the private sector in using their grass-roots expertise for the rehabilitation of dispossessed peasants.

The construction of the real estate development project has dispossessed farmers from their land in exchange for cash compensation. Only a few households have been able to contract or informally buy additional land. Even now, the dispossessed peasants feel insecure about their holdings of the small homesteads, as there is no guarantee against double displacement from their dwellings and farmland. Similarly access for the procurement of food crops will get worse as the coming of new urban 'elites' to the area escalates prices in the local market.

The replenishing of household assets, notably through the purchase of additional livestock, is an alternative means of sustenance being followed by the dispossessed households. However, there is no bright future for the continuation of stocking as farmers are facing problems of grazing land and lack of alternative cattle feed.

The number of households that were dispossessed from their dwellings was 27 percent. The project helped these households to obtain building permits within the project colony. But these poor rural households may not be able to live as neighbours with the urban middle- and upper-class families. Their intention is therefore to sell their dwellings once their construction is completed. The undertaking of the project has not affected the dynamics of social institutions such as *Iddir* and *Iqub*. However, the expansion of drinking places and the earning of wage income are affecting the young peasants. Access to common natural resources has been reduced by diminishing forest and grazing lands.

Migration has appeared as one of the means of searching for a sustainable livelihood. A few dispossessed households who were among the rich have bought and kept livestock among their distant kin and relatives and are pursuing rural-rural migration. There is also migration of urban labourers into Yeka Taffo. This could saturate employment opportunities and might create new slum areas or squatter settlements. Out-migration is unlikely, given limited skilled labour in masonry, carpentry and painting and limited opportunities available for these categories. However, lack of means of survival might force dispossessed peasants and young people to leave.

Urban development policies should be farmer-friendly and take into account the views of the peasants in the formulation of urban land-lease policy. The planning methodologies should be strengthened with social engineering skills that will analyse the effects of displacement at different stages of the project cycle and in multi-variable ways. For this, the incorporation of the Cernea and Scudder-Colson models into their planning approach would be very useful. Furthermore, the following implementation mechanisms are worth incorporating: (a) *preparation of comprehensive rehabilitation action plans* to identify the problems and needs of the various cross-sections of the affected communities and to design a comprehensive action plan for their rehabilitation; (b) *a policy and legal framework* to define rights and entitlements and outline the legal procedures and resource allocation for implementation; (c) *changes in methods of compensation evaluation* to shift the assessment of lost assets from measures based on market value to those based on replacement value in order to enable project-affected people to replace their lost assets; (d) *grievance redress mechanisms* to institute grievance-redressing forums and procedures at various levels; (e) *special advice and counselling services* to help project-affected people cope with their new lives; (f) *increasing involvement of NGOs* to facilitate communication, mobilization of resources and the speedy recovery of project-affected people; (g) *participatory monitoring and impact assessment mechanisms* to set up in-built and on-going participatory monitoring for better understanding of the impact of development projects on the lives of project-affected people.

The lease development or investment promotion offices need to institute a responsible unit in charge of the re-establishment of rural households. The planning skill of the urban planning team needs to be strengthened in the areas of participatory social assessment and management of rehabilitation operations.

This study started with existing models, notably those by Scudder-Colson and Cernea. However, it has shown that there are differential effects rather than an organic uniform response. Households and individuals have adopted different mechanisms to cope with their dispossessions and to use their cash compensations. Cernea's model of risk assessment is found useful to analyse the threats; however, the variables are very much interdependent and difficult to distinguish one from the other. For instance, the dispossession of land directly affects food security, the lack of common resources and the style of off-farm activities and vice versa. In order to have a sound project that aims to restore livelihoods, the minimization of risks variables mentioned by Cernea is essential. The inclusion of a 'migration' variable could broaden the dimensions of the analysis. The consequences of displacement can be explained better if the Scudder-Colson processual model is harmonized with Cernea's models of assessing the anticipated risks that arise out of displacement and of the 'migration' variable.

Notes

1. The first model is that of Scudder and Colson's five stages of a successful resettlement cycle. They explained successful resettlement in terms of five stages; (i) recruitment; (ii) site preparation; (iii) transition; (iv) potential development and community formation and (v) the consolidation stage. This model therefore emphasizes temporal and processual aspects (Scudder 1969, 1990; Colson 1971). It assumes that communities act in common organic ways during resettlement. It fails to explain the different strategies pursued by individuals, households and groups in coping with the consequences of displacement and resettlement.

2. Cernea outlined eight sub-processes through which resettlement makes for impoverishment: unemployment, homelessness, landlessness, marginalization, food insecurity, loss of access to common property, erosion of health status and social disarticulation (Cernea 1990). According to this model, a focus on the 8 sub-processes could transform the impoverishing tendencies into potential 'reconstruction' and enrichment.

Part IV

THE EXPERIENCE OF STATE-ORGANIZED RESETTLEMENT

Nine

Why Did Resettlement Fail?

Lessons from Metekel

GEBRE YNTISO

Introduction

Of an estimated 600,000 people resettled in Ethiopia in the 1980s, over 82,000 were relocated from drought-affected and overpopulated areas to Metekel (Northwestern Ethiopia), a place already inhabited by the Gumuz shifting cultivators. At the time of the resettlement, the population of the Gumuz was estimated at 72,000 (Dessalegn 1988, in Agneta *et al.* 1993:256-7). Of the total 250,000 ha of land designated for resettlement, over 73,000 ha was cleared for cultivation and the establishment of 48 villages. In 1986, large-scale development programmes were launched with financial and technical assistance from the Italian government. In the late 1980s, the resettlement area was portrayed as an oasis in the middle of wasteland. Salini Costruttori (1989: 14), a contractor for the Italian cooperation, reported, 'Food self-sufficiency represents the prime objective of the Tana-Beles Project. This objective has already been reached, at the end of 1988.' Today, the once popular Metekel (Pawe) resettlement is nothing but a failed project and a reminder of despair.

This chapter examines the 1980s resettlement to find out why the project failed and what lessons could be learnt. The outstanding flaws and deficiencies may be summarized as follows. The Pawe resettlement lacked clear conception, a feasibility study, proper planning, adequate physical preparation and responsible management. Neither the settlers nor the host people were consulted or involved in the decision-making. The ambitious development projects initiated by the Italians terminated before the settlers had re-established their lives. The overall impact on the settlers and the Gumuz was tremendously painful.

Rationale for the resettlement

Planned resettlement schemes were introduced in Ethiopia in 1958 (Eshetu and Teshome 1988: 167). However, until the establishment of the Relief and Rehabilitation Commission in 1974 and the nationalization of rural land in 1975, few resettlements were established. Beginning in 1975, however, the military government intensified resettlement programmes with the objective of addressing ecological, economic and social issues. In the early 1980s, the number of resettlement sites reached 88 and the number of settlers were estimated at 150,000 (Pankhurst 1990:121). The programmes failed to achieve the intended goals, in particular the attainment of the self-reliance of the settlers (Pankhurst 1990; Brüne 1990). Instead, despite high government expenditures settlers in some schemes (e.g. Gode and Bale) became totally dependent on food aid (Dawit 1989). Eshetu and Teshome (1988: 176-82) criticized the process of establishing and expanding settlements on account of high cost, mismanagement, and low levels of labour and land productivity.

Why did the government initiate new resettlements in 1984 after the earlier projects had failed? The official objective was to prevent famine and attain food security. Given the sudden rise in the number of famine-related deaths in 1984, and the slow response of the international community in providing relief aid for ideological reasons, resettlement was seen as a justified durable solution to the crippling food crisis. However, critics not only questioned the sincerity of the government position, but also indicated alleged hidden motives. The government was suspected of suppressing insurgent movements by depopulating their mass base (Clay and Holcomb 1986: 29; Colchester and Luling 1987: 5; Dawit 1989: 289,298; Keller 1993: 233), using resettlements to control opposition movements in the destination areas (de Waal 1991: 221; Colchester and Luling 1987: 5), and reorganizing the peasantry into producers' cooperatives (Dawit 1989: 289).[1] Most of the settlers came from northern Ethiopia and resettled in the southwestern, western, and northwestern parts of the country. Some writers viewed this movement as a pattern of state-sponsored migration that began a century ago (Scott 1998: 248; Clay and Holcomb 1986: 28). The former Commissioner of the Relief and Rehabilitation Commission (RRC), Dawit Wolde-Ghiorgis (1989: 289), suggested that the rationale was:

- to establish model producers' cooperatives;
- to place people who had accepted the Revolution along sensitive parts of the border;
- to promote the integration of various tribes and nationalities;
- to develop vast fertile areas that would produce food surpluses;
- to remove the unemployed from the urban centres;
- to rehabilitate politically undesirable people; and
- to depopulate rebel areas and deprive the rebels of support.

There were counter-arguments aimed at invalidating some of the above criticisms because of weak evidence.[2] Although evidence is scant, it can be surmised that famine was the central concern, while the government may have planned for collateral advantages of resettlement, such as state control of the peripheral regions, counter-insurgency, the establishment of collective farms, and regional development (Gebre 2002b).

Flaws and deficiencies of the resettlement

RESEARCH AND PLANNING

In 1984, the Ethiopian government adopted a ten-year perspective plan. Resettlement was considered an integral part of the overall development strategy for the country (Kirsch *et al.* 1989: 102). In September 1984, the governing party approved a broad resettlement plan proposed by the RRC and projected the relocation of 115,000 people during the ten-year period. Two months later, however, the government decided to resettle 300,000 households (1.5 million people) in nine months (Dawit 1989: 288). No research and no prior plan existed for this massive relocation. In December 1984, the Ethiopian Highland Reclamation Study, financed by the United Nations Food and Agricultural Organization, was reported to have supported the resettlement programme on environmental grounds (Alemneh 1990: 96), although there is no indication that the study was used in planning the 1980s relocation.

How were the resettlement sites (such as Metekel) selected? Dawit (1989: 294) noted, 'While the National Planning Committee was reviewing settlement sites, Mengistu started travelling around Ethiopia looking for sites on his own.... He made on-the-spot decisions on settlement sites without any research.' Other writers also subscribe to the idea that the Head of State may have selected many of the sites based on aerial maps, helicopter tours, and information from lower party/government officials (Dessalegn 1988a,b; Pankhurst 1990). There are accounts that Metekel was chosen as a suitable settlement site as early as 1981 (Viezzoli 1992: 166; Berterame and Magni 1992: 307). Nevertheless, no evidence suggests that the selection of Metekel was based on adequate feasibility research to assess its suitability for agriculture and its capacity to accommodate large number of settlers. The following quote from Dawit (1989: 290) sums up the initial flaw:

> Mengistu's resettlement plan was the result neither of research nor of long-term planning. It was a spontaneous act designed to take political advantage of the people's suffering...

MANNER OF THE RESETTLEMENT

Initially, the government insisted that the resettlement process was entirely voluntary. The authorities claimed that the government was supporting and organizing the self-motivated spontaneous reaction of drought victims. Dawit (1989:294) conveyed this message to the international donors' conference in Addis Ababa.

However, the initiative was certainly forced because in October 1984 the government decided to resettle 1.5 million people without the consent of the potential settlers. The reaction of the settlers to the resettlement was mixed: those recruited in late 1984 and early 1985 volunteered to be resettled, while those enlisted after mid-1985 were relocated against their will (Gebre 2002b). Among the so-called voluntary migrants, there were significant differences in terms of their motivations, decisions and expectations. Some embraced the relocation programme out of desperation. The first group to be resettled in Metekel included people who had temporarily migrated to Gojam to survive the famine, but whose hopes were shattered by lack of charity and decreased demand for wage labour. Other volunteers included famine victims in poorly equipped and unhygienic relief camps, where the incidence of morbidity and mortality was high. There were also those who were still living in their homes barely surviving the famine and who opted for temporary out-migration. Although the intentions of many of these relocatees were temporary migration, they were trapped in a permanent residence arrangement.

Some were attracted to resettlement through deception and sustained inducements. Berterame and Magni (1992: 316) wrote, 'In some cases, the promises and the guarantees given by the authorities removed the last doubts and made the people decide to go.' Reports from other resettlement areas suggest that enticements attracted many settlers, particularly the younger generation (Pankhurst 1992a). Some people volunteered when their loved ones or group members decided, were persuaded, or were forced to resettle. In short, the migration decisions of most of the so-called voluntary settlers were dictated by factors other than perceived gainful opportunities.

After mid-1985, willingness to be resettled declined because the long awaited rains arrived, crops ripened, distribution of food aid improved, and disturbing rumours spread about the resettlement areas. At this stage, Peasant Associations (PA) were given new recruitment guidelines. In Wollo, for example, PAs were instructed to recruit households unable to feed themselves for six years to come, and those without sufficient productive resources (oxen and land). In some places, quotas were imposed. This resulted in the use of physical force, which the authorities justified as *bego tetsi'ino* (well-intentioned coercion). In the absence of checks and balances, the empowerment of PAs to dislocate individuals and households led to corruption, favouritism, vengeance, and other forms of power abuses. There were people resettled because of their disagreement with local officials, refusal to give bribes, and reluctance to join producers' cooperatives. Many reported having been arbitrarily rounded up from homes, market places, streets and farms, resulting in family separations.

PHYSICAL PREPARATION

Settlers were promised that their adjustment would be smooth. They were told that the new land was unoccupied and fertile, the rain abundant, and basic services and facilities, such as houses, schools, clinics, water supplies, agricultural tools, household utensils, and transportation means all ready. In 1984/5 alone, over 53,000 people arrived in Metekel only to witness a completely different reality. Since there were no habitable houses, the migrants had to erect their own huts. Two to five households were forced to live in congested single rooms for several months to over one year. During the initial adaptation lasting over a year, food rations (cereals, flour, salt, and pepper) were insufficient, irregular, and nutritionally inadequate. Consequently, the settlers experienced severe food insecurity. Informants reported having eaten wild plants to save their lives.

Salini Costruttori (1989: 4) reported:

> More than 70,000 people had just been settled in the area. Most of these people were weakened by malnutrition while others were victims of tuberculosis and malaria and the area had not even the most basic health facilities… The few plots of land that had been cultivated were in a disastrous condition and gave negligible yields. There was no drinking water, no road…not even the most elementary materials to start farming.

Although beginning in mid-1985 the Ethiopian famine began to recede and the supply and distribution of food aid improved, there was a surge in the food crisis and increased mortality in the resettlement area. The incidence of sickness was so high that thousands of people perished without receiving medical attention. Due to the high mortality[3] the dead were buried in mass graves. The causes of sickness and death were explained in relation to undernourishment, malaria, tuberculosis, and lack of clean drinking water. The settlers were so destitute that they could not afford to buy coffins or proper funerary clothing.

ITALIAN ASSISTANCE

As a result of agreements between the Ethiopian and Italian governments, emergency aid was to be accompanied by development activities. Between 1986 and 1990, Italian governmental and non-governmental agencies[4] assisted the Metekel resettlement. The Tana-Beles Project, sponsored by the Italian government, provided relief assistance and initiated two major development activities. While the production sector focused on highly mechanized agriculture, forestation, livestock, fishery, agro-industry, and a pipe factory, the infrastructure works included water supplies, roads, bridges, housing, stores, an airport, health, education, etc.

The Italian assistance to the Tana-Beles Project made significant differences in food supply, childcare, health provision, basic education, housing and water supply. Settlers enjoyed privileges that were never available to ordinary rural residents, and were better-off during the Italian operation than in the initial period of adaptation. Some admitted that they were better-off than in their homelands. However, 31 percent of the sample population (368 respondents) reported inadequate food intake during the second half of the 1980s. Although gross food availability increased in the resettlement area, the settlers consumed nutritionally inadequate diets. Thus, malnutrition remained high.[5]

The settlers did not have any say in production decisions or control over the fruits of their labour. They worked as daily labourers for food rations distributed according to family size. This discouraged personal initiative and motivation to increase productivity. In 1988, a points system was initiated to reward devoted workers and raise productivity. Team leaders were selected from among the villagers to record attendance, evaluate work performance, and assign points. However, there were no clear efficiency-assessment techniques and no qualified personnel to perform an objective evaluation. The overall result was that the income of many settler households declined and production did not increase. Worst of all, the project was unsustainable and most of the activities collapsed following the Italians' withdrawal. The collectivization of agriculture and the introduction of mechanized farms into an archaic agrarian order completely failed after making the settlers more dependent and poorer.

POST-1991 HANDLING

When the Italians withdrew, free provision of modern production inputs ended; agro-industrial plants and the pipe factory were closed; kindergarten establishments were abandoned; the airport reverted to bushland; and the number of clinics dropped from 45 to 13. The dam on the Little Beles river had technical problems that could not be fixed by local experts. Because of silt formation and lack of maintenance, shortage of clean drinking water became a problem. Grinding mills were either out of order or villagers had to pay for the service. In 1999, most settlers were living in thatched houses because they had sold their metal roofs to survive the post-1991 crisis.

The transitional government took over the responsibility of running the Tana-

Beles Project. Because of budget constraints, the project's operation was limited to maintaining essential staff and providing limited assistance. In 1991, it supplied food to settlers and during the following two production years, all resettled households were given land planted with crops (first 0.5 ha and later 0.75 ha per household) to weed and harvest. The objective was to enable settlers to have their own farmland as opposed to working on collective farms for food rations. Meanwhile, many settlers left Metekel, abandoning their crops and plots. While those who decided to stay in the resettlement area worked hard, the undecided, the sick, and the aged failed to take proper care of their crops. The amount of harvest and the level of household food security therefore depended on the amount of labour each household invested. The overall production declined and many households became food-insecure.

In 1994, the project asked settlers to pay for tractor services, fertilizers, and seeds. Most settlers are reported to have received the project's services by paying the initial instalment. Some settlers had to rely on their labour and hand tools, as they could not afford the service charge. In 1995, the project offered to continue to provide tractor services on condition that the settlers made their payments immediately, before receiving the services. The project toughened its rental policy as many settlers had defaulted on the preceding year's payments. Most settlers were unwilling and/or unable to pay the service fees at once. The immediate consequence was a production shortfall and the spread of famine throughout the resettlement area. The concerns of the settlers failed to attract significant attention, as evidenced by the delay in delivering food aid. By the time a small quantity of grain was sent hundreds of people were reported to have perished. Food aid continued to be inadequate and people continued to die until 1996.

In the mid-1990s, those farmers who had decided to stay in Metekel were left with one alternative: a return to plough agriculture. This involved a multitude of obstacles, including shortage of oxen for ploughing, cattle diseases, scarcity of farm labour, inability to buy fertilizers, frequent invasion of armyworm and striga weed attacks on maize and sorghum. The prices of meat and legumes were so high that most settlers survived on carbohydrates. Malaria, tuberculosis, shortage of clean drinking water, and malnutrition remained the major causes of sickness and death.

The settlers, who were pleased with the reinstitution of private property, employed different strategies to cope with the hardships. These included expansion of land holdings, use of cows for traction, hiring of labourers from Gojjam, introduction of sharecropping arrangements, production of finger millet as a staple crop, production of sesame as a cash crop, and participation in petty trade and other off-farm activities. In 1999, dynamic economic diversification and differentiation were noticeable. Similar developments were observed in other settlements (Pankhurst 2002a). In Metekel, some settlers became more than self-reliant. However, for the majority the resettlement ordeal is far from over because of production and health risks. Thousands of households in many villages are still anguishing in poverty.

HOST POPULATION

Policy-makers, funding agencies, and displacement researchers often overlook the implications of resettlement for the receiving host populations. Settlers and refugees usually receive aid, research coverage, and/or policy attention, while the plight of the hosts remains largely unnoticed. The 1980s resettlement programme in Metekel is a case in point. Neither the Ethiopian government nor the Italian cooperation paid attention to the concerns of the Gumuz shifting cultivators. The resettlement severely affected their lives; they were forced to give up their farmlands, hunting/gathering grounds, and fishing sites (Gebre 2003).[6]

Some villagers were physically uprooted from their homes and lands more than once. For example, the residents of Manjeri village were removed from their homes three times. The first dislocation occurred in 1986 when an epidemic of an unspecified diarrhoea-related disease broke out in the resettled villages and spread to the Gumuz village. When the deadly disease killed many of their members, the Gumuz moved to a new village. In 1991, the first major clash between the settlers and the Gumuz mourners broke out, and more than 50 settlers are believed to have died. To avoid retaliation and further bloodshed, the Gumuz moved further away and established a new village. In 1993, this village was destroyed and its inhabitants were forced to move further away due to another clash with the settlers.

Land dispossession removed the foundation upon which people's productive systems and livelihoods were based. In the absence of an alternative source of income, the decline in agricultural production led to severe periodic grain scarcity in Gumuz. As Gaim (2000:316) noted, common property resources 'play a significant role in the livelihoods of the rural poor; consequently their loss may deprive the latter of important sources of income, biomass, raw materials, and way of life.' The sudden decline of access to game, wild plants, fish, and honey worsened food insecurity among local communities in the vicinity of Pawe. The land dispossession and marginalization triggered local resistance and consequent bloody confrontations between the Gumuz and the settlers. Apart from isolated retaliatory slayings, nine bloody clashes occurred between 1985/6 and 1993/4, in which both sides lost many lives and much property.

ENVIRONMENT

The Metekel resettlement was carried out without any regard for the environment. Massive deforestation was the most conspicuous consequence. According to Viezzoli (1992:168), on average 50,000 ha of land was bulldozed to establish 48 villages. In addition, 23,000 ha were cleared for mechanized agriculture (Salini Costruttori 1989: 14). Between 1985 and 1990 alone, therefore, the dense vegetation cover was wiped out from 73,000 ha of land. Tens of thousands of thatched houses were built, which required the felling of trees from the remaining forests. Most settlers reported having completely changed or substantially repaired their houses every three to four years, due to termites that destroyed the mud walls and grass roofs. Besides the total reliance of settlers on wood for fuel, the intensification of logging and carpentry as sideline activities accelerated the on-going deforestation.

The substantial removal of vegetation cover exposed the fragile sub-tropical soils to rain and wind erosion. Although the extent was not known, erosion had tremendously increased and the yield per unit of land continued to decline. The deforestation process contributed to the disappearance of wild animals and a variety of edible wild plants.

Discussion: contradictions, dilemmas and obscurity

INTENTIONS VERSUS OUTCOMES

When resettlements are envisaged, their intentions often appear noble and honourable. The contradiction is that the outcomes are often contrary to expectations.

In Ethiopia most resettlements were undertaken with the objective of promoting economic development and improving people's living standards. During the Imperial era, the planned settlements aimed at utilizing idle land and water resources for development, and addressing the concerns of landless peasants, unemployed persons, and people affected by drought and overcrowding (Eshetu and Teshome 1988: 168). Similarly, the military government's resettlement objectives were to prevent famine, reduce demographic pressures in the densely populated and highly denuded highlands, and promote agricultural production in the sparsely populated lowlands.

Recently, the regional governments of Oromia, Amhara, Tigray, Benishangul-Gumuz, and Gambela have plans for new resettlements. Their stated goals are fundamentally similar to those of previous governments, i.e., relocating people to improve their living conditions. However, it is important to recognize that resettlement as a feasible strategy for bringing about socio-economic development has been questioned. This chapter and other contributions in this volume clearly demonstrate how the previous resettlement adversely affected the resettled people, the hosts, and the environment. In spite of the fact that people were resettled on fertile lands and were provided with production inputs, many programmes failed. Other projects were doomed because pre-relocation promises to provide services remained empty rhetoric. The question today is whether the past mistakes will be repeated or averted. Before implementing any resettlement plan, regional and federal governments should examine and re-examine their resettlement initiatives to ensure that the proposed plans are truly voluntary, affordable, attainable and sustainable.

ETHICAL DIMENSIONS

In Ethiopia a large number of households have been displaced from their homes and familiar environments due to development projects, such as the construction of dams and roads, the protection of national parks, and the development and expansion of urban centres. The country needs such projects to create employment opportunities, provide improved services to the public, conserve natural resources, and promote socio-economic development. Given the increased need for power generation, irrigation schemes, wildlife conservation, and expansion of infrastructure and social services, development-induced forced resettlements are expected to increase in the future. The dilemma is that such resettlements often disrupt the livelihoods of the affected people and restrict their ability to make life choices. Development projects may result in decline or loss of income sources, breakdown of social networks, disintegration of cultural identity, outbreak of health hazards, escalation of conflict, loss of cultural sites, and environmental degradation. To the disappointment of the local people, the new projects may benefit people and regions far from the project area. For example, towns and cities located in distant places may enjoy the electricity. New jobs are likely to be taken by labour migrants and skilled workers from other places. Proceeds from large farms, mining firms, and national parks will go to corporations, private investors, or government agencies rather than to project-affected people. As Cernea (2000: 12) correctly argued, the outcome is an unjustifiable repartition of development's costs and benefits: some people enjoy the gains of development, while others bear its pains.

It would be against development philosophy to create a new poverty regime while claiming to avoid it. It would also be against elementary codes of ethics and morality to let people suffer by depriving them of their own resources. When development projects entail population displacement, the consequent resettlement programmes should be viewed as an opportunity to improve the living standards of the affected communities. In other words, the plan should be based on a development approach that transcends replacement and restoration of the existing living conditions. Instead of being condemned to bear the pains and become worse-off, development-induced displacees should be enabled to share the gains and become better-off than they were before their displacement.

CONCEPTUALIZATION OF MIGRATION DECISIONS

Conventionally, migrations have been conceptualized as having two distinct forms: voluntary and involuntary (Hansen and Oliver-Smith 1982:4; Cernea and Guggenheim 1993:3). Guggenheim recognized that the distinction is more theoretical than empirical (1994:3). Previous studies of the 1980s Ethiopian resettlement programme seem to have taken the conventional approach for granted. Similarly, the authorities characterized the programme as involving voluntary relocation and well-intentioned coercion. However, the migration decisions of most of the so-called voluntary settlers were inconsistent with the conventional definitions. In the Ethiopian context, the strict voluntary-involuntary approach obscured important dimensions of migration. It failed to uncover and explain resettlements that occurred when people embraced forced relocation out of desperation. Deception and inducement that characterized the 1980s resettlement programme also remained invisible.

Elsewhere, I proposed a modified conceptual tool capable of capturing most population movements (Gebre 2002b). The new approach identifies four major types of migration. These include voluntary, induced-voluntary, involuntary or forced, and compulsory-voluntary movements. Voluntary resettlement occurs when the migrants have (i) the power to make informed and free relocation decisions and (ii) the willingness to leave their original location. Induced-voluntary movement takes place when people leave their place of residence to resettle elsewhere due to deliberate acts of inducement perpetrated by outside agencies. Although the migrants may maintain the decision-making power, the facts on which their decisions are based are analysed and provided by other agencies. Involuntary migration refers to forcible uprooting of people from their original place of residence. The force agents could be natural disasters and/or humans. Compulsory-voluntary migration occurs when people accept forced removal out of desperation, and when voluntarily resettled people are denied the right to leave the resettlement area.

What is the theoretical and practical importance of redefining migration processes? First, this initiative is warranted by the need to provide conceptual clarity, which is lacking in the conventional dichotomous approach. Second, the new model has practical relevance, as it raises the question of responsibility and remedy. Who should be held accountable for which type of migration? What remedial measure is appropriate for which migration type? The conventional wisdom provides that voluntary migrants are responsible for the consequences of their decision to move. Voluntary migration is confused with induced voluntarism, and the authorities tend to portray resettlements attained through deception and/or inducement as voluntary, thereby avoiding responsibility. The new model enables us to argue that (i) the two forms of movement stand apart, and (ii) any agency that lures people to leave their homes and resettle elsewhere should be held accountable for the consequences that ensue.

Compulsory-voluntary migration may also be confused with forced relocation. The two types of movements have clear differences of practical relevance. The policy prescription for forced migrants could be not to displace them in the first place or to let them return to their original homes. Such remedies may not work (unless accompanied by rehabilitation programmes) for compulsory-voluntary migrants, who are willing to leave their homes for better safety and security. The second difference has to do with the reactions of the people to forced resettlement initiatives. Compulsory-voluntary migrants would embrace such an offer, while involuntary migrants tend to resist it. Resistance to forced resettlement tends to affect the pace and degree of re-establishment in the new environment. In Metekel, most voluntary and compulsory-voluntary migrants appeared materially better-off than most involuntary relocatees (Gebre 2002a). From this it is evident that resettlements that involve reckless acts of deception, unrealistic inducement, intimidation, and force are likely to fail.

Conclusion and recommendations

In Ethiopia, the outcomes of the planned resettlement programmes have almost always been disappointing. The Metekel resettlement programme caused livelihood deterioration, major health risks, and deadly conflict over resources. This happened because the programme had numerous flaws and fundamental deficiencies. It lacked feasibility studies, proper planning, and adequate physical preparation. Moreover, the resettlement authorities failed to respect the life choices and human rights of the settlers; to formulate compatible and sustainable development projects; to address the concerns of the host people, who lost their means of livelihood; to provide safeguards to deal with adversities; and to prevent environmental losses. It is in the best interest of the country and its peoples for policy-makers and planners to review such lessons to avoid committing similar mistakes in the future. The ideal solution to avert resettlement-induced impoverishment is to avoid forced relocation. When resettlement is unavoidable for justified reasons, it is important to ensure that the programme is affordable, attainable and sustainable.

Clear national policy and legal frameworks should guide resettlements. Plans should be based on comprehensive feasibility studies, assessing the human, economic, social, cultural and environmental impacts of the resettlement. The potential settlers and host populations should be consulted to secure their consent and participation in the decision-making process. Compliance should not come through deception, inducement, intimidation or the use of force. The construction of homes, the development of infrastructure and social services, and the commencement of production should start before the relocation to make the transition smooth and less disruptive.

The citizenship and human rights of the affected people should be protected. People's rights to life, dignity, liberty, and security should be protected. Moreover, their freedom of movement, expression, belief, association, and customs should be respected.

All resettlement plans should be based on a development approach that transcends mere compensation to replace or restore the existing living conditions. Plans should aim at improving the life choices and living standards of the affected communities.

Notes

1. The pre-1984 resettlements are suspected of having been executed with the objective of breaking up homogeneity (Wood 1982), using resettlements for counter-insurgency (de Waal 1991), using settlers as a defence force along troubled borders (Dawit 1989), and modelling settlements on producers' cooperatives (Eshetu and Teshome 1988).
2. According to Jansson (1990:65), for example, the allegation that the resettlement aimed at depopulating the Tigray Peoples Liberation Front's support base was unfounded as only 15% of the 600,000 settlers came from Tigray. Official statistics show that the largest and the second largest number of settlers came from Wollo and Shewa, respectively, rather than from Tigray (Dawit 1989; Alemneh 1990; Pankhurst 1992a). Pankhurst (1992a: 79) noted, 'Recruitment from areas not under central rule was considered unwise.' Alemneh (1990: 96-97) asserted that the objective of the resettlement was 'to restore the loss of productive land affected by drought and to use the vast amount of land in the fertile southwestern region to increase food production and generate rural income.'
3. De Waal (1991: 225-6) reported: 'RRC figures for recorded deaths during the first year of resettlement indicate heightened death rates: 110 per thousand in Gojjam [Metekel], 68 in Illubabor, 42 in Keffa, 38 in Wollega and 34 in Gonder. ... The same RRC data indicate that in Pawe resettlement, Gojjam, death rates in the first four weeks of registration were equivalent to 332 per thousand per year – almost 20 times normal.'
4. The International Committee for the Development of Peoples / *Comitato Internazionale per lo Sviluppo dei Popoli* (CISP), sponsored small-scale multisectoral programmes from 1986 to 1999, covering only a small portion of the resettled people. .
5. Antonioli (1992: 387) reported: 'In return for their work on the approximately 20,000 hectares of the agricultural land pertaining to the "Tana-Beles Project", the settlers were given their monthly food rations. These rations consisted basically of cereals...and small amounts of oil seeds... plus allowances of sugar, salt, and oils. Very clearly an unbalanced diet was being provided, especially as regards protein and particularly vitamin requirements.'
6. Dieci and Roscio (1992:120) wrote: 'With the arrival of approximately 75,000 settlers, a large part of the Gumuz left the resettlement area...several Gumuz villages were seen to disappear from several localities in the Beles area between June 1986 and October of that same year.' Berterame and Magni (1992:307) stated: 'When the [Italian] project started the Beles area was considered by the authorities as virtually unoccupied land with agricultural potential, although this definition does not seem accurate since the ...Gumuz were scattered over the area in complex land-use and land distribution system.'

Ten

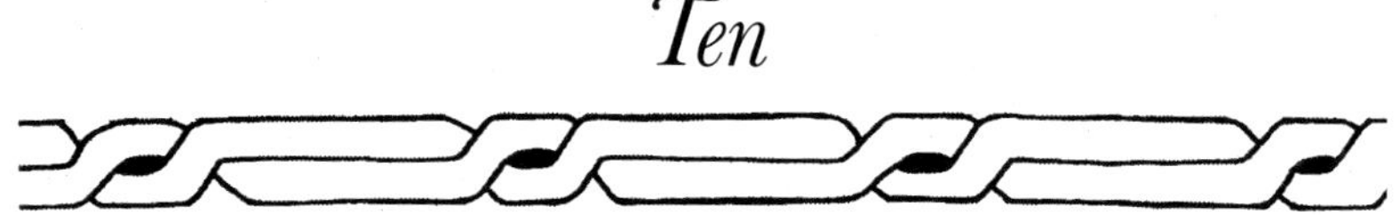

Social Impact of Resettlement in the Beles Valley

WOLDE-SELASSIE ABBUTE

Introduction

This chapter examines the social impact of the state-sponsored resettlement of the 1980s in the Beles Valley (Metekel), northwestern Ethiopia, imposed and driven by mixed motives to do with famine and drought prevention, food production, security and population control. The Beles Valley resettlement area is located along a tributary of the Abbay (Blue Nile) River, southwest of Lake Tana in the Metekel Zone of the Benishangul-Gumuz National Regional State. The area has a lowland altitude range of between 1000 and 1200 masl. The scheme is one of the biggest state-sponsored programmes of the 1980s and hosted people resettled from the drought-prone area of north-central Ethiopia and 'over-populated' areas from the southwest. The initially planned scheme was around 250,000 hectares (Salini Costruttori 1989: 8). The resettlers were relocated along the banks of the Beles River in 48 villages with an average number of 500 households each. At the peak of the process in 1987/88, the population reached a total of 82,106 (21,994 heads of household with 60,112 family members). The ethnic composition is very heterogeneous including: Amhara (from Wello, North Shewa, Gojjam and Gonder), Kambata, Hadiyya, Oromo (from South Wello and North Shewa), Wolayta, Tigraway, and Agaw (from Wello and Tigray), with a mixture of cultures from many parts of the country.

Social disintegration and livelihood impoverishment

In the process of the emergency mass relocation of the 1980s, the propaganda that described the new homes as if comforts were awaiting the resettlers deceived many. In June-July 1985 I witnessed local authorities telling Kambata and Hadiyya peasants that the land would be cultivated by tractors; that fully furnished iron-roofed houses were already built awaiting them; and that they would be given food, clothing and the necessary implements. Many peasants joined the scheme, disposing of their property. The would-be resettlers sold their domestic animals and other valuables at very low prices. Many used up the last of their money while waiting in temporary shelters for transportation. Immediately after their departure, their plots were redistributed to newly married and land-short farmers. These resettlers' initial contacts with the new sites were characterized by insecurity and precariousness, creating great disillusionment. They had to build new houses because those built by students and university staff campaigners were already crumbling. Disillusioned by the denial of their expectations, the resettlers began a hard life, aggravated by acute malaria and other epidemics. They underwent painful experiences in adapting to the new socio-cultural, economic and biophysical environment. The scheme led to the breaking down of long established social structures, dismantling of production systems, and destruction of traditional coping mechanisms. The planners and implementers neglected the web of institutions in which the resettlers were linked in manifold ways in their original location. The resettlers experienced the disintegration of social institutions leading to uncertainties and desperation in their daily lives. They therefore repeatedly recalled their pre-resettlement living conditions in a positive light.

The relocated peasants were alienated from family and community control, and their social, political and religious leaders were impotent to prevent the social disintegration and disruption of their livelihoods; the roles of elders and religious leaders as facilitators of the processes of marriage, burial and other rituals were disrupted. The spiritual festive associations like *mahber* and *senbete* of the Orthodox Church followers were curtailed. The crucial roles of elders in the overall village community lives and livelihoods were absent. The administration of the village was left solely in the hands of the political cadres and Peasant Association (PA) committee members.

In their home area, the resettlers belonged mostly to related kin groupings living in neighbouring villages and hamlets. Village communities were also known by their respective parish, mosque, clan or village groups. They were coherent and intimate with spiritual ties and a sense of belonging through a common origin. In the planning and implementation of the resettlement the potential of kinship relationships, neighbourhood networks, and a common ethnic background in sustaining the resettlers' livelihood was underestimated. The villages are made up of residential houses with only a 0.1 hectare homestead plot for each household (the only farm area managed by the farm household). In no case was an entire village community relocated together. They lacked community mutual associations. Free observation of religious holidays was constrained. Social organization of production was disrupted and social institutions no longer functioned.

Resettlement brought about the break-up of families. It has affected the family set-up of couples. One of the partners often abandoned their spouse by leaving or remaining behind. Moreover, after tasting the bitter experience in the resettlement area, many resettlers again abandoned their partners to return. Marriages that were established during the height of the problem were rather loose and resulted in abandonment and separation. In particular, many of the abandoned or separated women have had difficulties in finding new partners. In the case of divorce, men had a higher chance of re-marriage, and resettlement has worsened the situation of women and there were more widows than widowers.

The resettlement scheme has brought resettlers from the highlands to the lowlands. The Beles Valley's hot and inhospitable climate had adverse effects on the adaptive adjustment of highland resettlers, resulting in increased morbidity and mortality due to health problems and malnutrition.

The scheme has increased state control over the resettlers, with government, party, and executing agencies taking control of their resources and lives. At all levels, they were heavily guarded to prevent escape. They were strictly forbidden to travel out of the area. In 1988, village-to-village travel was possible only through pass letters obtained from the village authorities. Agricultural collectivization was imposed upon the resettlers and their labour time was strictly controlled according to the points system devised for producers' co-operatives. Individual initiatives and private trade were restricted. The overall administration was put under the tight control of village political cadres. As a result, the scheme has involved 'notable human costs higher than those caused by famine, in spite of large investments to install the infrastructures' (Sivini 1986: 235).

The diverse origins of the resettlers resulted in interactions of different ethnic groups and diverse cultures. In some of the villages, resettlers belonging to the same ethnic groups were relocated together, whereas, in others, resettlers belonging to different ethnic backgrounds were resettled together. The resettlers from the north-central parts of the country were intensive cultivators of cereal crops, with their main staple food being *injera*. The resettlers from the southwestern part of the country are mainly *enset* and tuber crops cultivators with an additional specialization in income-generating activities, with their main staple food being *qocho*.

In the resettlers' home areas, land was 'individually' owned and the household was the main unit of production and consumption. In the new setting, the highland crops and cropping seasons have been changed, and resettlers have to readjust to lowland farming systems. In line with the change in the type of crops produced, the food habits of the resettlers were also changed. Both southwestern and north-central groups of resettlers were critical of feeding maize porridge to their wives during maternity as opposed to the barley porridge provided in the north-central areas and the *bu'lla* porridge in the southwest. According to the views of the respective resettlers, both *bu'lla* and barley have high nutritional and cultural values.

Resettlement brought resettlers into direct contact with the autochthonous Gumuz population. The Gumuz used to lead a quite different socio-economic and cultural way of life. Resettlement has taken away the traditional resources of the Gumuz whose livelihood is based on shifting cultivation combined with gathering, hunting, fishing, and honey collection. The marginalization and expropriation of resources that belonged by tradition to the Gumuz resulted in fierce ethnic conflicts that caused loss of lives on both sides. This is one of the bitter experiences for both hosts and resettlers brought about by the resettlement scheme in contrast to their previous more secure way of life.

In particular, following the 1991 political change in Ethiopia, many resettlers were forced to evacuate the Beles Valley due to the adverse environment, new dietary habits, suffering caused by the prevalent diseases (malaria, tuberculosis, and asthma), nostalgia for the homeland and wish to reunite with separated relatives, and especially ethnic conflicts with the hosts. However, despite all the adversities, a substantial number of resettlers remained. Part of them moved and regrouped within the different villages in the scheme where many had left. The size of the resettled population dropped from 82,106 in 1987/88 to 26,660 in 1993/94. However, the number increased again to reach 30,513 in 2002 (Wolde-Selassie 2002: 154). Among the 17,849 new settlers 6,858 were immigrant farmers of the 1990s, and 10,991 dwellers in the emerging three small towns, searching for new opportunities.

Social rearticulation and livelihood reconstruction

After the initial phase of emergency and transition, the resettlers began adapting to the new context. They established complex social relations both within the resettlement area as well as with the neighbouring population through marriage, religion, work groups, land exchange, bond friendship and fictive parenthood as well as on the basis of the individual's entrepreneurial ability. Through the marriage ties, affinal kin groups began to be established between the families of the spouses. The role of elders has regained importance in marriage ceremonies and other aspects of village life. For example, elders in the respective communities now have a role in settling disputes arising between and within households and at the village level. Increasingly, they advise, guide, and punish defaulters according to custom and take responsibility for teaching the importance of culturally accepted values and norms. Elders encourage and motivate self-support among the resettlers; they visit the weak and disabled, console the families of the deceased and perform other vital social services.

Associations based around the Orthodox, Protestant and, Catholic churches and Muslim mosques in the sites have emerged to extend support to their weaker members and in many cases have become the main source of livelihood. Hand-in-hand with the re-establishment of the different churches, church leaders, consisting mostly of the elderly, have also re-emerged. They strongly preach being faithful to one's own religion and observing the proper performances of followers respecting its precepts. They perform the daily prayers for the salvation of the souls of the dead. Moreover, they have a key role in consoling bereaved families through their frequent prayers and visits. The very re-emergence of the belief systems has created an optimistic feeling of hope among the resettlers and is contributing to their adaptation.

Iddir, which were totally absent in the 1980s, have managed to be revitalized, with the household as the basic unit for membership. The present *iddir* of the villages cross ethnic and religious boundaries based on the composition of the respective village inhabitants. Apart from the well-established *iddir* for burial and mourning, there are now *iddir* for oxen (a kind of insurance mechanism), and for transporting the sick to hospital (the stretcher society). The different *iddir* are administered by an elected respected *dagna* (judge), and those who fail to make contributions to the services are punished severely.

Resettlers also managed to re-establish *mahber* and *senbete*, mutual religious festive associations among the followers of the Orthodox Church. The *mahber* members meet once a month in each other's houses, rotating in the name of a selected saint, and enjoy food and drinks at the same time as performing prayers. The *senbete* members meet every two weeks, rotating among members, holding feasts in the compound of the village church together with those disabled and weak members who come in search of food. At the same time, priests perform prayers. Both the *mahber* and *senbete* are formed across ethnic boundaries, and mutual support is extended to members as demanded both on good and bad occasions.

With the re-establishment of smallholder household production systems, resettlers' social organization has also re-emerged. The social organization of production among resettlers is centred on various work groups. These include *dabo* (festive labour), *wenfel* (reciprocal labour), *amicha* (affinal kin-based festive labour), *balinjera* (intimate friendship based on festive labour which is also known as *elfinna-qaso* among the southwestern resettlers), *waari/maarfeja/toori* (supportive labour for the weak in the early hours of the morning before the resettler-farmers go to their daily tasks), and *lim-maano* (full-time supportive labour mostly for the disabled needy). Local community-level self-supportive organizations have been strengthened, mainly based on the re-establishment of the smallholder cultivation requiring mutual support. For instance, oxenless resettlers obtain ploughing support through their kin, and those without cash can gain access to loans. Based on established kin, some resettler traders mobilize village-level grain purchase for merchants and earn commissions. In the field of agricultural activities, resettlers who have established better social networks are capable of mobilizing a considerable amount of festive labour, which makes a significant contribution to the success of livelihood strategies.

Initially, only those activities considered by the planners as marginal were left to the resettler households. However, in the absence of support and encouragement, resettlers showed initiative and independence through the management of activities with conscious evaluations of the benefits of supplementary income. Despite the local authorities' efforts to hamper them, periodic markets developed to trade home gardening products, handicraft products, grain, livestock, spices and clothing. Entrepreneurial activities such as trade and market exchange were found to be one of the best adaptive strategies. Though markets signal economic activity in the new context, they were highly controlled by the authorities, being considered as distracting occasions, which affect campaign cooperative work in the field. Despite the effort of the authorities to curtail them, markets emerged and displayed significant economic dynamism. Resettlers opted for alternative adaptive strategies because the sparseness of the rations was not sufficient to guarantee their survival. Their engagement in exchange, trading and similar activities strengthened their social networks within the resettlement villages and neighbouring areas. The resettlers proved to be innovative and dynamic in their adaptive strategies. Thus, the re-emergence of the household economy coupled with the individual initiatives and industriousness acted as key elements in the resettlers' adaptation, revitalization, and reconstruction of livelihoods. As resettlers adjusted their social arrangements and their productive activities, the socio-cultural rearticulation propelled economic recovery and livelihood reconstruction.

Social institutions in resettlers' livelihood adaptation

The early disarticulation and the later rearticulation of local institutions enabled the often-invisible complex web of institutional arrangements and their multiple roles to become visible to outsiders as well. Meaningful re-instituting processes of institutions were properly realized with the collapse of collectivization and the re-establishment of smallholder production systems. Resettler households embedded in these local institutional frameworks channel access to different livelihood resources, which are essential for their survival. These strategies are in turn linked to the multiple institutional settings in which the households are embedded. However, livelihood adaptation and coping strategies depend on wealth categories.

ACCESS TO LIVELIHOOD RESOURCES

Local institutions mediate and channel the resettler households' access to a wide range of resources and serve as gateways to livelihood security. The livelihood strategies of the very rich and rich households mostly have favourable local institutional opportunities for further improvements. Their livelihood strategies are based on institutional arrangements such as sharecropping-in and renting-in land; mobilizing large festive labour (*dabo, amicha,* and *balinjera*); hiring-in farmers for a cropping season and daily labour during peak seasons; generating income from diverse sources (cash and food crops, livestock and its products, interest from cash and grain loans, trading grain and livestock, etc.); exchanging oxen for labour, cash and grain, or land; and exchanging grain for labour. In their social rankings, they are highly respected and extend generous welfare support to the weak members of the village through several local institutional arrangements. They organize feasts on annual holidays (*mahber, senbete,* and *kristinna*) attended by the weak members.

Less extensive, the production strategies of medium households depend on institutional arrangements such as pooling reciprocal labour through *wenfel* or *qaanja*. These households generate average income from diverse sources to augment the field produce and organize feasts only on major occasions. However, they seldom mobilize festive labour. They do not demand the welfare support of others and can only occasionally extend moderately generous support to the weak members of their neighbourhood.

The main coping strategies of poor households are based on institutional arrangements such as exchange of land for oxen; exchange of labour for grain or oxen; taking grain and cash loans; getting access to inputs and oxen through social networks; and collecting support from friends and neighbours. In addition, the poor households get access to oxen and/or credit (cash or grain loan) through local institutions such as bond friendship, fictive/foster-parenthood, affinal kinship, and *yezimdina balinjera iddir.* However, the survival strategies of weak and dependent households are based on institutional arrangements consisting basically of the generous handouts of the village community as well as visiting places of feasts for mere existence. The very poorest families merely survive on the generous welfare support of the better-off households.

SOCIAL SECURITY AND SAFETY NETS

Local institutional arrangements provide social security and safety nets for the community. *Iddir* is the most important exemplary institution. Through *yeafer iddir,* funeral processes are facilitated and closely attended, the financial expenses are covered, and multiple forms of solidarity and support are offered to the mourning family. Cattle-owning members support each other through *yekebt iddir. Yebetsira iddir* enables community members to construct residences with fewer burdens. *Yeqareza iddir* enables transporting their sick members and helps in saving lives. Members of *yezimdinna balinjera iddir* use their institutional resources for fulfilling several goals of self-help in their daily lives in addition to extending extra mutual support during funerals and mourning. Membership in the basic neighbourhood *iddir* is equally open to all village community members without any differentiation of status.

The religious belief institutions are basically meant for the spiritual gratification and social security of the community. Members of *mahber* and *senbete* enjoy secure social cohesion and extend mutual support within each. Through the religious institutions, followers extend welfare support to the poorest and weak. The priests and *qaadi* play key roles in creating and maintaining cohesive relationships in the community. They have a strong capacity to apply pressure in conflict resolution. They play an important role in maintaining stability within the community through prayers.

The role of elders in the community is indispensable. The conflict-resolution capacity of elders is vital in creating stability and security. Elders facilitate the process of extending welfare support to the weak members of the community through their traditionally valued blessings. They advocate important values of mutual trust, co-operation and sharing. Using their traditional wisdom, elders care for the safety and security of all community members.

LOCAL SELF-GOVERNANCE

Local institutions have a well-established and traditionally proven role of facilitating forums for local self-governance through popular participation and community empowerment. They facilitate a free, safe and enabling environment, serving as vehicles of community participation. They enhance the freedom of community members as masters of their own affairs. Since the loyalty and accountability of local institutions are to their community, they boost the trust, motivation and self-esteem of the community, revealing its proven capacity to organize and manage its own affairs.

Social institutions open up opportunities of participation at the local level especially for those marginal groups of the community such as the poor, women and artisan caste groups. The different types of local institutions have an indispensable significance in the processes of local-level community self-governance. The council of elders customarily discusses issues of community concern in public. Its conflict-resolving procedures are considered to be fair and binding with careful compromise and tolerance, preventing either litigant from being a total loser or winner. The council has a role in the management of common resources such as grazing areas, village forests, front yards, footpaths, and similar commonly owned properties, though its customary role seemes to have been neglected in some cases by the peasant association leaders. However, in most of the villages, the peasant association administrators are unable to make a final decision with respect to defaulters before the traditional elders exhaust their methods through the appropriate local institutions. Peasant association administrators confirmed the fact that, without the elders' councils, their role would have been insignificant. The most frequently cited context is the comparison of self-governance between the time of 'political cadre administration' and the more recent situation. At the initial stage of resettlement, almost all the local institutions were displaced and dismantled. After relocation, the cadres were the only authorities in village affairs. Under the local cadre administration, the communities had no freedom whatsoever to make decisions by themselves and their social institutions of interaction were disintegrated, increasing the stresses.

The community recalls that period with hatred. Since 1991 there has been an improved re-articulation of local institutions. *Iddir* creates an appropriate forum for discussing issues of common good. Members, while attending a mourning family, discuss and settle matters of community concern. The whole process of electing leaders, voting, running meetings, keeping discipline, etc. reveals the local potential in governing community affairs.

Conclusion

The resettlement scheme in the Beles Valley has brought about complex changes in socio-cultural, economic and environmental conditions in the area. The resettlers from the highlands, the host population, and the eco-system are all affected. The resettlement scheme initially disintegrated the resettlers' social organizations, which bind their web of relations and interactions in manifold ways. The scheme disrupted the resettlers' production systems and impoverished their livelihoods. As a consequence, the uncertainties and desperation of the resettlers increased. However, after undergoing the initial painful difficulty of adaptive readjustment, they began re-instituting social institutions. The rearticulation of social networks in turn played a central role in the process of the resettlers' livelihood adaptation, reducing the uncertainties in their daily lives and recovering stable livelihood strategies. Thus, the social impact of resettlement reveals the centrality of social institutions in an involuntary resettlement context, from an initial social disintegration to a subsequent uneasy community reintegration.

Eleven

Revisiting Resettlement under Two Regimes in Ethiopia

The 2000s Programme Reviewed in the Light of the 1980s Experience

ALULA PANKHURST

Introduction

Over a million people have been resettled in Ethiopia in two phases: over 200,000 households representing a little under 600,000 people in 1985-6 under the Derg and about 190,000 households and around 627,000 people[1] during 2003-7 under the EPRDF. This chapter considers the following nine questions: Was it a coincidence that resettlement was promoted at times of famine in the mid-1980s and early 2000s? Why was further resettlement deemed necessary when the earlier resettlement was known to have been a failure? What are the similarities and differences between the two programmes? Were the mistakes committed in the earlier resettlement avoided? How far has the current resettlement adhered to the principles and guidelines set out? Have the economic costs and financial implications of resettlement been taken into consideration and properly analysed? What are the longer-term consequences of resettlement? How could resettlement planning and practice be improved on the basis of the current and past experience? Is there an alternative model that might work better?

The Derg resettlement has been the subject of considerable research including three PhD theses (Pankhurst 1989; Gebre 2001; Wolde-Selassie 2002), several books (Alemneh 1990; Dieci and Viezzoli 1992; Pankhurst 1992a; Wolde-Selassie 1998; Dessalegn 2003) and a large number of reports and articles. The problems and failings of the 1980s resettlement are discussed in the chapters in this book by Gebre and Wolde-Selassie and in the introductory and concluding chapters by the editors. The EPDRF came to power with a clearly negative attitude towards resettlement. The drastic consequences and injustices of the Derg resettlement, the coercion, high death rates, and escapees from the resettlement camps were often alluded to. The TPLF was particularly aware of how supporters were rounded up and taken by force and how many escaped and became refugees in Sudan. The weight of the evidence suggests that the programme was flawed in its design and hasty in implementation, involving human rights abuses and untold suffering to settlers and peoples living in areas where the resettlement was carried out with grave social, economic, political, cultural and environmental costs described in the introduction to this book and the chapters by Gebre and Wolde-Selassie. Even those costs which might have been measured, notably the financial and economic aspects, were generally overlooked in the planning and hidden in the implementation largely by diverting resources and personnel from ongoing projects and programmes, and have been the focus of limited attention (Prunier 1994; Pankhurst 1992a), as is often the case in resettlement projects (Cernea 2008a).

Early reviews of the current resettlement were rather limited and comprised mainly brief reports by the government, United Nations agencies, international organizations, non-government organizations and commissioned researchers, produced largely on the basis of short fieldtrips to a few sites (Pankhurst 2003b). The most thorough of these was by Hammond and Bezaeit (2003), the conclusions and recommendations of which were published (Hammond and Bezaeit 2004). There have been few comparisons of resettlement between regions except between Amhara and Oromia (Abraham and Piguet 2004a), Amhara and SNNPR (Tranquilli 2004), and more recently Amhara and Tigray (Kelemework 2008). However, there have been a number of in-depth studies including ten recent MA theses on the subject produced at Addis Ababa University, eight in social anthropology, and one each in geography and regional and local development studies.[2] Moreover, a project sponsored by the Forum for Social Studies carried out comparative case studies in eleven resettlement sites in four regions (FSS 2006). Some of the insights from recent theses and studies are discussed below. However, in 2006 and 2007 the interest in resettlement both on the part of government and of potential settlers seems to have waned, with a reduction in comparison with planned numbers and less resettlement being carried out than had been expected with regional variations. This may be in part because some of the problems of the current resettlement have been realized, there are fewer volunteers in some of the 'sending areas', and the campaign approach that is almost a national statal trait has meant that energies were mobilized elsewhere.

This chapter focuses on the recent resettlement in comparison with the earlier phase and also seeks to draw longer-term lessons from the latter. The chapter has five sections. In the first the recent policy shift is documented and an account is given of the federal and regional planning and implementation. In the second the current practice is reviewed in the light of the pillars, principles and approaches laid out in the document of the Coalition for Food Security in Ethiopia. In the third section the longer-term consequences of resettlement are discussed in relation to what happened to the 1980s resettlers. In the fourth section resettlement is considered as a process involving three phases: first, the planning and preparations; second, the move and conditions of reception; third, creating sustainable conditions. For each of the phases and aspects involved, suggestions are put forward on the basis of past and current experience for improving future resettlement planning and practice. The final section returns to the questions raised in the introduction and makes a case for an alternative more participatory, efficient and sustainable model within a broader migration framework.

The policy shift: from rejection to an integral part of the food security strategy

The EPRDF opposed resettlement during its armed struggle and reaffirmed this position once in power. However, within a decade a gradual shift in policy took place.

With the increasing numbers facing food insecurity in the early 2000s, resettlement came to be considered not only a potentially viable option, but even a necessary aspect and crucial component of food security. Resettlement had been alluded to in key policy documents, notably the National Food Security Strategy (1996), the Second Five-Year Development Plan (1999), the Federal Food Security Strategy (FDRE 2002a), the Sustainable Development and Poverty Reduction Programme (SDPRP), Ethiopia's first Poverty Reduction Strategy (PRS) (FDRE 2002b) and the Rural Development Policy and Strategies (MoFED 2003).

The SDPRP mentions the need for resettlement in the context of alleviating pressure on drought-prone areas and developing areas with uncultivated land. Under the section 'Proper Use of Land' the document states that: 'Voluntary resettlement programmes can also be used to alleviate land shortages as well as helping to develop hitherto uncultivated lands' (FDRE 2002b: 54). The document adds: 'Resettling people from drought-prone areas to areas where there is land and adequate rainfall is a strategy that would help realize the objective of food security quite expeditiously in the medium and long term' (*ibid.*: 56). This view was said to have come out of *wereda* and regional consultations. Implicit in this shift in policy is the idea that what was wrong with the Derg resettlement was the coercion and hasty and badly planned implementation. In other words it was not resettlement as such but the way it was carried out which was considered faulty. The SDPRP concluded: 'The main defect of the Derg's settlement programme was that it was not voluntary. The other shortcoming was that it was done hastily and was not integrated with regional development efforts and programmes' (*ibid.*:57). Another major criticism was that resettling people across regions created inter-ethnic conflict; it was therefore decided that the new settlement programmes should be conducted within rather than across regions. However, beyond general statements there was no clearly stated framework, specification of regions, numbers of settlers, modalities, timeframe or costing on the agenda till 2003, when resettlement suddenly became a high priority for the government.

From mid-2002 the serious drought affecting millions of people led the government to rethink its food security strategy. In June 2003 the government held a high-level workshop with donors on food security and resettlement at which the figure of 2.2 million people to be resettled in three years was raised. There was concern among donors, notably the European Union and USAID, at the large predetermined scale and short timeframe (Lind and Jalleta 2005). The World Bank suggested an alternative incentives-based model focusing on enhancing food security through improved access to land by providing infrastructure, access to land with secure tenure and grants to stimulate labour mobility. In July a joint technical group involving members of government and donors was formed, which incorporated some aspects of the World Bank design and produced a report by September on urgent food security actions. This was developed into the New Coalition for Food Security in Ethiopia (NCFSE) report which was presented to donors at a workshop in December 2003. Volume II was dedicated to the Voluntary Resettlement Programme. Resettlement was justified on the grounds that millions were facing food insecurity and even in good years many were unable to feed their families throughout the year, whereas there was underutilized land in the west and southwest. It was argued that as a result of the drought affecting 14 million people, some in the worst-hit areas were moving spontaneously into forests and national parks, which may not improve their own or the nation's welfare. The proposal retained the figure of resettling 2.2 million people or 440,000 households in four Regions[3] over three years.[4]

By the time the NCFSE document had been produced, 45,000 households had already been resettled in 2002/3 in three regions in a 'pilot' phase and were said to be able to establish better livelihoods (NCFSE 2003b:1). To administer the Food Security Programme of which resettlement was one component the Food Security Coordination Bureau (FSCB) was established at federal level under the Ministry of Agriculture and Rural Development along with regional offices (MoARD 2004), although the Disaster Prevention and Preparedness Agency (DPPA) also has Settlement Programme Desks at regional level in Tigray (Fosse 2006).

Unlike the SDPRP, the second PRS, the Plan for Accelerated and Sustained Development to End Poverty (PASDEP), has a specific section on resettlement as part of the food security programme. Resettlement is justified on the grounds that 'a large portion of the population has lost the capacity to be productive mainly due to land degradation and high population pressure, while at the same time Ethiopia has a considerable amount of land currently underutilized but still suitable for farm activities' (MoFED 2006: 95). The figure of 2.2 million people or 440,000 households is mentioned, along with the report that by the end of 2004/5 50 percent had been resettled. However, rather than within three years it was suggested that the rest would be resettled by the end of the PASDEP period (2010) at a cost of 1.2 billion *birr* (US$115 million). The PASDEP acknowledged that some problems were encountered in the early implementation especially in the first year, but suggested that the majority of settlers had become self-sufficient with improved livelihoods and that the programme had proved to be a reliable alternative ensuring food security and would therefore be expanded to accommodate as many settlers as possible. However, changes in the planning suggest a reduction of numbers, with no further resettlement in Tigray and very little in Oromia, with a continuation in Amhara and an increase in SNNPR.[5]

The PASDEP First Annual Progress Report for 2005/06, produced in June 2007 (MoFED 2007a) noted that 149,000 households had been resettled and that there was some 'underperformance' in 2005/6, with a little over 15,000 households resettled in three regions instead of the planned 30,000, one of the reasons being delay in preparatory work on the newly identified resettlement sites. The PASDEP Second Annual Progress Report for 2006/07, produced in December 2007 gave a slightly higher figure for 2006 of 28,794 households resettled, which was 50 percent of the annual target (MoFED 2007b). The overall target of resettling a further 291,000 households was retained to meet the total of 440,000 (MoFED 2007a: 36,98). The Ministry of Agriculture and Rural Development Food Security Coordination Bureau's review of food security produced in July 2007 noted that a major concern was 'graduation' i.e. reaching the stage when settlers no longer need basic support. According to the report 88 percent had graduated. Difficulties in the initial years were 'largely attributed to spontaneous movement of settlers in Oromiya Region', which was seen as a reflection of the voluntary nature of the programme and which was addressed by the government with donor support, notably to deal with malnutrition. The report concluded that 'these problems have now become things of the past' (MoARD 2007:6).

In conclusion, it seems that resettlement, which was viewed negatively in the early 1990s, given the injustices, coercion, suffering and failure of the Derg resettlement, began to be considered as an option to promote food security and development in policy documents from the mid-1990s, and general planning began from 2000. The following factors may have had some role in this shift: (i) increasing population resulting in land-holdings reaching a viability threshold in some areas; (ii) a growing awareness of the limitations of potential for land redistribution: (iii) a sense that redistributions affect tenure security; (iv) problems facing the peasantry as land-holdings reach critically low levels; (v) a sense that the extension programme has not solved the livelihood problems in drought-prone areas; (vi) a regional and local awareness of some spontaneous resettlement; and (vii) requests for voluntary resettlement by destitute farmers. This last factor is related to the previous ones and it is noteworthy that consultations at the *wereda* and regional level in the context of the drawing up of a poverty reduction strategy brought this issue to the forefront. However, it was the context of drought and food insecurity in 2002 that triggered a change in gear. By mid-2002 resettlement became a top priority agenda for government in spite of donor misgivings, as occurred in 1985. Despite the major differences in circumstances, there are similarities related to the pervasive logic of dealing with drought by finding more lasting solutions of exploiting less intensively used areas. The need for purposive and lasting action is therefore arguably a driving force pushing for rapid emergency resettlement rather than a gradual and carefully planned approach. The costing of resettlement to be borne largely by the federal government at 75 per cent built in a strong incentive for regions and especially receiving *weredas*, whose contribution was limited to 5 percent, to host resettlement programmes.

Resettlement planning and trends in the Regional states

Regarding regional planning, the earliest initiatives were in Amhara Region and the best planning was carried out in Oromia. In Amhara the process began in mid-2000 with resettlement planning seen as a means of resolving food insecurity, and it gained urgency with the emergence of a so-called Internally Displaced Persons' (IDPs) crisis by the end of the year. The Region was concerned that there were 2.5 million food-insecure vulnerable people in 48 *weredas*, and considered resettlement as a necessary part of a food security strategy. In June 2000 a reconnaissance survey was carried out by the Region's Food Security Coordination Office, which identified three *weredas*: Metemma, Tsegedie Armachio and Dangla, and areas within them for potential resettlement sites. In the meantime in April, June and December 2000 there were clashes in Gidda Kiremu *wereda* in East Wellega Zone of Oromia Region, between Oromo and settlers who had been resettled there from Northern Ethiopia in the mid-1980s.[6] By December some 12,000 former settlers in about 4,200 households had congregated in West Gojjam Zone of Amhara Region in an emergency relief camp outside Bure town.

In December 2000 the Region's Food Security Programme Coordination Office (FSPCO) held a meeting with the Ethiopian Society of Sociology Social Workers and Anthropologists (ESSSWA) in Addis Ababa and a workshop was organized to discuss resettlement in Bahr Dar in February 2001 (Seyoum 2004). In March 2001 the Region's FSPCO organized a six-day mission to Metemma *Wereda*, with European Union representatives visiting proposed resettlement areas. The team noted a range of constraints relating to roads, water, health, livestock and natural resources, and recommended a gradual approach with settlement villages not exceeding 150 households; it stressed the need to respect the rights of the local Gumuz people, and concluded that further studies by development experts were needed. The initial plan of the Region was to resettle a total of 3,300 households, assumed to represent some 15,000 people (Vivero and Beernaert 2001). However, the IDP crisis in Bure required a hasty solution and the first resettlement in the Region involving 12,000 resettlers from Bure was carried out in April 2001 in the lowland site of Jawe in Dangla *Wereda* of Awi Zone of Amhara Region (Getu 2005, Tesfaye 2007).[7] Amhara Region increased the plan for 2003 to 20,000 households assumed to comprise 100,000 people, and resettlement began in February 2003. A two-months study suggested a figure of 40,400 households to be resettled in 2004 in North Gonder Zone, but this figure was increased to 80,000 at a conference of officials in October 2003 (Zelalem 2005: 69-70).

In Oromia planning started in December 2000 and the Food Security Coordination Office (FSCO) approached the UK Department for International Development (DfID) for advice and assistance to study the feasibility of resettlement. A consultancy in March 2001 suggested the need for a more in-depth study. The FSCO carried out its own study in July suggesting a figure of over 25,000 households or over 146,000 people to be resettled (OFSPCO 2001) and asked for further assistance from DfID. The School of Geography of the University of Leeds therefore carried out a study in January and February 2002 followed by a workshop in August leading to a final report in October 2002 (RSO 2002). This thorough report investigated 31 potential resettlement sites, rejected seven as not having enough land or moisture or requiring uneconomical inputs, and three as requiring further detailed studies, and divided the rest into four categories: (i) five sites with potential for immediate resettlement under rain-fed crop husbandry; (ii) six sites for possible eventual resettlement if preconditions are met; (iii) five sites viable only with sustainable irrigation; and (iv) five sites in which resettlement would be part of a planned frontier expansion. The report considered four types of resettlement: (i) in-fill resettlement under rainfed agriculture; (ii) in-fill resettlement under irrigation; (iii) resettlement on former state farms; and (iv) frontier expansion, and divided the sites into six immediate-priority sites and 14 second-priority ones. The study also proposed three models of resettlement: (i) assisted community-led resettlement involving the most basic level of government support; (ii) local authority-coordinated in-fill schemes with an intermediate level of government support; and (iii) government-led river valley settlement requiring a higher level of support and investment.

In Oromia too, 'spontaneous' movement mainly from Harerge to Bale created an impetus and trigger for planned resettlement. In Mana Angetu *Wereda* in Bale Zone, settlers were estimated to amount to over 1,000 households in 2000, and had reached 12,000 at the beginning of 2002 and 33,000 by the end of the year. They came as a result of adverse conditions in Harerge, including land shortage, recurrent drought and environmental degradation. Settlers were also attracted by success stories of earlier migrants in 1995, some 500 of whom obtained land and were given food and medical supplies by the authorities for two years. It was also suggested that they were hoping to gain access to land before others came or before they were resettled further away. A number of NGOs became involved in providing emergency assistance to the IDPs (RSO 2002; Abiy 2004).

Planning began in Tigray in 2001 with a pre-feasibility study in parts of the Western Zone by the integrated food security desk. The study considered potential areas as well as possible constraints. The latter included that the areas are used for free grazing and watering of livestock, a practice of farmers migrating seasonally to plough land in the lowlands called *wofri zemed,* that the settlements are close to a wildlife reserve and the Eritrean border raising possible conflict and security risks, and that there is a shortage of infrastructure (Fosse 2005:56) Resettlement was carried out on a small scale in Tigray starting with a pilot project near Badime in 2002; by June 2003 some 15,000 had been resettled in 14 sites in the lowlands of Kafta Humera Zone, near the western border town of Humera , and about 15,000 people were moved in 2005 from all five zones in Tigray (Hammond and Bezaeit 2004; Fosse 2005). Planning in the Southern Region and Beni-Shangul-Gumuz was limited and as in Tigray did not involve donor support. In the Southern Region resettlement was postponed till 2004 except in Wolayta Zone, where it began in 2003 and 618 were resettled in six *weredas* by June (Wolde-Selassie 2003; Tranquilli 2004). The planned resettlement was not carried out in Beni-Shangul-Gumuz.

Over the period 2002-7 a total of a little under 194,000 households have been resettled, representing 44 percent of the target. Whereas this represents about three-quarters of the targets for Tigray and Oromia, it is less than a third of the targets for Amhara and SNNPR. In regional terms over the five years it is striking that resettlement was stopped in Tigray from 2005; in Oromia there was a drop in 2005 after criticisms of resettlement in 2004 but a resumption in 2006, when 43 percent of the annual target was reached. In Amhara there was a big increase in 2004 but a drop in 2005 and 2006 when there were fewer volunteers, and 48 percent of the annual target was met. In SNNPR there was an increase in 2003 but a drop in 2004, with slight increases in 2005 and 2006, representing 88 percent of the annual target (MoFED 2007b:57).

Table 11.1: Number of households planned and resettled 2002-7

Region	Target	2002/3 (1995)	2003/4 (1996)	2004/5 (1997)	2005/6 (1998)	2006/7 (1999)	2002-7 1995-9	% of target
Oromia	100,000	19,432	31,641	6,845	3,035	14,931	75,884	75.9
Amhara	200,000	6,298	5,639	31,918	8,505	7,203	59,563	29.8
Tigray	40,000	6,058	11,810	12,089	0	0	29,957	74.9
SNNPR	100,000	971	14,184	2,740	3,567	6,660	28,122	28.1
Total	**440,000**	**32,759**	**63,274**	**53,592**	**15,107**	**28,794**	**193,526**	**44.0**

Source: MoARD (2007); MoFEDb (2007)

Government figures have concentrated on the number of households rather than the number of people resettled. This is because in some regions at some points male household heads were resettled on their own with the family members assumed to join subsequently. However, even when family members were resettled together it seems that the average number was smaller than in the home areas with an overall average of about 3.3. members per household, suggesting a strategy of some members remaining behind.[8]

Table 11.2 based on figures collated by UNOCHA up to the end of 2005 suggests that there are regional variations; the lowest average household sizes were in Tigray with 1.4 members per household, followed by Amhara with 2.1 members, and the highest was in Oromia with an average of 5.3 members.

Oromia Region had considered resettling some 25,000 households in its prefeasibility study (OFSPCO 2001). The study produced by Leeds University suggested a figure of some 27,000 households. Of these some 22,000 households were in sites that did not require irrigation; a further 3,000 households could be added with irrigation in Bale Zone and some 2,000 additional households in West Shewa Zone in areas unoccupied by investors.

Table 11.2: Number of resettler households, family members and household size by Region

Region	households	family members	total members	household size
Amhara	53,090	56,848	109,938	2.1
Oromia	60,579	259,622	320,201	5.3
Tigray	32,129	12,636	44,765	1.4
SNNPR	14,444	41,289	55,733	3.9
Total	**160,242**	**370,395**	**530,637**	**3.3**

Source: UNOCHA Resettlement Monitoring Matrix, December 2005

Table 11.3: Proposed and actual resettlement in Oromia Region

Bale Zone	Proposed	Actual 2003-5	Proportion
Agarfa	1455	1573	1.08
Goro	923	133	0.14
Berberie	7351	662	0.09
Mena Angetu	9243	17	0.00
Other *weredas*		1155	
Sub-total Bale	**18,972**	**3,540**	0.19
West Shewa			
Ameya	2339		0.00
Nono	224	1488	6.64
Dano	1584	1824	1.15
Sub-total West Shewa	**4,147**	**3,312**	0.80
West Welega			
Hawa Welel	800	7979	9.97
Gawo Dale	1200	1956	1.63
Dale Sedi	132	660	5.00
Lalo Kile	300	761	2.54
Other *weredas*		4488	
Sub-total West Welega	**2,432**	**15,844**	6.51
Illubabor Zone			
Gatchi-Borocha	2200	3482	1.58
Other *Weredas*		17713	
Sub-total Illubabor	**2,200**	**21,195**	9.63
East Wellega Zone		**11,865**	
Jimma Zone		**4645**	
Guji Zone		**178**	
Oromia Total	**27,751**	**60,579**	**2.18**

Source: RSO 2002, Tables 2 and 6.

In practice the total number of households resettled by the end of 2005 was over 60,000, representing more than twice the numbers suggested by the study, and by 2007 the number was over 71,000. The resettlement was also carried out in zones not included in the study, notably East Wellega and Jimma zones, accounting for over 16,000 households or 27 percent of the total. Within the zones that were suggested, the proportions resettled were significantly lower than those suggested in Bale and West Shewa, but six times higher in West Wellega and almost ten times higher in Illubabor.

Resettlement practice in relation to policy guidelines

The NCFSE document provided useful principles for undertaking resettlement, although some resettlement had already been carried out during the previous year. The following section considers the 2000s resettlement on the basis of recent MA research and the FSS case studies in relation to the pillars, principles and approaches laid out in the document. The four pillars are that resettlement must be: (i) voluntary; (ii) on underutilized land; (iii) in consultation with host communities; and (iv) carried out with proper preparation.

VOLUNTARY RESETTLEMENT

A major improvement in principle of the current resettlement is its aspirations to be voluntary. Settlers can return to their homeland if they are unhappy and will be eligible to receive the assistance they were receiving before they left. They are to be guaranteed land-use rights for their holdings in their original area for 3 years (NCFSE 2003b:5). The studies confirm that the resettlement has not involved direct coercion of the type for which the 1980s resettlement was criticized. However, the extent of voluntariness and ability to make real choices was constrained by four factors: (i) desperation resulting from increasing land shortage, drought and destitution; (ii) the idyllic picture presented of the resettlement sites and the exaggerated promises of support; (iii) warnings in some areas that food aid would not continue in drought-prone highland areas; and (iv) social pressures from peer groups, kin, neighbours, and community members often affected the decision-making of individuals. The resettlement can therefore be characterized as having elements of indirect compulsion and inducement if not outright coercion. There were also allegations in some cases that the land of departed settlers was being registered for redistribution. After the three-year period settlers in some cases were asked to produce 'clearance letters' from their place of origin in order to confirm their choice and officially register in the new settlement areas.

UNDER-UTILIZED LAND

The current resettlement planning started at a federal level, and involved regional and *wereda* administrations. Sites were selected based on initial surveying by regional and zonal experts, who consulted with local administrators and community representatives. This was done with more consideration than during the 1980s resettlement when some sites were selected in extreme haste with no planning whatsoever. However, there was limited time and resources for careful planning and assessment of land availability and existing uses. In some cases sites were selected hastily, new or alternative sites were added such as Qwara in Amhara Region, or much greater numbers were resettled than were proposed by the study teams, as happened in some sites, notably in Amhara and Oromia Regions. The theses and case studies therefore suggest that the availability of under-utilized land is questionable. In most cases the land selected was used either by local groups for grazing and forest resources, or by earlier resettlers or self-organized resettlers, notably former state-farm workers, who were evicted as illegal resettlers. Where land was not in intensive use for cultivation or grazing, the settlements have been established at the expense of rapidly dwindling forest reserves, which are often used by local communities for coffee and honey production.

CONSULTATION WITH LOCAL COMMUNITIES

Consultation with local people took place at a local level with a view to obtaining their consent. However, this was generally restricted to attempting to persuade local communities to accept the resettlement and mobilize them to prepare for the resettlers' arrival by building shelters etc. Apart from one case where the local people wanted resettlers as a buffer against wildlife, the locals were generally not in favour of the resettlement and some even tried to oppose the idea when it was repeatedly presented to them at meetings. In some cases they argued that they had landless young people among them who should be given priority, and that the proposed settlement area was on land that was used for grazing and non-timber forest products. In one case in Tigray the local people had thus distributed land prior to the resettlers' arrival which was later taken away and redistributed to the resettlers.

Meetings were sometimes held with *Kebele* leaders, elders, or only with a section of the community. In some cases certain groups such as the Gumuz in Oromia and the Sidama in SNNPR were not consulted. In three sites in Oromia resettlers on former state farms were evicted on the grounds that they were illegal resettlers. In the three sites in SNNPR consent was either not requested, not obtained or only a section of the population agreed under pressure. The Sidama population in Humbo did not know about the resettlement, in Bilate they complained to no avail, and in Salamago among the Bodi pastoralists only the elders reluctantly gave their consent as they felt they had no option. Where objections were voiced, sometimes at repeated meetings, such as in Qwara in Amhara and Qeto in Oromia these were overruled and the resettlement went ahead regardless.

In some sites in each of the Regions displacement of local people occurred on the grounds that the local people were not sedentary cultivators, or were illegal resettlers or migrants. In several cases, sites were located on land left fallow or used for grazing by pastoralist groups, notably in SNNPR, close to or in forest reserves with wildlife particularly in Tigray and Amhara, or in previous state farms or earlier settlement areas, notably in Oromia. In no cases was compensation provided. Broader dislocatory effects included settlements affecting access to water points and forest products, notably coffee and bee-hives. In almost all the sites tensions developed over the use of land, water, forests and grazing resources, and conflicts have occurred in eight of the eleven FSS study sites, resulting in incidents leading to deaths in two sites.

PREPARATIONS AND PROVISIONS

The guidelines emphasize the need for proper preparations. These can be considered in terms of recruitment and briefings in the sending areas, and preparations in resettlement areas notably of roads and access, shelter and housing, food and other provisions, water and sanitation, allocation of land and oxen, and health and education services.

Briefings in sending areas. Meetings were held in sending areas to inform communities about the resettlement option. The resettlement sites tended to be portrayed in ideal terms. Promises included two hectares of fertile land, a pair of oxen for cultivation, reasonable standard housing, adequate health and education services, up to three years of relief aid, agricultural inputs and in some cases irrigation. Some of these promises were not in the resettlement guidelines or had been misinterpreted at a local level or by resettlers. Nonetheless, differences between expectations and the reality of conditions in the resettlement sites were a major factor leading to significant numbers of resettlers leaving shortly after arrival and dissatisfaction among others. In particular, complaints included in some sites land shortage and conflicting claims by locals; provision of at best one hectare of land rather than two and one ox between two households; either temporary shelters or hastily built and poor quality houses; lowland diseases notably malaria and trypanosomiasis rendering ox-plough cultivation precarious; difficulties of access in the rainy season with serious consequences for the provision of rations and heath care; no or limited schooling in often crowded conditions; rations limited to grain, with oil and supplementary feeding either not available or reduced after a short period; delays in rations initially and during the rains, and stoppage after eight months before large numbers of resettlers had become food-secure.

Roads and access. Feeder roads existed or were cleared to all the sites. However, some are only dry-weather and the sites are cut off during the rains with serious implications, particularly in the first rainy season, for providing timely rations, and health care referral.

Shelter and housing. Local people were mobilized to build shelters or houses for resettlers as was the case in the 1980s resettlement. However, in some sites there was inadequate shelter and in several cases resettlers were dismayed to find that they had to build houses after their arrival. Even where houses had been built, as in the earlier resettlement, these were often of poor quality and had to be rebuilt.

Food rations. Food aid was distributed in the form of 15-20 kg of grain per person per month (wheat, maize or sorghum) and in some cases 0.5 kg of cooking oil. In a few sites additional rations included beans, sweet potatoes, peppers, salt and soap. In other sites 20-50 *birr* (US$2-5) cash was provided. However, in some cases food had not been pre-positioned prior to the resettlers' arrival, and the local population had to be mobilized to provide food for up to a week. There were also cases of interruptions during the rainy season due to roads being cut off, leading to serious malnutrition, and supplementary feeding was either lacking or interrupted in most sites. There was some variation in type, amounts and duration of rations even within regions. In most sites rations were stopped after eight months. However, in one site they continued for two years. Resettlers often sold some rations to purchase other basic foods to vary and spice the diet, and in some cases food types were different from the staples to which the resettlers were accustomed.

Other provisions. Resettlers were provided with utensils such as jerry cans, pots, plates and cups, textiles mainly in the form of blankets, bed-nets against mosquitoes, and in one case clothes and locally made shoes, and farm tools including hoes, sickles and axes, and in some cases seed and fertiliser. There was variation in amounts, and some complaints were voiced about distribution on a household basis, especially of one blanket and bed-net for the entire family, and about the quality of some of the utensils which were said to wear out quickly.

Water and sanitation. Water sources include rivers, springs, and wells. In several sites distance from rivers and reduced flow in the dry season are constraints, and use of water by animals as well as humans for drinking and washing presents potential health risks. Where there are pumps several of these have not been repaired or have fallen into disuse leading to queues forcing people to walk further to rivers.

Land allocation. Resettlers had been told about being allocated two hectares of cleared farmland. In some cases resettlers had to clear new land, and in general obtained a maximum of one hectare owing to land scarcity. In other cases there were complaints about water-logging and that the land distribution did not take account of family size or land quality. Most significantly there were in most cases prior claims to the land and disputes sometimes led to conflict with local people who tried to defend their claims.

Oxen. Settlers were either provided with an ox for one or two households or given credit to buy one. There were complaints particularly where only one ox was provided for two households since four households had therefore to form a team to plough. Trypanosomiasis and other livestock diseases present serious challenges to effective cultivation; some settlers who feared losing cattle sold oxen after the harvest and had to buy them at a higher cost the following ploughing season.

Health and nutrition. Health posts are available in the sites, and were either already in place or were built by local people. However, in the initial period relatively high child malnutrition was reported in some sites, particularly where and when supplementary feeding was not available, limited, interrupted during the rains, or withdrawn. The health posts suffer from limited facilities, staff, rooms, equipment and medicine. Lowland diseases, in particular malaria, despite spraying and due to limited bednets, and kalazar present serious challenges to adaptation. Reaching clinics and hospitals for referral is a problem in sites cut off during the rainy season, leading to severe malnutrition in some sites especially in the first year. In one site in SNNPR the health post was withdrawn after the bulk of the resettlers left. In one site in Oromia local people were not allowed access to the health services provided for settlers. There has not been any significant attention to family planning issues or the threat of HIV/AIDS in any of the sites.

Schools and education. Schools are available in most sites. However, in a few cases these are distant, in one case in SNNPR eight kilometres away involving four hours walking. In many cases the schools are crowded, with high student-teacher ratios and up to 150 students per class in one case in Oromia. In a few sites students still learn under trees or temporary shelters. In one site the host community's children do not attend the school for settlers, and in another the schools attended by local children have become crowded due to additional resettlers' children.

Principles and approaches and their implementation

The NCFSE document also outlined principles and approaches, the most important of which were intra-regional resettlement; environmental concern; the development process; partnership; self-help and cost-sharing; transparency; an iterative process; capacity-building; self-reliance; income and employment creation; community management; and minimum infrastructure.

INTRA-REGIONAL RESETTLEMENT

A major principle of the current resettlement has been intra-regional resettlement with a view to avoiding linguistic/ethnic differences between settler and host populations. As planned, resettlement has been intra-regional, which has to some extent reduced ethnic variation. However, in all four regions some ethnic, cultural and/or religious differences exist between the highlands and lowlands. Among the case studies in Amhara there are Gumuz and Agaw populations as well as Amhara; in Oromia Region there are Gumuz and Amhara as well as Oromo; in Tigray there are Amhara and Kunama as well as Tigraway. The most obvious cases of completely different ethnicities and identities are in the SNNPR where Kambata were resettled among the Kaficho, Wolayta among the Sidama and Konso among the Bodi pastoralists (Asfaw 2005; Mellesse 2005; Feseha 2006). In terms of religion in Oromia Muslims from Harerge were resettled among Christians in Wellega. More significantly, the somewhat greater ethnic/religious homogeneity of the current resettlement has not *in itself* avoided tensions and conflicts since these are largely over resources, notably agricultural and grazing land, forests and non-timber products, and water points. The intra-regional nature of the current resettlement has therefore not prevented the eruption of conflicts between settler and local communities, and the process has resulted in further marginalization of lowland pastoralist groups, as well as earlier migrants and resettlers.

ENVIRONMENTAL CONCERN

The need for environmental care and conservation associated with resettlement is clear. The resettlement has led to considerable deforestation for land clearing, housing construction, and firewood, resulting in soil erosion, reduction of bio-diversity and potential climate change. It is of particular concern that some of the sites were selected in or very near to, some of the few remaining forest areas in the country, resulting in the virtual disappearance of certain indigenous tree species and wildlife. Riverine forests in many areas have been adversely affected. Local people have also expressed serious worries about the tendency for resettlers to fell large trees and produce charcoal as a survival or business strategy. Uses of forest areas by local people for non-timber forest products such as coffee and honey have not been respected and these areas were often handed over to the settlers without compensation. Where indigenous natural-resource management systems exist, they have also been adversely affected. No natural-resource conservation measures or joint management systems between resettlers and hosts were reported in any of the sites, and forest and wildlife protection measures are almost non-existent.

DEVELOPMENT PROCESS

The guidelines suggest the need to promote not just food security but marketable surpluses to improve livelihoods. The studies show that in the first year most settler households had difficulty in achieving food security and that the stoppage of rations, generally after eight months, had a detrimental effect on confidence, and placed stress on the more food-secure who had to support those who had not attained food security. Female-headed households, the elderly, weak, disabled and those suffering from chronic and/or lowland diseases have often faced particular difficulties. However, certain households have been able to succeed much better than others, and have attained food security faster than in previous resettlements. This has been due mainly to resources brought from home areas, notably in the case of settlers from Harerge in Oromia. Some have been able to invest in increasing production through share-cropping and have focused on cash crops, notably sesame. The more successful are generally male-headed households, with good social capital and linkages with the community through informal associations, as well as with administrators and with local people and investors. They have been able to purchase livestock, especially oxen to plough with, and some have been involved in additional agricultural production through share-cropping or rental and/or trade. Many have improved their quality of life and wellbeing, through purchasing livestock, consumer goods, household equipment and better clothing and being able to afford better medical care and education. A few have even been able to group together to purchase grinding mills.

PARTNERSHIP

Partnership between government, donors, NGOs, private enterprise, hosts and re-settlers was advocated. However, partnership was limited. Most of the costs of resettlement were borne by the government. International organizations, donors and NGOs have played quite a limited role. A few international organizations such as WFP and UNICEF have been providing support through their regional and sectoral programmes. Some donors such as USAID and the EU have been involved in monitoring activities. The only NGO actively involved was MSF-Holland in health care in one region. There seems to have been a mutual lack of trust on both sides. The government's partners have not been forthcoming in providing funding, and access to resettlement sites has been relatively restricted. A UNDP project to provide support for food-security activities was under consideration. Partnership with investors has also been advocated and in some areas settlers have been working as labourers on large farms. However, there have been some tensions over land, due to unclear demarcation of which land is for settlement and which for investors. There have also been some complaints by administrators about settlers working as labourers rather than on the land allocated to them. Partnership with local communities has also been quite limited. Local communities were mobilized to construct houses for settlers and in some cases provided them with food for up to a week after their arrival. Some settlers work for local people or are involved in share-cropping with them. Market exchanges are also common and have benefited local communities, notably due to increases in livestock and grain prices. There have been some improvements in infrastructure and services. However, local health and education services have been stretched in some cases, and access for locals has been restricted in others. The most serious problems are, however, over land and other resources, notably forests, grazing areas, water points, coffee and bee-hives. This has led to tensions in all sites, conflicts in many sites, and clashes in a few. Social and cultural relations and integration between local people and settlers at individual, household and community levels are fairly limited.

COST-SHARING AND SELF-HELP

The NCFSE document estimates the cost of resettling 440,000 households at 1,867 million *birr* (US$217 million). The funds were to be allocated within the federal budget for food security. Regions were to draw on the funds according to their demonstrated readiness to implement and match them with a portion of regional funds. The federal contribution was set at 75 percent, the Regions at 20 percent and the host *weredas* at 5 percent. This provides significant incentives for regions and *weredas* to become involved in the resettlement programme. The guidelines also stress the need for resettlers to avoid dependence and to become involved in the resettlement process through their labour. This was clearly evidenced by the fact that resettlers have had to build or rebuild their houses, and have often had to clear land, although in some cases tractor services were provided. The costs have been borne largely by the government, the local communities and the settlers themselves with limited donor and external agency involvement. Some resources were diverted from existing programmes and reallocations from sending to receiving areas were planned. The programme relied on a campaign approach with the risk of absorbing and diverting energies and resources from ongoing and planned activities.

TRANSPARENCY

The guidelines stress the need for adherence to rules and for active information to be available to partners. In fact the haste and campaign approach which have characterized the resettlement process have hindered keeping to some of the rules set out in the guidelines. An important provision in the current resettlement, and an improvement on previous practice, was to allow delegations to be sent to visit selected resettlement areas. However, the delegates tended to be taken to model sites which were not necessarily those to which their communities were sent, resulting in complaints, and in some cases the moving of resettlers happened without visits or started even before the delegates had returned. The consent and involvement of host communities tended to be nominal, minimal, and in some cases non-existent. Genuine participation was hampered by serious concerns about resource alienation and competition, leading to conflict and clashes. Relations between the government and its partners have been characterized by a degree of mutual mistrust which has hampered collaboration and potential resourcing of the resettlement process.

AN ITERATIVE PROCESS

The need to learn and adapt the resettlement practice on the basis of learning from experience had been emphasized. The resettlement process was carried out on a large scale with a fairly standardized design rather than on an experimental basis with a flexible and regionally and locally differentiated approach. The government carried out reviews after the first year which was considered to be a 'pilot' year. Although significant changes to the resettlement planning and implementation do not seem to have been introduced in the second year, there was a reduction in scale, particularly in Amhara Region which may be accounted for by high return rates and the limited interest of volunteers. Most of the departures in all the sites took place in the initial weeks after arrival. These were largely due to; (i) mismatches between expectations and conditions in the sites; (ii) high initial morbidity and mortality due to malaria and other health risks; (iii) harshness of the physical lowland environment to which highlanders were not used; (iv) conflicts with locals and security concerns; (v) relocation to other resettlement sites due to insufficient or poor quality land; and (vi) unfavourable comparison of the resettlement sites with the home areas. In the FSS study sites departures ranged from 5 percent to 87 percent. In seven sites they were above a fifth of the settlers, and in five sites above a quarter, including all three sites in SNNPR and the one in Amhara Region. In three sites departures represented over 40 percent. Although a few of those who left returned later, the majority did not. However, currently it seems that most of those who have stayed wish to remain, as evidenced by hard work on farmland, investment in livestock, construction of better houses, and moving families to settlements in cases where the men had moved there first. Nonetheless, fears of conflict with local people are a serious concern in some sites, notably in the SNNPR. It is noteworthy that in 2006 Oromia and Tigray decided on a moratorium on further resettlement and a consolidation of existing settlements.[9]

SELF-RELIANCE

Breaking the 'dependency syndrome' and fostering self-reliance have been important aims of the programme. In this respect most of those settlers who have remained are on the path to self-reliance and may no longer need support unless they are faced with drought years, which does happen in the lowland environment. However, self-reliance will depend on the ability to keep oxen for cultivation which requires better veterinary support. Moreover, sustainable self-reliance will require resolving conflicts with local people and developing positive political, economic, social and cultural relations between settlers and hosts.

INCOME AND EMPLOYMENT CREATION

The guidelines stress the need to promote not just agricultural production but also off-farm activities and small businesses. The evidence regarding successful cases shows that a number of settlers in all sites have been able to engage in trade and become relatively prosperous in a short time. Some have been able to invest in productive assets, notably livestock and particularly oxen, and a few have even purchased grinding mills, and have been able to build houses with corrugated iron sheet roofs and set up shops not just in the settlements but also in local towns. They have also been able to gain access to more land and increase their production and productivity by hiring labour or through share-cropping, and have succeeded in increasing their income and wellbeing significantly through the production of cash crops, notably sesame. This positive development has been made possible by settlers bringing capital with them or obtaining finance from produce on farms in their home areas, particularly in the case of settlers from Harerge in Oromia, suggesting that linkages between areas of origin and resettlement have a positive impact.

COMMUNITY MANAGEMENT

The guidelines suggest that settler communities should be 'in the driver's seat' and be actively involved in planning, implementation and monitoring. However, to date the resettlement has been been characterized by a top-down and campaign approach in which decision-making has tended to come from above. There has been only limited community management. In ten of the eleven FSS case-study sites the resettlers are under local administrations run by the host communities and are therefore not adequately represented in the political process. The limited community participation is further exacerbated because settlers even within the same site come from different areas and from a surprisingly large number of different *weredas* and *kebele* administrations within the same zones. They therefore need time to get to know each other and develop trust before they can work together effectively for joint development. Furthermore, mistrust and tensions with local populations have also hampered effective joint community management, particularly of natural resources.

MINIMUM INFRASTRUCTURE

The guidelines suggest that the infrastructure should be similar to that in the areas of origin and that there should not be a deterioration in service delivery. There is some variation in comparisons between areas of origin and resettlement partly because some resettlers even within the same site come from more remote areas than others. However, in many cases the resettlement areas are fairly remote and the infrastructure in term of roads and communications is less developed than in the home areas in the highlands, and inaccessibility during the rainy season is a major constraint in some sites, particularly for health referral. Lack of facilities, personnel and drugs is compounded by lowland diseases, and settlers have to adapt to new environments in addition to coping with other health problems. The guidelines also suggest that infrastructure and service provision for host populations should not be inferior or be affected detrimentally by the arrival of settlers, and that the local population should be able to take advantage of facilities established for settlers on a fee-paying basis in order to avoid conflict from the start. In some cases the arrival of settlers has put a strain on existing health and education services, increasing student-teacher and patient-health worker ratios. There are also cases where local people have been denied access to health posts, schools and mills established for settlers. Access to certain resources, notably forests, rivers and water points, and grazing areas, has also been restricted for local people in some sites.

Longer-term consequences of resettlement: lessons from the 1980s

Resettlement is envisaged as a 'durable solution' in contrast to emergency food aid. However, in general not much thought goes into the longer-term effects and consequences. It is often assumed that resettlers will require some initial assistance in the short term, in particular with shelter, food aid until their first harvest, agricultural equipment and basic health and education services. After that it is assumed that they will 'graduate' and it is presumed that the problems will go away, and that the settlers will become self-sufficient and locally integrated. Most studies of resettlement are carried out in the early first few years and the impact after a decade or two is less often a subject of investigation.[10] In practice, resettlement often ends up being far more costly than was initially expected (Prunier 1988; Pankhurst 1992a) and settlers tend to require support for longer than was assumed.

In the case of the 1980s resettlement many of the changes that occurred in a decade and a half have been dramatic and largely unpredictable. The settlements are almost unrecognizable, not only in terms of the transformation of the physical layout, but also in terms of the changes in the material conditions of the settlers who have remained, in the ways they view themselves, and in the differences which emerged or became accentuated (Pankhurst 2002a; Wolde-Selassie 2002). An increasing proportion of the settlers have been born in the settlements or have little recollection of a previous homeland. This is likely to bring about a significant change as the majority begin to be those whose experiences are grounded and rooted in the realities of life in the resettlement villages.

The following ten issues emerging from a longer-term view of resettlement need consideration: (i) political changes in the conditions of resettlement; (ii) changing environmental conditions in settlements and home areas; (iii) impacts of the settlements on the livelihoods of local people; (iv) impacts of settlers' surplus on the local economy; (v) relations between settlers and local people; (vi) provision of services and relations with the government; (vii) impacts on the settlement environment; (viii) relations between the settlers and their areas of origin; (ix) inter-generational issues; and (x) investment in new livelihoods and changing identities.

(i) Political changes in the context of resettlement. Already in the late 1980s changes in the political context had fundamentally altered the dynamics of resettlement in Ethiopia. A move away from collectivization led to a gradual shift from complete dependence on cooperative production towards a mixed economy with more scope for private enterprise. Over the years settlers were gradually allowed to have access to more individually managed plots of land beyond their household garden plots. There was also a welcome move away from major reliance on alienating mechanized agriculture,[11] towards the more familiar use of oxen, although the trypanosomiasis challenge in many cases limited the potential for oxen traction, and remains a serious threat to the viability of many settlements. In social terms the greater freedom also had a significant positive effect, notably in that settlers were able to organize their work and social events rather than having work norms set by the cooperative. They were able to build churches and mosques and to celebrate religious occasions.

The defeat of the Derg in 1991 further radically altered the context of resettlement. The majority of settlers left the resettlement areas since there were no longer any controls on movement, and they feared that the context of insecurity would lead to reprisals against them. Indeed, attacks against settlers occurred repeatedly during this period, notably in the Metekel area. In the post-Derg period news that returnees had been given access to land in their home areas also encouraged many to leave. Those who returned before the change and/or before redistributions were carried out often gained access to land, whereas those who came later tended to join the ranks of the landless relying on share-cropping or wage labour unless relatives had been able to keep their land or they had connections to officials (Pankhurst 2002a). The picture regarding returnees is complex and this relates partly to their ambiguous legitimacies, which could be negotiated at a local level. On the one hand, they could be portrayed as victims of coerced resettlement, but on the other they could be branded as collaborators of Derg policies. How families fared depended in part on how they negotiated their ambivalent status, the degree of family support and their connections with those in power at the local level. However, many returnee settlers expressed disappointment with how they had been treated not only by local officials but even by close kin. It also seems that where a large proportion of the population left resettlement and returned together they had a better bargaining position.

In the 1990s further changes affected the political context of resettlement. The major impact was prompted by the regionalization policy and the delimitation of regions on an ethnic basis. In this context settlers coming from other regions were considered as not belonging and in some cases were victims of moves to expel them (Tesfaye 2007). A further consequence was that the language policy resulted in education being in regional languages. As a result, most settlers found that they needed to learn local languages to benefit from education, and there is some evidence of a reduced interest or investment in schooling. The land redistributions carried out in 1997 in Amhara Region also had an effect on settlers since some of the returnees were able to obtain access to some land. However, the pattern seems to have been uneven, and many settlers complained about not receiving enough land to survive. Moreover, in areas where redistributions were not carried out, settlers who arrived after the change have tended to be able to get access to land only through share-cropping, through special arrangements with relatives, through influence with officials or, in cases where land was returned to the *kebele* administration when a household head died without successors.

(ii) Changing environmental conditions in settlement and home areas. Patterns of settlers leaving resettlement areas were affected already in the late 1980s by their perceptions and reports from visitors about the environmental conditions and the extent of good rainfall or famine in the areas they came from (Pankhurst 1991). After the bulk of the settlers left around the time of the fall of the Derg, those who remained were able to have access to much larger amounts of land (up to 2 hectares). Although in the early 1990s there were a series of favourable years in the northern highlands, many returnee settlers were not able to get access to land, since their former holdings had been redistributed and they were too late to benefit from the redistributions. As a result, many settlers who had left the resettlement areas subsequently returned there. In the 1990s there were a number of localized drought years in the highlands (notably 1994, 1998 and especially 1999). This resulted in a tendency of some relatives of settlers and new migrants seeking to join them in the hope of benefiting from a share of the land. However, these returnees or new migrants were sometimes considered illegal immigrants or 'squatters' by the local authorities (Piguet and Dechassa 2004).

(iii) Impacts of the settlements on the livelihoods of local people. The potentially adverse effects of the settlers' presence on the livelihoods of local people had already been noted by Dessalegn (1988a) in the case of the Gumuz and have been highlighted by further studies (Wolde-Selassie 1997, 2002; Gebre 2003). In particular, the swidden form of cultivation practised by the Gumuz based on shifting agriculture allows for areas that have been cultivated to be left fallow and regenerate while new areas are cleared. The introduction of a high density of settlers with a more intensive form of land exploitation, and the clearing of large areas for fuelwood, had pushed the Gumuz and other lowland groups into withdrawing from the settlement areas, and their livelihoods have been compromised. Likewise, the clearing of forests has reduced the scope for game hunting, bee-keeping, collection of wild fruits and fishing. Similar findings have been reported for the Anywaa in Gambella (Kurimoto 2005) and the Berta in Assosa. Conflicts over coffee and bee-hives have also been noted in many contexts (Pankhurst 2002a).

(iv) Impacts of settlers' surplus on the local economy. From a situation of dependence on food aid, the settlers soon began to produce a surplus and the major problem they faced

was a trend of dramatic falls in the prices of crops, notably maize and sorghum, in the post-harvest period. Local markets were flooded and in the early days private traders were not allowed to purchase grain from settlers. More recently, the main limitation has been the ability of private traders to collect and transport the surplus produced by settlers, although this has been a source of lucrative trade from which some settlers have benefited as middlemen. In some cases settler traders have even been able to purchase sewing machines, mills or generators, and their activities have stimulated the growth of small towns.

(v) Relations between settlers and local people. Perhaps the area that is given least attention in resettlement planning, and is arguably the most important and crucial in terms of the longer-term prospects for resettlement, is relations between settlers and local people. Here the experience of how spontaneous settlement takes place provides useful lessons which could be considered in any resettlement planning (Assefa 1999; Berihun 1996). In general, spontaneous settlers seek to establish social relations with important people among the local population, who then become their patrons and who provide them with security and through whom they can gain access to land through share-cropping, lease, rental or other arrangements. In some cases such relations may be further developed through commensality, joint participation in social and religious events, involvement in each others' life-cycle events, through bond friendships, and occasionally through intermarriage, religion and ethnicity permitting. Tension between settlers and local people has tended to relate in the first instance to use of natural resources. Often disputes flare up in the context of markets where disagreements over exchange and the consumption of alcohol can lead to fights between individuals, which may rapidly escalate (Wolde-Selassie 2002). Resentment towards the settlers had already built up in some cases before their arrival, when administrators made local people build shelters for the settlers. The delimitation of areas of land, notably with access to rivers, and forests where coffee and wild products were obtained, as being part of the settlement areas exacerbated tensions.

In general the sphere of exchanges between settlers and local people in many settlement areas has tended to be restricted to economic exchanges in the market place. Initially settlers sold food aid and personal belongings such as jewellery in exchange for basic commodities such as food aid, salt, coffee, and spices. After their first harvest settlers began to sell crops and mainly sought to buy livestock. Gradually, as they began to become more established and produced more, they have been buying and selling a greater range of products, and a number of settlers have become involved as middlemen between settlers and local traders. In some cases a few settlers have become very successful and even wealthy, involved in longer-distance trade, renting houses in town and providing services on a larger scale. Their success has often generated a sense of resentment and envy on the part of local people, since the settlers are sometimes perceived or portrayed as having prospered at the expense of local people. Some settlers have reached agreements with local people to share-crop or lease additional land. In some cases relations between settlers and local people have gone beyond the economic to social and religious interaction. The building of joint religious edifices has been an important linkage between settlers and locals of the same religion in the case of Orthodox Christians and Muslims, and there are a few cases of settlers who have converted to local Protestant churches. However, further individual relations and intermarriages are rarer, at least in the larger settlement areas where most social relations tend to be within the settlements.

(vi) Provision of services and relations with government. The settlers were over-privileged in the early years after the 1985 resettlement and benefited from much greater assistance than the local population. Indeed, the services provided in terms of agriculture, health and other extension were greater than those available to the local population and sometimes even than the national average. However, this also had considerable negative effects for the settlers, since it allowed for greater control and the imposition of the resented collectivization. Nonetheless, the limited planning of integrated services severely hampered the potential for developing occasions and fora in which settlers and local people could meet, carry out joint activities, and move towards a better understanding and mutual respect. Moreover, the support settlers received was often not extended to local populations so that joint education and health care occurred in only a few cases. However, the level of support was gradually reduced and settlers began to pay taxes and lost their privileged status. The reduction in agricultural extension services had the advantage that settlers became freer to manage their own affairs, though the reduction in health-care support gave them a sense of having been abandoned by the government. Under the EPRDF there were attempts to integrate the settlers within the local structure, in terms of extension, health care and education. The education policy resulted in a situation where tuition was not in the settler children's mother tongue. This may have led to some opting out of education, and in some cases a focusing on church education carried out in Amharic.

(vii) Impacts on the settlement environment. The potentially negative effect of resettlement on the local environment has been highlighted in a number of studies (e.g. Alemneh 1990; Mengistu 2005). In many of the lowland areas where the resettlement was undertaken the soils tend to be fragile and subject to erosion, and the concentration of large numbers of people resulting in the clearing of land for cultivation and firewood has led to considerable deforestation with potentially irreversible negative consequences. In the lowlands, sites were selected in areas assumed to be 'virgin', but which were often used by indigenous peoples for shifting cultivation, thus not excessively exploiting the fragile soils. The land-use rights of local people were ignored and settlements were established without local consultation, consent or compensation for lost resources (Pankhurst 1998: 551-4). Sites were selected without land-use planning and were often abandoned after much investment and wasted energy, owing to a lack of water, or conversely water saturation (Alemneh 1990: 107-8; Pankhurst 1992a: 111-12). However, in most cases fortunately the bulk of settlers left at the time of the change of government, thus substantially reducing the pressure on the environment. In some cases there has also been evidence of tree planting, especially in homestead plots of eucalyptus and fruit trees such as bananas, papayas and mangos. However, tree planting is largely close to homesteads so that, although the villages have become more wooded, a wider circle of the surrounding area has tended to be deforested and the distances women have to go to collect wood have increased. More recently there have been reports of increased clearing of land and bush both by new settlers and by local people wishing to stake claims as a result of rumours of new resettlement (Piguet and Dechassa 2004).

(viii) Relations between the settlers and their areas of origin. In the early days of the resettlement travel was restricted by checkpoints and settlers had the feeling of being prisoners. Nonetheless, many managed to escape by various means and some were able to visit their home areas and bring back news and letters (Pankhurst 1992a). There

were large numbers of settlers leaving in the first couple of years, and then a tendency for them to leave after the harvest period when they had sold their crops, despite attempt to prevent them from doing so. The bulk of the settlers, in many cases up to three-quarters, left at the time of the change of government due to lack of restrictions and fears of insecurity, and in the early transition period. Departures were also related to news about opportunities in their home areas, notably favourable climatic conditions in the early 1990s and the hope of obtaining land. However, a small proportion who left during the transition returned once they felt it was secure and because they were not able to gain access to land in their former homelands and felt that opportunities in the settlement area might be preferable. More recently there has been a trend of some former settlers returning to settlements and established settlers bringing relatives to join them. In addition to the former settlers who returned, a new wave of people began to seek ways to join the settlements, notably during years of drought and famine in northern Ethiopia. There have also been recent reports of people from the highlands who had not been settlers coming as seasonal wage labourers, seeking better opportunities. Some have been able to find ways of remaining by working for settlers and others have been clearing new land; despite attempts by the local authorities to try to discourage this trend, there have also been migrants coming in groups with their livestock (Wolde-Selassie 1997; Piguet and Dechassa 2004).

(x) Inter-generational issues. A key aspect of the longer-term consequences of resettlement relates to generational change. Already after a decade children born in the settlement had no clear sense of a different homeland, and even the teenagers only knew of a previous home through the tales of their parents and visitors. By now, two decades later, most of the people living in the settlement were either born there or were too young to recall an earlier life. This change has considerable implications for the future of resettlement. The younger generation has a greater sense of rootedness in the environment in which it grew up and does not have the same sense of exile felt by many of the older generation, even if they have adapted successfully and become prosperous. The younger generation is also less likely to envisage leaving the settlements unless it is forced to do so, and within a few years there will be a change in the balance of power between the generations, as the younger generation which grew up in the settlement begins to take on more responsibilities.

(x) Investment in new livelihoods and changing identities. As the years went by and settlers had spent more than a decade in the resettlement areas, their view of themselves and their livelihood underwent changes. Signs of greater investment in their new lives became more common. These include both material physical and social investments. Settlers built larger and more permanent houses with fences and larger granaries, and planted trees in their compounds. Settlement villages tended to regroup according to preferences often based on previous backgrounds. Settlers saved more assets, notably in terms of livestock and household goods, some items becoming status symbols such as radios and bicycles. There is also some diversification with some settlers specializing in particular occupations such as craft production and tailoring, and a number becoming involved in trade, including longer-distance trade. Already after a few years settlers began to resent the label 'settlers'.[12] In particular, once they started paying taxes, many felt that they were entitled to be considered like other farmers living in the area. Along with a tendency to downplay their settler status, differences between them in terms of religion and former background seem to have become

more accentuated. Thus, where there have been differences in religion and regional backgrounds, socializing and the formation of agricultural work groups and burial and credit associations have tended to reflect these differences.

Lessons from resettlement experiences: the need for a processual phased approach

Resettlement and migration can be seen as complex processes which need to be understood in phases. The following discussion divides the resettlement process into three phases. The first relates to measures taken to prepare for resettlement, including the planning, costing, settler recruitment, site selection and preparations. The second phase concerns the move and conditions of reception, including timing of relocation, organizing departures and transport, and monitoring guidelines for infrastructure, services and assistance. The third phase considers creating sustainable conditions and adaptations to lowland conditions, relations with local people, environmental concerns, and assessment of self-reliance and sustainability.

PLANNING AND PREPARATIONS OF RELOCATION

In the first phase, prior to the relocation the following issues deserve further consideration: (i) planning the process; (ii) costing the programme; (iii) settler recruitment; and (iv) site selection and preparation.

(i) Planning resettlement: the risks of an emergency response. Many studies as well as the document of the NCFSE suggest that resettlement should not be pursued as an emergency campaign, but rather as an element in an integrated food security strategy linked with the country's poverty reduction strategy. The problem of food insecurity is critical, and clearly solutions are urgently needed. However, resettlement is a complex operation that requires careful planning and sufficient timing, even if it is undertaken on a relatively small scale. It may therefore be argued that, rather than as part of an emergency response, resettlement should be considered as part of a longer-term migration strategy including a range of measures, packages, options and incentives, notably preparing the basic infrastructure, services, credit, etc. required to attract settlers.

Insofar as resettlement planning is linked to a response to famine, the experience from the mid-1980s and the early 2000s suggests that there is a tendency to move from a planned, gradual and medium-term approach to a more immediate, rapid and increased scale. In the 1980s this had consequences for site selection, preparation, transport of settlers, provision of food and delivery of services, all of which were difficult to organize rapidly, at short notice at a time of famine when resources were stretched. Moreover, it was difficult to coordinate all the aspects required for resettlement during a time of crisis. This resulted in poor site selection, lack of adequate preparation and problems of timely transport of settlers, food and other provisions, leading to much unnecessary suffering which contributed to the failure of most of the settlement schemes in that period. Despite the differences of the current resettlement, and the good intentions as reflected in the *Resettlement Programme Implementation Manual* (FDRE 2003), standards set were often not met, as noted in the FSS report (2006). Many sites were cut off in the rainy season resulting in problems with provision of food and health crises, notably in the first year. As in the 1980s local people were mobilized to build shelters and houses, though in some cases the settlers had to build houses after their arrival, or to rebuild poorly constructed ones. Food aid was provided with full rations of 15-20 kg of grain per person per month, and in some cases edible oil and additional rations. However, in some cases insufficient food was prepositioned or there were interruptions of supplies during the rains. With regard to other provisions, in some sites there were shortages of blankets and anti-mosquito bednets, or of cooking utensils or agricultural tools, and especially oxen for ploughing, with one ox given on a credit basis for one or two households.

It would therefore be important to ensure that in any future resettlement the principles, approaches and guidelines of the NCFSE and the *Resettlement Programme Implementation Manual* are followed, since more careful planning and preparation prior to settlers' arrival can increase the likelihood of a better adaptation for more settlers in a shorter period. A modified resettlement approach could seek to facilitate migration by providing incentives and ensuring that roads are constructed and other infrastructure is in place prior to resettlement. Such a model would need to consider joint infrastructure and service development for both local peoples and settlers.

(ii) Costing the programme: including the hidden costs. The emergency programme of the Derg set out a budget of 531.92 million *birr* (US$257 m.) of which a quarter was to go on resettlement. Thus some 133 million *birr* (US$64 m.) was to be allocated for resettling some 300,000 households or 1.5 million people, which would give a figure of 443 *birr* (US$214) per household or 89 *birr* (US$42) per capita. In fact, expenditures for the resettlement component alone were much higher and a government study estimated a cost of 564.3 million *birr* (US$272 million), which would give a per capita amount of 951 *birr* (US$460). An eminent scholar suggested that an estimate of 600 million *birr* (US$290 million) would be more realistic (Dessalegn 1989:75). This would put the amount at about 1000 *birr* (US$483) per capita. Estimates did not take account of inputs by the Ministries of Health, Education and Water Resources, and all the hidden costs of thousands of campaigners sent from centres of higher education and government departments, and the mobilization of 'mass organizations'. Ministries were instructed to provide extension staff; tractors were diverted from other areas, food from relief, seeds, fertilizer and pesticides from allocations of the Ministry of Agriculture, and medicine from the Ministry of Health budget. Settlements were over-privileged with higher proportions of extension staff and considerable state-supplied inputs. When support from foreign bilateral and international organizations, NGOs and religious organizations is added, an estimate of a billion *birr* or about US$483 million would probably be conservative. This would give a per capita figure of 1,686 *birr* or US$814 in a country with a per capita income at the time of US$123 per annum (Pankhurst 1992a:74-5). The resettlement venture was thus a costly business even in strict financial terms.

As noted earlier, the recent resettlement was estimated to cost 1,867 million *birr* (US$217 million).[13] This would imply a cost of 4,244 *birr* (US$493) per household or 849 *birr* (US$99) per capita if the estimate of 5 persons per household were correct. Insofar as exact figures on what has been spent exist they do not seem to have been made publicly available. The extent of hidden costs borne by existing programmes, ministries, settlers and local communities has also not been estimated. The SDPRP of 2002 put the figure for the remaining budget required from 2005 to 2010 at 1.2 billion *birr* (US$115 million). The document suggests that half the target had been reached by then, which would imply an increased figure of 5,454 *birr* per household (US$631) for the remaining 220,000 households or 1,090 *birr* (US$127) per capita for the remaining 1,100,000 people, assuming five persons per household. This would suggest an increase in the cost estimate, possibly due in part to inflation.

The current resettlement plan was clearly costed more carefully than that during the earlier phase under the Derg. The overall planned cost was slightly lower but the per capita estimate more than twice as much (when converted into US$). In fact the Derg resettlement ended up being much more costly, in part because the numbers resettled were significantly lower than planned and the household size smaller than anticipated. If we consider the hidden costs, the overall expenditure is considerable, especially in terms of per capita income. Details of the costs of the current resettlement are not readily available, though the planned estimated costs seem to have been revised upwards in the SDPRP, and constitute large expenditures both in aggregate and in per capita terms for a poor country.

(iii) Settler recruitment: voluntariness and numbers. The experience from the mid-1980s suggests that, even where initially the principle of voluntariness is stated, there is a danger of targets turning into quotas as overzealous officials seek to impress their superiors, and as some local leaders seek to abuse resettlement to victimize opponents. Such risks are related to the top-down approach adopted by implementing strategies based on 'campaigns' leading to targets turning into quotas, and the temptation to use food aid and distribution points in the resettlement site as incentives to persuade people to move. The abuses and coercion in the 1980s resettlement in this respect have been amply documented. Once resettlement is defined by government as necessary, there is a tendency to portray the settlements as idyllic visions of modernization, development and prosperity. This can lead to disappointment, disaffection and desertion. In the 1980s settlers were promised fertile land, corrugated-iron-roofed houses, clothing, tractors and implements. They were also induced to resettle by food aid being allocated to the resettlement areas and being reduced or cut back in areas of origin and famine shelters. Some settlers in the 1980s therefore talked of the famine shelters as 'rat traps' (Pankhurst 1992a).

A major improvement in principle of the current resettlement is its aspirations to be voluntary. Several theses and the FSS study have confirmed that the recent resettlement has not involved direct coercion such as occurred during the Derg resettlement. However, the extent of voluntariness and the ability to make real choices was found to have been constrained by four factors: (i) desperation resulting from increasing land shortage, drought and destitution; (ii) the idyllic picture presented of the resettlement sites and the exaggerated promises of support; (iii) warnings, in some areas, that food aid would not continue in the drought-prone highland areas; and (iv) some incidents of food aid being withheld while resettlement registration took place. The resettlement can therefore be characterized as having elements of indirect compulsion and inducement if not outright coercion.

Moreover, the question of voluntariness is not straightforward, and individuals' decision-making is embedded in social, economic and political factors. Even where an individual volunteers to be resettled, this may go against the wishes of other family members. Parents, spouses or children of the decision-maker may find themselves pushed into resettlement. Women often face tough choices of whether to remain with parents or leave with husbands or vice versa. Beyond the family, peer and kin pressure, as well as the decisions of influential leaders, members of social and religious organizations, and local residential groups, can influence others' decision-making, leading to a kind of chain reaction of community pressure in which the wishes and choices of individuals are over-ridden, leading to social coercion (Pankhurst 1992a). Gebre Yntiso (2002a) suggests that the distinction between 'voluntary' and 'involuntary' migration is too simplistic. He defines voluntary resettlers as those who are in a position to decide freely, and are willing to leave, and involuntary resettlers as those who were coerced into leaving. However, he suggests the need to take account of two additional categories: (i) 'induced-voluntary settlers', who are pressurized by external agencies; and (ii) 'compulsory-voluntary' settlers who willingly accept forced resettlement out of desperation. Gebre suggests that 'voluntary' and 'compulsory-voluntary' settlers adapted better than 'involuntary' and 'induced-voluntary' settlers, therefore concluding that use of direct force as well as unrealistic inducement is likely to fail.

According to the FSS study, in the recent resettlement, meetings were held in sending areas to inform communities about the resettlement. The sites tended to be portrayed in ideal terms. Some of the promises were not included in the guidelines or had been misinterpreted locally by administrators or resettlers. Differences between expectations and actual conditions were a major factor leading to many resettlers leaving shortly after arrival and dissatisfaction among those who remained. Complaints included land shortage and competing claims by locals; provision of at best one hectare of land rather than two; assumptions that oxen were to be provided as grants rather than loans[14] and disappointment that there was only one ox per household or between two households; either temporary shelters or hastily built and poor quality houses; lowland diseases notably malaria and trypanosomiasis rendering ox-plough cultivation precarious; sites being cut off during the rains with serious consequences for the provision of rations and heath care; lack of or limited schooling in often crowded conditions; rations restricted to grain, with oil and supplementary feeding either not available or reduced too soon; delays in rations initially and during the rains, and stoppage after eight months before many resettlers had become food-secure.

If the principle of voluntarism is to be preserved, the decision-making of potential settlers should be kept *at an individual level* as far as possible. This means ensuring that people are free to choose to participate or not, and that enticements, threats and warnings are avoided. Within the household, care should be taken to ensure that the decision is taken jointly and not only by the household head, and that members who do not wish to resettle are not coerced to do so. There has been a debate as to whether households should resettle as a unit or whether single heads should be the first to go. There are advantages and disadvantages in both options, and this may be best left to individual choices. Both possibilities could be entertained simultaneously, with the choice left to those directly concerned. The rationale for men going first is that conditions may initially be harsh for women and children. However, given the sexual division of labour, men tend to find it difficult to live on their own, and if they are to settle first it is important that they are joined by their families fairly soon. The danger of the spread of HIV/AIDS as a result of resettlement may also be heightened, notably with a large single male population, and this may exacerbate the already high HIV/AIDS incidence, with significant effects on the economy and society (Pankhurst and Kloos 2000).

The evidence from many studies therefore suggests that, rather than seeking to plan numbers to be moved in advance, it may be more realistic to provide the incentives and prerequisites in advance and allow settlers to assess the potential themselves and make decisions based on reconnaissance visits to potential settlement areas. Such an approach that would seek to facilitate and encourage migration by potentially successful settlers might prove to be a more cost-effective and sustainable strategy in the long run, and more likely to receive donor support. An approach which starts by assessing the interest and willingness of host communities to accommodate settlers, and of potential settlers to move, and then works out appropriate incentives and provides basis infrastructure and services, is less likely to result in attempts to persuade or pressurize people to leave, and possible resistance.[15]

(iv) Site selection and preparation: implementing realistic guidelines. Resettlement requires careful and systematic planning, particularly in the selection of sites and the verification of land availability, existing land-use rights, and potential for settlement. In the 1980s this was not done. Most of the sites were selected on a very hasty basis, often with no clear criteria or prior feasibility studies. In a number of cases the selected sites were completely unsuitable owing to lack of water, waterlogging, insufficient or infertile land, leading to their being abandoned after the settlers arrived and resulting in wastage of resources and preventable suffering. A crucial and recurrent issue in this respect is accessibility, in particular the risk of sites being cut off during the rainy season, which can have serious consequences for the provision of assistance, notably in the first year when settlers are dependent on food aid.

The recent resettlement planning started at a federal level, and involved regional and *wereda* administrations. Sites were selected based on initial surveying by regional and zonal experts in consultation with local administrators and community representatives. However, limited time and resources hindered detailed planning and assessment of land availability and existing uses. In some cases sites were selected hastily, new or alternative sites were added or much greater numbers were resettled than was proposed by study teams. As noted by Dessalegn (2003), the widespread availability of under-utilized land is questionable. In many of the cases documented by the FSS study, the land selected was either used by local groups or earlier settlers or migrants as fallow areas, for grazing and forest resources, or was close to dwindling forests often used for coffee and honey production.

Land-use and socio-economic studies of the conditions and concerns of local people carried out in receiving areas may provide more realistic figures for phased resettlement, identification of potential sites and numbers of settlers that can be accommodated, projections of assistance needed and timelines for achieving self-reliance. Uniform standards are needed that take into account both internationally recognized minimal standards and essential basic needs, and the limited capacity of Ethiopia's infrastructure and social services, notably in terms of health and education. These standards should be used to evaluate conditions. It is also important to seek a compromise between what settlers had been used to in terms of infrastructure and services in the areas they came from with higher population densities and better facilities, and the need to improve conditions for settlers and local populations in the receiving areas, so that the resettlement does not become a burden on the limited resources and services available in the resettlement areas, but rather leads to integrated development for the existing population as well as the settlers. Standards should also be progressive: the goal should be that the resettlement should improve the infrastructure facilities and services for local people in the lowlands as well as for the settlers, so that gradually the standards in the lowlands catch up with the higher standards in the more densely populated highlands.

In the 1980s settlers in some areas arrived in settlements where only flimsy shelters had been constructed either by local people or by students mobilized on campaigns. In some cases even such rudimentary housing was not available prior to their arrival. The lack of adequate shelter resulted in much hardship, the spread of epidemics and a high initial mortality rate. Other facilities and basic equipment were minimal in most areas. In many cases land had not been cleared, requiring much labour and resulting in delays that meant that the first year's harvest was inadequate and settlers became dependent on food aid for more than a year.

As in the past, the question of infrastructure remains crucial in the current resettlement programme. In some sites, resettlers have been brought to the site before finalizing the preparation of water points, clinics and schools. Contributions were requested from the local population to help the newcomers, particularly for food and to prepare housing. To improve resettlement practices, once sites are selected, guidelines about levels of basic infrastructure (feeder roads, health posts, water points, schools, and in some cases houses) should be monitored before the transport of people is undertaken. It is also particularly important to ensure that any services provided are available to local communities as well as to settlers, to avoid antagonism and promote integration and joint development.

Resettlers had been told about being allocated two hectares of cleared farmland. In fact, in some cases they had to clear new land, and households generally obtained a maximum of one hectare due to land scarcity. In other cases there were complaints about water logging and that land distribution did not take account of family size or land quality.

An alternative model could consider facilitating migration to designated sites, with the consent and involvement of local people who would stand to benefit from the development of infrastructure and basic services and would undertake to become involved in joint development ventures. In other words, such an approach would start by assessing the interest of local communities to host migrants in return for access to funds and programmes to develop infrastructure and services. This is in line with the vision in the PASDEP of resettlement areas becoming centres of development, where investors, along with settlers and local people involved in off-farm activities and agro-processing could be agents of regional development.

THE RELOCATION AND CONDITIONS IN RESETTLEMENT AREAS

In the phase of moving settlers the following three issues need consideration: (i) timing of relocation; (ii) organizing departures and transport: and (iii) monitoring infrastructure, services and assistance.

(i) Timing the move: taking account of the agricultural calendar. Resettlement timing is a key factor in the ability of settlers to adapt rapidly. Given that resettlement tends to be planned as a hurried response to famine, there has been a tendency to resettle people during the agricultural peak season. In the 1980s this resulted in settlers being unable to produce enough food to survive the first year, so that they were dependent on food aid for several years. Similar problems of late relocation occurred in the 2000s resettlement, affecting the ability of settlers to clear and cultivate sufficient land to become self-reliant within the intended one-year period. A strategy of preparing population

transfers over a longer period and starting earlier in the year could enhance the chances of increased success. In relation to agricultural timing, resettlement should be completed before February to allow time to clear land, construct houses, and gather essential inputs (oxen, seeds, tools, etc.) for preparation of farmland.

Agricultural inputs, tools, seeds and credit need to be planned in advance, if settlers are to become food-secure rapidly. Given the major constraint in the lowlands of livestock diseases, notably trypanosomiasis, and the key role that livestock breeding plays in improving nutrition and asset development, the issues of credit and veterinary support deserve to be given emphasis and priority in planning. The timely, affordable and fair provision of seeds, fertiliser and credit is vital, since delays or bottlenecks can result in missed opportunities, given the short window for agricultural production at the commencement of the rainy season.

(ii) Departure and transport: assets, land rights and property transfers. The 1980s experience shows that, prior to departure, some settlers sold their assets such as livestock, household equipment and even housing at very low prices, and certain individuals profiteered. The majority of settlers from the mid-1980s left the resettlement sites in the late 1980s and especially in greater numbers just after the defeat of the Derg in 1991. When they returned to the areas they came from they found that their land had been redistributed and most of those who did not have relatives to fall back on, or who were unable to use networks or patrons to gain access to land, joined the ranks of the rural landless or urban destitute (Pankhurst 1992a, 2002a). This raises the question of an 'exit option' and whether resettlers are entitled to retain rights at least temporarily in the areas from which they came, which became an area of policy debate in the 2000s resettlement.

As in the 1980s, during the 2000s resettlement candidates often did not have enough time to prepare themselves, and in some areas settlers sold assets hastily at low prices. This would suggest that measures could be put in place to guarantee minimum prices for the sale of livestock and other assets. Unlike in the 1980s, the current resettlement practice, as noted in the NCFSE document, in principle allows the possibility for settlers to retain rights over land in areas they came from for up to three years. However, there were claims that in Hararge resettlers' plots were registered for redistribution shortly after their departure. It would be important to ensure that settlers are informed of these rights and that they are respected. A related issue is the involvement of the very poor and destitute in development schemes based on food for work and employment-generation schemes. Settlers who opt to return to their previous homes should be entitled to reregister to take part in development projects. In the 1980s returnees lost rights and tended to become economically among the poorest landless categories, surviving by cutting wood and the production of charcoal, or casual work in towns. They were often also socially outcast and even stigmatized by relatives and friends as those who had left and abandoned them. The assurances of the current resettlement that rights of return will be respected are a significant improvement on previous resettlement, provided they are put in practice. It remains to be seen whether returnees from the current resettlement will be able to reintegrate and regain rights to land that they had left, and whether they will be able to avoid the tendency of joining the ranks of the destitute like former returnees.

In the 1980s none of the settlers had the possibility of seeing beforehand the places to which they were going. The 2003 resettlement programme stipulated that communities' delegates should visit schemes prior to resettlement. This is an important improvement, and some visits were organized for community representatives. In the sending areas meetings were held to inform communities about the resettlement. However, as in the 1980s, conditions in the resettlement areas tended to be portrayed in ideal terms. Some promises were not in the guidelines or had been misinterpreted locally by administrators or resettlers.

One of the major flaws of the 1980s resettlement was the conditions of transport, notably the abuses of sending settlers in unpressurized planes, and crowded and unsanitary conditions in transit shelters on the way and in reception centres on arrival in the resettlement sites. In the 2000s the conditions were much better, although in some cases settlers were crowded in trucks rather than buses, and in many cases they complained about not having enough room to take essential belongings with them. This suggests that adequate standards for transport of people and their belongings need to be worked out and adhered to. Appropriate standards for transit and reception centres also need to be implemented, and careful planning of provisions in terms of food, shelter, sanitation and medical care need to be prepositioned prior to moving large numbers of people.

A migration strategy that allows for gradual migration, with households making their own decisions to move at their own pace, could minimize some of the costs and risks of large concentrations of people in transit and reception centres. A broader and more holistic approach to migration could envisage two-way flows and exchanges between highlands and lowlands, with families keeping members in both zones. This has been an effective traditional coping strategy which could be enhanced and strengthened by the government and other agencies. Such an approach could make individuals, households and communities more resilient in finding their own solutions to the problems they face.

(iii) Monitoring assistance: implementing realistic standards and guidelines. In the 1980s settlers were initially disadvantaged compared with local people in terms of assistance since facilities were not in place. Later in some areas they benefited for a while from more assistance than was available for the local people, giving rise to resentment, especially when and where facilities for settlers were not available to the local population. However, along with greater services the government imposed more control, particularly of agricultural production and civil liberties. In the late 1980s, in most areas, settlers were increasingly left to their own devices, with much less support but greater freedom (Pankhurst 1992a, 2002a; Gebre 2001; Wolde-Selassie 2002).

The fact that some areas are cut off during the rains is a major constraint in providing assistance, especially in the first year when settlers are largely dependent on assistance. This led both in the 1980s and in the 2000s to severe malnutrition and morbidity in some sites. A greater emphasis by the government and donors on improving roads prior to resettlement could provide a major stimulus to migration, and on its own might be one of the most important measures in promoting successful resettlement and migration.

Appropriate standards of assistance need to be worked out in detail, from the provision and pre-positioning of food, shelter, and household and agricultural equipment through to basic services of water, health, education, and to the provision of agricultural support and credit. The government has already provided useful guidelines in the NCFSE and the *Resettlement Programme Implementation Manual.* However, the question of standards should be worked out in a realistic and progressive manner, which allows for regional variations and plans for gradual improvements over time.

A key issue in this respect is to establish guidelines that take account of minimum international standards that are grounded in the reality of Ethiopia, and adapted to regional considerations. Furthermore, there are disparities between the highlands and lowlands, in terms of agricultural and cultural practices and beliefs and with regard to infrastructure and services. The establishment of standards and guidelines also needs to take into consideration existing facilities for the local people. Provision should be made to upgrade facilities for local people through an integrated approach with the settlers, and the aim should be gradually to attain regional and eventually national and even international standards.

For resettlement to be successful, a monitoring framework should be devised as was suggested by the NCFSE. A proposed draft was developed, on the basis of a 24-month cycle, featuring a series of annual in-depth evaluations, linked by quarterly monitoring exercises (Hammond *et al.* 2004). Evaluations would start with a baseline assessment of existing conditions, planning and preparations for assisting the resettlement operation. A mid-term evaluation would be conducted twelve months after resettlement had begun. Two years afterwards a potential final evaluation would be carried out to determine whether 'graduation standards' had been met. Every three months regular monitoring would be conducted to track basic humanitarian indicators. The proposal suggests that monitoring and evaluation be carried out by multi-agency teams composed of representatives of government Food Security Offices, donor and UN agencies, and NGOs operational in resettlement sites. The cooperation of Resettlement Task Forces at all levels would be particularly important as collaborators both in gathering information and in helping to institutionalize a response mechanism. Information would be passed to the Ministry of Agriculture and Rural Development and to a coordinating body made up of all stakeholders, for analysis, dissemination, and action.

CREATING SUSTAINABLE CONDITIONS IN THE RESETTLEMENT AREAS

Once settlers have been resettled the following four issues deserve consideration: (i) adaptations to lowland conditions: (ii) relations with local people; (iii) environmental concerns; and (iv) self-reliance and sustainability.

(i) Adaptation to a lowland climate and diet. Resettlement sites have tended to be located largely in the lowlands since this is where the population is less dense and it has been assumed that relatively more land is available. But there are equally good reasons why such areas tended to be less populated, especially due to human and livestock diseases, less reliable rainfall, and shallow and fragile soils for which swidden (shifting) cultivation and extensive agro-pastoralism were rational adaptations by local peoples that did not overexploit the resources.

Most of the resettlers of the 1980s came from the highlands and found adapting to a hotter, more arid climate in the lowlands arduous, and they suffered from the prevalence of diseases, particularly malaria and kalazar, with some of which they were unfamiliar. Moreover, the lowland climate was conducive to growing only a limited range of crops, notably sorghum, maize and beans, and this represented a change and a reduction in the variety and quality of the diet. Wolde-Selassie (2002) noted the particular hardships faced by settlers coming from areas where the *enset* plant was their former staple. The question of nutrition, especially until the settlers can produce a greater variety of crops and raise livestock, presents an important challenge. In particular, child malnutrition is a serious issue, and the risk of sites being cut off during the rainy season, resulting in delays in food-aid provision, is a recurrent experience, which needs to be avoided. Furthermore, some of the resettlement areas are in potential surplus-producing areas. The introduction of food aid on a large scale can depress prices, affecting local producers and traders. The possibility of purchasing grain locally as a partial alternative to food aid should therefore be given due consideration.

Given lowland diseases and the need to vary the diet, one of the most important forms of intervention to facilitate resettlement and migration would be to provide credit for livestock acquisition and to enhance veterinary services and their provision. Such measures would in themselves provide important incentives for resettlement.

(ii) Relations with local peoples: towards a joint development model. Several contributions to this book and other studies point out that resettlement in the 1980s resulted in tension and conflict with local peoples who were not consulted, involved or compensated for the loss of resources they used and on which they depended for their livelihoods. Shifting agriculture, which relies on a wide expanse of land with areas left fallow to regenerate, and pastoralism, where large pasture areas and dry-season access to riverine areas are necessary, were often disrupted by resettlement schemes, and local people were restricted in their agricultural and transhumance patterns. In particular, conflicts over riverine water use, forest resources, coffee and honey, have been common. The negative impacts of settlers on the local environment and their lack of respect for indigenous rights and conservation practices, have been a recurrent complaint, and conflict over resources has led to a number of violent clashes.[16] Moreover, in some cases native people such as the Gumuz have been dominated and marginalized by settlers who are better connected with government structures and services, and traders and markets. Some of these concerns abour local people losing land and resources, becoming marginalized and entering into conflicts with settlers have also been raised regarding the recent resettlement.

If the likelihood of conflict between groups is to be minimized, joint administration and close communication between settlers and local hosts needs to be promoted, in order to bridge the divides of language, culture, religion and ways of life, reduce resource competition and reach negotiated solutions. Settlers and local communities should be represented and involved in joint administration. Services including health and education available to settlers should be open to local people and vice versa. This can affect decisions about where water points, schools and health facilities should be built or improved. Both settlers and local communities should receive community-based assistance, in ways similar to UNHCR's policy of offering support to refugees as well as the host population facing difficulties. Women's and youth associations as well as informal burial, credit and religious associations have been shown to ease adaptation (Pankhurst 1990; Gebre 2001; Wolde-Selassie 2002). Such institutions can also play a role in conflict management and the development of integration. Likewise, elders can play an important role in traditional forms of arbitration, and customary dispute resolution is often relied on by the formal justice system and should be involved in negotiations (Pankhurst and Getachew 2008). Most importantly, joint development projects should be devised to involve settlers and locals in ventures in which they benefit from working together.

The intra-regional resettlement currently undertaken might be seen as reducing the likelihood of conflict between different ethnic groups. However, differences in culture, language, religion, social institutions and livelihood patterns between the highlands and lowlands are common features in Ethiopia. Moreover, most of the conflicts are over resource use, and demographic changes and pressure on resources are likely to result in some competition and possible conflict, so that measures to forestall confrontations need to be considered. In particular in the Southern Region, where there are a number of small ethnic groups, the risk of their being swamped by more numerous settlers competing for resources over which the local groups believe they have prior rights, could lead to clashes.

Given shortage of resources, limited options for assistance, unreliable climatic conditions and potential conflict, the scaling back of resettlement could be considered in certain areas that do not seem to have the necessary prerequisites for sustainable resettlement. Where surveys of resettlement sites have been carried out such as the study in Oromia (RSO 2002) the recommendations should be followed in terms of avoiding unsuitable sites and keeping numbers limited. Settling people in environments that do not meet minimum standards may also result in disaffection, and ultimately could jeopardize the programme. Resettlement planning has often not given much thought to the question of integrated provision of services such as health, veterinary and education services, infrastructure, market and credit support, which need to be made available on time through mechanisms that ensure fair distribution. It should also be recognized that local groups on the periphery are often marginalized and disadvantaged in terms of language and education, and this may require affirmative action. In other words, settlements have tended to be conceived of as isolated project islands that are often divorced in the minds of planners from the social, economic and political environment in which they exist. A more integrated approach that does not prioritize the interests of settlers over locals, and that highlights joint development within regions, is likely to be more successful.[17]

(iii) *Environmental concerns: mitigating risks of aggravating degradation.* Seasonal and longer-term spontaneous migration continues to be significant in Ethiopia, as migration push and pull factors promote further movements from the highlands. In most resettlement areas deforestation and environmental damage are conspicuous phenomena. A major problem is the disparity between traditional natural-resources management practices of local people and the short-term exploitative approach of migrants and settlers, who may not have a long-term commitment to conservation (Assefa 2002). Resettlement can therefore represent a threat to the rights of indigenous people by alienating resources, which have been vital to their livelihoods (Gebre 2003). Expansion of cultivation is being practised by earlier migrants and settlers, as well as by new migrants some of whom are joining resettlement schemes. This has resulted in some areas in a reaction by local people, particularly the younger landless generation, arguing that they should make claims to land and clear forest areas before the settlers come (FSS 2006). This raises the need for regulation of resource use in relation to the potentially negative aspects of in-migration.

Environmental protection and rehabilitation are needed not just in the areas from which settlers have come but also in the areas they have moved to so that the criticism of resettlement as reproducing the destruction of the environment from the highlands to the lowlands does not become a reality. In resettlement areas, safeguards need to be put in place at the outset of the resettlement programme to ensure that harvesting of forest products and other resources is regulated and sustainable; forest and wildlife areas need to be protected from the risks resulting from an increase of population through migration and resettlement. Given the fast disappearing remaining forested areas of Ethiopia, a migration policy requires participatory conservation measures (Pankhurst 2002b). Migrants and settlers would need to abide by natural-resource management regulations involving both customary and state-formulated rules. An important area that should be given more emphasis is devising and implementing natural-resource development projects to be undertaken jointly by local communities and settlers. Funding for such ventures should not await a period when settlers become food-secure – by which time much of the damage may already have been done – but should be initiated from the outset of the resettlement, and should be an integral part of initial planning and subsequent implementation, monitoring and evaluation.

Likewise regarding the parks, projects involving local communities rather than excluding them should be given priority over any resettlement plans. Local communities can be committed conservationists and appropriate guardians of wildlife, as shown from experiences in other African countries and noted in other contributions to this volume, as long as they see clear benefits from conservation. They can be involved as guides, guards and casual and skilled workers. They can obtain income from services to tourists and sale of crafts, etc. Moreover, a fair proportion of the benefits from tourism should be used to enable the development of local infrastructure and services.

(iv) Self-reliance and sustainability: economic, social and environmental development. The 1980s resettlement sites took at least a couple of years if not longer to attain basic food self-sufficiency. Given the constraints of collectivized production, self-sufficiency at a household level took even longer. The question of measuring the sustainability of resettlements is complex, and includes environmental, demographic, economic, social and cultural aspects. Gebre's chapter in this book notes a reported decline in soil fertility and yields. The bulk of the 1980s resettlers left the settlements around 1991, thus reducing pressure on the environment, but since then some have returned and the number of new settlers has slowly been increasing in some areas. Areas near settlements are becoming increasingly deforested, as evidenced, for instance, by the distances women have to go to fetch wood. Some tree planting is occurring, mainly of eucalyptus and fruit trees, but these tend to be limited to homesteads, and the need for afforestation has not been prioritized and is likely to be a major ongoing concern.

A concerted and sustained effort to provide incentives to reduce population growth is needed, in combination with efforts to diversify the livelihood base of the rural population. Reducing the population growth rate may help buy some time to diversify the economy and enable rural residents to achieve self-reliance through additional means, notably off-farm activities, crafts and agro-industries with appropriate involvement of investors. In the medium term, the main question related to the demographic transition in Ethiopia is when and how fertility-rate decreases can be expected, and resettlement cannot be considered as a solution to the potential population crisis.

In addition to environmental issues the question of economic sustainability in terms of agricultural production patterns, types of crops grown, the risk of declining yields, crop rotation and fallowing, markets for settlers' produce and the promotion of non-agricultural livelihoods deserves consideration. However, the success of resettlement may well mainly depend on, and be best measured by, its *social* sustainability in terms of developing positive relations of coexistence, exchange and joint development between settlers and local people. This may require changes in attitudes in order to alter the existing stereotypes on both sides, and to work towards forms of interaction, cooperation, mutual respect and cultural understanding. In the final analysis the success of resettlement depends on settlers remaining in the settlement areas and improving their livelihoods, together with local people whose quality of life should be enhanced by assistance to resettlement areas, while protecting and developing the environment.

Conclusion

Resettlement had been opposed by the EPRDF when it came to power, given the excesses and abuses of the Derg resettlement. However, recently it has become an important component of the food security strategy, due to increasing population, decreasing land holdings, and limitations of other options such as land redistribution in a context of some 'spontaneous' migration and the eviction of former resettlers. However, it was the serious drought in 2002 and the need to be independent from food aid that prompted a change of gear and led to resettlement being considered a national priority in spite of donor opposition, as happened in 1984.

There are striking similarities but also significant contrasts[18] in the resettlement programmes carried out in the mid-1980s by the Derg and in the early 2000s by the EPRDF. Regarding the similarities the following twelve points may be made:

(i) In both periods resettlement was promoted to a high-priority agenda after a serious drought, which led the government to consider implementing a large-scale emergency resettlement programme. In both cases some general consideration of resettlement had been part of earlier policy, but the threat of famine triggered a change to a fast-track large-scale model, involving pronouncements by government officials at the highest level.

(ii) In both cases resettlement was planned primarily to address food insecurity in a lasting way, especially in order to avoid dependence on foreign food aid.

(iii) An additional logic in both cases was to develop areas that were assumed to be under-populated and where it was claimed that underutilized land was available. However, in both cases this claim has been challenged by eminent scholars, notably Dessalegn (2003).

(iv) Ambitious targets of numbers of households to be resettled were set with a predetermined timeframe, with insufficient consideration of the estimated and hidden costs, and the government assumed full responsibility to organize the programme. In both cases the overall estimates of the costs of the programme were less than the amount expended, and the household and per capita costs were high, especially for a poor country. Moreover, the official costs did not take into consideration the secondment of personnel and reallocation of resources from government institutions, or indirect contributions from donors and NGOs, let alone the contributions of host communities and the settlers themselves.

(v) Donors were sceptical in both periods and support was not forthcoming, but the government went ahead regardless, and was subject to criticism from some donors and NGOs.

(vi) The resettlement was carried out in both cases with haste in a campaign approach with limited time for planning.

(vii) In both cases plans about numbers that could be resettled within specific areas were ignored and larger numbers were resettled.
(viii) Resettlement was carried out primarily in the lowlands and borderland where human diseases, notably malaria and kalazar, and livestock diseases, particularly trypanosomiasis, are serious constraints.
(ix) Participation of settlers in the planning process was limited and the resettlement model was state-led.
(x) The resettlement sites were portrayed to prospective settlers in idyllic terms and unrealistic promises were made, some of which were not fulfilled, leading to disappointment and frustration.
(xi) Consultation with communities living in areas designated as resettlement sites was limited, and compensation for alienated land and other resources was not provided.
(xii) In both cases tensions and conflicts with local people emerged, particularly over rights to land and other resources.

However, there are also significant differences in the design and implementation, some of which were noted in policy documents and in official speeches.[19] The following twelve differences may be highlighted:

(i) The 2000s resettlement stressed the voluntary nature of resettlement. In general, this principle was adhered to, unlike under the Derg.[20] However, we have seen that in practice several factors have constrained voluntariness, notably the limited choices of famine victims, social pressures from peers, kin, neighbours and community members, allegations that food aid would not be available continuously or would be restricted and promises of idyllic conditions in resettlement areas raising expectations. The dichotomy between voluntary and compulsory is too rigid as Gebre notes, and there may be intermediary forms of 'induced voluntarism' and 'compulsory voluntarism' (Gebre 2002a,b). Nonetheless, it is clear that types of direct coercion that were a part of the 1980s resettlement were avoided.
(ii) Settlers have been given the right to return to their areas of origin and reclaim their land for a period of up to three years. This is an important provision, and, unlike under the Derg, when there were attempts to prevent settlers from leaving, currently there is relative freedom of movement and there have certainly been large numbers who have left the resettlement areas, particularly in Amhara Region. However, there has not been much evidence of how far this guideline has been adhered to; there have been rumours of resettlers' land being registered for redistribution, and little is known about how returnees fare and whether they are able to obtain food and other assistance, as set out in the guidelines. After the period has elapsed settlers are expected to obtain a 'release letter' from their area of origin and confirm their choice by formally registering in the settlement areas.
(iv) Policy statements clearly stipulated that resettlement must be within regions since the cross-regional resettlement during the Derg era was viewed as a cause of inter-ethnic conflicts. This policy guideline was adhered to. However, differences in ethnicity, religion, livelihoods and culture are common between the highlands and lowlands within the regions, so that differences between settlers and locals are prevalent in most of the current resettlement sites. More significantly, conflicts over resources are the key issue rather than cultural differences, and have also been a serious problem in many of the current resettlement sites.
(iv) In terms of planning and costing, there was more consideration given in the 2000s

resettlement. Moreover, the process of site selection was given more care and time, and the principle of finding underutilized land was given more prominence. In Oromia DfID and in Amhara the EU provided support for planning. However, in the current resettlement also numbers to be accommodated were increased, disregarding local plans. Moreover, studies show that much of the land that has been designated for resettlement was used by local groups, former settlers or investors for agriculture, grazing and as forests, resulting in resource conflict and potential environmental degradation.

(v) Unlike under the Derg, in the current resettlement prior visits were organized to resettlement areas by community representatives. However, this was often not to the sites the resettlers ended up going to and was not done systematically.

(vi) Unlike previously, consultation with local communities was carried out. However, at many of these meetings there was considerable opposition from local people who claimed that there were many landless and that the allocated land was being used by them or that they should be given priority in allocations. Moreover, as with the previous resettlement, compensation for lost resources was not provided.

(vii) Preparation for the settlers was carried out with much greater care than in the 1980s resettlement. However, shelter and housing were often very poor or not available, in some cases insufficient food was prepositioned, and there were shortages of health equipment, personnel and drugs, and of household utensils, blankets, bednets and farming tools. Some sites were cut off during the rains, leading to hardship and malnutrition in some sites in the first year.

(viii) Settler transport was generally in buses, unlike the 1980s resettlement that also included transport in unpressurized planes. However, some settlers were transported in trucks and there were complaints about shortage of space for belongings.

(ix) Land was allocated to settlers on a household basis rather than to cooperatives as under the Derg, but in many sites there was not enough land to allocate the promised 2 hectares per household.

(x) Oxen were provided to settlers rather than tractor services as under the Derg; however, in most cases one ox was provided for two households, and there was lack of clarity as to whether these were provided as a grant or a loan. There were also serious threats from trypanosomiasis.

(xi) The elements of control under the Derg, including the enforced cooperativization and the restrictions on travel and religious practice, are clearly not part of the recent resettlement.

(xii) Assistance to settlers under the Derg was unsustainable and costly initially, and services and support much greater than to the local population. During the recent resettlement the assistance package was minimal and within a year food aid was stopped in most sites. The government claims that 88 percent of the settlers have 'graduated' to become self-reliant. However, studies suggest that while large numbers are food self-reliant, and many have surpluses invested in livestock and other goods and some have prospered through selling cash crops, there are also large numbers who remain vulnerable to food insecurity, especially given the uncertainties of production in the lowlands. Moreover, longer-term issues of environmental sustainability and developing cooperative relations with local people have not been given sufficient thought.

To conclude, in comparing the 1980s and 2000s resettlements, many of the abuses, shortcomings and failures of the earlier phase were avoided in the current programme and the coercive elements in the selection and in the settlement model were largely absent. Moreover, the settlers adapted faster to their new circumstances and some have prospered. However, a range of similar problems re-emerged and large numbers have left some sites. A major reason for the reoccurrence of many of the problems may be the basic similarities in the design of the resettlement as a state-planned and -led large-scale relocation from the highlands to the lowlands in the context of serious food insecurity, with insufficient consideration of integration with people already living in the area.

In the second section the discussion considered the pillars, principles and approaches set out in the NCFSE document that sought to include the views of both donors and government. The comparison with the implementation practice shows clearly that the ideals of the guidelines were not always adhered to. Some of the problems may have emanated from the guidelines referring to a more participatory, demand-driven, consultative, processual, iterative, and community-managed resettlement concept that the donors were advocating rather than the actual state-led, pre-planned model put into practice.

The third section considered the longer-term implications of resettlement, which highlighted changes in the political contexts of resettlement, in relations between settlers and government, between settlers and local people, between settlers and their areas of origin, between generations among resettlers, and in the identity of settlers. There is a need to consider the longer-term viability of resettlements in terms of environmental, economic and social sustainability, and in particular joint development from the outset with local people already living in the areas designated for resettlement if resettlement is going to be a success in the longer term.

Although resettlement has been seen as a means to achieve 'durable solutions', planning has been based on an emergency logic which seldom considers the longer-term implications and consequences. The complexity of the process involving a range of actors with contrasting and contradictory views often results in tensions and conflict, and resettlement tends to follow an unpredictable and uncontrollable logic of its own. Many of the changes that have occurred since 1985 were dramatic and largely unpredictable, leading to fundamental changes in the context of resettlement. The changes in political conditions from mechanized collectivization to smallholder oxen-based production, and the effects of changing environmental conditions in the settlement and home areas, affected settlers' decision-making about staying or leaving. Relations with government also changed beyond recognition. At first settlers were over-privileged in terms of support and services, resulting in resentment by local people, but they were also the victims of imposed collectivization. As support was withdrawn, the differences in treatment as compared with local people were reduced and settlers gained more autonomy. After the defeat of the Derg and the definition of regions on an ethnic basis, in some cases settlers were perceived as unwelcome migrants from other regions, resulting in cases of evictions (Tesfaye 2007). More generally, there have been changes in relations with local people, with continuing conflicts over access to resources, at times erupting into fighting, but an increase in exchanges notably in the markets, although there has been limited development of social relations on an individual basis. In terms of the local environment, the settlements have resulted in severe deforestation and ecological degradation. However, the departure of the bulk of settlers has eased the pressure. Settlers have been engaged in some tree planting although this is mainly in homestead plots and consists largely of eucalyptus and fruit trees. As the settlers approach the end of their second decade, there are some indications of more investment in the settlement environment both in physical terms in their homesteads, livestock acquisition, tree planting etc., and in terms of social relations. More importantly, with an increasing proportion having been born and brought up in the resettlement context, there are indications of changes in identity, partly in terms of a greater sense of belonging to the settlement environment, but also paradoxically a resurgence of differences between settlers in terms of religion and former regional background and in forming networks and groups.

Looking at resettlement from the vantage point of what happened to the 1985 settlers, resettlement planning needs to adopt a broader longer-term vision. There is also a case for learning from spontaneous migration which privileges social relations with local people, and maintains linkages between settlement and home areas, rather than seeking to create rigidly planned isolated units. The myth of vast fertile and uninhabited areas is still believed in, despite the weight of substantial academic studies to the contrary, and resettlement thinking still privileges the technical-fix approach concentrated on the settlers, which ignores or abuses local peoples' rights, particularly those of marginalized minorities on the peripheries of the state where most resettlement is planned.

Future resettlement planning and implementation could be improved by a more careful processual approach that gives greater consideration to the sequential phases of resettlement, allows for proper planning, costing, preparation, settler recruitment, and site selection; improves the conditions of the move and reception; and from the outset builds in ways of addressing concerns with adaptations to the lowlands, creating sustainable conditions and favourable relations with local people, and addressing environmental issues. A range of suggestions at each stage of the phases has been put forward in the fourth section. However, for this to happen in the future, resettlement will need to avoid a large-scale campaign approach with predetermined targets and an over-ambitious time-scale.

There is a case for taking a more processual human-centred and interactive approach to resettlement. This would seek first and foremost to promote understanding and joint development initiatives in which 'host' communities' rights over land and resources are respected and settlers' usufruct rights are negotiated for and by settlers. Moreover, rather than discouraging interaction between the highlands and the lowlands, which has been a major survival and development strategy built into the Ethiopian ecological and social context, settlers should be encouraged to develop relations with their home communities. Such a twin interactive approach promoting linkages between settlers and hosts and between settlers and home communities would reduce the risks of the logic of resettlement in Ethiopia turning into a self-fulfilling prophecy. The repeated cycles of disaster have brought famine and conflict into closer relation through the unintended consequences of well-meaning but socially blind development planning.

A more flexible and human-centred approach would recognize the importance of social rather than technical relations in the resettlement process. This could help avert the likelihood of failure, which has tended to be the norm rather than the exception in resettlement planning worldwide. Ultimately, in the longer term the viability of resettlement does not depend merely or primarily on attaining economic self-sufficiency or even environmental sustainability, but rather on the promotion of social integration which respects diversity and complementarity, and promotes joint development at local, regional and national levels.

There has been a tendency to repeat the prevalent model of resettlement that involves large-scale, high-input, state-sponsored and -organized movements. This is seen as having the advantages of mobilizing resources, creating new programmes, solving land shortages and exploiting under-utilized areas. However, the record world-wide, and in Ethiopia, suggests that this is often a costly approach economically, socially and environmentally. Moreover, the assumption that the poorest and most destitute, in particular landless or famine victims, necessarily make the best migrants who can succeed in a harsh environment is questionable. The study carried out by FSS (2006) found that the more successful were generally male-headed households, with good social capital and linkages with the community through informal associations, as well as with administrators, local people and investors. They were able to purchase livestock, especially oxen for ploughing, and some have been involved in additional agricultural production through share-cropping or rental of land or tractors, and/or trade. Many improved their quality of life and wellbeing, by purchasing livestock, consumer goods, household equipment and clothing, and were able to afford better medical care and education. Thus it may well be that the kinds of migrants who can make a success of starting a new life in resettlement areas are more likely to be the more enterprising with experience, expertise, and some resources to fall back on. This would suggest the need to consider ways of influencing the decision-making of potential migrants, to encourage those most likely to succeed.

Given the recurring problems of resettlement in Ethiopia, the difficulties of sticking to guidelines, the heavy direct and indirect costs and the longer-term concerns with the social and environmental viability of resettlement, an alternative model should be given a chance. It may be argued that, rather than part of an emergency response, resettlement should be considered as part of a longer-term migration strategy including a range of measures, packages, credits and options to attract settlers who are likely to become successful migrants. A modified approach could seek to facilitate migration by providing incentives and ensuring that roads are constructed and other pre-requisites are in place prior to resettlement. Such a model would need to consider joint infrastructure and service development between settlers and local people, who would stand to benefit from the development of infrastructure and basic services and would undertake to become involved in joint development ventures. In other words such an approach would start by assessing the interest of local communities in hosting migrants in return for access to funds and programmes to develop infrastructure and services. This is in line with the vision in the PASDEP of resettlement areas becoming centres of development, where investors along with settlers and local people involved in off-farm activities and agro-processing could be agents of regional development.

The evidence from many studies suggests that, rather than seeking to plan numbers to be moved in advance, it may therefore be more realistic to provide the incentives and prerequisites and allow settlers to assess the potential themselves and make decisions based on reconnaissance visits to potential settlement areas. Such an approach that would seek to facilitate and encourage migration by potentially successful settlers might prove to be a more cost-effective and sustainable strategy in the long run, and be more likely to receive donor support.

A migration strategy that allows for gradual migration of households making their own decisions to move at their own pace could minimize the risk of political and social pressures and some of the costs and risks of large concentrations of people in transit and reception centres. A broader and more holistic approach to migration could envisage two-way flows and exchanges between highlands and lowlands, with families keeping members in both zones. This has been an effective traditional coping strategy which could be enhanced and strengthened by the government and other agencies. Such an approach could make individuals, households and communities more resilient in finding their own solutions to the problems they face.

The ultimate success of resettlement and migration depends very largely on coexistence, exchange and joint development between settlers, migrants and local people. This calls for devising joint development projects for which mixed communities of hosts and migrants could seek funding from government and donors. The strengthening of joint formal and informal institutions that involve local people and migrant settlers together in collaborative ventures would be an important measure for creating conducive conditions to enable longer-term social integration and sustainable development.

Resettlement and migration is ultimately a human rather than a technical process. In addition to being able to produce enough to survive and prosper, migrants need to adapt to local conditions and seek ways of coexisting and integrating with communities in areas they move to. Social and cultural adaptation and interaction therefore deserve to be given more consideration and should be at the forefront of the development of a migration policy. There is a need to go beyond the tendency to assume that resettlement is only about food security and technical agricultural solutions, and to include promotion of social and cultural incentives to migration in the design of a more inclusive, participatory and human-centred approach to migration. It may be hoped that this chapter and book can provide ideas for the development of a migration policy and strategy in Ethiopia.

Notes

1. The official total number of households in mid-2007 was 193,526 households (MoFED 2007b). The plan estimated an average of 5 persons per household which would mean over 967,000 people resettled. However, average household sizes by the end of 2005 were about 3.3 members which would suggest a total of about 638,000 people. The household size was under 3 persons in the 1980s resettlement.
2. Of these four were on resettlement sites in Oromia (Abdurouf 2005; Areba 2005; Asfaw 2005; Driba 2005), three in Amhara Region (Zelalem 2005; Getu 2005 and Solomon 2005), and three in the SNNP Region (Ayke 2005; Mellesse 2005; and Feseha 2006).
3. 200,000 in Amhara, 100,000 each in Oromia and SNNP and 40,000 in Tigray.
4. 100,000 in the first year, 150,000 in the second year and 190,000 in the third year.
5. Table 7.12 in the appendix has a target of 161,108 further households to be resettled by 2009-10 (and 1.5 million to become 'food secured'), suggesting a possible drop in planned numbers. In Regional terms none of these are in Tigray, 3500 in Oromia, 40,000 in Amhara and 117,600 in the Southern Region.
6. For the complex and inter-related environmental, political, socio-cultural, legal and economic causes of the conflict see Tesfaye (2007:78-106).
7. There were 3,600 households and 12,263 persons resettled in Jawe, an average of 3.4 persons per household which Piguet and Dechassa attribute to some settlers returning to Wellega to get their belongings and female-headed households leaving for towns (2004:144).
8. Even in Oromia with the highest average of 5.3, the Region in its prefeasibility study had estimated an average of 5.7 (OFSPCO 2001).
9. However, whereas Tigray did not carry out further resettlement Oromia did in 2006-07 but on a reduced scale.
10. Colson and Scudder are exceptions in continuing to study the effects of resettlement on the Gwembe Tonga (Scudder 1996).
11. This was best summed up by metaphors about being treated like livestock. The settlers used

expressions such as: 'We have now become the oxen that have been yoked', and references to being 'counted like sheep in the morning and evening' (Pankhurst 1992a: 149, 160).

12 When I expressed surprise at this new-found identity, one man wryly noted that the word for settler, *sefari*, rhymes with *assafari*, meaning 'shameful' (Pankhurst 1992a: 270).

13. The largest component (39%) was for household packages including food rations of grain for 8-10 months and additional 'nutritive food and spices', farm implements and hand tools, household utensils, and seeds. The second largest item was for oxen (24%) which were expected to be repaid within five years. The third largest component (16%) was for 'community packages' including water, health, veterinary, educational and warehouse and grinding mill services. The fourth component was transportation at 11%, and the fifth was for drugs and health services at 6%.

14 It would seem that in the end only those who decided to leave were expected to return the money.

15. For a discussion of resistance to displacement see Oliver-Smith (2002).

16. See, Gebre (2001), Wolde-Selassie (2002) and Assefa (2002).

17. On understandings of social integration see Cernea (1985).

18. For discussions of similarities and contrasts see Zelalem 2005: 54-100; Gebre 2005: 376-7; Feleke 2003.

19. Prime Minister Meles Zenawi stated: 'Our resettlement programme is totally different from that undertaken by the Derg. For one thing, the Derg's resettlement programme was a forced one, while ours is being carried out on a voluntary basis. In our programme farmers reserve the right not to be involved in the programme and also to return to their previous localities if they are not comfortable in the new environment. For this purpose, the land that a resettler used to cultivate in his or her original place is reserved for three years in case he/she returns. So this programme is a voluntary exercise totally different from that of the Derg, which was carried out without the consent of the resettlers.' (May 2004, quoted in Zelalem 2005:70.)

20. It should be noted that the Derg resettlement plan also had the criteria that prospective settlers should be willing to resettle, and that there was voluntary resettlement especially in the earlier period in 1984 prior to the rains in some areas and that the types and degrees of coercion varied over time and place (Pankhurst 1992a).

Part V

THE DILEMMAS OF REFUGEES, RETURNEES & DISPLACED GROUPS

Twelve

In the Mouth of the Lion

Working with the Displaced in Addis Ababa

LEWIS APTEKAR & BEHAILU ABEBE

Introduction

Critiques of humanitarian assistance (Duffield 1995; Maren 1997; Timberlake 1986) have often been written from a distance. In contrast, the view here is close-up; the smells, sounds and sites of Kaliti, a camp for the displaced outside Addis Ababa, will engage the reader, often but not exclusively unpleasantly, with actual people, many of whom live in dire circumstances.

Humanitarian assistance almost always involves people from the developed nations offering assistance to impoverished people with different cultural traditions. Inherent in this work is a continual flow of moral conflicts. Decisions have to be made often affecting people's lives. The central motivation of the aid worker, trying to give to the needy, is not easy. It is often frustrating and difficult for well-meaning people to continue working in the field. A good deal of this has to do with how people who are receiving the assistance cope with their own life circumstances. I am a Western psychologist, my colleague an Ethiopian anthropologist. Together we discuss how our views, and the coping styles of the displaced in Kaliti, influenced our attempts to begin a mental health programme during our nearly two years of ethnographic fieldwork.

The size of Kaliti camp was 4,125 square meters.[1] To get a sense of the physical conditions, if the camp were one square kilometre there would be nearly a million people living in it, making the density of living space (including private living areas, public buildings like the school-house, latrines, and stores, and public walkways) about one person per 1.98 square meters. This meant that a step in any direction involved bumping into someone or having to take a side step.

Before they were displaced most families made a decent living as civil servants. The men were married to women from Tigray, so when the war ended[2] the women were given a few hours to choose either Eritrean or Ethiopian citizenship. If they chose Eritrean citizenship, they could remain close to their families of origin, but they would not be able to stay with their husbands and children because they were considered to be enemies. If they accepted Ethiopian citizenship they could continue their lives with their husbands and children, but they would have to leave their original families and homelands. The people in Kaliti left their homelands to start new lives with their husbands and children.

Kaliti was composed of two groups of people, one from Assab and the other from Asmara. To get to Addis the people from Assab were forced to trek through the hostile Danakil Depression, where temperatures reached 50 degrees centigrade in the shade, without water. Because they were forced to leave with only what they could carry they made the march with insufficient water. Almost everyone bore witness to relatives and friends who perished from thirst.

Woizoro Zewde, a middle-aged woman from Assab, told us that that it took her family 20 days to cross the Danakil. They had one jerrycan of water per day; she and her husband had eight children, and three perished on the march. They continued until they were close to the border. When they stopped that night a small group of Islamic fundamentalists told them they would not be allowed to continue, which meant that they were obstructing the path of life. Two men in Zewde's party complained, and their throats were slit. During the night they remained captive. In the morning they were allowed to continue walking, which Zewde interpreted as a blessing from God.

GETTING STARTED

At the time Woizoro Zewde was a member of the camp committee. On our first visit to the camp we explained to her and other committee members that we were working with the Dutch government and the Department of Psychiatry at Addis Ababa University to conduct research on the mental health of the people traumatized by war. We asked for their help in allowing us to carry out a survey. We also wanted to train some camp members to help others with mental health problems. Some of these trainees might become part of our 'core group' who would become proficient enough to train people in other camps. In return, we would pay for a school teacher for the youngest children, supply the services of a nurse and, because we were working in the Department of Psychiatry, help them with whatever psychiatric needs they might have.

They listened and made a few comments, the men taking the lead in the conversation, the women waiting for the men to speak before adding their comments. Then came the big question, what material benefits would they get, and we said, unfortunately we cannot supply material benefits, such as housing or food. After this they do not tell us directly whether they are going to accept or reject our proposal. Perhaps, this is the reason why we feel obliged to add that, by helping us gather information, they would be helping others in similar situations. Then for further leverage we tell them we are part of a worldwide effort to discover cultural differences in people's reactions to war-related trauma. We continue to sit and make pleasant conversation until we have to leave, and they tell us again they need medicine and food.

As time went on there was a constant negotiation between what we could offer and get for them, and what we promised (or what they thought we promised). Whether this was based on their past experiences with different types of projects that made promises that were not kept, or a symptom of post-traumatic stress, or an honest expression of their fear of dying because of lack of resources, was difficult to know. What was clear was that coming to an acceptable agreement about what the programme would do for them, and what they would do to help themselves, was an ongoing test that determined the nature of our working relationship.

In spite of the tenuous contract we had with the people of Kaliti, we were being asked by the home office in the Netherlands to take European visitors. Early on a European woman and an Ethiopian man, both of whom were on leave from their work in Rwanda, came to Kaliti. When the four of us entered the camp, the children gathered around as usual. The question of whether or not the visitors would contribute something arose without being mentioned.

The first person we saw was Solomon, a tall slender orphaned young man in his early twenties. When we entered his tent, he was too sick to sit up to talk to us. He had diarrhoea continually and he was asking us for *Bactrim*. He could not get the antibiotic, because he had no money to buy it, and without it he could not keep going. Because he was an orphan he had considerably less help.[3] In his case this meant that when he was sick, there was no one to get him food, let alone prepare it for him. Nor was there anyone to place within reach the used tin can that was his latrine, nor even anyone to hold his head when he was too sick to lift it and the vomit rolled down his chin under his clothes.

As we were leaving I asked the woman visitor if she would like to give Solomon money for food. She immediately became anxious and turned to her Ethiopian colleague for help; however, even before receiving a reply from her colleague, she asked me how much I thought would be appropriate. I said about 10 *birr*. (I should have suggested a higher figure.) Then she asked her colleague to give it to him for her. She did not want to give it to Solomon herself, she said, because 'it will just reinforce the stereotype of white people giving money to black people'. But there was more behind this; to give was at least to begin to accept the reality of what one was encountering.

As the four of us drove back from the camp, the visitors from Rwanda began to express their reactions. They were overwhelmed by the poverty, disease, and what they saw as deep despair. I thought what they saw here would have paled in comparison with what they had seen in Rwanda. The people of Kaliti were suffering from something more mundane yet far more frequent – no machetes severing limbs, no children surviving only because they were able to kill their mothers and fathers. The truth was that the scenario of Kaliti is far more common among the world's 40 million refugees and displaced people than the highlighted atrocities that my visitors had been working in (see Daniel and Knudson 1995; Duffield 1995; Summerfield 1998).

Post-traumatic stress disorder

Because of their ordeal we expected to see many people with post-traumatic stress disorder (PTSD). The best-known symptoms of PTSD are either flashbacks during the day or bad dreams at night. Because the sufferer remembers the trauma when s/he encounters similar events, s/he begins to change his/her normal life patterns to avoid stimuli that provoke distress. Another typical symptom is a numbing response; highly charged emotions with important people (like family members) are dealt with without feeling. Also, many traumatized people are hyper-vigilant, presenting too strong a response to benign stimuli. The normal degree of response is replaced with the extremes calibrated to protection based on the body's fight-or-run response. This heightened level of alertness is sustained by emergency biochemical changes. At some point the body can no longer maintain its level of alertness and begins to turn against itself, eventually reducing its ability to cope and ultimately leading to a physical and mental demise. When coupled with lack of adequate nutrition, this eventually leads to illness (see WHO 1995).

Throughout the study we went from believing that the people were suffering from PTSD to believing they were not, and later coming up with a broader, and we believe a more accurate, assessment of PTSD, one that would encompass their psycho-social problems, which finally we could not dismiss as benign. These subtler, yet still debilitating, psycho-social manifestations of trauma included many physical symptoms, difficulties in facing new challenges, and problems associated with engaging unnecessarily and self-destructively in petty disputes. All of these symptoms overrode the process of coming to terms with the larger issues of grief and rejuvenation that the people of Kaliti would have to face. They were therefore, particularly given their duration, important symptoms of mental disorder.

The main trouble was how to figure out the interplay between post-traumatic symptoms, personality changes due to malnutrition, AIDS-related dementia (ARD), the psychological sequel of TB, and the side-effects of untreated epilepsy. Nearly half the people with full-blown AIDS show some signs of ARD, which is a clinical syndrome consisting primarily of dementia (a loss of memory and reduced mental concentration, including loss of other intellectual functions). Patients with ARD often suffer from mania and panic attacks with psychosis, and many have depressive symptoms often associated with the realization that they are losing their functions and dying. In fact, depression and apathy are often early manifestations. Also, AIDS patients who are on anti-psychotic medication are likely to experience an anti-cholinergic delirium, which is characterized by visual and/or tactile hallucinations, confusion, and, at times, agitation. All these symptoms were apparent at Kaliti. There were other manifestations of suffering as well; but there were also many people who were coping, so we had to ask, could it be possible that the people in Kaliti, in spite of being traumatized and not having assurance of shelter, food and medical care, were managing better than expected? If they were, why was this?

Also, what, if any, was our role in helping them deal with these difficulties? At the outset of the work, we attended a party given by a man in charge of a national aid programme. Our host asked us about our work. When we told him we were working in the field of mental health, his response was that what we were doing was a laughable enterprise. He said that, if he were giving money for aid to Ethiopia, mental health would be far down the list, certainly below immunization, shelter, sanitation, primary health care, etc. His list went on for an uncomfortable amount of time. Although we were taken aback, we were not able to dismiss his point. The people's poverty was so striking that their mental health could be viewed as an addendum.

Yet we were to learn that a single person with a major mental disorder was a significant financial drain on their family and community. Not only were the mentally ill unable to contribute to the family income; they also caused family members to lose time from their own work in order to care for them. Moreover, their families had to cope with additional day-to-day expenses such as costs of medical care, transport, medicines, etc. Here we are only talking about people with severe mental disorders. When we took into consideration the lost productivity due to depression and anxiety, and linked with alcohol and *chat* dependence, the costs rose even further.[4]

International assistance programmes are usually run by Westerners trained in social science who have accepted a hierarchical scale of needs drawn up by Abraham Maslow, the American psychologist who defined the basic requirements beginning with food and shelter and moving up to community and spirituality. We have come to believe that all of these needs are basic, and that, without being able to satisfy the so-called higher needs, people are unable to compete for the lower ones. Mental health was what made the people in Kaliti competitive in continuing life. With each continued round of diminished humanitarian assistance, and without adequate mental health, they took a seat further back. In Kaliti, and places like it, there was not much room for people at the lower end of the line.

The next time we arrived in the camp we were taken to see Astra, a small dark-skinned Oromo woman in her mid-thirties. She too was so acutely ill that she could not raise her head to acknowledge us when we entered her space. She had a fever and was dehydrated. Her friend Checkla told us that she had not eaten for several days. Frazer, Astra's son, who we were told was her only living relative, sat by her side, remaining with her night and day, a witness to her demise. Checkla helped her turn over; when she did, the plastic grain sack that was her blanket slipped off, revealing her reed-thin body. Checkla covered her gently, while we tried to take down her history. Astra's immediate concern was that she did not have enough food with which to take her medicine; each time she tried she vomited. Grunting with physical effort that was more signs than words, she pleaded with me for money for injections which could be taken without food.

Astra had already spent all her resources on medicine, which was bought with the money supposed to have been spent on food. By our figuring, there were three ways for her to get money: (i) she could borrow it from her family or a friend; (ii) she could borrow it against her future grain rations; and (iii) she could get money from us. Her first option was no option. Her family had all perished except for her son, Frazer, who was already contributing as much as he could by shining shoes. Her neighbours had already loaned her some money; they could give her more but only by jeopardizing their own lives. Her second option was also not viable, because she had already borrowed once against her future grain rations. If she did this again, she would have no hope of being able to repay her debt which, upon her death, might be passed on to her son. This left the third option: us.[5]

A few days later Astra was admitted to Mother Teresa's home for AIDS victims. Her friend Checkla, who took her there, was staying with her because she needed constant care. Unfortunately, a problem emerged; since Checkla would be away from the camp, who would take care of Checkla's children? Several people gathered around us to talk about the situation. Before long, the conversation became heated. Amarech, a flamboyant super-charged stout middle-aged woman from Assab, screamed at us to get out of the camp. We were not helping them, she shouted, only causing more problems. Why should she give up her grain ration for Checkla's two children when we could give them money?

Within a few weeks word came to us that Astra had died in the Mother Teresa home. We sat in a tent while people were talking about what to do with Frazer, her surviving eight-year-old boy. Astra's friend Lulu agreed to take care of him, until something more permanent could be worked out. Some people thanked us for helping Astra get into the home, but others were not pleased that we were not assuming financial responsibility for Frazer. As we left the tent there were a dozen or more women in a heated discussion outside. One was arguing that Astra's body should be left at Mother Teresa's, which would mean that Astra would not receive a proper burial. This woman based her position on the costs of bringing the body back to Kaliti. She believed that all the resources Astra had (she had some 100 kilos of *tef*) should go to taking care of Frazer, now an orphan.

Leading the opposition against this was Woizoro Amarech, who wanted Astra's body returned to Kaliti and prepared for a proper funeral. She claimed that since Astra had been in the camp with the rest of them for six years, she should be buried among them. Did the argument stem from ethnic tensions – Astra was from Tigray and the people who were complaining about the costs of giving her a proper funeral were from Amhara – or was it because Astra did not belong to an *iddir*, and therefore there was no financial responsibility to help her?. It was also possible that the argument was fueled by the tension diverted from their continual psychological stress and had less to do with community associations or ethnicity than with coping with difficult stress factors. There was even another possible reason, which was to discredit the woman who was arguing against a proper burial because her opponents felt that she was getting too much from us. They reasoned that if she could be demoted someone else would be in favor, which, through association by friendship, family relations, or ethnic affinity, might well provide them with a possible source of income. Even if the income was meagre it was potentially important, maybe even life-affirming.

TO GIVE OR NOT TO GIVE?

We knew that material assistance would not solve their emotional trauma. We asked them rhetorically 'how many of the people in the camp who lost loved ones would feel better about their losses by receiving material assistance?' In spite of what was given, most of them would have to come to terms with being less comfortable, more hungry, and suffering from far too many physical woes than my money could solve. Whatever degree of destitution they faced, we wanted them to know that what would separate the resilient from the desperate would have more to do with their human spirit than with whatever material benefits they received from us.[6]

Our reasoning for helping materially boiled down to the following. It was necessary to give them material aid because: (i) we were doing research with them, so they were earning it; (ii) it was an important aspect to building up a therapeutic trusting relationship with them; and (ii) because we had it, and they needed it, we had no ethical alternative. We were aware that this approach flew in the face of what would be acceptable therapeutic behavior in the West, where engagement by the counsellor is frowned on and material assistance unheard of. As time went on we abandoned the secular Western professional stance, and moved into communicating more on the spiritual and symbolic level.[7]

STRESS FACTORS: IS THERE A DOCTOR IN THE HOUSE, OR SHOULD I EAT?

As we continued to go to Kaliti on a daily basis we began to know more people. One was Tsehaynesh, a displaced Tigrayan woman in her late thirties, who lived in one of the three large tents donated to the camp by the EU. She shared her space and wheat with Hirut, a pregnant widow, and her 12-year-old son, David. Together they lived in a two by three meters space, the same size as a prison cell. She spent almost all her time lying on a dried mud and straw bed over which hung a photocopy of a religious painting in bright pastels and several figures of attractive young white women cut out of fashion magazines. Her belongings were stuffed into two cardboard boxes at the foot of her bed, each of which doubled as a stool. Her single set of extra clothes hung from the part of the tent's eucalyptus rafters that was in her space. The three of them shared a blue plastic five-gallon container for water, and a black long-necked ceramic coffeepot with six small, white ceramic cups for the coffee ceremony. When we asked about her health, she said that today was a good day, meaning that she was only bleeding intermittently and not continually.

Tsehaynesh, not atypically, saved her money for food instead of using it to go to the doctor. She told us that, to get the money needed to see the doctor, she would have to sell her monthly grain ration in advance. The 'businessman' who would lend her money, against the collateral of her grain, asked for a 15 percent monthly interest rate. Pointing across her living space to the other bed, she told us that her 'room mates' had already sold more than a year's supply of their grain ration in advance and no one could or would front them any more.

Tsehaynesh, like so many others in this camp, had two identities. Her official one was based on obtaining as much as possible from her status of being a displaced person. In this official identity she inflated the number of people in her family (saying that her husband was alive and they had two children) because aid was assigned according to family size.[8] Personal identities were more secret. Before we found out that Tsehaynesh's husband had died before the march, and that she was supporting herself and her only child by being what was called a 'bar girl', serving drinks and being friendly to the foreigners coming into the port of Assab, we would have to develop a significant degree of trust.

She reached under her soiled blanket to bring out a small piece of folded paper, and opened it to show us six yellow pills; resuming her crying, she said, 'The pharmacist at the clinic is stealing our medicine and selling it'. She and others thought the pharmacist at the clinic was giving them cheaper or outdated medicines or smaller doses, and making a profit by selling the better drugs.[9]

In fact, medical care and the changing rules about the Food for Work Programme consistently reduced the amount of food that the work brought in. Also, the changing position of the government about allowing grain to come into the country untaxed prevented people from knowing if it was going to come at all. This kept them in a constant state of anxiety, resulting not only in hoarding, but also in continual accusations and bad will towards the people in power, including themselves.

ARE THEY OR ARE THEY NOT DISPLACED?

Another stressor was the worry over whether or not they would remain eligible for benefits and compensation for losses. This depended upon their official status of being registered as a displaced person. They never knew if the camp would be torn down and they would be forced to leave (the camp burned to the ground in 2003, United Nations Regional Information Networks, 27 May 2003). With sticks constantly being used behind them, carrots were dangled in front of them. They were offered money, start-up fees, etc., if they left and agreed to certain restrictions. Again, this contributed to living in a constant state of turmoil. In this case, this proved to be an important reason why they could not heal their wounds from their trek across the Danakil nor leave the camp to start a new life.

When we first met Yodit, a 21-year-old diminutive Oromo woman, who weighed no more than 40 kg, she had the beauty of a doll special enough to be treasured. But her life was anything but protected. Her parents were divorced and for much of her childhood she was raised in Asmara by an aunt. When her aunt died she accepted an arranged marriage at 13 years of age, but her husband left her before she was 15. Then she voluntarily married a soldier, and they built a house on the outskirts of Asmara where they lived together. She re-established her relationship with her mother. They had some household property and personal belongings, and she was able to tell her friends that she was happy with her life.

During the war the army division of her husband was mobilized. When Asmara was about to fall, Yodit went to inquire about him at the military barracks where he had been stationed, but he had already joined the front. Moments after she walked into the camp, it was closed, and people were banned from leaving. The next day, all the residents of the camp including Yodit and the others who happened to be there at the wrong time were made to leave Asmara. She was given no opportunity of saying goodbye to her mother.

Miraculously, a few months later she was reunited with her husband in Jan Meda, the main transit camp for the displaced in Addis Ababa. He was living with his parents who were in Cherkos, a working-class quarter of the capital. The young couple tried living there, but her husband's parents refused to accept Yodit because, being from Tigray, they did not look kindly on Oromo. The ethnic difference was enough to lead to their demise as a couple. The problem was that by this time she was pregnant. Shortly after their baby was born she was forced to leave, and having no place to live she moved into Kaliti. Within six months she was diagnosed with TB.

When we saw her six months later she was so depressed that she stared into space, never budging from a near-catatonic posture no matter what the topic of conversation. She complained of being hot. Her arms from the elbow down were flat, like pieces of cardboard rather than flesh. The skin on her face was scaly and blotched and her feet curled up under the covers, so that from head to toe she was no more than a reduced replica of an adult woman. Her now 12-month-old baby daughter was lying next to her completely covered with what appeared to be soiled towels.[10]

As we began to talk she took off the cloths that veiled the baby and, looking into the child's face, we could see its eyes bulging from a nearly hairless head, its mouth gasping for the milk that Yodit did not have. With her own health failing, when she put the baby to her breast it could find no more milk and stiffened, wailing in silence. The doctor, she said, had told her the baby was fine, except for being malnourished. This had soothed her into thinking that her child could be saved.

Yodit's history overflowed with such adversity that it was impossible to tease out the influence of each component in her current mental state; and maybe it was not important to do so. As time progressed our work with her became a topic of constant discussion. For one thing, she raised the issue of whether or not it was possible to work with the people in Kaliti without offering them some material help. For another, Yodit was ready to go back to her mother in Asmara, but she could not quite make the move.

Yodit also demonstrated the problems of being ill in Kaliti, where the types of sickness meant living on the edge of life, because coupled with physical illness was the fact that the people in Kaliti were malnourished, and for many their immune systems were seriously compromised. This was why victims of typhus and typhoid and TB patients died. There were no antiviral drugs to slow the opportunistic infections brought about by the disease and no drugs to reduce the side-effects of dementia or depression. There was nothing to interrupt the dance of death between AIDS and TB here. We could no longer avoid the degree of illness and death in the camp. The people would have to get more medical attention and better food or they would die in multitudes. Many of these people would also have mental health problems, some of them were related to their past trauma and others to physical illnesses. Many cases were probably HIV-related.

Different views of health and illness

People in the West doubtless follow the scientific reasoning that is the origin for understanding our bodies and our mental status. While at first it seemed that this was not the case among the Ethiopians, whose beliefs about mental health and illness seemed strongly influenced by what the West referred to as the spiritual world, we also saw many similarities (Vecchiato, 1993b).

In Kaliti two spirits were particularly important, the *buda* and the *zar*. When the *buda*, the Amharic word for evil eye, possessed its victim, not only would the person become physically ill, but s/he would also succumb to a hysterical collapse consisting of shaking and incoherent vocalizations. The people in Kaliti assumed that Amarech had been possessed by the evil eye. Someone possessed by the evil eye could pass it on to others, so if Amarech was possessed she had the power to possess others. Some people thought she was a sorceress, capable of giving someone the evil eye.

People devised rituals, often consisting of highly structured behavior, to protect themselves against the spirit world and thus ward off mental illness. For example, there were those who believed that if one neglected one's responsibilities to the elderly one would suffer the wrath of the *buda*; so the elderly were rarely left alone. Children, particularly attractive and happy ones, were considered the most vulnerable to the *buda*, so they had to be protected. Some mothers placed something made of iron at the head of their child's bed to ward off the *buda*; almost every mother had an amulet attached to their child for protection. Many adults in the camp wore silver bracelets on their left wrists; some tied a string on to their left thumb. Chickens were sacrificed, and the blood used to avoid the *buda*.

Almost everyone observed dietary restrictions, including avoiding eating pork. We heard about people deliberately avoiding urinating at dawn, because they could be ambushed by a spirit. Also the spirit had an affinity for living in streams or lakes, so many people avoided fresh water, as they did walking through a graveyard, or being out alone at midnight or midday.

The second important spirit was the *Zar*, thought to have originated from Eve in the Garden of Eden. It was said that Eve had 30 children, and hid 15 of them from God when he brought the apple to her attention. When God discovered the 15 hidden children, he made them live forever in the dark and gave them power to possess humans. From these 15 came 82 *Zar* spirits. They were not necessarily considered evil, but they were the bearers of physical and mental illnesses, including typhus, typhoid, smallpox and seizures, all of which were seen as coming from *Zar* spirits. If a woman had a disabled baby, it was considered that a *Zar* spirit had impregnated her.[11]

In spite of the differences about what causes mental illness in Ethiopia and in the West, the behaviors that describe the mentally ill in Ethiopia are comparable to those of the West. The term *ibd* is used for people who wander naked on the streets and whose language is unintelligible, who are aggressive and talk to themselves. *Wofefe* refers to people whose mood fluctuates suddenly. *Bisichu* describes people who respond to life's problems with a great deal of irritability, intense gloom or severe anxiety.[12]

To ward off these powerful spirits, particularly if they are associated with mental illness, about 80 percent of Ethiopians go to traditional healers (see Araya and Aboud 1993). Some rules for traditional healing were originally written in Ge'ez texts, illustrating a long-standing religious history of traditional medical care. These texts included empirical medical care such as the use of herbs. There were 300 or more materials from plants, animals, and the earth that served as medicines (Vecchiato 1993b). For example, coffee was often consumed as a relief for headaches, eucalyptus leaves were stuffed into the nostrils for the relief of cold symptoms, and skin and arthritic conditions were often treated with herbs or leaves. The texts were also filled with magical religious prescriptions such as the power of the number seven, which repeatedly turned up as significant (as it did in the Old Testament). A person might be instructed to take seven leaves from seven different plants to reduce an illness or to avoid it altogether.

Sorcerers (*tenkway*) used divination of leaves, brewing herbs, eating ash without water, beating and burning, animal sacrifices and the application of animal blood to cure clients. In severe cases hot metal was applied to the client's face to make burns of certain patterns. There were also shamans (*balezar)*, demons (*ganel genach)* and seers. The *tenkway* was a sorcerer who treated illnesses caused by the *buda* and *djinn (*evil spirits) by invoking spirits through singing and dancing, fasting and animal sacrifices. The *dabtara* wrote messages that were put into amulets. The patient wore the amulet to prevent getting an illness (Vecchiato 1993b). There was also a new class of healer, one who treated the dreaded never-mentioned HIV virus, by using injections; sometimes the substance they injected was no more than distilled water advertised as holy water.

The first line of medical care for most people in Kaliti against the *buda* or *Zar* spirits was to seek out holy water (*tebel*).[13] The belief was that this water had special qualities, which helped towards shedding the power of the spirit that was causing their illness. In addition, people went to church to be healed, where they found many similarities with the *Zar* healers. The Ethiopian Church, like the *Zar* practitioners, believed that people were in the throess of a constant struggle between God and Satan, between angels and demons, or from uninvited malevolent spirits. Both types of healers saw their work as reducing the influence of the devil and increasing God's presence. *Zar* counselling and a session in the Orthodox Church were similar and started with a prayer.

Because priests and *Zar* healers worked to install God in place of the despised devil, they were less interested in case histories than in church attendance, and curing the client had less to do with restoring health than with eliminating symptoms.[14] The *Zar* healer, following a prayer, would open up his coffee tray (*ganda*) and offer a coffee ceremony, which in effect was like opening the Tabot in the Orthodox Church or the Torah in Judaism, signifying entry into the religious world. Then the *Zar* healer would ask the possessed person if they 'saw a dream', and if so to tell it. By recalling the dream and by the way the person expressed their recollections, the healer would make a diagnosis about what *zar* spirit had possessed them. In the church the client would also be asked to talk about what ailed them, and again in the language of demons and spirits.[15]

As counseling progressed the *Zar* healer and the client would go through a series of negotiations, the healer asking the patient to tell him what was wrong, the patients deferring and asking for help from the healer. Then the healer would tell the client that he or she would get better but that to do so they must follow a certain regime. The threats, pleas and promises that made up the negotiations ended in the client's promise to participate. It was hoped that the client would make a commitment to the *Zar* therapy, which meant that, in exchange for regular payments, the client would begin a type of exorcism that was supposed to end in being symptom-free (Kahana 1985; Messing 1965). The process in the church was not all that different. In fact, I was not so sure that Western counselors would describe their process very differently.

Although most mental illnesses were thought to be curable through exorcism, both parties generally assumed that the mentally ill person would only be temporarily cured. It was thought that the possession could not be broken, but that the traditional healer knew how to help the spirit and the victim live in harmony. To stay healthy it was necessary to visit the *Zar* healer regularly. Because clients went over and over again they formed their own therapeutic community. The patient thus became part of the *Zar* community, which meant paying a continual fee, in order to avoid being repossessed (Messing 1965). *Zar* healers through the organization of their rituals gave hope to the ill, and provided coping strategies for the daily strains of life and effective group psychotherapy, as well as education on how to live. In short, it sounds much like the therapeutic communities in the West, including Alcoholics Anonymous.

Treatment for spirit possession also occurred as a matter of course in Orthodox churches either as part of the normal service or at special services, in which case several people who were designated helpers, one of them usually the priest or his designate, the *dabtara*, would meet the client. The *dabtara* was extremely powerful, being able to talk to spirits, drive them away, and change their purpose. People who wanted to be cured had to attend church regularly and follow the directives given by the *dabtara*; not very different from Western-oriented cognitive therapy.

Having seen so many similarities, it is also important to mention the differences as well. In Ethiopia mental health services were most often provided in the church or in an area which was designated for its spiritual value, whereas in the West they were more likely to be provided in the doctor's or clinician's surgery, both of which were non-sectarian spaces. When Ethiopians went to church or to a traditional healer for psychological problems, they subjected themselves to God or to other forms of the supernatural. In the West the client wanted to consult a professional, and expected healing to come from theories based on natural scientific principles. The philosophy of the practitioner in the West was considered to be secular humanism and the practice was democratic, while in Ethiopia the practitioner was religious and authoritarian. In Ethiopia the client had no power in the counseling relationship, and trusted his weakness to the all-powerful priest or traditional healer, while in the West counseling was conceived of as a partnership between counselor and client.

The reasons for becoming a healer in Ethiopia were secondary to one's true calling which was to do God's work, while in the West one specialized in caring for people's mental health, not very differently from any other service profession. To become a healer in Ethiopia one went through the rites of passage and the training of a religious indoctrination. This was different from attending graduate or professional school, which meant, in addition to other differences, that the Ethiopian training called for accepting the unknown, while the Westerner trained to find rational truth. Ethiopian healers were more likely to receive insight into the clinical process from prayer than at academic conferences. This was clear in the different idioms used in therapeutic communication. In the West clinicians used rational language, whereas the language of the Ethiopian healer had its own semiotic idiom, one of trance and possession.[16] Spirits always spoke during the healing process, although the spirit was not the person from whose mouth the expression emerged; it was always someone else.

There were also different explanatory models of causation, which in the West were environmental and physical, while in Ethiopia they were spiritual and animistic. In Ethiopia mental illness was believed to be caused by evil spirits, each with its own name and *modus operandi*, while in the West the causes of mental illness came from childhood traumas or perceptions of them, ongoing mental stresses, and physiological dispositions.

The medical disease model of the West versus the spiritual orientation of the Ethiopians meant that the focus of treatment, which in the West was individual or family-oriented, was in Ethiopia in group form and religious. Counseling in the West was commonly an individual affair, one client seeing one counselor, while in Ethiopia it was almost always done in a group. People went into a space that was shared with others, and waited while the traditional healer or church person attended to them.

Therapeutic expectations in the West involved occasional emotional arousal, but mostly well thought-out recollections of past and current events, while traditional Ethiopian clients were expected to be taken over by what we might refer to as a hysterical trance, or what they referred to as spiritual possession. In the West the mechanisms of change involved the client's learning to react to social situations differently, or to control their behaviour and make cognitive changes, while among traditional Ethiopians the client followed the instructions of the priest's or traditional healer's religious or spiritual persuasions. In the West the client listened and contemplated, in Ethiopia the client listened and followed directives.[17]

Given the comparisons between mental illness models, the role of therapists and the expectation of the clients, it was not totally surprising that it was not uncommon for people in the camp to abandon traditional healers if they were not getting better and go to Western healers, and of course, vice-versa.[18]

Having gone through some similarities and differences between beliefs concerning the origins of mental illness and the reasoning behind the counseling for mental illness we are now ready to apply this information to behaviors we saw in Kaliti.

SYMPTOMS IN KALITI

While stress, tension and mental disorders were part of the public fabric, they rarely showed themselves straightforwardly at least to Western eyes. There was the case of the widow who lived in poverty while hoarding her wealth under her mattress. Was this example a sign of post-traumatic stress disorder (PTSD)? There was a group of young men who spent their days playing cards. How were we to assess their avoidance of helping the civic polity? Was this symptomatic of poor mental health or was it what was culturally expected of men's behaviour? How should we look at the constant bickering between the different factions in the camp? For example, were the arguments about what to do with Checkla's two boys while she was taking care of Astra in the hospital, or what to do with Astra's money after she died and left her orphaned boy, Frazer, evidence of healthy coping or symptoms of PTSD? There were also the insistent demanding expectations directed towards people who were trying to help, which contributed to driving almost all the potential helpers away. Was this also a sign of PTSD?

When events became overpowering, we developed a strategy of leaving the person's tent while we went on to see another person. This time we went to see Nani, because we were told she and her daughter Amelok were quarreling. We found Nani overcome with sadness, tears gushing from her eyes, because Amelok had told her that she was going to leave the tent to live elsewhere. Nani, in addition to being terminally ill, was so close to having no material possessions, that today she had only eaten berbere chilli mixed into a glass of non-potable water.

Abay and Dagnachew, two of the young men in the camp with whom we were working, responded to Amelok's threat to leave home with a lecture about taking better care of her mother. We tried to get them to be quiet, but it was not easy. Our point was that the emphasis in our counselling should be on Amelok's needs and not her mother's, which flew in the face of their view. We told them that Amelok's mother was going to die soon, either of illness or starvation or both, while Amelok still had to make a life, not only for herself but also for her little brother. While they could appreciate this point, it was not easy, because we were asking them to accept the opposite of what they had grown up with, namely to take care of their parents at all costs.

We avoided seeing Woizoro Tsehaynesh for a week or longer, because she was so sick we knew we could do nothing for her. When we finally went to see her we found we were able to be more honest, almost as if we had needed this time to prepare for honesty. We gave her 50 *birr* to bring in a priest for what was left unsaid, to give her last rites. This made her cry, we hoped in gratitude and not fear. She told us that we were the only ones to help her. We told her to look carefully at her roommate. She had been helping her every day. What a pity that she could not take advantage of it; maybe they lived too close to each other, or were too similar in status to be helpers?

We went to have coffee with Zewde. Mulu, the best friend of Zewde's daughter, came in to tell us that she had decided to 'give my child to my parents'. Mulu's stepfather, Ato Biru, was holding the child up and letting him stand on his own, which he was barely able to do, even though he was far beyond the appropriate age for this. As soon as he saw Mulu, he began to cry for her. Mulu did not intervene or pick him up. We were at a loss to understand what was happening. It was clear from what we had seen of them together that she had loved this boy. Were these ties so easily broken by the decision to give him away? Maybe by giving her child to her parents her parents' pleasure would be increased, and this would relieve Mulu of the guilt of not having been able to care for the baby herself? If this were true, maybe it was in the interests of both child and mother.

Tsehaynesh was getting weaker. She was too tired to talk. We had to ask her to remove her single blanket, which she had over her head, so that we could communicate with her. The flies were getting more abundant every day. We were told that the priest had visited last Sunday and spent an hour with her, giving her water and praying with her. We were glad of that. We asked Abay, another of the camp students, to look in on her every day. He asks me what he should say to her. We tell him that he should just talk to her and be with her while she is in need. He does not have to choose or avoid any topic.

The next day Woizoro Tsehaynesh died. When we saw her sleeping yesterday with the blanket over her head and the flies swarming around her, it was just hours before she passed away. Evidently, she woke up only one more time, around 5pm, asking for water and a bit of food. Then she died in her sleep. The priest came to get her ready for the funeral and they buried her without a coffin near the local church. More than 100 people from the camp were sitting outside her tent mourning. There was no coffee, so we gave them money to get some. We learned that her daughter, her only living relative, was not informed about her death. We were sorry that the two of them had no chance to see each other one last time. All we could say to the mourners was that Tsehaynesh was at peace when she died. Several people told us that we had done a lot for her. We told them that they also had done a lot for her. After about 20 minutes we got up to leave. We were sad, but we got on with our work as a way of not feeling it; we were bolstered by the idea that they said we had done a great deal to help her. Dagnashew gave the best solace, 'It is better to say she is resting than that she is dead, better to think of her as having what she wanted near the end, some peace, rather than to think that she will never get what she deserved.'

Solomon looked awful; once again he was sick in bed and not able to get up. His teeth were protruding from his sunken face. He lay on his bed, his rags over him for covers, and the same gray jacket done up tight for warmth. We found that we did not really want to be inside the tent, but not to be outside either. We compromised by leaning against the opening. We told him that we were going to bring in a *ferenj* nurse who might be able to get him into the Alert hospital. He indicated that he was glad, but he was too weak to talk. We told him to hold on, that God loved him, but what we really wanted to say was that we loved him, but we were too embarrassed. We were sorry that he had not taken the oral rehydration solution we had given him, especially when it could have made him feel better. We realized that this kind of care was not a high priority for him.

No one was removing his waste (urine and faeces). If Solomon could not do it, then it was his family's responsibility. If he had no family, we hoped that there was enough civil responsibility to take care of him, or that the health committee would become involved. In fact, someone should be turning him in his bed so that he will not get bed sores, and someone should see to it that he is warm, and make sure he gets enough water. We really wanted to be clear about this, and to tell them that, with so many men playing cards all day, they ought to be able to find a way to do this kind of civic work. Had we made no progress towards the community's mental health?

We talked to several of the camp students about the fact that Solomon might have AIDS. The general feeling among them was that it was OK for him to have a test, but that we should keep it very low-profile, namely, not mention the word to him or pass it on to anyone else. When we talked to Solomon about it he said he wanted to go for the medical examination. While we talked, a cockroach roamed across him without being knocked away, and he said he considered himself lucky to have the chance.

When we finally took Solomon to the clinic he was dressed in a clean sweatshirt and had a broad smile. It was nice to see him this way, as if he had come back from the dead. When we got to the clinic he told the doctor that he had had sex eight years ago, but not since. He was in Assab at the time, which had a high incidence of HIV. Then the doctor examined him on the table, and said, straightaway, that maybe his problem was that he was starving. This struck a nerve with us; could it be that, after all this concern, his problem was profoundly simple? He needed more food. Ten days later we took Solomon back to the doctor. His lab test showed that he had a bacterial infection in his lungs (pneumonia), anaemia; the doctor suspects TB, and finally said the dreaded word, HIV. Solomon was treated for the bacterial infection with antibiotics, and given iron pills for his anaemia, and we were told that in ten days time he would undergo a further blood test and chest x-ray, and then we could decide what to do.

Solomon had been getting food from Zewde. However, since the grain was late she could not afford to give this to him any longer. Her family had no reserves. We begged her to give him food for ten more days. Zewde said they (meaning her collective family) could not do this. In spite of having worked so long with Zewde, we still could not get her to help Solomon. When the strings were drawn tight, they took care of their family and let the weak die. Maybe this was the way it had to be, that the food must be saved for the healthy, and that the sick had to be left to die. We wondered if Mulu ever thought about cutting out the food for one of her children.

We wanted Solomon to have some protein, at least lentils or beans, but this was beyond what most healthy people in the camp received. We were ready to settle for at least enough food for him to be able to keep his medicine down. We were even willing to come up with 90 percent of what he needed, no, make that 99 percent, but we still could not find someone else to come up with the 10 percent or even the 1 percent. We were convinced that we had made no progress at all with the counseling, and that the very family we had given so much to, was not willing to repay us in kind. Were all our efforts wasted?

The lab results confirmed that Solomon was HIV-positive. Should we tell him, and if so should we advise him to keep the information secret, or to share it with friends and the community? The majority thought we should not tell him, on the grounds that not only would it be bad for him, but also the people in the camp would avoid him if they knew he was HIV-positive. Many people would be afraid of touching him, and would probably not even speak to him. We were not sure if they were right; maybe Solomon could be better healed and more of a help to the camp by telling people about his status? However, since we were soon to be leaving because the project had run out of funds, we were in a bind. We did not want to tell Solomon about the results and then leave, nor did we want to not tell him, or give the results to someone else to tell him after we had left.

As we left camp for the last time he told us that he was only suffering from the fear of being alone, and the fear that the pain would linger on. We felt awful that at the moment when he was ready to face his death we were so close to leaving. He tried to cry repeatedly but never really broke down into tears. We held hands, and he said that he had not had sex in six years, and what bad luck this was, and we agreed.

Conclusion

After working in Kaliti we had to examine and calculate the degree of mental health of the inhabitants and the degree and kinds of mental disorders that existed in the camp. We found that, in spite of the obvious trauma they were living through by Western standards, it paled in comparison with the highly traumatized people in several other non-Western contexts. No inhabitants of Kaliti that we knew of had seen their loved ones murdered, and no one had been made to maim or kill their relatives in order to survive. Nor had they been through the kind of genocide that was associated with Rwanda.

What the Kaliti residents experienced was the abrupt forced exodus from their homes and the horrendous journeys to safety on which many of them died of thirst. Since arriving in Kaliti they had been under severe pressure, living in extreme poverty, and not knowing if they would continue to receive help. In spite of their problems, by comparison with the accounts of genocide in the international press, they had experienced a common run-of-the-mill kind of horror. This was what I think took the experts from Rwanda visiting Kaliti by surprise, and they did not therefore think the people of Kaliti were *bona fide* psychologically traumatized. Did the trauma in Kaliti, much more a feature of the 80 million displaced and refugees in the world, fade by comparison, so that the visiting experts from the worst 'stations of Hell' could not find the manifestations of trauma in the more common spaces of Hell?

We would have to explain the mental health of the people in Kaliti that would include the people who shuffled through one day and then another, leaning on the weight of promises made and broken. What could we say of their mental health as we saw them being forced to bend again and again to the vagaries of the ongoing climate of despair and hope? What characterized the people of Kaliti was being able to eat only one meal a day – and this no more than a threadbare *wet* and *injera.* To obtain medical care they were forced into a demeaning posture for even the minimum service. Having been promised compensation for what they had had to leave behind, or perhaps more succinctly holding onto the possibility of what they thought they had been promised, they also lived with the fear of giving up what claims they had. They were unwilling to leave Kaliti because they knew it would certainly mean forfeiting their claims and therefore the possibility of being able to return to the lifestyle they once had. As a result, many remained stuck in a deadly place and unable to leave it.

We found ourselves coming back to the question; why did they not leave? Even though life in Kaliti was rough, there were rational reasons for staying. They did not stay only because they were trapped, or because they were mentally ill. Of the people in Kaliti, it was the adolescents who seemed the strongest and the most willing to stay in the camp. There were several factors underlying the relative lack of psychopathology among the adolescents (Aptekar *et al.* 2000). One was the community's openness to allowing a non-traditional lifestyle among them. This was particularly true of females who were given nearly full adult status to socialize. Adults allowed the young people to open up to each other and made living in such a high density less of a burden. Sex in the camp between unmarried young men and women was not uncommon. In the past this would have brought considerable problems between parents and their adolescent children, but no longer. This change of attitude on the part of parents was the opposite situation to that adolescents and their parents faced under the Derg, when the *Kebele* held regular youth meetings, which it was in essence mandatory to attend. If the parents did not send their children to the meetings they were labelled as anti-government. Yet, if the parents did send them, they faced the prospect that the police, because they had so much power, might do something awful to their adolescents, including allegedly raping their daughters. Parents were scared of their children, because the *Kebele* could force them into testifying against them. Camp life provided an opportunity for parents and adolescents to get back to living together without fearing each other. This was not to be forgotten in trying to figure out why people stayed in the camp, and in enhancing the relationships between the generations.

Having learned from the time of the Derg, many parents in Kaliti chose to treat their adolescents as partners. This helped keep them at home. The two generations took care of one another; the adolescents contributed to their parents' hopes, so that their parents, even when they were reduced to near-hopelessness, found strength in seeing their children happy and took comfort in knowing that they could still help them, still make it up to their children. As Zewde said, 'Our children have God's good graces, look at them!'

The second reason for the relative lack of adolescent psychopathology came from the adolescents themselves. They took solace in making a comparison between their own and their parents' adolescence. When they did this they had much to be thankful for. Many adolescents told us that by the time their parents were pre-teenagers they were restricted to their homes. The young women were always under supervision until husbands had been chosen for them. They recalled their parents being routinely prevented from playing with the opposite sex, and even playing among their own gender. In contrast, they enjoyed the benefits of living in close community with many other adolescents in a relatively open way.

A third reason for their mental health was that they took care of one another. Although this care had its limitations, often from lack of knowledge, when we watched Bereket care for Solomon, or Yodit being ministered to by her friends, or Amelok caring for Nani, we came to understand how the very act of providing care to terminally ill friends or family gave the carer a reason to live. In Kaliti the good and the bad existed together. Illness and disease provided the awful drama of slow and tortured death, as well as the opportunity for love and care. The latter was a force of empowerment, and, when coupled with their spiritual traditions, helped them deal with what we in the West could not imagine, save for our most horrific literary images of Hell. Those who gave care found that they were also maturing and finding their own meaning in life.

OUR REGRETS

We should have told our host that, in Kaliti, getting what Maslow referred to as the necessities, i.e. food and shelter, was a competitive effort requiring both psychic energy and mental alertness. The winners were the most healthy mentally. In Kaliti they were the ones who had more will to live, more faith in what the future held, and less daily fear and anger. They were highly spiritual. They could enjoy life. They could find meaning in work, even if it was unpaid work. They found a reason to fight for justice, they enjoyed helping others, took pride in their positions of authority and continued to fight for the wellbeing of their offspring or their parents. These people represented important markers for understanding the nature of mental health.

In contrast, the people who were not prospering had less will to live, were not well integrated into the community, were self-centred and self-serving, and less appreciative of what they had or received. To understand our point about Maslow's theory was to see the crucial circularity: mental health became problematic as basic needs were unfulfilled; and basic needs were not met because of poor mental health. As time wore on, it became more and more apparent that the level of a person's mental health was what separated those who succumbed from those who survived. The physical wellbeing of the displaced, ultimately the question of who lived and who died, was dependent upon mental health.

It was a pity that, when donor agencies were making their choices about how to spend their limited funds (or, for that matter, when NGOs were seeking funding from the Western governments or international aid organizations), they had such a hard time persuading donors to give money for mental health. Our work suggested that this was shortsighted. To be sure, it was not necessary to have separate mental health clinics or individual counseling, but it was necessary to support a mentally healthy community, which meant acknowledging spirituality and altruism. To increase the will to live of a community like Kaliti meant not only giving them food, shelter, and health. To survive, the community must learn to seek its own justice by standing up to its government for what it deserved, to oppose those who were unethically taking away what they should be getting, and to help each other cope with their circumstances. Without food, shelter and medical care, it was impossible for the community to succeed; but even with these, success was not likely unless the varied attributes that made life meaningful existed.

Notes

1. We use the past tense because our census was taken in 1997. See Aptekar *et al.* (2000).
2. At the end of the civil war in 1991, the new Eritrean authorities chased out numerous civilians, and in 1998 such measures recurred both in Eritrea and in Ethiopia.
3. Solomon was one of about 160 male adolescents in Kaliti camp who were in many ways a third group of migrants. Once children without parental supervision reached Jan Meda in Addis, they were given special resources because they were without their parents. 'Orphan' was an official status of the international aid community, but it was a less definitive term than in the West where it means that both parents are dead. Some like Solomon had one live parent, that he had not seen, because of rejection due to problems with a stepfather or stepmother. Most orphans in Kaliti shared a common history. They entered the army because of the promise of being given food and money to attend school, functioning in a capacity best described as a mascot. The soldiers liked having them around, and they took care of the boys. In exchange the boys helped by washing clothes, cooking, making beds, cleaning shoes, etc. Most of the boys, although not Solomon, looked back at this time with pleasure, particularly in comparison with their material resources in the camp.
4. Some research indicates that a person in a developing country who has a mental illness may be considered 'recovered' more easily than a person in an industrialized country. The reasoning rests on the assumptions that many types of manual labour, such as those in agriculture and construction, allow lapses in consistency of work. Under these circumstances, such a person may be more easily re-integrated into the work community. However, in the developing world the ratio of employment to job-seekers is so severe that even people with mild to moderate cases of mental illness, where by definition the ability to *sustain* a work level or to work *continuously* is impaired, are likely to incur losses even in unskilled work, and the income flow that might be possible will, at best, be variable. Thus in the developing world, where cash flow is imperative and its reliability less secure, people with mental disorders are likely to suffer serious consequences (see Westermeyer 1984).
5. We were continually faced with having enough money to bring her ordeal to an end, but not enough to solve all the problems in Kaliti. We not only had to decide to whom to give, but also how to give. Stacked against the constant need is the common demand. Every person we encountered wanted to lay a claim, to ask for something, to get some help; they all needed some hope. In total it was more than enough to drain our good will. Any answer we gave was out of psychological necessity a promise on which they laid their hopes for life over death. While we were trying to separate ourselves from the promises that had already been made by the programme and were not being kept, it appears we were only getting more deeply involved. We couldn't blame them and we couldn't continue helping them.
6. There was another side to giving. The first author was often obsessed by the idea that the people only saw him as someone who gave them things: photographs, notes of 10, 20 or 50 and, very occasionally, 100 *birr* and sometimes providing access to assistance that might not otherwise have been available. What bothered him about this was that they were not getting from him what he thought he really had to offer. He had hoped to give them something of his professional knowledge, and the wisdom he had garnered in working in various cultures with people in difficult circumstances.
7. However, as the above situation showed, giving material assistance meant that many, if not all, of our interactions with them were based on the potential to get something material.
8. When the people first arrived they were given wheat from international emergency aid. Later this was replaced with a governmental Food for Work programme, which allowed one member of each family to work in the public sector (often repairing roads) in exchange for 15 kg of wheat per month per person in the family. See Pankhurst (1992a) on how the delivery of aid after the 1984 famine changed family structure.
9. A few years back, the clinic had an outpost in Kaliti, but it was closed after a few months. There were many rumors about why this was done. The displaced claimed that having the clinic in the camp was less profitable for the clinic because it was harder for the clinic staff to steal;

the clinic staff claimed that the health assistant in Kaliti was selling the medicine rather than dispensing it to the clients. Opinions on both sides are strong and contradictory. Nothing was verified and probably not verifiable either, but the clinic refused to reopen its service, although, very occasionally, a doctor would make a professional visit to the camp.

10. Covering babies was often done to avoid having the baby get the 'evil eye'.

11. See Alem *et al.* (1995); Aspen (1994); Giel (1967); Assefa Hailemarian and Kloos (1993); Hodes and Azbire (1993); Kahana (1985); Levine (1965); Pankhurst, R. (1990); Vecchiato (1993a).

12. A study conducted by the WHO suggested that there were one million Ethiopians who suffered from mental disorders (Endale 1996). Another study estimated the rate of mental illness at 2.6 adults per 100 and about 3 million children (Araya and Aboud 1993).

13. Most people in Kaliti took advantage of many types of traditional healers. They went to baptizers (*atmaki*), midwives (*yelimd awalaj*), herbalists (*yemedhanit awaki*), and uvula or tonsil cutters (*yeintel korach*).

14. Several authors, Jacobsson and Giel (1995); Giel *et al.* (1968); Vecchiato (1993b) reported that many illnesses, including neurotic disorders, were improved by church attendance.

15. See Singleton (1996) for an account of this in the Protestant church.

16. The image of mental illness caused by a *Zar* spirit was that of a rider (the spirit) and a horse (the mentally ill person). The healers thought that if they could get the riders off the backs of their clients (through exorcism), the riders would not ride their clients to death. If the healers could not get control of the spirits, the prognosis could be death.

17. See Kleinman (1988) on comparing mental health causes and therapies across cultures.

18. Taking advantage of both traditional and modern health was not new. Menilik II, who ruled from 1890 to 1913, suffered from a lifelong illness that he treated first with traditional medicine, and then with modern Western medical experts invited to Ethiopia for that purpose. At the end of his life, when Western medicine had failed to help him, he went to Debre Libanos to take the Holy Waters. The public knew of his illness and ways of coping with it, and considered him as a modern leader. To this day it is not uncommon to have traditional and modern healers share patients. In spite of the fact that the Orthodox Church believed that most mental illnesses were the result of the devil and that cure was in the purview of the Church, most priests would refer certain clients to medical facilities. Singleton (1996) reported a woman who went to an Evangelical church for help. 'When the priests began to minister to her she became very disruptive, physically attacking them and throwing furniture around. She would not allow the Priest and his helpers to pray with her. After some time and additional efforts to help, they referred her to a psychiatric hospital for treatment.'

Thirteen

Returnees' Experiences of Resettlement in Humera

KASSAHUN BERHANU

Introduction

This chapter examines the merits and drawbacks of resettlement as a feasible alternative for addressing problems affecting ex-refugees (or returnees) and other vulnerable groups. The heavy dependence on the agricultural sector rendered rural land settlement increasingly attractive to policy-makers and planners as a means of overcoming a host of problems. In embarking on resettlement, it is assumed that prevalent problems such as food insecurity, rural unemployment, and land fragmentation and marginality can be overcome. Policy-makers expect that moving people to areas with agricultural potential can offset the disadvantages accruing from the concentration of population in localities where intensive farming has long been heavily entrenched. Since the 1960s, Ethiopia has adopted planned resettlement programmes in the hope of solving all kinds of socio-economic and political problems. Planned land settlement in Ethiopia gained wider currency from the mid-1970s following the revolutionary process. Prior to this, resettlement programmes were mainly designed to address isolated local problems with limited objectives.

The chapter highlights aspects of resettlement relevant to concerns relating to returnees based on a case study of two returnee resettlement schemes in the Humera District, Western Tigray. The study considers efforts in rehabilitating the settlers by assessing the impacts of interventions made by the Ethiopian government and multilateral agencies notably the United Nations High Commissioner for Refugees (UNHCR), the World Food Programme (WFP) and the Relief Society of Tigray (REST).

The viability of planned versus 'spontaneous' resettlement

Resettlement as a strategy for rehabilitating vulnerable groups and promoting different socio-economic objectives is becoming increasingly contentious. The relative merits of two types of resettlement, namely planned and 'spontaneous', are debated, and opposing positions can be characterized in the following two cases, both of which claim that their respective approaches could be instrumental in realizing efforts towards self-sufficiency.

CASE 1

Tom Kuhlman (1994a: 122-35) is among those who view organized settlement as disadvantageous. He attributes the dispositions of governments favoring organized settlements to the lust for control and use of the settlements for the purpose of attracting funding and other forms of assistance. The proponents of this school of thought claim that concentrated visibility of needs allowing for speedy procurement of support is the underlying reason for opting for organized settlements. Citing figures suggesting that numbers of refugees that have settled on their own in Africa are greater than those in planned schemes, Kuhlman asserts that organized settlements are doomed to fail and thus any argument in their favor cannot hold. He also argues that the cost of initiating and running planned settlements is so high that they become liabilities to both the international community and the country that embarks on the venture.

Kuhlman (1994b: 47) supports Harrell-Bond's (1986) generalization that depicts organized settlements as highly artificial communities that are devoid of autonomy and subjected to the control of camp authorities. He argues that it is possible to assist self-settled refugees at less cost, enabling them to achieve the same standard of living as those in organized settlements whose maintenance is far more expensive.

Other proponents of spontaneous settlement (Gaim Kibreab 1985: 100; Chambers 1982: 22) lament the prevalence of the mentality of dependence in organized settlements. They claim that unplanned settlements have a better chance of developing self-management and self-reliance. Mekuria (1987: 33-34, 1988: 195) views organized settlements as hotbeds of conflict and antagonism among settlers themselves and between settlers and the host population. He argues that they are often designed to promote ulterior motives other than those openly stated. Scudder (1985: 126) claims that spontaneously settled groups have fared better in terms of becoming more productive. Dieci and Viezzoli (1992: 80) claim to have identified poor performance in agriculture in organized settlements.

CASE 2

Proponents of organized settlements view unplanned settlements as unrealistic. Rogge (1981: 200-207) lists the advantages of organized schemes as instrumental in providing the means to be self-sufficient, ensuring security of land tenure and enabling refugees to live in their own communities and under their own leaders, without facing the threat of alienation in a new environment. Mazur (1988: 51) feels that those favoring self-settlement are either unaware of the existence of planned settlements or have opted for less useful alternatives. He also dismisses the possibility of self-settlement itself, given the prevalence of a situation where there does not exist a 'no-man's land' since all private land is owned by individuals and companies, and public land is under the custody of governments. Implied in this argument also is that self-settlement amounts to forfeiting leverages that could originate from the intervention of the institutional actors. Clarke (1986: 42) goes further by affirming his belief that the advantage of planned settlement is not limited to those directly involved. He argues that the whole country could benefit as a result of more production, fewer people in need of assistance and hence diminished relief-aid requirements. In a study conducted in the Sudan, Wijbrandi (1986) concludes that organized settlements have fared far better than spontaneous settlements.

Oberai (1988: 24-25) identifies a definite potential in organized settlements, which could be further developed by overcoming certain weaknesses like lack of coordination and cooperation between the different actors, and promoting alternative employment opportunities in and around settlement areas. Zetter (1995: 51) envisages positive outcomes from organized settlements that are close to existing population centres; Pitterman (1984: 136) anticipates possibilities for prosperity in organized settlements, provided broader economic integration is fostered. Alemneh (1990: 109) indicates the existence of legitimate causes for initiating planned settlements, suggesting that they should be carried out on the basis of imaginative planning and willingness to be relocated on the part of target groups.

Some notes on Ethiopia's experience in undertaking resettlement

Prior to the revolution of 1974, resettlement was mainly undertaken as a result of isolated and local actions by both voluntary and governmental agencies without posing as major concerns in government plans (Pankhurst 1989: 319 and 1992a: 14-15). In the 1960s and 1970s, a number of settlement schemes run by government departments and non-governmental organizations had invariably been small-scale in size, *ad hoc* in nature, and were mainly designed for different beneficiaries. These were aimed at alleviating specific and limited objectives (RRC 1985: 157; Tegegne 1988: 82; Pankhurst 1997: 540). Prior to 1974, spontaneous settlement undertaken by individuals and small groups took place more frequently than those sponsored by governments and other actors (Wood 1977). The underlying reasons for such a state of affairs seem to be the non-availability of public land to be used for relatively larger settlement schemes and resistance by the landed gentry against such undertakings. Wood (*ibid.*.: 78-80) lists the following as accountable for the proliferation of spontaneous settlements during the three decades prior to the revolution:

(a) stagnation of the Ethiopian economy in general and the consequent deterioration of the quality of life for urban dwellers;
(b) proliferation of mechanized farms that led to incidences of eviction necessitating migration to other places;
(c) availability of information on opportunities that abounded in localities endowed with unutilized and underutilized land;
(d) population pressure and marginality of land in the highlands where intensive agricultural activity has been in operation for several centuries.

Planned resettlement gained currency and gathered momentum only after the initiation of the revolutionary process in 1974. At this point in time, there had been only 20 settlement sites comprising some 7,000 households and representing less than 0.2 percent of all rural households in the country (Wood 1985: 92). The post-revolution period witnessed dramatic advances in the pace of resettlement over a ten-year period (1974-84). Some 46,000 households comprising about 180,000 people were resettled in over 80 sites in eleven regions, which could be explained by such factors as the Land Reform of 1975 that made public land available to be used for resettlement purposes, famine recurrence at short intervals calling for durable solutions in the form of embarking on resettlement in areas with marked agricultural potential, and the establishment of institutions and agencies that were made responsible for implementing resettlement programmes. However, the total cultivated area in all settlements in the decade following the revolutionary upsurge amounted to 40,000 hectares, representing 0.4 percent of the total cultivated land in the country.

Adopting resettlement as a panacea for the problem of recurrent food insecurity in Ethiopia is based on three assumptions: (i) the exhaustion of potential in the home villages of the settlers; (ii) the capacity of the settlement areas to sustain the insertion of thousands of newcomers; and (iii) the compatibility and appropriateness of the already existing agricultural techniques and skills of the settlers for productive activities in the new areas.

Given that the resettlement undertakings initiated in connection with the 1984/85 famine were more of an emergency operation conducted in the middle of an ongoing catastrophe, the planning aspect of the whole enterprise was done in haste. The attempt was, therefore, ridden by a series of setbacks. First, consultation between policy-makers, implementers, the settlers, and the host population was minimal. Second, high-handedness in implementing plans entailed resentments which were often quelled by coercive methods, and thus undermined possibilities for commitment and conviction on the part of the target groups. Third, the resources and socio-political support necessary for bolstering the chances of meeting stated targets were not optimally rallied, and hence disorganization and confusion unfolded. The disarray in this regard had its costs in the form of a staggering rate of attrition expressed in deaths, separation of family members, escape to the Sudan, and spontaneous and 'illegal' return to original home villages (Dawit 1989: 304). Brüne (1990: 27) indicated that the government acknowledged certain drawbacks of the exercise, caused by poor planning and faulty implementation rooted in the haste with which it was executed. This led to declaring a temporary moratorium on resettlement in March 1986 and was expressed in downsizing the numbers to be resettled.

Institutional development relating to resettlement took shape following greater policy prominence. The establishment of the Relief and Rehabilitation Commission (RRC) and the Settlement Authority in the mid-1970s is illuminating in this regard. The following could be said, albeit in general terms, regarding resettlement in Ethiopia:

(a) resettlement characterized by large population movements has taken place in response to threats caused by famine and conflict;
(b) incidences of 'spontaneous' settlement were more frequent in occurrence and far greater in scope than the ones that were institutionally sponsored prior to the 1974 revolution;
(c) planned resettlement gained wider currency and gathered momentum after 1974 as a response to natural and man-made calamities often expressed in famine and conflict episodes;
(d) new developments experienced in the post-revolution years led to a number of basic assumptions anchored in the availability of public land which justified resettlement as a means for tackling a wide array of problems associated with landlessness and unemployment, food insecurity, and natural-resource management.

Returnee rehabilitation in two resettlement schemes in Humera

BACKGROUND

The discussion in this chapter is based on findings from a study (Kassahun 2000) of two planned resettlement schemes in the Humera area, Western Tigray Zone, Ethiopia. The settler population in the two schemes are Ethiopian ex-refugees (returnees) who were repatriated to their country of origin after a prolonged stay in the Sudan. The majority of the returnees fled to the Sudan amidst threatening circumstances triggered by a mix of conflict and famine episodes around the mid-1980s. The then confrontation between the Derg regime and the Tigray People's Liberation Front (TPLF) was compounded by a devastating famine prompting mass flight across the border.

Following the ousting of the military regime in mid-1991, voluntary repatriation of the ex-refugees and their subsequent rehabilitation became a major preoccupation of the Transitional Government of Ethiopia. Repatriation was initiated according to standard procedures based on a tripartite agreement that involved the host government (Sudan), the government of the country of origin (Ethiopia), and the United Nations High Commissioner for Refugees (UNHCR). In addition to the agreement, the expressed willingness of the returnees to be repatriated and resettle in their country of origin led to subsequent undertakings aimed at their rehabilitation.

THE STUDY LOCATION, SAMPLE POPULATION AND OTHER DATA SOURCES

The location of the study is the Humera area in Western Tigray Zone of Ethiopia. Humera is bordered by Eritrea in the north and Sudan in the West. The area is famous for including large tracts of land suitable for agricultural activities, which made it attractive for initiating returnee resettlement schemes. For the last thirty-five years, the locality has accommodated several commercial agricultural firms specializing in the production of cash crops like sesame, cotton and sorghum. Following the 1974 revolution, these undertakings were disrupted as a result of nationalizations effected by the pro-communist military government.

The two returnee resettlement schemes considered are Mai-Kadra and Rawyan. In 1996, they hosted a total of 746 and 18,107 returnee households, respectively. While the Mai-Kadra scheme, which is 30 km from Humera town and located in a relatively remote spot, had 400 inhabitants in about 100 households at the time of the arrival of the returnees, there was no host population in the immediate vicinity of the Rawyan area, apart from the residents of Humera town, 6 km away. In Mai-Kadra, the majority among the host population was resettled in the area around 1975 by the Derg regime because of the drought-induced famine.

A total of 300 returnee household heads in both sites were randomly selected to constitute the sample population representing over 10 percent of the total returnee households in each settlement site. Interviews were also conducted with officials and field-staff of participating organizations (governmental, non-governmental and the UNHCR), site administrators who are ex-refugees posing as returnee representatives, community elders and selected household heads from the host population.

ADOPTING RESETTLEMENT AS A STRATEGY FOR RETURNEE REHABILITATION

Resettling returnees in organized settlements was believed to lead gradually to their self-sufficiency. This resulted in a partnership between different actors (governmental, non-governmental and multilateral). Accordingly, the relevant departments of the Ethiopian government at the central and local levels, the UNHCR, the World Food Programme (WFP) and the Relief Society of Tigray (REST) participated in the different phases of the rehabilitation programme. They were responsible for the implementation of the repatriation effort and agreed to assist subsequent endeavors that could result in durable solutions to achieve an acceptable level of self-sufficiency.

In deciding to resettle the returnees, the government made a number of assumptions presumed to lend feasibility and viability to its resettlement programme. These included: availability of large tracts of underutilized land in the selected areas that were sparsely populated; compatibility of the skills and experiences of the beneficiaries as peasant producers prior to their flight with engaging in farm activities; viewing target groups as politically correct, given their close ties with the ruling political Front prior to fleeing to the country of asylum and during their sojourn in the Sudan; and existence of possibilities for attracting external assistance that could support the government's rehabilitation plan through relocation. In deciding to agree to being resettled, the returnees also considered a number of factors presumed to be advantageous to them: obtaining larger and more fertile plots than could be available for them in their original home villages; accessing interim institutional assistance; and a greater chance of off-farm and non-farm gainful employment opportunities during slack seasons for which the Humera area was famed.

Recognizing the fact that most of the returnee households were originally engaged in farming prior to their flight, it was decided to settle them in areas where public land could be made available for agricultural undertakings. Thus the two settlement sites in the Humera area were singled out as appropriate. The following implementation arrangements were agreed on and expedited:

(i) The Ethiopian government allocated farm-plots and land for homesteads by making use of available public land under its custodianship. It also assisted by covering the costs of land clearing and tractor services for ploughing farmsteads, and mobilizing the relevant units of its departments to extend the required services in line with their respective specialization and competence;
(ii) REST contributed by extending transport facilities and warehouses for food storage and deployed its experienced staff for overall coordination of the resettlement effort;
(iii) UNHCR agreed to cover infrastructural costs relating to the construction of schools, clinics, water points and dry-weather feeder roads;
(iv) WFP, through the Relief and Rehabilitation Commission (RRC), provided food rations for nine months that could be used by returnee settler-households during the interim period;
(v) The host population contributed labour and construction material for temporary shelters in which the returnees could be housed.

ON FEASIBILITY/VIABILITY OF PLANNED RESETTLEMENT

Assessment could be made of the merits of planned resettlement as a useful strategy for rehabilitating vulnerable groups, using a number of variables including types and amounts of assistance provided, impacts of inputs provided on drives made to realize stated goals, conditions of other categories of returnees who are not included in the settlement programme, implications of 'spontaneous' settlement for the lives of host populations, and rational use of environmental resources.

Analyses of the empirical data collected on the situation of beneficiaries included in planned land settlement, on the one hand, and conditions pertaining to the non-settler returnee groups, on the other, led to the following conclusions:

(a) The betterment in conditions of life seems much greater and markedly experienced as regards returnee settlers affected by the planned intervention.
(b) There appears to be considerable preference for assisted resettlement programmes on the part of groups of returnees who have either reintegrated into their original home villages or attempted to earn their livelihoods on their own. This seems to have been caused by the marginality and diminished amount of land, entailing low yield and hence a reduced standard of living for those who are reintegrated in the highlands, and an absence of a dependable means of livelihood through the use of land for other non-settler returnee groups in the vicinity of the resettlement sites.
(c) Planned resettlement is accompanied by institutional assistance lending added leverage to the endeavors of returnees in their effort to adjust to, and cope with, the challenges in the new environment. The returnees not included in planned resettlement programmes have encountered various forms of deprivation, owing to absence of satisfactory access to land , and lack of concerted institutional assistance.
(d) Trickling multiplier effects and incidental benefits accruing from planned settlement schemes in the localities in question are expressed in the laying down of physical/social infrastructure and increased attention of the government and donors to the settlement area. This proved advantageous to the receiving localities, despite constraints in the use of existing facilities following the insertion of several thousands of 'illegal' settlers into the receiving areas.
(e) Planned intervention in resettlement programmes in the study location is marked by the low level of settler participation in important issues and decisions affecting them. Priorities of the major providers – the government and its partners – were given primacy over the settlers' concerns. Furthermore, the preferences of the providers were given more weight than those of beneficiaries.

Despite misgivings regarding the diminished participation of target groups and the prevalent influence of providers in decision-making, the intervention of institutional actors is considered to be preferable in returnee rehabilitation, when comparing the situation of returnees in assisted resettlement schemes with that of those who did not benefit from planned interventions.

ON ATTAINMENT OF SELF-SUFFICIENCY BY SETTLER HOUSEHOLDS

Appraisal of the overall condition and performance of the returnee settler households is made on the basis of amount of yield obtained, income from sale of crops and other sources, satisfaction of household needs, and possession of cash savings and other assets. Analysis of data on the subject led to the following conclusions:

- Settler households managed to support themselves by meeting family food requirements and other basic needs through the use of products obtained from their farms.
- Dependence on external support in the settlements has been effectively discontinued following the termination of assistance, provided *ad interim*, in accordance with the terms of prior understandings and arrangements.
- Institutional assistance provided by the involved actors in the form of service facilities, land resources, agricultural inputs and consumables was crucial in bringing about the ability to cater for oneself, which could have been very difficult or impossible in the absence of organized enabling support at the initial stage.
- Apart from meeting the basic requirements for maintaining smooth family life, institutional support has enabled settler households to develop capacity for financing community infrastructural development endeavors in their respective localities.
- Conditions of life in the settlements may be considered better compared with the situations in both original home-villages, and in exile in Sudan, since settlers were provided with larger and more fertile plots, which accounted for greater yields, resulting in improvements in their living standards. This is considered as the necessary price paid for enduring the inhospitable climate of the Humera lowlands, and bearing with health hazards caused by such endemic diseases as malaria or kalazar.

Regarding the attainment of self-sufficiency by settler households, the goal of realizing a modest level of self-sufficiency has been more or less achieved. However, whether this is the result of the impetus provided by the initial enabling assistance, or whether it is a logical outcome of settler efforts that could progressively persist in the years to come, is difficult to tell at this stage. Nevertheless, there are already signs showing that several factors are likely to pose serious challenges militating against probable opportunities for a progressive increase in the betterment of livelihoods.

ON SUSTAINABILITY OF ACHIEVED SELF-SUFFICIENCY

Findings on the possibility of maintaining and/or broadening the achieved level of self-sufficiency warranted the following conclusions:

- Sustainability through maintaining and/or expanding a given level of self-sufficiency could be realized only under conditions where the variables that have led to the specific situation remain equal and constant.
- Sustainable self-sufficiency for those engaged in agricultural production could be adversely affected by such factors as unfavorable climatic conditions, poor transportation networks, fluctuating demands and prices for farm products, and preferential treatment favoring some market forces at the expense of others, on the basis of discriminatory official policy and practice.
- Organization of producers based on clearly articulated interests and access to market information (on demand and price) could serve as safeguards against an artificial fall in producer revenue.

However, prospects for sustainable self-sufficiency are in the process of being negatively affected as a result of a host of unhealthy developments. These include a fall in producer prices entailed by constrained market outlets, an administrative fiat limiting options for producers and aimed at entrenching the hegemonic position of favored syndicates, and an influx of several thousand non-resettled returnees entailing considerable pressure on forest resources and existing services and facilities.

Moreover, the Ethiopian-Eritrean border conflict in the environs of the research location will undoubtedly affect the chances for sustained self-sufficiency. This is due to the fact that Eritrea had been the most important market for Humera's agricultural products. In addition, the location of the settlements within the range of Eritrean artillery firepower forced the evacuation of the settlers, thereby entailing disruption of activities, albeit temporarily.

In summary: maintenance and/or expansion of a given level of self-sufficiency is conditioned by the existence of factors including favorable natural conditions (rainfall), existence of market information and outlets, communication infrastructure, avoidance of artificial tampering in the logical interplay of market forces, and prevalence of peace and stability allowing for normal productive activities and unhampered transactions in goods and services.

ON PREDICTABILITY AND REPLICABILITY OF RESETTLEMENT AS A STRATEGY FOR RETURNEE REHABILITATION

Most resettlement programmes in Ethiopia initiated between the late 1960s and mid-1980s were beset with problems that undermined efforts towards building production capacities leading to self-sufficiency. A combination of various factors like faulty management, poor planning, and cultural and environmental impediments is held responsible for low production and income in planned settlement schemes. Thus the self-sufficiency of settlers as the intended outcome of past resettlement efforts did not materialize. Despite the fact that it was relegated to the background in the first decade of the post-1991 period, resettlement in the study area seems to have fared better in many ways compared with previous similar undertakings. This is evidenced by such facts as the termination of outside assistance within the specified time-limit, the ability to fulfil family food requirements, the capacity to finance community infrastructure, and the ongoing propensity to create assets that could serve as risk-buffers in times of need.

It appears that achievements in the two settlement sites are the outcomes of a combination of factors including: a) availability of relatively large tracts of fertile land for household agricultural production; b) favourable climatic factors which led to obtaining a significant yield throughout most harvest seasons; c) favorable market outlets, as witnessed in 1994/95 harvest year; and d) initial enabling institutional inputs that lent leverage to good performance during the take-off stage.

Another variable that could help in establishing the replicability of such an undertaking relates to the cost component. Estimates from a study (FAO 1984) dealing with previous resettlement undertakings indicate that the costs of resettling a household amount to various expenses including transportation, feeding in transit, enabling interim assistance in the form of food rations, household utensils and farm tools, and infrastructural development undertakings such as land clearing and paving roads, etc. However, since land was declared public property and is not subject to sale, the market value of land is not included in the estimates.

From the foregoing, it is possible to conclude that resettlement as a strategy for returnee rehabilitation could be replicable in terms of ensuring a modest level of self-sufficiency, provided the factors responsible for its achievement remain constant. In addition, resettlement as a strategy for rehabilitation could be replicable when considering a total cost of US$700 as the expense incurred to establish a settler household in a new locality. It could be argued that by making use of available idle land and mobilizing domestic and international support, it is possible to resettle at least 5,000 families every year by expending less than US$4 million.

Information obtained during the fieldwork on future trends of maintaining and/or broadening the achieved level of self-sufficiency, however, do not warrant predictability in the long run. The following could render such an assertion plausible:

(a) Since the returnee settlers engage in rain-fed agricultural production, there is the possibility of a decline in yield during some harvest seasons owing to adverse natural conditions (poor and erratic rainfall, pests).
(b) Compounded with limited market-outlet and policy drawbacks, price fluctuations characterized by a decline in the value of, and demand for, primary products negatively affect producer revenue.
(c) Poor communication networks deprive settlers of access to big market centres and information on price and type of commodities.
(d) And a possible decline in production could result from the use of traditional farming practices characterized by marginal use of improved inputs and techniques.

It could, therefore, be argued that predictable self-sufficiency based on productive agricultural engagement in settlements depends on the existence of capabilities that could offset the vagaries of nature, implications of wrong policies, and diminished and distorted market outlets and structures.

Conclusion

In general, planned land settlement carried out with imaginative planning, foresight and feasible assessment of concrete conditions may provide partial solutions to Ethiopia's perennial problems associated with food insecurity and rural unemployment, but at considerable cost. The country has approximately 13 million hectares of expandable land suitable for rain-fed agriculture (Tegegne 1995: 25). Such a potential could double current production under the existing system of farming, while at the same time creating employment for a labour force of 16 million. Outcomes could be further augmented by making significant capital investment in farming techniques, agricultural inputs, human-resource development and production infrastructure. Nevertheless, replication of resettlement on a wider scale is likely to lead to environmental hazards due to ever increasing encroachments aimed at fulfilling various requirements like preparing farm plots, homesteads, energy needs, laying of physical/social infrastructure, etc.

Land settlement experiences elsewhere involve a mix of success and failure in the different aspects of the same undertaking. Whereas certain achievements feature in a given component, drawbacks and failure appear in other dimensions. For example, land settlement in Tanzania undertaken by launching the *Ujamaa* scheme failed to bring about the intended self-reliance and development. This appears to have been caused by defective and arbitrary site selection, faulty physical planning and intensive use of coercion rather than persuasion. Such shortcomings led to the abandonment of several settlement villages and failure in attaining the expected level of agricultural production due to low productivity, inefficient marketing and a poor transportation network (Tegegne 1989: 17; Maro 1988: 243-251; Lundqvist 1981: 338). However, *Ujamaa* settlements have registered commendable success in the field of social-service delivery, which was used by the Tanzanian government for inducing people to move voluntarily to the villages (McHenry 1979: 128).

Planned land settlement in Malaysia succeeded in bringing about a boom in agricultural production and transforming traditional farmers into cash-crop producers (Bahrin 1988: 109). In the Philippines, expansion of agricultural land to frontier areas has brought an increase in food production for a rapidly growing population (Paderanga 1988: 143). On the other hand, the overwhelming majority of settlements in Indonesia experienced production levels that could not be justified as economically viable (Oberai 1988: 16).

It is thus possible to conclude that the impact of planned settlement on agricultural production and employment generation is diverse, varying from place to place and conditioned by various factors including imaginative planning, voluntary participation, availability of communication networks, adequate market outlets and economically feasible policy frameworks. In situations where performance appears to be dismal, it is necessary to probe into the circumstances that led to the proliferation of drawbacks, which might help in putting things right through applying corrective measures.

Given the currently prevalent problems in Ethiopia expressed in the form of food insecurity, poverty, and unemployment, and provided that the claim of availability of adequate land for relocation is authentic, resettlement could be considered as an option for addressing pressing predicaments that underpin the lives of a major portion of the population.

Fourteen

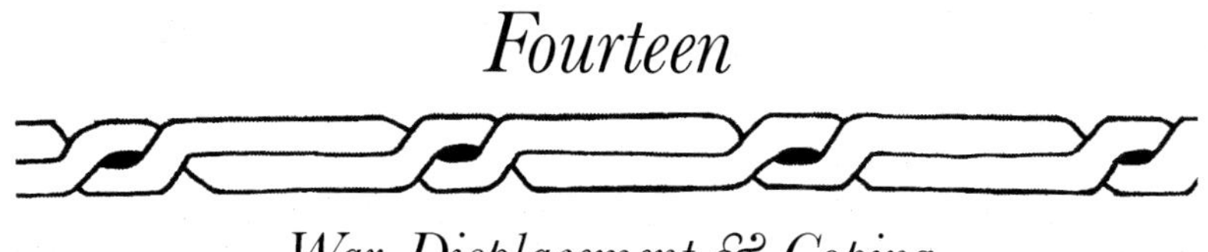

War, Displacement & Coping

Stories from the Ethio-Eritrean War

BEHAILU ABEBE

This chapter covers war stories from villages and describes cases of families affected by the 1998–2000 Ethio-Eritrean conflict, divided into three parts relating to the situations before, during and after the war. Differences between a town and two rural villages are discussed. The chapter concludes with a discussion of the impact of war on border villages in relation to identity.

Before the war: competition for economic and political dominance

Zalanbesa, a small border town, was an economically fast-growing centre in North-Eastern Tigray. Statistics put the population at 6,059, of whom 2,756 were males and 3,303 females (CSA 1995b). Zalanbesa benefited from being situated on the main road between Adigrat and Asmara. Commercial activity in the area gained momentum, after Zalanbesa became a border town following the independence of Eritrea. Food items and livestock were smuggled across the border to Eritrea while goods such as textiles and beer were brought to the Ethiopian market. Many of the town's residents benefited directly or indirectly from these activities.

Zalanbesa reflects in microcosm the difficult relationship between the two countries following Eritrea's independence. Only an estimated one-fifth of the population was Eritrean, but they were dominant among the well-off and trading classes. As a border town, Zalanbesa also represented the continuities and mixtures of identities. The socio-cultural homogeneity of villages and the cross-border bonds of kinship made the relationship more complex. Zalanbesa was an enclave of Ethiopian political administration in an area where identities were difficult to disentangle. Fluid identities were partly responsible for creating confusion over the rights and obligations of the two nationalities. Eritreans living in the town considered themselves Eritrean as much as Ethiopian.

Unlike other areas of Ethiopia, Zalanbesa was peculiar in its treatment of Eritrean nationals in the town after relations between the two countries deteriorated. Elsewhere, strict distinctions were not made between Ethiopian and Eritrean rights in many spheres of activity such as jobs, casting votes and being elected. Solomon explained, 'Eritreans could live and work in Ethiopia and enjoy the same rights and privileges as Ethiopians' (Walta Information Centre 2001: 7). The situation was different in Zalanbesa, and Eritreans were increasingly excluded from most political activities. Most of these measures were not well received by Eritreans, who wanted to participate in local affairs.

There was fierce competition in trade and investment, with many traders operating from Zalanbesa in both duty-paid goods and smuggling. Both Ethiopian and Eritrean townspeople alike benefited from this trade, but the political authorities wanted to control the illegal trade and there was often conflict across the border between militias. This conflict had political ramifications. With customs checkpoints in the area, traders used various illicit methods of getting goods through, including the manipulation of social networks. The local authority in Zalanbesa took certain measures that changed the economic dominance of the Eritrean minority in the town. It promoted a policy giving priority to Ethiopians in trade and investment; only areas not covered by Ethiopians were left to be occupied by Eritrean traders..

While relations between urban Ethiopians and Eritreans are influenced by conflicting political interests and economic competition, tensions in rural villages are reflected in the area of conflicting claims to farmland. I was often told about disputes between Eritrean and Ethiopian villagers living adjacent to one another. Villagers interpreted the current border war as a continuation of these conflicting claims that marred and shaped much of the relationship between Ethiopian and Eritrean peasants. One of these contested plots of land, located in the village of Sheshet, was claimed by the Eritrean village called Geleba as well as the Ethiopian villages of Ligat, Aga T'irqe and Mukhuyam. Priest Girmay narrated the myth as follows:

> The lord of the area was known as Hailedonay who taxed all peasants in the area and used to live in Ligat. There was a person from Shewa called Adey BealShewa who was born the son of an Amhara trader living in the area. He requested the hand of the daughter of Hailedonay in marriage but was rejected. This rejection sparked off conflict between the villagers and many died in the process. Fearing that he was the cause of the conflict, Adey BealShewa sold part of his plot to Hailedonay and part of it to his uncle. The latter asked Hailedonay to divide the plot between them. The lord had little regard for this man because he was not rich, and gave him permission to take as much as he could till in a single day. The man went and begged his relatives in Senafe to come and help him by wearing *Wech'eho* (black sheepskin). They all responded positively and he decided to start tilling in the night. He then made the sound of a lash as a sign to Hailedonay that he was getting towards the end of his work. The lord was taken by surprise as he did not expect what had happened but he did not go back on his promise. He hurriedly went on tilling as much virgin land as possible to maintain his holding, taking his 100 oxen and calling upon Ethiopian villagers to help in the task before all the land was taken by the Eritrean. The rule was that a plot of farmland would be the property of whoever tilled the most. The competition was fierce and those from Hailedonay's side made a sign on the plot by scratching because the other side began earlier and had already tilled and taken much land. In this way, Sheshet was shared between them: Hailedonay and the uncle of Adey BealShewa or between Eritreans and Ethiopians in the present context. The farmland taken by the Eritreans was known as Adey BealShewa indicating the locality of the first owner.

> When Hailedonay died, he vowed to be buried in Inda Aba Libanos monastery in Eritrea. He also transferred his *Gult* right to the monastery, stating that one-third (or *siso*) of the produce was to be paid as tax to the monastery while the land was to remain under the administration of the villagers of Ligat where his descendants lived. After the death of Hailedonay, villagers using the Sheshet farm plot used to pay tax to the monastery in the form of butter. Haile Adonay clearly passed the edict and warned both sides to stick to the rules and not break them even if there were a change in the balance of power between the two sides. He sanctioned his word of honour by Amdeworq and it was written in Wengele Werq (a register of tenure contracts in the church), which described all the *Gult* holdings of Ethiopia and could be found in Axum in the monastery of St Mary. Priest Girmay witnessed that he acted responsibly in paying tax to the monastery until the last days of Haile Selassie. The monastery did not lift its claim to the land, even when the land reform was in force with the transformation of power from the monarchy to the Derg regime. The villagers stood firm against the claim of the monastery by stressing that land was given to the tiller and that they were the owners. However, Sheshet continued to be contested during the time of the Derg and after, and the villagers thought that the monastery did not relinquish its interest in the land even during and after the recent war. They also perceive the recent war as the extension of disputes among villagers regarding plots of land.

This myth was a common lens through which rural villagers saw and analysed the current war with Eritrea. Since the war was addressed as a border dispute, they interpreted it as a continuation of the conflict that the villagers had with the neighbouring residents of the Eritrean village of Geleba. For them, it was a form of encroachment of the expanding village trying to take their land which was now supported by government forces. Often the figurative identification of Geleba was '*iquy*' or 'evil'. Many villagers told me that it was Geleba villagers who directed the invading Eritrean army into the interior of Ethiopia. While the myth narrated the traditional interpretation of conflicts among villagers over farmland, it also provided a perspective through which this war was understood and seen in the current context at least by villagers who still claimed to have unsettled disputes with Eritrean villages over farm plots.

Changes in the pre-war period

Relations between the two countries deteriorated after the issuance of separate currencies, and developed into an all-out war in Western Tigray, Badime, on 12 May 1998. Zalanbesa was attacked on 2 June. This interval gave both the government and the people the opportunity to take precautionary measures. Government offices in Zalanbesa were moved to a safer area, Qerseber. Schools and health centres were also moved. These actions encouraged many to leave the town before it was too late.

Prior to the war, Zalanbesa was not entirely peaceful, and an exchange of gunfire occurred just before the incident at Badime. An Eritrean guard shot into the sky one night. The Ethiopian militia responded and chased the Eritrean forces up to Senafe but were ordered to pull back; many were killed from both sides. This incident alarmed many people and convinced them to leave the area, including those from some rural villages. The weeks preceding the war were known for being chaotic because of the movements of people to Adigrat and surrounding villages. However, reactions differed from one village to another due to the relative distances from Zalanbesa. Movement from the villages was generally less than that from Zalanbesa town. Town residents were moving any possessions they could not keep with relatives. For Abeba, the difference between rich and poor extended to access to information. The rich were well informed and therefore better prepared to take precautions than the poor:

> The rich were informed by the local administration of potential trouble and could therefore remove their possessions before everything went wrong. People like me carried some of their property with them; one of my two beds went to rural areas and the other to Adigrat. I spent a night in the village and when I returned to Zalanbesa I found the town deserted. My possessions were lost when the EPLF forces took control of the area. Eritrean farmers who came to help in constructing trenches for the Eritrean army took most of the possessions stolen from the town. Even if displaced persons said that they did not remove their property, at least they tried to take some when they left the town at the last minute. Most of the property in the rural villages was also lost and few items were returned by the Ethiopian army after retaking Zalanbesa. It was difficult to determine who owned the property. The army tried to give items to people who came to claim lost property but they were not interested in taking things that did not belong to them.

There were differences in taking precautions and leaving the area before the war erupted. The majority (77 percent) of Mukhuyam villagers remained in the village when the fighting reached their doorsteps unlike many of the sample from Dongolo (70 percent) who fled their village. Most of the Ethiopian Zalanbesa residents (95 percent) left the area before the war began. This generally indicates preparedness. With the exception of Mukhuyam, they were aware of the approaching danger and took precautionary measures. This action reduced the level of stress felt by the people and the meaning they accorded to it. As Kelieber and Brom have suggested, 'aspects such as the anticipation of the event substantially influence the way in which the shock itself is experienced and how people react' (1992: 129).

Eruption of the war: displacement from Zalanbesa town

For some families the recent war is not by any means their first experience of conflict. Some understood it as a problem created by the same former enemy who drove them out because they were not part of the new Eritrea. It was the same process of leaving home and property, and starting life again from scratch. The big difference between the 1998 war and the displacement in 1991 following Eritrean independence was that the government saw the problem as different and therefore responded differently. In 1991, most of the displaced were treated as part of the old political system and no rehabilitation programmes were provided for them. The recently displaced people were treated as victims of aggression and received all the necessary support. As the following cases show, families passed through two displacements, coping the first time by using local resources, mainly social networks and with a combination of government assistance and local resources.

Three cases follow, two selected from Zalanbesa town and one from Mukhuyam village. The first concerns a woman who was displaced twice in less than ten years. The second was a single woman from Zalanbesa who was displaced less than ten years after she had been repatriated from Sudan where she spent much of her life in the refugee camp. The third was a displaced rich family from Zalanbesa.

ABREHIT WOLDU: WIDOW OF AN ETHIOPIAN SOLDIER IN ERITREA

Abrehit married a soldier and spent most of her time in Eritrea. She never had a child but she had a good relationship with her husband, who had retired before the EPLF took control of Asmara in 1991. When Eritrea got its independence, their life was disrupted and they were forced to leave Eritrea, abandoning their belongings. They settled in Mukhuyam where her relatives live. They were given a plot of land where they built a house and were soon able to integrate themselves into the local community by joining religious associations and participating in other social events. Her husband had a pension from his service in the army and they kept sheep. When the recent war began, they had to leave their home for the second time but this time they took their sheep with them. They stayed in a place called Gergis with relatives to make it easier for them to find pasture. Since there were many livestock herded in the area following the displacement of large numbers of the rural population, pasture soon became scarce. In addition, her husband became sick. So they sold their sheep and went to Adigrat hospital where he died. This was the biggest shock for Abrehit who saw her husband not only as a partner but also as a father. Abrehit had her own theory regarding the cause of her husband's death. She said that her husband had been forced to rebury 21 dead bodies of soldiers because one of them was Eritrean and the authorities ordered a separate burial for the Eritrean EPLF fighter. She thought that her husband was afflicted by a *mitch* (spirit) while he was reburying the bodies. She grieved by not combing her hair for a year and stopped participating in religious associations and reduced her participation in other social occasions. She was one of those people in the village whose house was constructed in the first round of the REST-funded rehabilitation programme. She gradually came to terms with her situation and began her life as a widow.

Abrehit's lasting resource was the social support she got from kin living in Mukhuyam and neighbouring villages. She settled in her village, got a farm plot, and began a rural lifestyle. During the recent war, her relatives helped her by providing pasture and giving her solace when her husband died. She was deeply affected by his death, which she related to the traumatic event of reburying dead bodies ten years earlier. She was exposed to a series of distressing events but the loss of her husband, which she interpreted in spiritual terms, was the most disturbing. She was still grieving, but recovering with the support of her kin.

ABREHIT HAGOS: A FORMER REFUGEE IN SUDAN

Although she had spent much of her time as a refugee in the Sudan, Abrehit was politically active which was one of the reasons for her return to Ethiopia following the change of regime in 1991. She maintained her political allegiance to the government. Her participation in local politics gave her a chance to understand the seriousness of the problem, and she fled Zalanbesa earlier, thereby escaping danger. Hammond (2000) reported that repatriated Ethiopian refugees faced almost equal deprivation. Most did not have any property when they came back from the Sudan. Those who owned a sewing machine were, by comparison with others, richer. Thus, Abrehit could be termed rich, since she owned a sewing machine, but was poor in comparison with the living conditions in Zalanbesa. Despite her active role in politics in terms of which belief in spirits is considered backward and reactionary, she interpreted her unfortunate loss of many children in terms of spirits. She managed to continue her spiritual rituals secretly and apart from her public participation in politics.

Abrehit was born in a place called Hidaga Hamus, 15 km away from Adigrat. She was open and keen to talk about her life. She was around 45 years of age and had had three children by three different men. Abrehit spent a significant part of her life as a refugee in the Sudan. She left Ethiopia in 1973 and returned to Adigrat in June 1991. While in the Sudan, she was active in support of the TPLF, and her daughter joined the liberation struggle during the civil war. She had good prospects of leading a better life and decided to return to Ethiopia after the downfall of the Derg regime. Abrehit used to earn a living as a tailor in the Sudan. On her way back to Zalanbesa, she sold her sewing machine in Adwa. When she returned from the Sudan, the government gave her a house made of corrugated iron sheets, 40 kg of wheat and other cereals as well as cooking oil for a month. After she was displaced, she got 60 kg of wheat and oil. While she was in Zalanbesa, she trained as a traditional birth attendant for three months and still serves in this capacity in Adigrat. She also used to have a small poultry farm with up to 30 chickens. She attempted the retail sale of oil and bean flour using credit that she got from a women's association.

Abrehit continued her participation in her local community and was well aware of the looming danger of the Ethiopian-Eritrean war, and decided to leave before it was too late and to take her belongings with her. A week before Zalanbesa fell to the EPLF she was received by her sister in a village called Meda Agame and stayed there for a week and then rented a house. She had no problem during the march. She thanked God for her safety despite all the loss she suffered. Abrehit still wanted to work as a tailor but it was difficult for her to go back into debt to buy a sewing machine. Previously she had received 1000 *birr* (US$140) credit and had had a hard time paying it back. She preferred running her small poultry farm to other activities and had strong confidence in her skills. Another source of support for her and others was work in the grain mill. Since these workers were paid in the form of flour, they always had a surplus which they wanted to exchange for money. When she is short of food, she borrows from these people and pays them back in cash at the rate of 3 *birr* a kilo.

Networks of mutual support were one of the resources that the displaced used to ameliorate the hardships of living in Adigrat town. These involved the reciprocal borrowing of food items, which works on the basis of mutual interest and trust, with no formal agreement between the partners. This arrangement provides further evidence that the poor had to rely on mutual support to cope with poverty exacerbated by the war.

> Abrehit said that life was difficult with the added responsibility of bringing up children, though the government provides exercise books for her children and food rations for her family, which helps a lot and makes life easier. She also sold some utensils given to her by a government emergency programme, for instance a water container, one of two big spoons, and one of two blankets. Abrehit also told us how people prepare food using their rations. They mix wheat flour with barley and salt to make porridge. This mixture is available in the market and costs 50 cents a kilo. Abrehit told us she knew many people in Zalanbesa and it was therefore easier to find someone who could help, but it was difficult in Adigrat because so few people knew her. Her income was better in Zalanbesa than it is now and she did not pay house rent there. She wanted her children to have a better life than hers and she believed that schooling was the way to achieve this. She hurt her leg slightly when she ran from artillery fire targeting Adigrat during the war. Abrehit stressed the shortage of money that every displaced family faced, and was desperately seeking to borrow money even with interest, but was unable to do so. She is often not able to pay the rent on time. She told us that there were many female-headed families displaced from Zalanbesa, who are worse-off than male-headed households. She rated her recent experience as one of the worst because she lost all she had. She said that relatives helped her to some extent but that did not last long. Her sister is in relatively good economic circumstances but she is not as helpful as she was before. She was also asked to pay 40 *birr* more for her present house but she could not afford that and was moving to another house with no electricity for 50 *birr* a month.

Abrehit was active in spirit possession rituals and in politics, which she dealt with separately. Much of her thinking and interpretation of suffering seems to be influenced by her belief in spirits. She also used her political allegiance to obtain information and some benefits from the government. She easily found a house when she was displaced by using her network. She was resilient despite the hardship she had been through and she knew which resources to tap for her different problems.

> While a refugee in the Sudan she gave birth to eleven children, but she lost eight due to natural causes. She associated her ordeal with punishment by a *wuqabi* spirit, which possessed her and which she failed to appease with the necessary ritual. She came to understand this after she lost her children and consulted a ritual leader. She claimed that she sometimes communicated with spirits in dreams and often went to ritual leaders in Adigrat. She did not want to practise her ritual spiritual activity openly to avoid punishment from the local authorities. Since she is politically active in the women's association, the rules could be stricter on her if her spiritual activity were disclosed. She also interprets the dreams of others who ask her for help.

ZEHAFU: EXCLUDED FROM REHABILITATION AID

This case depicts the tensions that existed in Zalanbesa. Political allegiance is understood in parochial terms. Some families were worried about being associated with current political figures, not necessarily because of shared political ideas but because of similar regional backgrounds. Zehafu left Zalanbesa on these grounds. The family escaped the danger but their economic loss was huge. They began life again from scratch and ran a drinking house and other small activities to make a living.

Zehafu lives with her husband and still owns a drinking house. Her husband served as a broker and cart driver in town. The couple used to be one of the rich families in Zalanbesa, where they had 20 bedrooms to let. Zehafu came from Adwa District. Many Eritreans living in the town suspected her of working for the government. After she heard about the incident in Badime, she left Zalanbesa before it fell to EPLF forces, taking with her her five children. Most of her children have progressed well in their education. One of her sons was in Bahirdar college, another at Addis Ababa University and her other son was in Adigrat town attending high school. When she came to Adigrat, she stayed with relatives for a month before moving to her present house located on the outskirts of the town within range of the artillery during most of the war. She said the owner, a relative living in Addis Ababa, allowed them to live in the house for two years free to look after it. Now he is asking them to pay 300 *birr* a month rent and she is looking for another house since they cannot afford to pay.

Zehafu reported that she had received 105 kg of wheat and 7 litres of cooking oil for her family of eight including her blind mother-in-law. She said that food is scarce but no one misses a day's meal even if there is a shortage of stew. She told us that food hand-outs come irregularly. She has two children going to a Catholic elementary school in Adigrat. The children received support from the school for things like exercise books, and 50 kg of *tef* at Christmas. Zehafu said that displaced people staged a demonstration in Adigrat last week asking the government to take rehabilitative measures; they wanted to return to their houses and the least they wanted from the government was plastic so that they could cover the roofs of demolished houses. It has been a long time, she explained, since they were displaced and they have become dependent on relatives and on the government. Even relatives have grown tired of supporting them. Zehafu explained that she was thrilled by the news that the EPLF troops had been defeated in Zalanbesa. Soon after that an Ethiopian soldier whom she knew came with the news that part of her house had been demolished and brought her some plants from the backyard. When she saw the plants, she was emotionally overcome and cried. The next day, she took some herbs and mustard with her and ritually cleansed her house in Zalanbesa. She also restored the door and used a plastic cover as a roof for the house. It is customary to ritually cleanse a house if it is spoiled with blood or if it is closed for a long time because it was believed to be dwelt in by spirits. She was struck by what she saw in her former town where most of the houses were reduced to rubble, but she did not cry again and felt lucky that her house was partly saved. She said even church buildings were not spared from demolition.

There was a persistent request from Zalanbesa residents to return to their homes but the government did not want to invest in the town's rehabilitation because this would depend on establishing a peaceful relationship with neighbouring Eritrea. The current stand-off was not irrevocably settled and further investment in the town was seen as a potential loss of resources. Zehafu accepted what had happened to her property because she was not the only person affected in this way. She took it as collective damage to all residents and was grateful that her house was not totally damaged. This existentialist evaluation of the situation helped her to come to terms with what had happened. What struck me about the family was their adjustment to the new situation. They were one of the rich families now reduced to poverty, and were attempting to rebuild their lives. The precautions that the family took reduced the stress level, whereas their use of social networks to obtain housing, and the localized social networks of the Zalanbesa people by going to drinking houses, helped them to move on in life.[1] The family lost their property but not the sympathy and social respect of their fellow villagers. The sympathy they received was one of the sources of solace for the family whose loss was huge as measured in material but not in emotional terms.. This situation kept the family on the same psychosocial footing where they still had respect in their community. The drinking house of the family was popular among Zalanbesa displaced people. Perhaps a hundred or more people were served four days a week when the local brew (*siwa*) was available. The case was also a further example of the importance of regional identity in Tigray and how this identity is used in political alliances. Zehafu came from Adwa and her regional identity made her suspect, and she was judged and regarded by others as such. This was a common view of many people complaining about Adwa's dominance in holding key political offices in Adigrat and other areas.

The war forced the people to disperse and the only occasions that bring them together are funerals. Despite the fact that burial associations are largely disbanded, people still manage to pass on messages and every one will turn up for a funeral. Zehafu said that her drinking house is a good place for people to meet and to pass on news, and she was always informed of deaths and funerals through people she knew who still come to her place to drink.

> Zehafu concluded that urban residents were not affected by shelling and cross-fire. More rehabilitative measures were taken to help the rural community than town residents; corrugated iron sheets, money, oxen, and other animals were given to displaced persons from rural areas but not to those from town.

Mukhuyam: a village taken over by Eritrean forces[2]

Eritrean forces attacked Zalanbesa on 2 June 1998, which has affected the surrounding areas. Mukhuyam is on the Eritrean side of the border and many people were in the village when the war began. Many of them knew that the war would soon start through rumours coming from the front and their networks across the political border. Rumours made a big difference as, during the border conflict, much of the news from the front line was largely carried by rumours.

One group of people in Mukhuyam took a risky precautionary measure. The households living in the centre of the village agreed to prepare a cover or shelter just one day before the fighting reached the village. The people staying behind were elderly men, women and girls. All the young people of the village left the area, deciding that it was not going to be safe for them to stay. The shelter was inadequate to protect the people left behind in circumstance of war, and it generated stress. This action represented their readiness to escape danger in an area where there was no retreat to their favoured cave, *Beati*. The village which is on the plateau had no good natural shelter in which to hide from the fighting, they had not expected defeat for the Ethiopian side, and since war was always in the area, they did not want to leave their homes. There was also no need to leave home because the war was between governments, and not between communities. They also did not expect the front line to come right up to their doorsteps, and least of all did they imagine that this war was going to target lives, homes and cultures.

The measure was a desperate act but also indicated the limited range of coping mechanisms available in a war situation. The risky move left its scar on the community but was also the only tenable option for those families who preferred to stay in their village. With the quickly changing situation in the area, some preferred to stay behind to avoid negative consequences such as the disruption of routine life and the loss of livelihood. It was a quick decision affected by stress, chaos, disorientation and bafflement. On 2 June 1998, the people woke up to the sound of artillery fire. They gathered at the spot they had prepared and waited. There seemed to be no respite from the fighting. In the afternoon, the very area where the civilians were sheltering was hit by artillery fire, killing one person on the spot and wounding five others. This was not the end of the people's ordeal and neither were they given safe passage for the wounded. When the fighting subsided in the evening, they took the wounded to their homes covering their injured bodies with pieces of cloth. Since most of them were still in shock, no one attended the burial of the dead girl the next day apart from her father, a priest and a neighbour. In between the fighting, many of those remaining decided to move away from the trap of being caught in the fighting. They all went to their preferred areas where they could receive shelter and support from relatives. Some of them had to run across the front line to reach safe areas.

TIRHAS: A MISSING EPILEPTIC WOMAN

Tirhas, aged 48, was living with her married elder brother, who was 55 and had four children. They were living in the middle of Mukhuyam village. Their main income came from ploughing their fields and the couple of animals they keep. Tirhas was epileptic and had fallen down many times, injuring herself. Her brother said that she often insulted neighbours for no apparent reason, and this was part of her condition. The neighbours understood her condition and believed that she was possessed by demon spirits and they sympathized with her. When the war started in June she was in the village, but her brother was unable to find her. Neither was she able to understand the danger of the situation and escape. She was never found after the war and her brother heard that she had been killed but he was not able to locate her body. He did the necessary bereavement ritual though he was unable to bury her, and accepted her death. Tirhas was one of those who were left in oblivion by the war never to be seen afterwards, and nobody was sure what had happened to her.

TIRFE MELES: A HOMELESS WIDOW

This case shows us how the rules within the village excluded some people from rehabilitation programmes. Rehabilitation was understood as compensation for those who lost houses and other tangible property but it did not redress the suffering caused by living in conflict.

Tirfe Meles is 45, widowed, and has had two children by two different husbands. She divorced her first husband and the second died of illness. Her first daughter is 13 and her son is five. Her husband did not have his own house and they used to live with his uncle. She gets help from her parents and her husband's relatives in ploughing her land. Unlike other families, she did not own livestock, and was working in a seedling nursery near the village. When the war started in the area, she hid in a cave located in Mukhuyam with her neighbours and later she went to a place called Adigudem and stayed there with her father until the war was over.

Her main support after the war was food hand-outs from the government, amounting to 45 kg of wheat, 3 litres of cooking oil and 1 kg of lentils. She returned to the village after the war but her condition as a widow and the fact that she did not previously own her house affected her entitlement to receive rehabilitation. One of the criteria by which the village committee selects beneficiaries, is that they have owned a house which was damaged during the war. Because of this, she was excluded from benefits such as receiving corrugated iron sheets and help in constructing a house. She was living in a makeshift house that her father put up for her. She did not try to get her field ploughed because the area was believed to be mined.

PRIEST LEGESE: LOSING SUPPORT

Legese was living in the large field called Ziban Hots'a. He had five children, five oxen, and about thirty sheep. He was one of the few people who constructed their houses along the main road, a *Debri* house. He is a dedicated priest and was known as a good farmer. Like other villagers, he is partly Eritrean. None of his family members felt this to be an identity crisis, and one of his sons is still a member of the army. Legese preferred to stay behind for the safety of his animals. In June 1998, the fighting in Zalanbesa reached his village and all his neighbours left. His wife and children went to Adigrat and he was living on barley porridge and cactus fruit from his backyard. For three months, his son, Hagos, brought food to him every night after passing through a dangerous war zone. The house was located at the midpoint between the Ethiopian and Eritrean trenches and no one came to the area because it was a no-go zone. Legese got used to the new routine of sleeping in the daytime and bringing in grass at night to feed his animals. After three months of this dangerous lifestyle, his animals escaped towards the Eritrean trenches. He went to recover them. He was fired on and his ox was hit, but luckily he was not injured. He retreated to his house and the next night his son came crying believing that his father had been killed and was relieved to find him still alive. This incident finally persuaded Legese to leave the area with his livestock. He joined the rest of his family and left his son behind in the neighbouring village to care for the injured ox and other animals. His son stayed in Dongolo with relatives who gave him and his animals shelter, but he had to find feed for the animals. This was because there was nothing left that could be used as pasture and everyone was relying on the stored straw because moving the animals was risky. His son later moved 15 km away, to Kirkos, where his mother's relatives lived. Grazing land was not available there either. He had to take the animals where they could graze in the fields or sometimes he purchased straw. When it became increasingly difficult to feed them, the son advised his mother to sell the animals, but they agreed not to tell Legese, who was very sad to learn in the end that his animals were sold. The family ultimately returned safely to their village, added an extension to their house, and rented out three rooms to teachers, the researcher and one for an office for REST.

This case shows the limitation of social support during the war. The area is rich in traditions of mutual support but this was diminished partly because of the war and partly due to the semi-arid conditions. Pasture was a scarce resource for rural families and this influenced many families to reduce the number of animals they kept during the war. Social capital did not provide the 'magic solution' for shortage of pasture.

THREE MINE VICTIMS

I met the family of Priest Andu because they were presented by the local authorities to any visitors as examples of victims. The family consists of three brothers, their wives, and their father living together in neighbouring houses at the edge of the river Afra bordering on Geleba, an Eritrean village. The second son, Hilluf, was conscripted into the Ethiopian army following the outbreak of hostilities and was not in the village when the war arrived. The rest of the family, and an aunt's son, left their houses with their livestock and moved to Ts'ehawa village where their relatives gave them shelter, food and comfort. The war did not reach that village. They stayed there until the war came to an end, and returned to their village in July 2000. Like others, they found their houses destroyed. They put up tents and makeshift houses made from corrugated-iron sheets in a place some 500 meters from their previous location. These makeshift houses were close to trenches used by the Eritrean army during the war. On 30 September, while playing in the area, three of the sons (aged 5, 7 and 12) stepped into a minefield. Their bodies were blown apart. One of the fathers told me that they buried the amputated parts of the boys in the evening. Only half a body of one of them was found and the remaining parts of the other bodies were put into a fertilizer sack and buried. This incident happened only three months after the end of the war and reminded villagers that they were still living in danger. The event shocked the community and put a halt to their hopes of returning to a normal life. One of the fathers told me that the deaths of the children made the grief very communal. Everyone coming to the funeral expressed their grief by weeping and crying; he said that they were really crying for themselves and their dangerous predicament. The whole community grieved for twelve days, sharing the grief and the cost of the ritual. This event represented the worst scenario of mine-related deaths and everyone in the village talks about it to outsiders as an example of what happened to the village.

Dongolo: a front-line village remaining under Ethiopian control

Dongolo means stone in Tigrigna and expresses the topography of the village – a rugged hill with lots of bare stones. Since it was located on high ground, it was used as a last line of defence by the Ethiopian forces. Around 200 families inhabit this rugged steep hill. The war spread by 4 June to this area. Dongolo was the target of EPLF artillery fire because of its defensive position. People living in the foothills moved to the upper plateau of the village's caves, and the hill was a safe haven for many of the villagers from surrounding areas. Since the direction of the fighting was not clear when it began, many of the residents were forced to leave the area. Nevertheless, many of them returned to the village after the fighting subsided, since they failed to find pasture for their cattle in other places. In many respects, Dongolo contrasted with what happened to Mukhayam, since few houses were damaged by artillery fire, a substantial number of residents managed to cultivate their land in safe places, many stayed close to their houses with their livestock, their village was not ransacked, and they provided support for others who were forced to flee. Many of them did not leave their homes entirely even when they were living in nearby caves. Moving to visit relatives, to receive food rations and to shop was common.

Dongolo was a front line as much as it was an example of a risky life under war conditions. Some localities of the village at the foot of the hill like Ts'ets'un were sites of confrontation, and residents from these parts were forced to leave. Its villagers always calculated and weighed the balance between risk and life when they decided to move to caves, to plough their land or to move between nearby villages and their own. With all these strains, some villagers at the top of the hill managed to till their land, harvest and thresh their crops even if the yield was less than in normal times. Movements and activities for those who stayed in the village had to be conducted at night in order not to attract artillery fire. The abnormal sound of artillery fire became part of their day-to-day activities and, unless there was real danger, people did not take it seriously. Fleeing the area and panic was the first stage of reaction to the war. Later people took the war as part of their life and dealt with it in various ways. For many of them, the advantage of remaining close to their home village outweighed that of leaving for practical reasons of finding shelter and feed for livestock. With all its negative repercussions, the war brought with it new opportunities of retail trade for the villagers, some of whom benefited by selling cigarettes, beer, alcohol, tea, etc. These opportunities created relationships between the army and villagers, some of which developed into marriages. These relationships were also useful for the villagers, giving them access to information about front-line situations.

The following two accounts illustrate differences between female- and male-headed households. Both demonstrate the readiness of families to cope with the changing conditions. These cases highlight the differences between Dongolo and Mukhuyam. There was definite awareness of danger and risk in Dongolo, protective measures were well organized, residents created new ways of coping with the risk such as storing food and minimizing loss. Reactions in Mukhuyam were hasty, chaotic and spontaneous, there was no chance of staying in the village and saving one's life was more important than minimizing loss. These differences characterized the communities' reactions in the wake of the conflict. The major problem for many dislocated rural families was finding animal feed. In the following case Hiwot's family fled the area after organizing themselves, and found a way of getting some animal feed in exchange for their animals' traction power.

HIWOT KIDANE MARYAM: A WIDOW WITH SIX CHILDREN

We met Hiwot in her *Hidimo* house; she was 40 and slim, lively and open. Her husband had died two years before and she had six children in her care. She moved to Dongolo from neighbouring Qetsqetsiya village after her marriage. The couple had been members of religious associations established in the village and she continued to participate in these associations. The main income of the family came from ploughing 1.5 *Gibri* of land and she owned two oxen used for traction. She supported her husband in farming and her son-in-law took over the task of ploughing after his death. The war characterized life events and activities but did not bring significant change in the household's economic condition. Before hostilities reached the area, her family made some emergency preparations. They buried their grain in the ground, keeping some to take with them. When the war reached their place in May 1989 the husband and wife fled separately. Hiwot said that she spent a night in a cave and met her husband the following day. Her husband took their animals, whereas she and the children carried other goods. The family sheltered in the neighbouring village of Ambeset Feqade with relatives.

Despite tensions her husband returned to sow his seeds in the evenings. This area is a plateau, and was behind the Ethiopian trenches shielded by hills. It was therefore relatively safe. Some people weeded their fields working by night and living in caves. They went back in November to harvest the field, worked for three nights, and piled up the crops on the field to dry. Before they could get organized to thresh their crops, artillery fire burned most of the crops on the field. Their main income after the war was food hand-outs from the government and support from relatives. Pasture was difficult to find and they lost animals owing to lack of grass. They rented out their oxen for various agricultural tasks, particularly threshing, and in return obtained animal feed. Cactus fruit was also an important source of food for the animals. During this period Hiwot's husband died from sickness and his burial was formally performed, though many people from the village did not attend the funeral. His death put the burden on her of caring for her children. When the war ended she returned to her village, to find everything in place but the stored grain affected by weevils and unusable. Disrupted activities, such as participation in religious associations, were resumed.

The next case shows us the strength and relentless struggle to plough and continue making a living in a dangerous environment. The common trend in the village was to return home and work in the fields until the war ended. This option was better than going to other crowded areas and competing for the already scarce resources such as pasture in the semi-arid areas.

What was the context of the war for the villagers as represented in Kelieber's model? Was it terrifying? Yes, it was dangerous, but still better to stay in the village than to starve and lose animals, particularly oxen, which are a scarce resource in Tigray. The reaction of the villagers in taking risks was therefore a rational choice. War led to panic but did not detach villagers from their lives and land, with which they were interwoven emotionally. As the war continued, the panic associated with it subsided and the emotional bond to their land drew villagers back to their homes. Returning to their villages was as much an economic urge as it was an emotional one. Risk-taking outweighed losing livelihood.

ALEQA TEWOLDEMEDHIN GEBRE YOHANIS: LIVING IN A CAVE

Tewoldemedhin is 44, married twenty-one years ago and a father of five. His main income comes from agriculture and working in the seedling nursery where he is paid monthly in the form of grain. He was a member of Medhanealem Religious Association, along with twelve other members from the same village. The association was suspended during the war and was reformed immediately after the villagers returned.

The war came in the middle of the agricultural season, and Tewoldemedhin decided to finish his tasks before fleeing the area. Like many others, he remained in the area, sheltering with his family in a cave. In July he decided to send his pregnant wife and children to his sister in a neighbouring village, and he followed them in September. His wife gave birth safely to their fifth child while she was staying with his sister. He sheltered in a cave two-and half-hours' walking distance from his field, eating ground barley and wheat flour. He again returned in November to harvest his field and stayed in the same cave for a month. The harvest of that year was burned by artillery fire. Tewoldemedhin sowed seed the following year and harvested 300 kg of grain. His wife and children helped him. In the first year of the war, he was entirely dependent on his sister to feed his animals and he later collected grass from far away when the supply in his locality ran out. He never ceased his agricultural tasks along with about fifty families who remained at the top of the village behind the Ethiopian defence lines. He was still getting relief food support from the government. As part of his commitment and support for the war, Tewoldemedhin helped the army many times by carrying food provisions and ammunition.

Tewoldemedhin's family were among the first to return to their village after the Eritrean forces were repelled. For him it was not a long stay away since he had been coming back to the village to work in his field. He used to visit the house and clean the floor. The top of the roof was slightly hit by artillery fire. He was able to return with his oxen and a couple of sheep and went back to his normal life. Since he had ploughed and harvested some grain the previous year, he was not short of animal feed. He had stored enough straw from the previous season.

FLEEING THE WAR

The war shattered village life, transformed the village into a dangerous location, destroyed trust and safety. Individuals react to war in different ways. This event was characterized by disorientation, panic and spontaneity. Sympathetic social gestures were common reactions from the people not directly affected by the war, and they were willing to host others shattered by it. The cultural value of extending a helping hand was a long-standing tradition in the region. Even if there are few resources, guests are always welcome and there is a well-established custom of giving in times of trouble. This was an important resource tapped by the displaced during the war, and especially while so many were on the move. It was common to see people giving food and other items to those who fled Zalanbesa and other affected villages. Some paid house rent for their displaced relatives and others stayed in rural areas while receiving monthly food rations.

Kidan was alone since her husband was at the front. Her husband was exempted from military duties as he was too old to continue serving. She left Zalanbesa but the war reached her area quickly and a shell dropped near her house. The fighting was very close when she was in Tegoza and sometimes they tried to cover the door with blankets to reduce the sound of gunfire, but this was a futile action stemming from fear. Everyone was in disarray and no one was available to help her move her child to safety so she had to do it on her own. She went to a cave nearby to escape the fighting and then to Adigrat the following day when the fighting subsided. Relatives welcomed her and gave her their kitchen as a shelter. When Adigrat was hit by artillery fire, her relatives left the town, leaving her the house. She was afraid to stay separated from her husband and relatives, but she did not want to leave the house unattended. Later the owners returned and she continued to live with them. Staying in a combat situation in Tegoza was stressful. She had prepared some food when leaving Zalanbesa, and was also given additional food by relatives in Tegoza. She was sheltered by her sister, and obtained food and other emergency support from the government after reaching Adigrat. This was helpful in coming to terms with what happened to them.

Fleeing the war was a common experience, but not all the people fled in the same direction. Some went to the interior part of Ethiopia and those who stayed behind were taken to Eritrea by EPLF forces. The issue has political dimensions as both governments were accusing each other of human rights violations. Older people and children were usually not maltreated during their stay in Eritrea, though the reactions of citizens varied over time. When there was news about the fighting or an offensive from the Ethiopian side, the displaced persons in Eritrea were subject to angry reactions. It was all too common for young Ethiopians to be conscripted and made to fight alongside the Eritrean army, or kept in prison to make them unavailable for conscription in Ethiopia. It was not uncommon to find Ethiopians imprisoned if they were suspected of working for their government or found to be active in raising funds for Tigrayan development activities. The following witness account was given by Priest Girmay who was held prisoner in Eritrea for two years. The displaced did not receive a warm welcome when they returned after the end of the war, partly because of the gossip that some of them had pillaged the properties of Ethiopians from the deserted Zalanbesa town and surrounding villages.

> Priest Girmay and other elderly persons remained in their village up to 28 June, a month after the EPLF took control of the area. Then they were ordered to leave the village. Girmay remembered when the church was hit by artillery fire from the Ethiopian side on 10 June. He said that the EPLF had three cannons near the church. They also saw when EPLF soldiers were hit by artillery fire from the Ethiopian side. After all this fighting, they left the area. Girmay stayed with his brother (*Aboy* Kahsay), who after the New Year returned to Ethiopia from Zalanbesa via Debre Damo. Girmay said that about 4,500 displaced persons stayed in a place called Amboha near Senafe. A Tigrayan man sent a truck of water to them from Asmara. The displaced were under the care of the International Red Cross and received tents, blankets, clothes and food. The EPLF authorities were in charge of the administration and they exchanged wheat for corn and gave it to them. Later, the ICRC took control of the food distribution and they got wheat. Food distribution was delayed for two months and Girmay had to purchase grain from Aga T'irqe villagers because they had good produce that year. He took his ox to Eritrea but not other property, which was taken like that of other villagers.
>
> Girmay said that the EPLF were lucky to arrive in villages like Ligat and Mukhuyam because the *Beles* was ripe and the corn in the field almost ready to harvest. The period was not good for the villagers as the EPLF forces harvested *tef* without sowing it. The displaced were in camps in Eritrea at a place called Amboha. They were free to travel within Eritrea but they had to pay 10 *birr* to get a pass permit. They obtained some money by selling grain from food hand-outs and some of them already had money. Other villagers sold property to get money. The displaced were divided into 13 *kebeles* and a bald man among them was ordered to register the young men to be armed. He reported that no one was healthy and fit enough to be registered. The EPLF official then hit the bald man on the head. Girmay said that the EPLF soldiers were irreligious and had no respect for the Church. They smoked cigarettes, stored heavy shells inside the church and used the building for radio communication. He claimed that most of the fighters were Muslim Tigre but the officers were from Senafe. The villagers did not expect that the church would be used as a fighting area. They sought refuge in the building at the beginning but left it after EPLF soldiers started to use it as a

fortress to fight from the high ground where it was located. At first the EPLF soldiers did not take property, but they soon began to loot the village, ransacking houses. It took them only one night to empty the houses. Armed men were carrying floor tiles and carpets from the church. People from Senafe were called in to demolish Zalanbesa town.

The displaced spent two years in a camp. When the Eritrean port of Mitsiwa was bombed by the Ethiopian Air Force, an angry mob came to assault the camp, but the Muslim administrator protected them. After the war they were allowed to go back home. They did not receive a warm welcome and no one asked them about the problems they had encountered, since they were associated with the enemy. No one gave them even a cup. They remained between the Ethiopian and the Eritrean sides and feared that they might be hit by artillery fire from the Ethiopian side targeting anti-aircraft artillery near them. They were afraid when they heard the news that the EPLF were fleeing the town of Adiqeye towards the end of the war. It was difficult to stay in Eritrea between May and June 2000 during the Ethiopian counter-offensive. The displaced were advised to leave Eritrea quickly and it was easier for Girmay as he had nothing to carry. Some handed over their property to someone else; others sold it or just abandoned it. Some purchased flour on a Thursday just before leaving on Saturday, and left it behind as it was too heavy to carry. They stayed at Abba Selama for 11 days in an open field before leaving by bus. When they returned to their village, they slept in bunkers and trenches made by the EPLF forces because all their houses were flattened.

The above case illustrates differences between those who were forced to go to Eritrea and others who fled to interior parts of Tigray when the war began. Even if they were forced and intimidated, the displaced in Eritrea were able to move freely to visit relatives, trade and work. These opportunities lowered the level of stress that could have been experienced. The biggest gap between those who went to Eritrea and those who remained within Ethiopia was the claim that 'the former participated in the ransacking of Zalanbesa'. This was the main tension between the two groups and was the reason for a cool and sometimes disappointing welcome for the families repatriated from Eritrea.

Finding refuge in caves and local constructions of home

Caves were part of war stories and the style of living during the war, representing a symbolic marker of danger, refuge and safety, as well as coping and challenge. *Beati* or cave was a common response when I asked people how they lived through the war. Sheltering in caves was considered abnormal but workable. Caves were also used to run schools to avoid the disruption of services. Since this war was partly a conflict of identity, taking risks was part of a response that the government promoted among the public. Thus, the use of caves for shelter, schools and other activities served to create the image of the war as a challenge. The notion of home is intrinsically linked with identity, social networks, and community life. This was even truer in the context of displacement and war where social life was defined and enacted in terms of meanings, values, and networks. It was the social networks and mutual-help mechanisms that made caves habitable (Hammond 2000).

The villagers used two related concepts: *Beati* or *Bereha*[3] to indicate a place where they fled the war. The former is used for a cave and the latter for any place not inhabited before or not suitable for human habitation. In many instances for those caught behind during hostilities, caves were the first and only easy way out from danger. The reaction was swift but the decision to live in caves depended on other conditions: the seriousness of the danger of war and the strength of social networks and their capacity to cover living costs in town. Some of the caves could accommodate a great number of people, but on the first day of the war the situation was chaotic and one informant put it this way: 'everyone was talking all night'. Everyone was terrified and there was not enough space to accommodate all those who sought safety. People appreciated the benefit of sheltering in caves because many of them had no alternative. On the other hand, they also spoke of the hardship of being in a cave. Gergis lived in a cave for seven months after Adigrat was hit by artillery fire. She said 'people took the place of monkeys'. She recalled all the hardships and the challenges including shortage of food, the cold, the use of stones as pillows, and over-crowding. What counted was for all to escape the war and stay alive. She said the capacity to face the challenges was proof of the saying: 'Humans and monkeys do not die quickly'. Monkeys are a symbol of strength and resilience, and the villagers were likened to them living through, dealing with, and overcoming hardships. War was not new to the region that had experienced civil wars for three decades. As the villagers put it: 'The northern land breeds war' or 'this land likes blood'. The degree may vary but every family had some experience of war. Some saw it as something unavoidable in the region, because they had no control of the political factors. This found expression in their belief system and led them to conclude that "the land liked blood'. The land or the supernatural beings were given the power of causing war and chaos.

Life in the caves had its own remarkable features. It was warm and more communal, though still uncomfortable and worrisome. Everything was shared: food, goods, labour, information, humour, and emotions. Cave-living required tolerance towards others, for there was no privacy. Those who lived through the cave experience appreciated the intimacy and unstructuring effect of displacement and cave life. People in the cave were largely from rural areas that could not afford the additional cost of living in town. Movement depended on the state of the war front and it was sometimes very dangerous to go out; excursions were therefore not allowed by the shelter administrators. Life, apart from being confined, was not bad. People went to church, visited relatives, received rations regularly, and went to the market in the evening. Sharing, giving, and caring in the cave were remarkable. People made a lot of jokes and had fun while they were together. However, their thinking was hanging on one thing: 'When will this be over so that I can go home?' Each shelling took people back to the tension and changed the mood of those in the cave from relaxed to tense and disturbed. '*Beati* was good to escape shelling and gave a sense of being safe but it was a different kind of living where no one wanted to stay long.'

The geographical proximity of living together was paralleled by the social intimacy and interaction that was seen among the shelter occupants. This metamorphic nature of sociality concurs with the view of Carrithers (1992) that emphasizes the human capacity for immensely varied and complex social behaviour, asserting that we are not just passive animals who are moulded by our respective societies and cultures but actively make and remake society into new ways of life and interactions.

Impacts of the War

The war between Ethiopia and Eritrea spread so rapidly that international organizations and the media were caught off-guard. Both sides attacked and retaliated with extreme force following the commencement of hostilities on 2 June 1998. By 5 June, the two sides were bombing towns from the air causing high numbers of civilian casualties. That the conflict was so violent is evidence that it was not a simple border dispute. It was instead a war of identities, continuity, deep animosity, history, and competition. The mood changed, support was rallied and the war gained momentum beyond the control of the two governments. It forced hundreds of thousands of people to be dislocated from their localities, while also causing numbers of casualties and great damage. At the micro level, the impact of the war on villages was huge and destructive. It obliterated houses, damaged farm fields, killed animals, made some areas unusable due to mines, and disrupted life in general.

In war there are things that can be said and things that cannot. It was therefore no surprise to have mixed images of why and what it was for. The reasoning behind the war, its associated damage, and the identity of the main perpetrators, remain unclear. This war was arguably waged at the heart of identity and its pressure on border villagers was immense. What is clear is that these answers will be as complex as the political and social relations in the area. Blame for events that occurred during the war has not been clearly and may never be fully assigned. Many evade it by saying, as Priest Hagos once explained, 'bygones are bygones', and do not talk about it. This was a period that should be put aside because it never resembled the village life cultivated and evolved over centuries, it was almost taboo. Letemedhin said: 'The period created animosity and incomprehension and the unusual act of harming each other'. Some said that the period was 'evil' or 'demonic', explanations deeply rooted in religious dogma and ideology. Everything exceptionally evil is considered the work of demons; and so is the evil of this war.

Apart from its political dimension and its link with identity, the war and its aftermath divided the displaced in opinions as to what happened to their properties. The division was more apparent between those who fled the war to the interior part of Ethiopia and those who were left behind and taken to Eritrea. This was contentious, for it disturbed relations between relatives living in the same locality. Gossip maintains that those who were left behind collaborated with the enemy and looted the properties of other Zalanbesa residents fleeing the war. In some cases, this created a schism between relatives and the issue was often avoided rather than being openly discussed. In fact, many became better-off after being displaced, particularly those who were left behind after the area came under the control of the EPLF and who managed to take out their own property, or looted that of others and sold it in Eritrea.

The most common impact of the war was impoverishment and this caused many independent families to become dependent on food hand-outs. Some families could not afford to live in town soon after the war began and moved to their rural villages if the area was safe. Others switched between rural and town residences to retain their displaced status so as not to be excluded from potential urban rehabilitation programmes. Many agreed that the war had no uniform negative economic impact on communities. Letebirhan suggested that some families became better-off and others worse-off. She classified the internally displaced in the following way:

- those who fled the war with their property or who did not take property with them;
- those who did not get food hand-outs in Zalanbesa but benefited from them now after they had been displaced;
- those who became better-off than their previous position in Zalanbesa;
- those whose position did not change, and who were not affected by the war or displacement.

Letebirhan said: 'We live by day and night with God's willingness.' By this she implied that it is not certain how she can make a living being dependent on government rations. She gets 60 kg of wheat and 4 litres of oil a month and when she gets a double month's ration, she sells half of that and uses it to pay rent and to buy food.

War and identity

The concept of identity and belonging is used in different ways (Barnard and Spencer 1996: 292). As Bauer (1973) remarked, regional identity has significance in Tigray and villages within this area. Gullomekeda *Wereda* falls in Agame proper: however, there is a slight difference. At first sight, the displaced population have no significant cultural and religious differences from the host community because they are all Agame. However, people from Gullomekeda inside Agame are seen as bearers of double identities: Agame and Eritrean, in contrast to people from Adigrat town district who consider themselves to be pure Agame in blood and cultural values. There were no major problems in relations between the host community and the displaced. Furthermore, identity differences were reflected as expressions of otherness rather than hostility. Some of these stereotypical differences were expressed in terms of style of speech and dialect. Cross-cutting kinship ties of Gullomekeda across the current political border are the core of their identities and they tend to be parochial and closed to outsiders. Barth (1996) underlines the importance of social behaviour and interactions in studying ethnic boundaries instead of limiting the focus to the cultural issues that enclose a group. Identity differences between Gullomekeda and other Agame groups are manifested in social interactions, based on shared values, customary law, kinship and mutual trust. After living among the people of Gullomekeda for more than eight years serving as a traditional birth attendant, Abrehit complained that none of her neighbours came to visit her even if they knew that she was ill. She said, 'The hearts of Gullomekeda people are never known to be open.'

In addition to dialectal variety, customary law provides Gulomekeda with its own identity. Gullomekeda and Sobiya can be said to be one region in terms of customary law and two in terms of kinship identities. Their names indicate that they were named after those who were believed to be founding fathers of the two settlements: Wede Harishay for Gullomekeda and Bilish for Sobiya. The law covered many areas of social life, reinforcing and homogenizing values and cultural forms. The law and the local polity were working in the area until 1974 and it is still used as a point of reference and a source of pride and identity. It also stood as a marker of local identity in the area in contrast to similar customary law utilized in neighbouring Eritrean villages (Tronvoll 1996). The use of primordial identities to mobilize followers in civil wars has resulted in more ingrained ethnic identities in the post-conflict era.[4]

The parties fought the civil war for political gains as much as for carving out new identities. There has been a primordial bond between Eritrean highlanders and their Tigray counterparts (Abbay 1998; Tronvoll 1996). This primordial bond was attacked before, though more profoundly in the recent war, which was in many ways a war against continuity of this bond; expulsion of each other's nationals and the selective use of negative stereotypes severed relationships. Retaliatory acts of demolishing houses and destroying livelihoods contributed to the widening gap. The war was actually an attempt to redefine the relationship between the two countries and this can easily impact on future relationships and the identity of each country. In villages, where fluidity of identity was a norm, social boundary markers were invisible or irrelevant and villagers indicated this by the analogy of saying 'Our seeds get mixed when we sow our fields'.

Before the war on border villages, the relations were based on long-established bonds. Preferred marriage partners on the Ethiopian side were always those coming from Eritrea rather than villages from the interior part of Tigray. One partner's group felt superior to the other, but that did not affect their relationship. There was conflict over plots of land but that was part of the normal rivalry and competition for local resources, and did not affect overall social interactions. For the villagers, the nearest economic centre was Asmara, though other towns also provided them with the opportunity of earning a livelihood in exchange for jobs ranging from working in the fields to the docks. Generally, the bond between villagers was very strong. For the sake of comparison, other villages in Badime were not so close; villagers came from both countries and settled recently and there was competition and animosity between them and cattle raiding was common. This is out of context in Gullomekeda and nearby areas and there was mutual sympathy and respect for one another. How did this war affect the common identity of villages that cut across recently introduced political borders?

The war shattered lives, wrecked houses, created new dangers, but at least at this stage failed to sever the relationships between villagers across the political borders of the two countries. Villages are linked across borders through kinship and other networks that have developed over time. They developed new forms of relationship across the border and maintained their bonds. These relationships were no longer open because they raised the concern of the local political authorities. There is no attendance for feasting from each other's villages, no longer weddings, no more walking to each others' markets. However, their animals still graze on the same fields, they still share information which is of mutual benefit, and smooth relationships continue in hidden forms and at the time of our fieldwork were normalizing. From the villagers' point of view, the political authorities brought the conflict. They were blamed for demolishing houses even though surrounding villagers were wary of participating in ransacking houses. Elders in Mukhuyam summarized their own view as follows. 'We are tied up intrinsically with our Eritrean neighbours by marriage, and we are one. Like them, we are close to our relatives but we are still Ethiopians'. This war-tested identity is shaken somewhat but not shattered, as evidenced by this quote. In order to demonstrate their loyalty to the state, and thus prevent suspicion based on their dual Ethiopian/Eritrean identities, many villages joined the militia army to support Ethiopia. The illusive impact of the war on identities may fade with time according to informants who added: 'Fire entered between us, otherwise they (Eritreans) are brothers. Like conflict between brothers, this will pass and we will meet again with relatives to live in peace as we did in the past.' As Cairns (1996) stated, the common social identity across the political borders of the two countries rather served as a mediating factor giving a perspective in which the war is seen and sensed, attributing accountability for all the misdeeds and destruction to the political authorities. Despite being in the forefront of the assault, the common social identity among villagers moderated animosities and restored social relations.

Conclusion

Zalanbesa gained significance as a border town following the independence of Eritrea, though this process itself created tensions in the town's identity and political administration. In Zalanbesa and the surrounding areas, village identities spoke louder than larger national identities. The socio-cultural homogeneity of villages and the cross-border bonds of kinship made the relationship more complex. Zalanbesa in some respects was an enclave of Ethiopian political administration in an area where identities were difficult to disentangle. For instance, if we take the myth of Hailedonay, we can see the ambivalence and fluidity of identities. Haledonay preferred to be buried in an Eritrean monastery while ambiguously dividing rights to the Sheshet farm between the Eritrean monastery and Ethiopian villagers. In Zalanbesa, whether with hidden intent or not, Eritreans had a stake in the political, economic and social life of the town. They felt Eritrean as much as they felt Ethiopian. Part of the confusion about the rights and duties of residents came from the fuzzy identity of the area and from the unclear status of citizens immediately after Eritrean independence.

The competition in trade and investment gave a more confused picture to the relations of the people living in the area, reflecting inherent political links between the two governments that continued before and after they came to power. This competition also brought into the limelight the two emerging nationalist trends that negated the old inclusive identity. Zalanbesa was a sphere of influence for surrounding villagers: it was their market, centre of social services, and source of income through trade, and an attractive magnet for labour. What happened in the town overshadowed views in the surrounding villages. Competition in trade and investments was expressed in terms of contesting claims for farm plots in rural areas. The competition to dominate characterized the relationships in towns, and the war was an extended expression of exerting influence.

Zalanbesa was one of the yardsticks for the deteriorating relations between the two governments. Controls on checkpoints and illegal trade became strict in proportion to the worsening political relations. Tensions were sometimes expressed in terms of exchanges of fire between militias and customs policemen. These incidents and the attack on Badime helped the government and people to take precautionary action by leaving the town before it was too late. This reduced the level of suffering and distress in the town. However, despite the existence of information about the impending danger, a large proportion of rural residents did not leave their areas. The war was not a surprise, but the extent of the damage and destruction was not anticipated. Mukhuyam villagers paid a heavy toll compared with others during the war. Many of the Zalanbesa residents left the area, whereas a substantial number of Dongolo villagers stayed behind.

The common pattern repeatedly seen in rural villages reinforced one fact. The strong grip of identity was expressed in terms of an emotional attachment to homeland. Expressions such as the following were common: 'It was a great chance to accept death in one's home village', and 'Death and weddings are graceful in a home village.' Many reasons were given for staying behind, some expressed in the love for animals, others underestimating the real danger, yet others not concerned about larger political changes and wanting to continue to live their routine life in the villages. Common identity was a condensed expression of all these reasons. Identity played the major role in moderating the effect of the war and in softening the danger of staying behind. The young left villages such as Mukhuyam because they were particularly targeted by the warring parties. Other categories such as the elderly, women, and children often stayed behind as they felt they were less likely to be harmed and were seen to be politically neutral.

The inclusive identity played a key role in writing a new script of the war in the minds of the villagers. This was quite different from what was commonly heard in the media about the opposing governments. The local narratives of the war provided a new view of changes in the political sphere in the area. The core of these narratives was the promotion of common kinship bonds, restoration of normal relations, nullifying any feeling of grudge and animosity, putting aside the past and rebuilding the future based on social structures that create the social fabric in the area. The script that said, 'We are brothers but fire came between us; we are one and mixed in blood and never will be separated.' passed on the message of tolerance and the restoration of trust between villagers.

The war was an all too common scene of suffering, destruction, loss of life and shattering of social fabric. It was also a scene of the extraordinary strength and capacity to cope of people whose lives were turned upside down by events but who continued to live in the hope of reversing their negative effects. The war was a story of loss but also a story of survival. The war destroyed towns, buildings and properties but not the spirit of the people. By the standards of the recent history of the region, the Ethio-Eritrean war was more damaging and costly than any others. The material devastation was unprecedented, but the capacity of the people and their resources to bounce back was also extraordinary. The most obvious effect of the war was impoverishment. However, the flexible and simple life of the people seemed to reduce the negative impacts of the war. The spiritual strength and emotional comfort of the people are found in the social context and relationships rather than in the material aspects.

The war stories were a witness to one fact. The reactions of people to terrifying events may not be the same. The responses to these events were influenced by various factors. Some of the Dongolo villagers fled the war, others stayed in nearby villages for a short period and returned to their village; yet others divided their families, leaving behind men to work in the fields. Some lived in caves throughout the war, others made repeated visits to their village to work and inspect their houses. These responses suggest that, even in situations as threatening as war, responses vary. The resources available to households including their networks are very important. Some avoided moving out because it was disadvantageous to keep their stock outside their area, due to the scarcity of animal feed. Many households demonstrated a great ability to adapt and survive dangerous situations. Some exploited opportunities to trade even if the situation was risky. This suggests that responses to stressful events depend on the context as much as on the reading of events by the actors.

Zalanbesa and its residents have gone through various changes. The town gained its importance and grew as a trading border town following the independence of Eritrea. Political situations changed and transferred the town to an area of competition and a route for smuggling goods. Developments that contributed to its growth soon deteriorated and contributed to the demise of the town, symbolically representing the atrocity of the fighting and the blind and destructive force of the war that spectacularly targeted more civilians than soldiers. The common identity of villagers was used in various ways to soften the impact as well as to restore future relations. In the midst of the crisis, people utilized their various resources to respond to the war. Thus within the same context of war, responses of households varied depending on many factors, notably social networks and the relative assessment of the economic costs of leaving or staying behind.

Notes

Much of the detail of this paper had to be cut due to space constraints and can be found in Behailu Abebe (2004).

1. Like many other places in Tigray, drinking houses were marked by a piece of coloured cloth hung from the doorframe. These cloths identify where the owner comes from. People tended to go to drinking houses owned by people, usually women, from their own locality. Drinking houses from Zalanbesa and Gullomekeda hung a purple piece of cloth whereas those from Adigrat hung a red one. This was an indication of the importance of regional identity.
2. Mukhyam was within the Ethiopian boundary until the recent verdict of the International Court based at The Hague. The verdict put Mukhuyam, like other villages surrounding Zalanbesa, within Eritrean territory. This study was conducted before this ruling and reflects the then situation.
3. Unlike *Beati* the word *Bereha* is also used to express the act of changing a residence to inaccessible places as a bandit, or more commonly joining the insurgent TPLF group during the civil war. It indicates abandoning civil life.
4. Primordial identities were also targets for those who wished to invent a new identity such as 'Hadas (new) Eritrea' as Abbay explained: 'The Eritrean and Tigrayan case studies show that the tension between the primordial identity and instrumentally-shaped sense of identity gets diluted by state mass violence. This is shown by the success and failure of the three political actors – the EPLF, the TPLF and the Derg – all of whom vied for a share of the political pie…three of them pursued divergent instrumentalist discourse. The EPLF, which did not find the primordial past serviceable, assaulted it. The TPLF summoned and effectively used it. The Derg pursued a policy of mass violence.' (1998: 221).

Fifteen

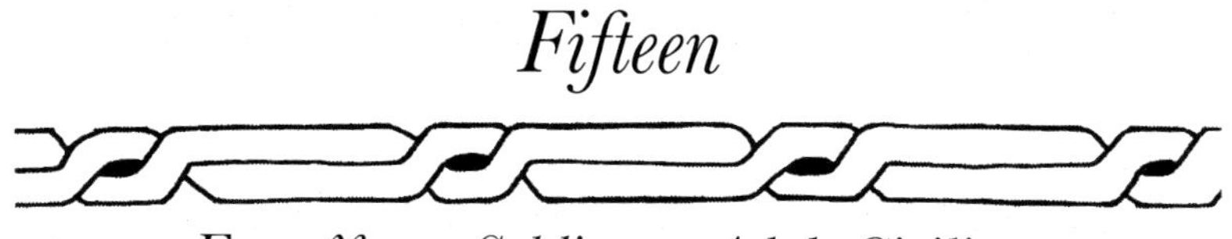

From Young Soldiers to Adult Civilians

Gender Challenges
in Addis Ababa Cooperatives

YISAK TAFERE

Introduction

After involvement in an internal conflict for two decades, the Ethiopian People's Revolutionary Democratic Front (EPRDF) overthrew the Derg regime (1974-91). The EPRDF army as a national defence force replaced the army that served in the Derg government and a programme was launched to facilitate the return of the ex-soldiers to civilian life. In June 1991, the EPRDF-led Transitional Government of Ethiopia established an institution called the Commission for the Rehabilitation of Members of the Former Army and Disabled War Veterans (CRMFADWV).

The Commission was given responsibility for the demobilization and reintegration of the ex-servicemen. Among the estimated 500,000 ex-soldiers, 326,338 were registered for institutional support in their transition. Some 156,710 preferred to assume urban life, 42,914 of whom settled in Addis Ababa. Different types of reintegration supports were provided including: return to their former employment, vocational training, certification of military skills to be useful in civilian activities, and credit schemes. Among those who settled in Addis Ababa about 1755 are engaged in 79 different cooperatives. Field research was based on two Addis Ababa cooperatives, one involving women who are engaged in food processing and the other men employed in household and office furniture production.

Some researchers, including Dercon and Daniel (1998) and Mulugeta (2000), have revealed aspects of the socio-economic reintegration of demobilized soldiers engaged in agricultural activities, though little was discussed about gender variations. This chapter investigates the socio-economic reintegration of ex-soldiers[1] who returned to a complex urban society. The challenge focuses on gender variations, which are complicated by many variables such as need for skills, housing and employment. Structured interviews were conducted among the 13 male and 9 female ex-soldiers. Five male and four female ex-soldiers were interviewed in depth to analyse the view of demobilized soldiers on demobilization, ex-soldiers' engagement in cooperatives, and military influence in the cooperative organizations. Other interviews with those involved in the implementation of the programme focused on policy challenges and economic and social reintegration.

Demobilization

From the end of the Cold War, African governments started to examine their military forces in relation to their domestic and international situations. It was argued that, in addition to the weak national policies, recurrent droughts, an increased debt burden, and civil wars have had a negative impact on income growth and development opportunities (Kingma 2000:7-9). One of the major issues considered for development was to return people in the army to civilian productive life. Such return of previously mobilized soldiers could be described as *de-mobilizing* them. What, then, is *demobilization*? What are the reasons behind demobilization?

Jakkie Cilliers (1995) describes demobilization 'as the process through which forces of a government and opposition parties shed themselves of excess personnel after a period of conflict'. Others give more emphasis to economic and security impacts in defining demobilization. It is considered to be 'the process by which the armed forces (government and/or opposition or factional forces such as guerrilla armies) either downsize or completely disband.... In many countries demobilization is a much broader transformation from a war to peace-time economy (transfer of resources to non-military sectors, restructuring of infrastructure, restoration of security)... and are often accompanied by structuring the armed forces' (World Bank 1993).

DEMOBILIZATION IN AFRICA

It has been strongly argued that African countries are unable to maintain huge armies in post-conflict situations. Decisions to demobilize in Africa had been initiated by specific military, political and socio-economic circumstances. The following are considered to be the most common reasons. (Kingma and Kiflemariam 1995 :5): (i) a multilateral, bilateral or national peace accord or disarmament agreement; (ii) defeat of one of the warring parties; (iii) perceived improvement in the security situation; (iv) shortage of adequate funding; (v) perceived economic and development impact of conversion; and (vi) changing military technologies and/or strategies.

Apart from their internal situations, African governments are also influenced by donor recommendations. As a response to economic problems, most African governments since the early 1980s have started to implement Structural Adjustment Programmes (SAPs). In the first decade of SAPs, little attention was paid to military expenditure. Demobilization was part of the conditionalities of SAP packages by the IMF/World Bank. Uganda sought to justify this to its citizens as an internal, home-grown government policy. Subsequently, the Uganda Army Council sitting in May 1992 decided to demobilize up to 50,000 soldiers from the then National Resistance Army (Byamukama 2000:3). In poor post-war economic situations, many are vulnerable to external influence leading to demobilization. For instance, `Chad's primary foreign sponsor, France, made it clear that demobilization was a precondition for future assistance`(World Bank, 1993).

DEMOBILIZATION IN ETHIOPIA

It is difficult to trace the process of demobilization in Ethiopia previous to the EPRDF era. In wartime, armed men were fed by their supporters or by the general farming community in cases of foreign aggression. There had been tendencies to return some of the army members to productive life. 'Emperor Tewodros (1855-68) attempted to return the armed bands and warlords to full time farming or other productive work' (Caulk 1977: 18). Emperor Yohannes (1872-89) more significantly showed an effort to mobilize his forces only in times of real national emergency and much of their time was spent in agricultural activities (R. Pankhurst 1963: 120). Emperor Menelik (1889-1913) tried to forbid his soldiers from forcibly taking farmers' property. Rather, he asked the latter to pay taxes for the upkeep of the army. Land was also distributed to those who had been in combat (Wood 1977: 52-3). Soldiers were given land at the end of campaigns under tribute systems which required the recipient to provide taxes and services to the state, such as guarding government offices. Hence, in those times leaders tended to try to handle the army rather than returning the soldiers fully to civilian activity.

Emperor Haile Selassie set up a new regular paid army in 1941; among others, soldiers came from the patriot warriors who had fought the Italians underground (Lefever 1970:143). There were no apparent practices of reducing the number of army members. At most, challenging soldiers or senior officers were either demoted or disciplined. This continued in the time of the Derg, which was practically a military government. But, immediately after seizing power, the EPRDF-led Provisional Government of Ethiopia decided to demobilize the army members who had been serving under the Derg regime.

The rationale behind demobilization

The Commission stipulated the main rationales for demobilization as: security, political, economic and the claimed 'will' of the ex-soldiers (CRMFDWV 1994).

Security. The Commission claimed that the brutal nature of the Derg had had some impact on its soldiers. If not handled properly, they would remain a major threat to the civilians. It was believed that the army which was in total disarray had time to harass unarmed civilians and cause disturbances. It was claimed, therefore, that demobilization was a necessity.

Political. The EPRDF Provisional Government had the ambition of peaceful co-existence with its neighbours, and the introduction of democracy within the country would require little force. That implied the unwillingness of the new government to maintain a large army personnel. Hence, immediately after seizing power, it declared: 'Ethiopia's determination to settle internal and external disputes through peaceful means, and viewed in light of this policy, the new Ethiopian defense force does not require to maintain a huge army'.

Economic. The army had been identified as economically harmful in three ways. It was unproductive, destructive of wealth and a high consumer of scarce resources. The Derg had reached a point where 48 percent of its expenditure went on the army in 1991 (World Bank 1995: 82). The new government was convinced that cuts in military expenditure were only possible by demobilizing the huge army.

Consent. The Commission claimed that most of the ex-soldiers were 'willing' to return to civilian life. The forced conscription by the Derg, especially in its final years, made the soldiers reluctant to remain in the army.

DEMOBILIZATION OR 'MEFENAKEL' (UPROOTING)?

The motives claimed by the government were categorically rejected and ex-soldiers gave demobilization completely different meanings. Soldiers who joined the army involuntarily may develop an interest and choose to remain, leading to the eventual rejection of being demobilized. Accordingly, most consider demobilization as 'a tool to punish enemies'. As opposed to its implementers' usage, the ex-soldiers called it '*mefenakel*', literally meaning *uprooting* from normal life.

Their justifications vary based on their differences in motives in joining the army and on their duties in it. Some base their argument against demobilization on their shock of a new experience in their long military service. One of them said: 'I have served in the army since the time of Emperor Haile Selassie. When the Derg came to power it let me continue. Why not the EPRDF? It was strange for me.' Others who had been involved in combat claimed that they were defending the interests of the nation. They believed that demobilization was necessitated because the Derg army was identified as an enemy. Those engaged in army technical and office work insisted that demobilization should be applied exclusively to those who were involved in combat activities.

Women had rather stronger arguments. They claimed that the Derg army was gender-biased and women were neglected in career development. While male colleagues progressed in rank and earnings, women rarely did. Moreover, their duties were non-combative and non-political. A female sergeant said:

> I have been working as a secretary for a male boss. My income was very small despite my long years of service. When I heard the EPRDF was approaching Addis Ababa, I hoped that my problem as a woman and low-ranking soldier would be solved. But when I was told that I was displaced from my job, I was shocked. I still associate the coming of the EPRDF with the loss of my job.

Female soldiers considered demobilization simply as a transition from bad to worse. The poor military life was worsened as the process of demobilization meant their losing their employment.

Other ex-soldiers considered demobilization as an interruption in their motivated upward mobility. Their long military service, which was supposed to bring them higher rank with associated economic power and honour, was interrupted. In addition, for those who were doing well in combat, their military status was disrupted. A major recalled:

> I had a successful period in the military and have achieved the highest possible rank in a short period of time. Only months after the EPRDF came to power I was due to move to the next rank, Lt. Colonel. Unfortunately, demobilization made it all come to nothing. My career was interrupted. Now my friends are either doctors or generals. But I have lost both.

Hence, the consequences of demobilization are manifold. It is considered as a break in livelihood, a disruption of motives, an interruption in upward mobility, etc. All share the economic consequences because they have lost their jobs and a regular salary. Moreover, long military service years ended up as null and void for they did not help them secure a pension.

The Cooperatives

GENET MALE COOPERATIVE

Genet Cooperative, organized in Addis Ababa, started with 19 members but only 14 remained. Ex-soldiers were initiated to organize themselves in cooperatives. The government agreed to help them if they became organized but at the same time gave them the liberty to select their colleagues themselves.

THE ORGANIZATIONAL STRUCTURE INFLUENCED BY MILITARY STRUCTURE

The general structure of a cooperative is provided in a Proclamation of 1978. Cooperatives are required to have a General Assembly, a Management Committee, a Control Committee and other necessary sub-committees. Non-skilled high-ranking officers took the initiative of organizing members of the cooperatives who approved their positions in the management committee when the first election was held. Military rank seems to have influenced the election. The management committee remained in power for eight years and not for four, as the proclamations and by-laws stipulate. Management committee members and a few others argue that the cooperative requires not only production but also management and that the acquired military leadership skills should be utilized in the cooperative as well. Others claimed that the management committee did not want to lose power. Being a leader means potential access to the resources of the cooperative, as management committee members run the financial and material resources of the cooperative on a daily basis.

The chairman of the Genet Cooperative told me that an un-elected officer tried to refuse to obey orders, recalling: 'One of the members, who was a captain, refused to wear the khaki uniform and carry goods with us. When I ordered him he replied, "I am an officer. How could you expect me to wear this uniform of a labourer and carry wood and metal? Let the ordinary soldiers do that. It is their duty". He never agreed to do that…then he left the cooperative.'

Bureaucratic experience had helped the officers to speed up the process and secure assistance to start production.. Most members preferred to choose the officers who were the organizers, consequently one became the chairman and another the general secretary.

TRANSPARENCY VIS-À-VIS BUSINESS SECRECY

The principles of cooperative societies advocate transparency among the members. Joint decision-making presupposes every member knowing all the activities. In the Genet Cooperative most members agreed that the management committee would do everything and the members had no say. Some doubt the financial accountability of the management committee. The committee argued that in competitive bids secrets are valuable and cannot be shared among all the members. Such a situation has created disputes between members and the leaders.

Policy change and challenges of adapting to the new Proclamation

The 1978 Proclamation advocates collective ownership in which members consider themselves as employed workers. The new Proclamation of 1998 has settled some difficulties and created others. First, under the previous Proclamation, it was difficult to give any compensation to members who left the cooperative. The whole property was declared to be indivisible. They were only able to give a certain amount through the decision of the general assembly. The new Proclamation provides for the determined individual shares, but at the same time fails to recognize individual claims on the fixed assets. Second, the new Proclamation provides for open membership in which the cooperative can sell shares to outsiders as long as no one share exceeds 10 percent of the paid-up share capital. This could be applied only when the cooperative faces a capital shortage. However, it was strongly opposed by the members who uniformly argued that the government provided the property for them and nobody should come in to share it. Third, the proclamation stipulates that members can serve on the management committee for no more than two terms of three years consecutively. Every member has the right to be elected. However, in practice the officers were re-elected and continued to manage the cooperative.

ANDINET FEMALE EX-SOLDIERS FOOD PROCESSING COOPERATIVE

The limited access of women army recruits to technical skills meant that they were also not given pre-job training. They were left only with secretarial skills and low paid jobs. Among the 79 cooperatives in Addis Ababa, not one was established to address the women's military skill in secretarial business. A few female members were included in the men's work in marginal duties, or they were required to organize themselves in cooperatives related to women's household duties. Female ex-soldiers were organized in food-processing activities on the direct recommendation of the Commission and members were recruited not by skill but through friendship. The management committee includes the chairwoman, general secretary, treasurer, purchaser, accountant and controller.

As in the case of male ex-soldiers, women who were active in the foundation of the cooperative were elected as management committee members. But in contrast to the men, this cooperative does not seem to be influenced by military rank. For instance, a sergeant is the chairwoman, whereas a captain is simply a member. The chairwoman of the cooperative explained why:

> In the army women are given limited access to rank and skill training. This could only help them to serve under certain male ranks. If I am promoted, it is to work for a man with a higher rank. As a sergeant I was working as a secretary for a man with the rank of major. Food processing belongs to everybody. Hence, at a cooperative level we are all equal.

But when the actual business activity started, women found it difficult to change their roles. One sergeant recalled:

> When we first started to sell tea, coffee and food, it was very difficult. We could not manage to be in front of customers selling cups of tea. For the first two days we failed to do this. Then we decided to hire daily workers who could sell for us. We began to follow them and started to help them bit by bit. After a few days some of us started to do the job. But some male customers regarded us as 'women ready for something else'.

The new dutirs led to this being understood as women who had changed their positions. They were considered as `prostitutes` rather than businesswomen. For those with husbands at home it was very difficult because they were afraid of rumours. One of them left the cooperative immediately claiming that she could not tolerate being called a 'bar lady'. But a better solution emerged when one customer who knew of the problem brought in a metallic advertisement to fix on the containers (shops) which read: 'Andinet Female Ex-soldiers' Food Processing Shop'. The chairwoman told me that since then customers have understood who they really were, and have started to be very friendly and helpful.

The removal of the shops: Re-displacement and survival strategies. After about seven years of settled business life, the female ex-soldiers were again displaced by the government. They call this *indegena mefenakel*, literally 'being uprooted again'.. According to the chairwoman, the removal of the shops was due to poor project preparation and neglect of the authorities that were supposed to help them. She recalled:

> In January 2001 the Addis Ababa Roads Authority Bureau removed the two containers in Mexico Square and Megenagna Square. Though we begged them crying they would not stop. Our containers were taken off somewhere to their stores. Since then we have been appealing to the Economic Department of the City administration every week. No solution has been achieved so far... What annoys us is that the containers of Ethio-Fruit Enterprise, which were also removed with ours, were replaced after one week. They told us this was done because it is a government enterprise. Who is the most needy? Are we not being displaced from our jobs by the government? Is it not the government which organized and gave us every support including the premises? How can a government deny its legal certificate? We are displaced again, this time for the worse.

Economic and social reintegration

ECONOMIC REINTEGRATION

According to Colletta *et al.* (1996), for ex-soldiers reintegration is a continuous, long-term process that takes place on social, political, and economic levels. Economic reintegration implies the financial independence of an ex-soldier's household through productive and gainful employment. Male ex-soldiers receive an average of 533 *birr* (US$63) as opposed to the average military salary of 354 *birr* ($42). In addition, a member of a cooperative earns about 60 *birr* ($7) *a* month for part-time work at the weekends and an average yearly bonus of 1,000 *birr* ($118). Each member also has an invested share worth 45,000 *birr* ($5,294). Such an individual income puts all the members ahead of the estimated annual average earnings of an ex-soldier, 642 *birr* ($76), and even that of the civilian Ethiopian working population, 1,161 *birr* ($137).

According to these estimates by the IMF and World Bank (Kingma 2000:145), the result implies that these ex-soldiers may be in a better situation as compared with other ex-soldiers and civilian counterparts. Nobody claimed any help from other people. Some even claimed that they help their needy relatives.

On the other hand, female ex-soldiers seem to have gone through stages of economic ups and downs. Initially, they had jobs and an income. When the food-processing co-operative was established, they began to earn some money. They were able to pay back 75 percent of their loan. And every member was getting 300 *birr* ($35) a month, equal to the highest salary some were able to earn in the army. However, their two shops were removed and the female ex-soldiers were displaced from their employment. Consequently their monthly income was reduced to about 100 *birr* ($12). It could thus be considered that male ex-soldiers were economically integrated, while their female compatriots seem to have failed. Why? Some of the basic reasons are outlined below.

Variation in initial assistance. Male- and female-based cooperatives were given different initial support. Genet Cooperative was funded with 340,099 *birr* ($40,000), only 10 percent of which was a loan, the rest being a grant. Each ex-soldier received about 17,000 *birr* as initial capital, an amount that abundantly exceeds the average reintegration assistance provided for an urban returnee with a per capita grant of 2,110 *birr* ($250) (Kingma 2000: 145). In contrast, 14 (the initial number) of female members were given an initial loan of 23,000 *birr* ($2,705), of which they were obliged to repay 18,000 *birr* ($2,120) up to the time the cooperative failed. Adding in the value of the containers at 9,000 *birr* ($1,060), the average initial capital was less than 2,300 *birr* ($270). A female was given less than 13 percent of what a male ex-soldier was provided with. Such variation definitely played a large part in creating differences in their eventual economic success.

Feasibility of the project area. Male ex-soldiers were provided with a free area of 660 square meters upon which construction was carried out, whereas the women were given three metallic containers to be used as shops, which were later removed by the city authorities. Accordingly, the men's project remained sustainable generating income, whereas the women's did not.

Conversion of military skills into civilian activities. Among the men, senior officers who had the opportunity to lead in the army were also able to control the positions of the management committee so that the military capabilities of leadership were transferred and have contributed tremendously to the success of the business. In contrast, the women were not given the chance to develop leadership skills since they were all engaged in secretarial work for their male bosses. Hence, they had limited skills to transfer to their civilian activities. This may have contributed to the management problems they faced. Their leaders did not have the capacity to control the activities of the members and develop a strong work discipline.

Male army members were provided with skills training, which had helped them in achieving economic self-reliance. In contrast, female ex-soldiers were not given the chance to gain important technical skills such as in metalwork and woodwork. Still worse, their vocational skill, secretarial work, was not accredited for transfer to civilian duties. Secretarial work belongs to both the military and the civilian sector, but the Commission failed to recognize this and obliged them to be engaged in so-called traditional female household duties.

Hence, male ex-soldiers had the access to acquire both managerial capabilities and technical skills that are easily transferable to civilian activities. A major said: 'I was commanding soldiers in a military uniform and now I am leading workers in a *kaki* uniform'. One of the male ex-soldiers recalled: 'I was producing chairs in the army and now I am doing the same.' In contrast, the women had little access to leadership and technical training within the army. Many claimed that the army was almost a waste of time. A woman sergeant said: 'We are back home and we have brought nothing from the army. We returned to food processing, the normal women's work.'

SOCIAL REINTEGRATION

Social reintegration may be broadly defined as the acceptance of an ex-soldier and her family by the host community. It is hardly possible to differentiate the process of economic and social reintegration. The whole process of economic adaptation is accompanied by the challenge to social cohesion. However, there are also other important attributes, which play an important role.

The resettlement area. Most ex-soldiers continued to live in Addis Ababa, where they used to live while in the army. They had already established networks. Moreover, the cultural diversity of the area of resettlement, Addis Ababa, eased their integration. Consequently, most of the ex-soldiers mixed easily with the civilians and have almost become *invisible as soldiers.*

But some have difficulties. The residential areas of the ex-soldiers seem to affect members' cohesion with the civilian communities. One ex-soldier said:

> The name of our cooperative was taken from our residential cooperative called Genet. It helped us to organize more members who were from the same residential area. But we now realize that people have continued to call our area *wetader* sefer [soldiers' area]. We are trying to mix with civilians in *Iddir* (burial associations) and *Iqub* (credit associations). But the difference is still there. I am personally considering selling my home and buying another elsewhere, if the difference continues.

The impact of the demobilization and reintegration process

As the reintegration of the ex-soldiers depends partly on the assistance of the government, any limitation or variation of the package would have an immediate impact on their lives. Demobilization had involved the assembly of ex-soldiers in centres where shelter, food, medication and orientation programmes were provided, and at which they were told not to expect much from the government. But the women, who were not given any chance of attending orientation programmes, remained with high expectations. They still assume themselves to be the most vulnerable group needing help.

Reinsertion support did not include clothing packages, which are not only economically but also socially important for people in transition from military to civilian life. Many stated that when civilians look at their military uniforms and shoes they easily identify them as ex-soldiers. For a long time, some faced difficulties in buying clothes since they had little money, and this contributed to the delay in their social reintegration.

Employment of the former soldiers in cooperatives of a civilian nature helped them in their process of integration. They worked alongside the hired civilian workers and they got income useful not only for consumption but also for widening social networks and reducing dependence. However, some, especially women, who did not get employment, face problems. Friends avoid visiting them and they are wary of visiting others for fear of being considered beggars.

COMMUNITY RELATIONSHIPS

The ultimate objective of social reintegration is the full participation of the ex-soldiers in the activities of the civilian communities. In return, the receiving communities should welcome the demobilized soldiers. However, there are some barriers on both sides. Former soldiers find it difficult to abandon their militarily influenced practices and lack the necessary civilian skills. Receiving communities may consider ex-soldiers as aggressive, and carriers of disease, and other social problems. Social cohesion requires adjustment to the existing civilian way of life and ex-soldiers may not find it easy to adjust rapidly.

One ex-officer described his problem of integration as follows:

> I joined the army when I was only 16 and served for 13 years. What I learned in the military was how to command my juniors and kill my enemies. In addition, I developed smoking and drinking addictions and other bad habits, which I still practise. I am not married so far. I do not participate in any local associations. Militarism is still within me. I am not actually a civilian, though I am trying hard to be one.

This case shows how ex-soldiers exposed to military life at an early age could find it very hard to adapt to the civilian way of life. Individual adjustment varies because of differences in personal ability to adapt, the age of recruitment, length of military service, type of duty a soldier was engaged in, etc. Another officer said:

> I stayed at the front for about 12 years without visiting my family. When I came back through demobilization, I felt alienated. I still prefer to communicate with my army friends rather than my family.

However, in general, ex-soldiers have received enormous support from the community. When government support failed in one way or another, family members, friends and community-based associations such as *Iddir, Iqub* and others were helpful. In particular, women needed support both in the demobilization period and when their cooperative failed. They continued to live with assistance from their relatives. Such help-based interaction might have helped them to facilitate their social integration. Accordingly, all, except two, of our sample participate in voluntary local organizations such as *Iddir, Mahiber* and *Iqub;* some even serve in positions of leadership.

THE IMPLICATIONS OF PENSION AND RANK

Only two members of our sample were pensioned. Pension payments provided much help for the most needy demobilized soldiers. However, many argued that it is not simply an economic issue. Most of the high-ranking officers and those who served for many years in the army claimed that pensions should be considered as recognition for serving their country. However, some see little economic benefit or social value in a pension. Those with lower ranks, and most women, opted for non-pension support. A corporal gave his view as follows:

> Despite my military service for nearly 20 years, I remained a corporal. If I were pensioned I would not join this cooperative. The pension payment is so small because it depends on the rank. I want to work as a civilian being called `Ato' and I am happy when people call me this. My rank is so low that it could not give me enough money or social status.

Most of the demobilized soldiers decided to accept downward mobility for the sake of survival. However, some members of the receiving community do not take it easily. A captain said,

> When I was working as a daily labourer, my friend accidentally came and called me by my rank. Since then, the boss could not order me as he used to. Then I left the job until I got another after a very long time.

Hence, those who support this idea insisted that rank and pension have little economic or social return once you are within the civilian community and you have access to other support. Rather, they claimed that pensions limit their economic and social reintegration.

Conclusion

Demobilization and reintegration programmes address broad issues of populations in transition. They may also contain valuable lessons for programmes that support the economic and social reintegration of other vulnerable groups, such as retrenched civil servants, internally displaced persons, and refugees.

The model of demobilization-reinsertion-reintegration as a one-way flow seems difficult to accept. Though the Ethiopian government had initially argued in favour of adopting the demobilization of army members because of the prevalence of peace and security, as well as the consent of those to be demobilized, the reality emerged differently. When a war unexpectedly broke out with Eritrea in 1998 a larger army was again needed. Among others, five of the ex-soldiers initially organized in the Genet cooperative volunteered and were re-mobilized.

The EPRDF-led government has undertaken three demobilization programmes in a decade, each with its own incentives from the donors (the Derg army in 1991, the TPLF ex-fighters in 1995 and in early 2000 the National Defence Force following the Ethio-Eritrean war). As the policy of demobilization is not based on the real situation of a given country, aid-initiated programmes tend to fail to achieve lasting solutions. Therefore demobilization may remain a cyclical rather than a one-way process.

Moreover, as soldiers may have technological and managerial know-how developed in the army, it would be important to try to convert this to the civilian life in demobilization. Human resource utilization during demobilization and reintegration refers to the effective deployment of existing skills, qualifications and competencies of ex-soldiers for the maximum achievement of individual, social, organizational or national goals and objectives of demobilization (Kingma 2000:52). This would contribute to the general development of a country pursuing demobilization. For instance, in the Genet Cooperative members were able to earn a living for more than 70 family members and, more importantly, they employed civilians who obtained incomes that could feed about 200 members. In this case, skills gained in the army were properly transferred into civilian activities.

In contrast, female soldiers had no access to technological skills training in the army nor were they exposed to management duties. The Commission has adopted a strategy of targeting ex-soldiers in their place of settlement (rural or urban) in planning their reintegration. In the final analysis, the variation in transferability of skills gained in the army has meant that women were disregarded in the overall development-initiated demobilization.

One way of integrating ex-soldiers was to organize them in cooperatives. Some claimed that government intervention was viewed as against the principles of cooperative societies. However, it could be argued, that needy people like ex-soldiers require intervention to start up a business. Governments which feel a need for planned change may intervene to bring in necessary resources for the beneficiaries. This study strongly substantiates this argument. All ex-soldiers have approved the intervention. However, national cooperative policies might need some flexibility to accommodate those vulnerable groups which require help to start up businesses.

Demobilization is considered to be an important part of a transition from war to peace in African post-civil war situations. It brings a reduction in military expenditure as well as achievement of security. Based on these objectives, ex-soldiers might be demobilized for different reasons. However, total demobilization may waste the human resources invested for a long period of time. Moreover, there is another source of doubt about economic and security justifications for demobilization. In the study about 85 percent of the ex-soldiers were engaged in non-combat activities. Such duties are more of a civilian type and have economic returns even within the army and are needed as long as military institutions exist. Hence, gross demobilization programmes may undermine the potential use of these skills.

If demobilization is ultimately motivated by economic development, the demobilized soldiers should be a central part of it. It entails not only the conversion of resources to civilian development but also the transformation of persons who were in the army to participate in civilian life. There has been little planning to help soldiers with specific objectives and within clear implementation periods. As a consequence, all the female soldiers failed to achieve economic adaptation. Women were not given opportunities for self-development either in the army or after demobilization. Moreover, they had little share of the economic investment earmarked both for modernizing the military and for implementing demobilization.

Note

1. The author prefers to use the term *ex-soldier* instead of *ex-combatant* which might not represent members who were not involved in the fighting.

Part VI

CONCLUSION

Sixteen

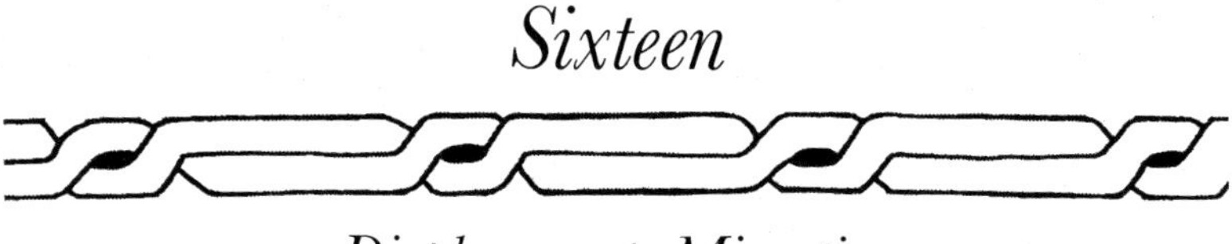

Displacement, Migration & Relocation

Challenges for Policy, Research & Coexistence

ALULA PANKHURST & FRANÇOIS PIGUET

In our Introduction we started by placing the key issues within a broader historical, geographical and theoretical framework of migration. We now return to the topic with a view to drawing insights from the case studies and recent research to provide suggestions based on past experience and current trends to inform debates on research, policy and practice.

To contextualize the issues, we start by providing an overview of the major topics discussed in the chapters, making the case for a more holistic approach that considers the various types of forced migration together and within the same framework as spontaneous and voluntary migration. For each topic we review recent developments and changing trends, noting that development-induced displacement in its various manifestations has become the most significant type of movement, replacing earlier concerns with resettlement, refugees, returnees and demobilization. This shift is beginning to be noticed by researchers but to date has no been sufficiently reflected in policy considerations. This may be in part because the forms of displacement are fragmentary and widespread and because development-induced displacees are among the poorest and most voiceless, whose rights may be in contradiction with national and international interests, and on whose behalf there is often limited advocacy within the country and internationally. We therefore argue for widening the current narrow focus on resettlement and displacement to pay greater attention to the various manifestations of development-induced displacement. This requires greater attention to the rights of displacees to consultation, adequate, fair and clear compensation and involvement in the planning and implementation of their resettlement.

A more inclusive and integrated approach to migration issues more generally implies, on the one hand, taking on board the need for preparations and incentives to promote and facilitate forms of migration which promote development, and, on the other, designing and implementing measures to safeguard the rights of local people and to protect the environment. The crux of the matter lies in the relations between hosts and migrants and their resource uses. Whereas there has been a tendency for the state to organize all aspects of migration and resettlement, we believe that more space should be given to local actors, individuals, households, and communities to take a leading role in decision-making and managing migration in partnership with civil society and non-governmental agencies, with support from government and donors.

Finally, given the tendency for migration to exacerbate resource conflict, there is a need to promote peaceful coexistence through joint development initiatives. Understanding the causes and consequences of conflicts and establishing the preconditions for their resolution must therefore become part and parcel of migration studies, policies and practices.

Reviewing the evidence: worldwide and Ethiopian experiences

In this section we review the major forms of displacement discussed in the case studies, as well as recent developments and research findings over the past five years. Some of these confirm trends noted in the last part of the twentieth century and the first few years of the twenty-first; others involve rapid increases, decreases, transformations or new departures. Development-induced displacement, which was previously overshadowed by issues relating to resettlement, refugees and returnees and had not been the subject of much research or advocacy or policy initiatives, has become a more significant trend in recent years with the country's drive to promote investment in agriculture, bio-fuels, hydropower and urban expansion.

RESETTLEMENT

As argued by de Wet and Turton in this book, the weight of evidence worldwide suggests that the resettlement of populations affected by conflict, famine and development projects is a risky process that often leads to impoverishment, rarely results in sustainable development, and sometimes involves abuse of basic human rights.[1] In Ethiopia at the time of the 1985 famine, the Derg carried out a draconian resettlement programme affecting the lives of more than half a million people. The findings of research presented in this book and other studies point to grave economic, environmental and social costs, and untold suffering. The shortcomings, excesses and limited successes of these resettlement projects have been well documented in academic studies which, however, have not been widely available within Ethiopia and internationally, and have not been within the reach of policy-makers.

The EPRDF opposed resettlement during its armed struggle and reaffirmed this position once in power. However, a shift in policy gradually took place to the point that resettlement came to be considered not only a potentially viable option, but even a necessary aspect and crucial component of food security. This position was reflected in key policy documents,[2] most of which have involved or been approved by international agencies and fora. In the face of recurrent famine, once again, the wish to find lasting solutions resulted in the planning and implementation of large-scale state-sponsored resettlement from 2003.

At the time of the ESSSWA–EUE workshop in early 2003, resettlement was on the cards, but had not yet been implemented, except to resettle groups that had already moved, either spontaneously or as a result of being forced out of areas in which they had been living (Piguet and Dechassa 2004). Very rapidly, however, in spite of concerns voiced at the workshop about the potential risks of rapid large-scale relocations, the pace and scale of resettlement planning and implementation increased. From 2003 to 2006 over 627,000 people were resettled in four regions, roughly the same number as were resettled by the Derg in the mid-1980s.

Unlike the resettlement of the 1980s, that has been the subject of in-depth studies (Pankhurst 1989; Gebre 2001; Wolde-Selassie 2000),[3] early reviews of the current resettlement were quite limited and comprised mainly brief reports by the government, United Nations agencies, international organizations, non-government organizations and commissioned researchers, produced largely on the basis of short field trips to a few sites (Pankhurst 2003b). A more substantial report with a range of useful recommendations to different stakeholders was produced by Hammond and Bezaiet (2004) and included in the workshop proceedings. More recently there have been half a dozen MA theses on the topic.[4] Moreover, a project sponsored by the Forum for Social Studies (FSS) involving masters students in social anthropology and staff of Addis Ababa University managed by one of the editors of this book carried out case studies in eleven resettlement sites (FSS 2006), as discussed in the chapter by Pankhurst in this volume. Useful policy measures and guidelines were developed and some of the mistakes made by earlier resettlement schemes were avoided. Nonetheless, many of the constraints remain similar and some of the problems have reoccurred.

However, in 2006 and especially 2007 the interest in resettlement seems to have waned with far less resettlement being carried out, and a reduction in numbers compared with the plans. Reasons include a realization of some of the problems of the current resettlement, limited donor support, and a shift of campaigning priorities, notably to ensuring food security support through the Productive Safety-net Programme rather than food aid.

REFUGEES, RETURNEES, DEMOBILIZED SOLDIERS AND THE INTERNALLY DISPLACED

Worldwide, at the end of the twentieth century refugees and people in refugee-like situations represented some 30 million people.[5] However, people displaced by development projects, though less visible and less protected, are much more numerous, representing about 10 million a year or 100 million people over the last decade of the twentieth century (Cernea 2000). In recent years, according to UNHCR figures,[6] refugee numbers have been decreasing and IDP numbers increasing.

Refugees. The Horn of Africa has long been a major producer and receiver of refugees and returnees (Allen 1996; Adelman and Sorensen 1994). Ethiopia moved from being largely a locus of exodus for hundreds of thousands of refugees to becoming mainly a host to large inflows of refugees, as well as returnees from neighbouring countries. In the past decade it has become an area from which returnees repatriated, with some return of diaspora Ethiopians. We can distinguish three major phases with different types of cross-boundary migration flows: (i) from the mid-1970s to the mid-1980s when Ethiopia was primarily a source of refugee exodus; (ii) the late 1980s and early 1990s when Ethiopia was mainly an area of refugee influxes from neighbouring countries and repatriation of Ethiopian refugees; and (iii) the late 1990s and early 2000s with repatriation of refugees from Ethiopia.[7] These phases are, of course, linked to the key political processes and changing relations between Ethiopia and it neighbours, particularly Somalia, Sudan and Eritrea, as well as shifting relations and alliances between the states and liberation fronts in neighbouring countries. Most significantly, the phases can be related to key turning points, notably the defeat of the Derg,[8] the collapse of Somalia, the independence of Eritrea, the war between Ethiopia and Eritrea, and peace negotiations in Sudan.

Though these phases provide a general sense of trends, in fact the refugee and returnee flows are more complex; at times Ethiopia has hosted simultaneously refugees and returnees.[9] This raises the question of the meaning of the labels 'refugee' and 'returnee' and who defines people's status in a context of complex kinship, social and political relations across borders, individual and household survival strategies, the potential to benefit from aid, the mandates of governments, international organizations and NGOs and the attempts to create cross-mandate and parallel operations approaches (Hogg 1997a; Ahmed 1997). It also raises the question of people's identities and livelihoods in the context of insecurity. Movement across borders, for example, has traditionally been common among pastoralist groups, for whom migration in search of better pastures, for trade and for pilgrimages to ritual sites has long been part of their way of life (Getachew 1996c; Piguet 1998; Schlee 1990).

Refugee numbers have been decreasing notably as a result of repatriation programmes. However, the consequences of their presence in the border areas have often been considerable. Most of the refugees from Somalia were repatriated prior to the 2006 crisis, and almost all the settlements in the Somali region of Ethiopia were closed down. However, the impacts of the refugees' presence on the local economy, society and environment may have long-term consequences (Bizuayehu 2004). The recent involvement of Ethiopian troops in Somalia and attacks by insurgent groups in Ethiopia have meant that population movements have been restricted. In the west, the repatriation programmes have been ongoing.[10] However, the refugee presence has exacerbated tensions between the Anywaa and Nuer. The conflict escalated in 2003, involving highlander settlers as well, leading to much loss of life and property.[11] In the north, continuing tensions with Eritrea have made the life and adaptations of displaced persons uncertain and heightened their sense of unease. The 11 camps around Addis Ababa, with some 17,000 people expelled from Eritrea, were closed down, some in 2003,[12] including the case described by Aptekar and Behailu in this book, and others in 2005 to make way for 'condominium' housing projects. Displacees from Eritrea who were still living in makeshift shelters along walls in the Jan Meda area of Addis Ababa were made to move, along with several thousand other beggars and people living on the streets, with the cleaning up of the city at the time of the millennium celebrations in September 2007.[13]

Returnees. The defeat of the Derg in 1991 and the restoration of peace paved the way for returnees in the lowlands of western Tigray, discussed by Kassahun in this book, based on his published thesis (Kassahun 2000), and by Hammond in her thesis and book (2000, 2004). These studies discuss the politics of return and the dilemmas of the integration of returnees, some of whom opted to go back to their home areas, but many of whom were persuaded to settle in lowland border area settlements. They describe the returnees' re-establishment and their resettlement in areas with which they had not previously been familiar, their strategies to rebuild their livelihoods, given the range of opportunities available, their endeavours to recreate a sense of identity and community and to negotiate their relations with the party, government and state.

Demobilized soldiers. The defeat of the Derg and end of the war with Eritrea also raised the question of the reintegration and resettlement of demobilized soldiers, considered in this work by Yisak in an urban context based on his MA thesis (Yisak 2002) and their resettlement in rural areas described by Mulugeta (2000) in his MA thesis. In his chapter, Yisak considers gender differences in reintegration and highlights the problems that female demobilized soldiers faced in forming viable cooperatives.

Although conditions in the early 1990s initially seemed to suggest that the problem of conflict and its outcome was less salient, the renewed war with Eritrea in 1998-2000 and the resulting tensions (particularly with the impending departure of the United Nations Mission in Ethiopia and Eritrea (UNMEE)) have again raised the question of the resettlement of displacees. This subject is addressed in this book by Behailu, based on his PhD research (Behailu 2005). His study documents the differential strategies and struggles of people who had been living in a border area, some of whom fled and others remained, and their efforts to re-establish their livelihoods.

Internally displaced. In the wake of the 1991 defeat of the Derg, the war with Eritrea and the reorganization of the country along federal lines based on ethnically defined regions, there was much internal displacement. The bulk of settlers left the resettlements and went back to their home areas (Pankhurst 1991). The chapter by Aptekar and Behailu deals with Ethiopians who had been living in Eritrea, were expelled and subsequently internally displaced within Ethiopia, ending up in a camp in the outskirts of Addis Ababa. They describe the plight of the displacees and their struggle to start new lives in difficult circumstances. Internal displacement resulting from conflict remains significant and has not received much attention apart from the MA thesis of Ephrem (1998) in which he highlighted the suffering and adaptation difficulties of the impoverished displaced without support who relied on charity around churches and on networks of self-help.

DEVELOPMENT-INDUCED DISPLACEMENT: DAMS, IRRIGATION, PARKS AND TOWNS

By its frequency, size and dire consequences, development-induced displacement has been acknowledged as the most important forced migration problem worldwide (Cernea 2000, 2005; Koenig 2001; de Wet 2005). However, in Ethiopia the issue has received comparatively little attention until recently. Some discussion of the displacement effects of parks took place at a workshop on Participatory Wildlife Management in 1995, but this book is the first attempt to present together various types of development-induced displacement in Ethiopia, notably resulting from the construction of dams, the establishment of irrigated agricultural development schemes, the creation of parks, and urban expansion. The different forms of development-induced displacement have been increasing in the past few years with greater hydropower and irrigated agricultural development, investment in parks including the attraction of foreign capital, and a vigorous policy of urban development and the promotion of private investment, notably by members of the Ethiopian diaspora.

Hydropower dam-induced displacement and livelihood impacts. The construction of dams for hydropower and irrigation can have four displacement and migration effects. First, the flooding may lead to the displacement of people living within the reservoir area, resulting in resettlement and concerns over re-establishment and adaptation as in the case of the Gilgel Gibe Dam discussed by Kassahun in this book, and the Dire Dam discussed by Demie (2007). Second, it can affect the livelihood of people living downstream as in the case of dams on the Awash River, which reduced the vital dry-season grazing land of pastoralist groups, notably the Afar and the Karrayu, as discussed by Ayalew and Getachew in this book. Third, the regulation, reduction or change in flows of the water can affect customary flood-retreat irrigation systems, notably in the Awash delta (Awsa) and Omo Basin. This is discussed by Melesse in his chapter on the Wayto Valley, where the irrigated farm of a private investor affected the livelihood of the Tsamako and Hor, resulting in unresolved conflict. Finally, the construction of dams can lead to a large migrant workforce during the construction, or as a result of opportunities created by irrigation schemes.

The construction of further dams as water reservoirs as well as for hydroelectricity seems likely to continue, with urbanization, industrialization, and potential benefits of electricity export to neighbouring countries, already under way to Sudan. Much of the discussion of dam-related displacement has so far focused on those displaced by reservoirs, as in the case discussed by Kassahun, or even the effects of the migrant labour force, as in the thesis by Teshome (2007) who considers how this resulted in the spread of HIV/AIDS. However, the effects on groups living downstream, notably in the Omo-Gibe valley where the livelihoods of the Dassenech, Mursi, Bodi and Kara are highly dependent on flood-retreat cultivation, are likely to become more of an issue with the construction under way of Gilgel Gibe III, and plans for a Gilgel Gibe IV. There are plans for up to nine power plants over the next ten years, and even claims that electricity might overtake coffee as the number-one export income earner.[14]

Irrigated development, marginalization of agro-pastoralists and resource conflict. Pastoralists relying on rivers for grazing during dry seasons and periods of drought have been marginalized worldwide, excluded from their best resources and subjected to sedentarization and resettlement (Salzman and Galaty 1990). In Africa generally, and especially in East Africa, notably in the Horn, relations with the state have been characterized by the encroachment of agriculture, the expropriation of pastoralists' communal resources, the expansion of protected areas, and the displacement of pastoralists to marginal lands (Markakis 1993; Mohammed 1999; Manger 2000). In Ethiopia, state interests in promoting irrigation, coupled with pervasive prejudices that view pastoralism as an irrational, outdated and inferior form of livelihood, have paved the way for the displacement of pastoralist groups from areas designated for irrigated development, the production of cash crops and wildlife conservation (Hogg 1997a; Ayalew 2001; Getachew 2001). There have been concerns with resettling pastoralists and pressurizing them to adopt a settled way of life. Development projects, starting from imperial times, have evicted and excluded pastoralists from crucial resources, notably dry-season grazing areas, especially in the Awash Valley. Settlement programmes were established from the 1960s and expanded during the Derg, and have continued to be implemented. Such attempts have tended to fail, and the irrigation projects have attracted the settlement of migrant labourers from the highlands, who competed with the interests of pastoralist groups, as suggested in the case studies by Ayalew, Getachew and Melesse based on their respective PhD research

(Melesse 2000; Getachew 2001; Ayalew 2001). Issues of land rights, compensation, conflict mitigation and joint development, which could have been the basis for a less confrontational and more cooperative environment, have often not been given the consideration they deserve.

Policy on pastoralism in Ethiopia historically has been primarily concerned with control, taxation, marketing livestock and settling pastoralists under the assumption that a sedentary way of life is superior and inevitable. The Second (1957-61) and Third (1963-67) Five-Year Development Plans were concerned with developing livestock production for export (Helland 1997: 43), and the imperial policy reserved all territories occupied by nomadic *zelan*[15] as state land (Yacob 2000: 30). The Derg land reform recognized in Article 24 '...possessory rights over the lands they customarily use for grazing or other purposes related to agriculture' (Ayalew 2001: 90); however, Proclamation 31 of 1975 included settling the nomadic peoples for farming (Helland 1997: 44), and a Settlement Authority was established in 1976.

Under the EPRDF the FDRE Constitution of 1995 in Article 40.5 states that 'Ethiopian pastoralists have the right to free land for grazing and cultivation as well as the right not to be displaced from their own lands'. However, as noted by Melesse in this book, there seems little awareness of these rights and a lack of legal provisions, guidelines and safeguards at federal and regional levels to ensure that they are protected. The National Five Year Development Plan (2000-4) as part of 'improving the nomadic life style', recommends 'sustainable settlement' with the introduction of small-scale irrigation. The Framework for Rural Development adopted in 2001 acknowledges that in the short term 'there is no alternative for agricultural development movement other than improving nomadic livestock husbandry'. However, the framework concludes that 'in the long term this cannot be a guarantee for a rapid and sustainable regional development', the argument being that 'it is impossible to provide efficient service of socio-economic infrastructure for nomadic people. Sustainable and rapid development can be achieved only if the people are settled' (FDRE 2001: 79).[16]

The Ministry of Federal Affairs set up a Pastoral Development Unit in the early 2000s, which issued a statement on pastoral development in 2002, advocating long-term voluntary settlement of the pastoral population. The SDPRP reiterated the position that 'selective settlement programmes are believed to be the only viable options in the long run' (FDRE 2002b: 72). In the course of the preparation of the World Bank-funded Pastoral Community Development Project, the Ministry of Federal Affairs issued a statement on Pastoral Development Policy in 2003, which considered phased voluntary sedentarization along the banks of major rivers, complemented with irrigation, urbanization and industrialization through small and micro enterprises. The major shift in policy terms is towards voluntary and longer-term settlement.

The recent PASDEP places much more emphasis on pastoralism, including an entire section on Pastoralist Livelihoods and Development (MoFED 2006: 191-7). It recognizes that pastoralists have been historically 'side-lined in the development process' and that 'policies and programmes have overlooked pastoralists' way of life and living conditions, and until recently they have experienced decades of socio-political exclusion'. It notes that because of this 'pastoralists have remained the poorest of the poor and become more vulnerable to a growing process of impoverishment' (MoFED 2006: 191). However, the PASDEP justifies the need for voluntary settlement on the grounds that pastoral mobility, resource competition and harmful traditional practices result in disputes as well as the need to provide basic services[17] and promote irrigation.[18]

Cash-crop production mainly of cotton and sugar cane which has affected the livelihoods of agro-pastoralists over the past half-century, has taken a new turn with the emphasis on the recently booming flower sector and bio-fuel production, based on sugar cane and drought-resistant plants such as jatropha, which has been stimulated by Western interests (*Seedling* 2007). The recent construction of a further dam on the Awash river which plans to irrigate about 60,000 ha is likely to result in further land alienation, displacement and potential conflict unless measures to ensure that local people benefit or at least are compensated adequately are instituted. The emphasis on private and foreign investment is an area where resource conflicts may emerge, unless clear policies regarding land rights and compensation are formulated, negotiated and implemented. Otherwise, further river valley development could have double negative resettlement effects. On the one hand, agro-pastoralist groups may continue to be displaced from high-potential resources near the rivers, thereby endangering the viability of their production system, exposing them to food insecurity, and resulting in the view that they need to be settled or resettled. On the other hand, irrigation is likely to promote the migration of highland workers to work on projects, and river valleys may be considered appropriate sites for the resettlement of highland famine victims.

The development of river valleys, on the grounds of 'the national interest', could therefore exacerbate resource competition, increase population pressure on the environment and aggravate conflict with and between pastoralists and agro-pastoralist communities. Constitutional provisions therefore need to be followed through with guidelines relating to international legal provisions. Moreover, practical safeguards and measures including compensation, negotiated resource-sharing and joint development should be envisaged from the planning stage through to the implementation of such interventions.

Parks, displacement and resource conflict. There has been a growing recognition worldwide of the value of integrating people and parks, whose habitat has often been shaped by interactions between wildlife, humans and their livestock. Southern and East African examples have taken the lead in this respect. However, so far such an enlightened approach to park management does not seem to have been followed in Ethiopia. In the Nech Sar case described in the book by Taddesse, the Kore were resettled by SNNPR Region whereas the Guji-Oromo have so far largely managed to resist resettlement in a context of negotiations between regional states.

The concession of the Nech Sar Park to the Netherlands-based African Parks Foundation (APF) in 2004 on a 25-year lease renewed the pressure for resettlement and restricted grazing. The further concession of the Omo National Park, also in the SNNPR, to the APF in 2005 posed a potential threat to the livelihoods of eight ethnic groups living in the park or making use of its resources for herding, cultivation, hunting, and bee-keeping.[19] In a bid to have the Omo Park boundaries gazetted, local people were asked to take part in a 'demarcation ceremony' in March 2005, at which their 'representatives' were persuaded to put their thumbprints on documents defining the boundaries. This could be interpreted as making people living in the park 'illegal squatters' on their own lands. But since those who signed the documents were not given copies of them, they were not in a position to obtain legal advice on the matter.

In December 2007 the APF made the surprise announcement that it had decided to terminate its management activities in Nech Sar and Omo National Parks. The reasons given included the 'unsustainable use by one or more ethnic groups, often in competition and conflict with each other'. The APF had apparently signed a restricted resource utilization agreement with the Guji living in the Nech Sar park in September 2007, but this was not sanctioned by the authorities. It also complained that unfounded criticisms by human rights organizations, particularly in relation to people living in and around the Omo park, had hampered its efforts and was likely to continue to do so (*Ethiopia: 7 Days Update*, 3 September 2007, p. 10).[20] The imminent departure of APF may provide an opportunity for negotiation and greater involvement of local peoples in park management, and indeed a group among the Mursi people have produced a proposal for a community-managed park.

Other tensions and potential conflicts concern the Awash National Park and the Babile Elephant sanctuary. The Awash Park, which is located between Afar and Oromia Regions, is another case where inter-state and inter-ethnic issues have arisen. The park is policed by Oromia Region and the Afar have complained that they are strictly excluded, whereas the cattle of the Karrayu are sometimes allowed to graze within the boundaries. In the case of the Babile Elephant sanctuary in East Hareghe, a concession was allocated in mid-2007 by the Ethiopian Investment Agency to the German company Flora Ecopower, for bio-fuel production in the vicinity of the sanctuary. This resulted in letters of protest to the Oromia Region from the Ethiopian Ministry of Agriculture and Rural Development, the Ethiopian Forum for the Environment, the Ethiopian Wildlife Association and international environmental and animal rights groups.[21]

All this raises the questions of the rights and involvement of local people living in areas that are considered to have high wildlife potential for conservation and tourism. An approach accepting that there is not necessarily an inherent conflict between people and parks and that local inhabitants can be the best conservationists has become conventional wisdom in other countries. The problems with foreign investment directly in parks or in competing agricultural ventures, and the difficulties in the management of parks in border areas between neighbouring states and different groups, suggest that the time is ripe to rethink the conservation and tourism policies and consider promoting more constructive and people-centred approaches.

Displacement resulting from urban expansion. Urban expansion through government development, road expansion, and construction of private and public housing and commercial buildings has impacted on two groups: the urban poor living in the inner cities, who tended to rely primarily on the informal sector, and peasants farming in the peri-urban areas, whose livelihood was tied to the land. Displacement has been increasing as a result of a number of development processes within cities and their surroundings, including: (i) the development of numerous suburban residential areas; (ii) clearing of whole areas in the centre of towns, notably the capital city Addis Ababa, to make way for private investment in high-rise buildings; (iii) the condominium housing expansion projects in the capital city centre; and (iv) considerable expansion of the road network, involving widening of existing roads and building of new ones. Feleke's chapter discusses the first of these in terms of the impacts on surrounding peasants, and how they made use of compensation for the loss of land, and their differential survival strategies.

Two further masters theses in social anthropology (Tadesse 2006; Zenaw 2007) and one in urban planning (Mekonnen 2002) show that more recent projects provided less compensation and resulted in greater hardships. The masters thesis in regional and development studies by Nebiyou (2000) and the PhD thesis in urban planning by Ashenafi (2001) discussed how those moved out of the centre because of the Sheraton Hotel project were trying to rebuild their lives in the new suburbs to which they were moved. Despite better housing in the suburbs, they no longer had employment opportunities in the informal sector on which they had relied in the city centre. They also had daily commuting costs, which were initially subsidized. Dejene (2005) discusses the impacts of the ring road which split communities and Fitsum (2006) and Ambaye (2006) the impacts on specific communities within the city resulting from inner city development. Prime Minister Meles Zenawi, in a public discussion with Addis Ababa residents on 21 December 2007 offered assurances that people would henceforth be able to obtain condominium housing in areas close to where they live. The pace of urban expansion has been growing and urban real estate projects are on the increase.[22] The recent literature suggests a need for more public debate and policy initiatives to protect the rights of displaced people from eviction particularly during the rainy season, and to promote the establishment of adequate and standardized compensation norms, access to alternative housing at affordable costs, and employment and credit options.

Major issues in policy and practice

This section considers the question of policy formulation and argues that much of the concern has been focused narrowly on resettlement without sufficient consideration of other forms of displacement and migration. The policy provisions do not give adequate consideration to protecting the rights of local groups and communities, in particular in the face of foreign and local commercial and financial interests. Refugee policy in Ethiopia has been generous in a spirit of hospitality and a Proclamation was approved in 2004. However, the provisions do not apply to environmental or economic refugees, let alone internally displaced persons or development-induced displacees.

BROADENING THE VISION, DEVELOPING NORMS AND PROTECTING RIGHTS

Policy with regard to resettlement, displacement and migration in Ethiopia has tended to be either non-existent or narrowly focused on technical solutions to resettlement. These were often prepared rapidly on an *ad hoc* basis as the need arose to justify ongoing relocation programmes. In so far as resettlement programmes were organized by the state, they tended to be closely associated with the objectives of successive governments. By uprooting people the state has often assumed the right to organize settlements in ways it saw fit. These were sometimes considered as experiments to promote a modernist vision of development (Scott 1998). The aim was to achieve a short cut to progress carried out rapidly and visibly through projects designed and implemented by the state, rather than by a long-term gradual approach to promoting initiatives of individuals, families and groups wishing to migrate.

Policy regarding displacement has until recently been very limited, though some compensation has been provided in certain cases of dam- and urban-related displacements, as noted in the case studies by Kassahun and Feleke in this book.

However, these were often also carried out on an *ad-hoc* basis with agreements brokered in specific cases rather than through the development of a consistent national policy taking into account international norms and standards. The rights of the displaced are often not known by themselves or others and there has been little advocacy by local, national or international groups in this respect. An important first step was the 'Proclamation for the Expropriation of Land Holdings for Public Purpose and Payment of Compensation' adopted in July 2005 (Proclamation 455/2005). This provides for the replacement costs of properties and relocation sites and for moving costs. However, it gives local administrations unlimited authority to 'expropriate rural or urban holdings for public purposes where they believe that it should be used for a better development project to be carried out by public entities, private investors, cooperative societies or other organs or where such expropriation has been decided by the appropriate higher regional or federal government organ for the same purpose'.[23] Moreover, the Proclamation allows the expropriating authority to allocate smaller and less valuable plots as replacement, and only provides for alternative land and the replacement cost of the building, not for lost income, or rental housing/relocation compensation. Though the Proclamation is one step in terms of at least allowing limited compensation, it is weak in terms of safeguarding rights and providing adequate compensation, does not yet seem to have been implemented systematically and lacks any avenue of appeal to an independent tribunal, court system or arbitration mechanism.

RESETTLEMENT

There was no resettlement policy in the imperial period, and measures were taken on an individual basis through the initiatives of local governors, religious missions and non-governmental agencies, and resettlement was used to promote a wide range of unrelated aims. During the Derg the land nationalization provided the state with the power to move people and the socialist ideology promoted villagization, collectivization and resettlement. However, no clear resettlement policy was formulated and the emergency programme in the mid-1980s which was carried out without much planning, primarily in the context of famine, was intended to promote agricultural development and imposed mechanized collectivization along socialist ideas of modernization. The Derg resettlement also involved strong elements of control of labour, markets and movement of people. Production was reorganized on a collective basis and an attempt was made to suppress religious practices. Most of the concentrated resettlement schemes were established in the western and southwestern lowlands, where, despite a harsh climate and relatively unstable environmental settings, local people have managed to make a living that often involved seasonal movements, shifting agriculture and pastoralism. Traditional customary rights of local peoples were not given any consideration, and compensation and/or joint development initiatives were not considered. The livelihoods of many of the indigenous peoples were severely affected by the resettlement process, as has been documented by a number of researchers who have described the local population as the 'hidden losers'[24] (Dessalegn 1988; Wolde-Selassie 2002; Gebre 2003). Moreover serious negative effects on the environment have been highlighted (Alemneh 1990; Mengistu 2005).

With the defeat of the Derg in 1991 most of the resettlers returned to the areas they came from. They found that their land had been redistributed to others, and no clear policy or guidelines were formulated as to how they should be accommodated. In some cases an interest in obtaining land, particularly irrigated plots, had even been a motivation for leaders to induce or force them to resettle in the first place. Often the land of settlers had been defined as belonging to the category of *yemote kedda* land, i.e. 'land of those who died and deserters', and redistributed to the landless, or the more powerful. When the bulk of settlers left the resettlement in 1991 and returned to areas they came from, they therefore found that their former land was occupied by others. Some who arrived before the redistributions, where these took place, obtained some land; others were able to use kinship and patronage to obtain access to limited land, but generally returnees joined the ranks of the rural landless or urban destitute, surviving on charity and wage labour, and were bitter about the 'lost years' (Erlichman 2000; Pankhurst 2001c).

In a context of federalism, regionalization and decentralization defined on an ethnic basis, the remaining resettlers in the resettlement areas in the west have at times been portrayed as unwelcome islands of foreigners, and some have been forced to leave, as in the case of settlers from East Wellega Zone of Oromia resettled in 2001 in Jawe Amhara Region (Piguet and Dechassa 2004; Getu 2005; Tesfaye 2007). In their case, too, no clear policy seems to have been formulated, and guidelines were not issued regarding their rights and options. However, in practice, in the resettlement areas economic realities and exchanges on the ground have often allowed for coexistence. Settlers have established relationships of exchange, have contributed to the local economy as agricultural surplus producers and tax-payers, and are involved in a range of economic, social and cultural relationships with local people (Pankhurst 2002a).

With the reorganization of the country on a regional basis defined largely in ethnic terms, policy statements and practice have excluded further *inter-regional* resettlement.[25] This decision was viewed as a positive measure, which could reduce potential conflicts over resources, which may be couched in the idiom of ethnicity, and lead to evictions as noted above. However, even with such a precaution, differences between the highlands from where most resettlers came and the lowlands where they were resettled, in terms of ethnicity, culture, religion, social institutions, agricultural techniques, natural resource management and livelihood patterns, are quite common. The comparative case studies of 11 resettlement sites conducted by FSS (2006) showed that in all four regions some ethnic, cultural and/or religious differences exist between the highlands and lowlands.[26] The greater ethnic and religious homogeneity of the recent resettlement has not *in itself* avoided conflicts since these are largely over natural resources. Despite being *intra-regional*, resettlement could still result in demographic imbalances and/or conflicts opposing natives and settlers, especially in the SNNPR. There is therefore a need to develop mechanisms for compensating local people for loss of resources and to promote joint development measures and common institutions, notably for conflict mitigation and working together for shared goals.

The 2003 resettlement programme has been presented as a means to achieve 'lasting food security' (FDRE 2003). The study carried out by FSS (2006) suggests that in the first year a significant proportion of settler households had difficulty in achieving food security. Female-headed households, the elderly, weak, disabled and those suffering from chronic and/or lowland diseases have faced particular difficulties. Stoppage of food aid rations after eight months had detrimental effects on confidence, and placed a stress on the food-secure households that had to support those who were food-insecure. However, certain households have been able to succeed much better than others, and have attained food security faster than in previous resettlements. This has been mainly due to resources brought from the home areas, notably in the case of settlers from Harerge in Oromia. Some have been able to invest in increasing production through share-cropping and have focused on cash crops, notably sesame.

Population relocations may not have a significant long-term demographic impact on reducing population pressure in the highlands, unless they are accompanied by a range of complementary measures, including family planning. Moreover, at least in the past, the bulk of settlers have returned to the areas they came from, and there have already been significant numbers of returnees in some current resettlement sites, particularly in Amhara Region. Such trends may continue unless the circumstances of resettlement are such that settlers feel their livelihoods are improving, and incentives, notably basic infrastructure, adequate services and affordable credit, are made available.

In the areas in which people have been resettled, the risk of aggravating environmental degradation is significant, as argued in a case study of Gambella Region (Mengistu 2005). Without strong conservation, environmental protection and development measures, implemented from the outset, the longer-term sustainability of settlements with large numbers of new settlers may be uncertain. In such a context resettlement, on its own, seems a risky strategy for furthering food security, unless it is complemented by a range of other measures, options and incentives, notably regarding infrastructure and services which can influence 'push and pull' factors in both 'sending' and 'receiving' areas.

In terms of food security, land settlement programmes in Ethiopia and other developing countries are often implemented with the ambition of offsetting the consequences of recurrent drought and famine, increasing access to land for the landless, and developing areas considered to be under-developed. Resettlement programmes are sometimes considered politically desirable as an expedient measure to involve large numbers of settlers by mobilizing them in campaigns, which have tended to be planned and organized mainly with a top-down approach. As such, resettlement is viewed as a radical measure that can achieve significant results within a short time. However, worldwide experience suggests that settlement programmes carried out on a large scale, in haste, have often fallen short of their expectations of attaining food security and sustainable livelihoods (de Wet 1995; McDowell 1996; Cernea 2000). Often they are undertaken with insufficient detailed assessments of land availability and potential, limited assessment of the willingness of host populations to accept settlers, too rudimentary a screening process to select motivated settlers, insufficient preparation and pre-positioning of infrastructure and services, and with limited consideration of joint development with people already living in the area. It is sometimes claimed, therefore, that resettlement may be considered more of a palliative to buy time for other policies to become fully operational, rather than a fully-fledged independent solution on its own. However, as part of a series of strategies, a range of options, and a number of packages, incentives and credits, as long as it is integrated with other measures, and implemented in a participatory manner with the involvement of both settlers and local people, resettlement may be considered as one potential component in a viable strategy for food security promotion, and could also be viewed as a means of promoting regional development.

Movements of groups of people, notably from the highlands to the lowlands and *vice versa*, have a long history and are continuous and ongoing processes to this day. This raises the question of whether government and other agencies should be seeking to regulate and/or to facilitate such processes. Influencing or expediting spontaneous migration with appropriate safeguards for the rights of local people and the environment may be a more effective, efficient and less costly alternative in addressing issues relating to the relationships between population and resources than organized and planned resettlement. Lessons can be learnt from the way spontaneous settlers plan and carry out their migrations. In particular, they tend to prioritize establishing social and economic relations with local people, by negotiating access to resources, entering agreements, and obtaining assurances of protection. This would suggest the need for planned resettlement to give more emphasis to promoting negotiated agreements and joint development between existing populations and new settlers, to avoid creating islands of resentment. In other words, there is a need to develop a more integrated, flexible, participatory and bottom-up approach.

Several case studies report the migration of large numbers of new settlers on their own initiative to planned resettlement areas. Measures to prevent such 'squatting' have been introduced in some instances. This raises the question of the relationship between spontaneous and state-sponsored resettlement, and suggests that there is a link between the two. It may well be that recognizing this link and establishing rules and guidelines for migration may be a more effective strategy than simply organizing large-scale resettlement programmes, on the one hand, and seeking to control spontaneous migration, on the other.

The current resettlement approach seeks to promote food security through population relocation involving large-scale planned resettlement where the state takes on almost the entire responsibility for organizing the relocation. An alternative could consider a wider migration framework with appropriate enabling and regulating policies where individuals, households and groups take more initiative. There is no doubt also an important role for civil society groups, NGOs and the private sector to form partnerships in resettlement ventures. This could include positive incentives to attract migrants as well as safeguards for local groups and the environment. Options for facilitating migration to make use of resources where they exist could focus on improving roads and providing the necessary infrastructure, basic services, minimal inputs and credit facilities. Options for regulating migration by pull factors could exclude certain areas, such as key forest and wildlife reserves, provide enforceable safeguards for the customary rights of local people, and seek to promote the regeneration and development of natural resources, and their sustainable use. Such an approach may end up being less costly and more effective and practical in the long run, and may be more in tune with current global perspectives on migration and therefore more likely to receive donor support.

REFUGEES AND INTERNALLY DISPLACED

The policies regarding refugees have been formulated in a spirit of inclusiveness and in relation to international conventions. Like other African states, Ethiopia has pursued a generous asylum approach, having signed the 1951 Convention relating to the status of refugees, the 1967 protocol and the 1969 Organization of African Unity Convention regarding refugees (Blavo 1999). A more substantial Refugee Proclamation was approved by the Ethiopian Parliament in 2004.[27] The Proclamation deals with asylum, protection and voluntary repatriation, as well as exclusion, withdrawal and cessation of refugee status, and issues of *non-refoulement*, expulsion, temporary detention, application procedures for refugee status and rights and obligations of asylum seekers and recognized refugees.[28] From a legal point of view this text is an important step forward in refugee legislation and has been described as a breakthrough (Bizuayehu 2004: 21).

However, the Proclamation is concerned with political refugees and does not consider environmental or economic 'refugees'; nor are internally displaced persons or development-induced displacees considered. There is an increasing view among international organizations, notably the International Organization for Migration, the International Committee of the Red Cross and the UN High Commissioner for Refugees that internally displaced persons (IDPs) have been neglected and deserve more consideration.[29] The UNHCR has suggested that its mandate should be widened to consider returnees, local civilian communities which are directly affected by refugees, stateless persons, and especially the growing numbers of IDPs. Within the countries of the Horn and East Africa, the Inter-Governmental Authority on Development has also been concerned with developing policy on IDPs, which were estimated at over 5 million in the member countries out of a total of 25 million worldwide (IGAD 2003). The African Union developed a migration policy framework in 2006 (AU 2006) and in 2008 held a ministerial conference on refugees, returnees and IDPs which produced a draft declaration addressing the challenge of forced displacement in Africa. The conference adopted a Draft Convention for the Protection and Assistance of Internally Displaced Persons in Africa to be considered by the AU summit in 2009 (AU 2008). However, despite often generous statements and declarations in tune with African notions of hospitality, the reality on the ground frequently involves competition and conflict over scarce resources, that require mechanisms for negotiated resolution.

Migration, relocation and coexistence

To conclude, as noted by Turton in his chapter, there is a need for an integrated academic and practitioner discussion of the field of forced migration. The distinction drawn between refugees and internal displacees can be considered rather artificial and unhelpful. Indeed, we may even go further and suggest that there is a need to think of migration frameworks and policy guidelines that do not consider refugees and other forced migrants in isolation from voluntary and spontaneous migrants, but rather seek to develop a more holistic and integrated approach to migration and population movement in general.

In the Ethiopian context much of the debate has centred on the specific question of the advantages, disadvantages, opportunities and risks of state-organized resettlement. We have argued that there is a need for broadening the discussion by contextualizing resettlement within a wider framework of historical and spatial migration in terms of highland-lowland dynamics, and in relation to the role of the Ethiopian state and its neighbours, particularly with respect to refugee and returnee flows and internally displaced groups. The limited focus on resettlement by government, international and non-governmental agencies and academics alike has, we believe, led to a tendency to overlook and underestimate the significance of migration processes over time and space, as well as the linkages between self, group and state-organized resettlement, and between forced and voluntary resettlement. In other words, there is a need to develop a better understanding of the complex dynamics in relations between people, space and the state.

Government efforts have largely been devoted to planning and implementing ambitious, complex and costly resettlement programmes with limited support from donors. In terms of policy on population, rural-urban balance and inter-relations, food security, poverty reduction, and development, more emphasis on a broader vision of migration could provide a framework that is more conducive to developing enabling, participatory and less costly approaches to resettlement.

Such a vision would seek a balance between two seemingly contradictory but equally important needs: on the one hand, there is a need to create favourable conditions, appropriate incentives, and an enabling environment to promote appropriate migration, which can play a positive role in stimulating development. This could include an emphasis on developing roads, basic infrastructure and adequate services with an emphasis on health care, addressing lowland human and cattle diseases, creating a viable economic environment for livestock marketing and providing credit services, particularly for non-agricultural income-generation. On the other hand, there is a need to ensure that safeguards are in place to guarantee the rights of local people and to ensure the preservation and rehabilitation of the environment. This could include measures to regulate the direction, size and types of migration, establishing enforceable means of protecting the customary rights of local people to natural resources, and working out participatory guidelines and mechanisms for the protection and enhancement of natural resources. The key to reconciling these apparently contradictory needs is, arguably, to emphasize the linkages between hosts and settlers. At an immediate and most practical minimal level, this should involve establishing or strengthening joint institutions for administration and conflict resolution. However, on a more positive note there should be promotion of joint development ventures, in which both local and migrant groups stand to gain from working together. Such initiatives should be designed in a participatory manner, such that individuals, groups and communities could apply to the local government, NGOs and donors for funding joint development projects. If the ultimate success of resettlement and migration lies in promoting sustainable development, we believe that such an approach has advantages and deserves to be given due consideration.

Despite a significant amount of research on resettlement, refugees, returnees, and development displacees in Ethiopia, many of the basic questions that need to be answered to devise more successful resettlement and migration policies, programmes and projects still remain unanswered. For instance, there are ongoing debates, but not yet clear answers, about what kinds of migrants are successful in what kinds of settlements and what the pre-requisite conditions are for attaining food security, let alone economic, social and cultural adaptation and the longer-term environmental viability of settlements.

The current context of concerns over food security and the promoting of cash crops and fuel alternatives has exacerbated resource conflicts between highland and lowland groups and among agro-pastoralist groups themselves in the lowlands in the east, the west and the south. Such conflicts often result in displacement and the use of force to justify claims to territory and access to resources. Peace-making initiatives by local elders, government, and non-governmental agencies have sought to address these conflicts, negotiate agreements and promote understanding and mutual coexistence. The context of greater decentralization from the federal to the regional and recently to the *wereda* level offers opportunities for bridging the disconnects, enhancing dialogue and negotiation between national and local interests and involving customary dispute resolution institutions in partnership with the formal justice system (Pankhurst and Getachew 2008). Greater cooperation, coordination and collaboration between local, regional, federal and international initiatives in this respect could improve conditions and forestall potential conflicts. Initiatives to promote peace-making, involving both formal and informal customary peace-making institutions and bringing the various stakeholders together, often have an important, and sometimes neglected, contribution to make. In the peripheral lowland areas, external conflicts have affected local populations and complicated peace-making processes. This widening context of conflict requires negotiations across borders, involves inter-state relations, and has become a concern of the Inter-Governmental Authority on Development (IGAD) set up by the countries of the Horn and East Africa, particularly in relation to pastoralist groups moving across borders.[30]

Displacement and voluntary migrations are at the roots of much conflict in Ethiopia and the Horn. Seeking ways of resolving these conflicts can benefit from the participation and negotiation of all stakeholders including government, civil society groups, the private sector, non-governmental organizations and donors, and the involvement of formal as well as informal customary institutions at various levels. It is to be hoped that initiatives at Addis Ababa University under the United Nations University for Peace, could enable the development of research programmes, which could provide contributions to understanding issues of migration, relocation, conflict resolution and coexistence that have become increasingly important in Ethiopia, the Horn and the rest of Africa.

Notes

1. For further discussions see McDowell (1996); Cernea and McDowell (2000); Robinson (2002); Newman and van Selm (2003); and Ohta and Gebre (2005).
2. Notably the Second Five Year-Development Plan (1999), the National Food Security Strategy (FDRE) (2002a), the Sustainable Development and Poverty Reduction Programme (FDRE 2002b), the report of the New Coalition for Food Security in Ethiopia (NCFSE 2003b), and the Plan for Accelerated and Sustained Development to End Poverty (PASDEP) (MoFED 2006).
3. Including three PhD theses in anthropology (Pankhurst 1989; Gebre 2001; Wolde-Selassie 2002). See the review in the Introduction and further articles in Pankhurst and Piguet (eds) (2004a).
4. These include those of Zelalem (2005); Getu (2005); Abdurouf (2005); Areba (2005); Ayke (2005); Mellese (2005); and Feseha (2006).
5. Towards the end of the twentieth century the number of refugees decreased to about 12 million and 20 million internally displaced persons (IDPs); those in Africa represented over a quarter (UNHCR 2002). At the beginning of 2003, out of a total of 10 million refugees, 3 million were in Africa, and out of a total of over 20 million 'people of concern' including asylum seekers, returned refugees, internally displaced and stateless people 4.5 million were in Africa (UNHCR 2003).
6. According to *2005 Global Refugee Trends*, published by UNHCR : 'By the end of 2005, the global number of refugees reached an estimated 8.4 million persons, the lowest level since 1980. This constitutes a net decrease of more than one million refugees (- 12%) since the beginning of 2005, when 9.5 million refugees were recorded. This is the fifth consecutive year in the global refugee population which has dropped and the second sharpest decrease since 2001. On the five years period, the global refugee population has fallen by one third (- 31%). Decreases in the refugee population are often the result of refugees having access to durable solutions, in particular voluntary repatriation' (p.3). 'At the end of 2005, UNHCR country offices reported 6.6 million internally displaced persons in 16 countries compared to 5.4 million IDPs in 13 countries one year earlier. This increase primarily reflects the IDP situation in Iraq (1.2 million) and Somalia (400.000)' (p. 8).
7. By March 2004, the number of refugees. especially Somalis. had decreased significantly, and the total was no more than 125,000 people, most of whom were Sudanese refugees.
8. In 1991 Ethiopia hosted over a million refugees; The number of Sudanese refugees was over

400,000 in 1991 and the number of refugees from Somalia had reached 594,000 in 1992 (Hogg 1996: 155).

9. For instance, in 1992 according to the UNHCR there were over 594,000 refugees and 117,000 returnees in the northern part of the Ogaden, and there were also an estimated 260,000 returnees living with relatives or friends who had been re-absorbed back into the local community (Hogg 1996: 155-6).

10. According to the Ethiopian Administration for Refugee and Returnee Affairs (ARRA), more than 20,000 refugees were repatriated in 2007, and about 36,000 remained in four camps in March 2008.

11. See in particular Dereje (2003, 2006a); Kurimoto (2005); and Van Uffelen (2006).

12 A fire broke out in Kaliti camp where Aptekar and Behailu conducted their field work and the camp was closed on 17 May 2003, subsequent to the authorities deciding in 2002 to close down all the camps around Addis Ababa (*Relief Web*, 29 May 2003).

13. Reported by AFP, August 28, in *Ethiopia: 7 days update*, vol. 14, no. 26, 3 September 2007, p. 10.

14. *Capital*, vol. 10, no 476, 27 January 2008.

15. A derogatory term for nomads, replaced during the EPRDF period with the term *arbito-adder*, 'those who live by breeding' as a parallel to the term *arso-adder* 'those who live by ploughing' commonly used for peasants.

16. The document concludes with the familiar Ethiopian stereotype of pastoralists as 'following the tails of their cattle'. 'When our people are liberated from moving following the tails of their cattle, that day will be a respected day, which brought a fundamental change in the development of our country' (FDRE 2001: 81).

17. 'Pastoralism as a mode of production requires movement across boundaries and within boundaries for search of water and pasture. This movement, when restricted, often leads to disputes between pastoralists and other neighbouring groups. The major causes of conflict are associated with range and resource limitation such as water and land, competition resulting from scarcity of resources, and due to HTPs. Hence, the necessary measures must be put in place to encourage pastoralists to settle voluntarily as well as for the provision of basic social services for those who prefer to travel and resettle in different areas' (MoFED 2006: 195).

18. '... irrigation development schemes must be introduced and strengthened for the willing resettlement of the pastoralists (MoFED 2006: 193).

19. These are the Mursi, Chai, Tirma, Nyangatom Dizi, Me'en, Bodi, Kwegu and Muguji. (http://www.mursi.org/national-parks).

20. See http://www.african-parks.org/apffoundation.

21. *Fortune* vol. 8 No. 369, 27 May 2007, 'Bio-diesel Project Encroaching on Elephant Reserve'.

22. The Ethiopian Investment Agency issued 7,326 real estate investment licences with a aggregate capital of almost 60 billion *birr* (US$6,500 m.) from 1992 to July 2007, with a steady increase during that period and a high proportion of foreign investment (about 590 projects worth 11.7 billion *birr* ($1,280 m.) (*Ethiopia: 7 Days Update*, Vol. 14, no 25, August 27, 2007, p.9).

23. Article 2.5 states 'Public purpose means the use of land defined as such by the decision of the appropriate body in conformity to urban structure plan or development plan in order to ensure the interest of the people to acquire direct or indirect benefits from the use of the land to consolidate sustainable socio-economic development.'

24. This term was used by Chambers (1986) to characterize the impact of refugees on poorer hosts.

25. This was noted in the Sustainable Development and Poverty Reduction Programme (FRDE 2002b), and the document of the New Coalition for Food Security in Ethiopia (2003).

26. See Chapter 11.

27. 'Refugee Proclamation of the Federal Democratic Republic of Ethiopia', Proclamation No 409/2004, *Negarit Gazeta*, 19 July 2004.

28. Proclamation No. 409/2004, *Negarit Gazeta*, Refugee 'Proclamation related to the status of refugees in Ethiopia'. Note that Ethiopia has expressed reserves regarding the 1951 Geneva Convention in connection with the labour market (art. 17, Wage-earning employment) and public schools access (art. 22. Public education).

29. This was stimulated by the Global IDP project of the Norwegian Refugee Council that pro-

duced a first global survey of IDPs in 1998 and a second edition in 2002. See also Cohen and Deng (1998), Korn (1999), and Robinson (2003).

30. Conflicts in the Horn have also taken on global dimensions due to the War on Terror, political, religious and social linkages with and migration to the Middle East and the presence of the Ethiopian army in Somalia.

Bibliography

AAMPPO (Addis Ababa Master Plan Project Office). 1984. 'The Metropolitan Development Scheme', Unpublished Master Plan Report, Addis Ababa.

Abate Jijo. 2004. 'Oromia Voluntary Resettlement Programme Feasibility Study: Preliminary Outline of Findings', in Pankhurst and Piguet (eds).

Abbay Alamseged. 1998. *Identity Jilted or Reimagining Identity?* Trenton, NJ: Red Sea Press.

Abdullahi Haji. 2004. 'Conflicts and their Resolution in Ethiopian Pastoral Areas: A Summary of the Situation in the Somali Region', in Pankhurst and Piguet (eds).

Abdulhamid Bedri Kello. 1989. 'Settling Semi-nomadic Pastoralists in the Awash Valley'. *Ethiopian Journal of Development Research*, 11 (1): 105-118.

Abdurouf Abdurahman. 2005. 'Resettlement and the Dynamics of Social Integration in Chewaka Resettlement in Ilu Abba Bora Zone, Southwest Ethiopia'. MA thesis in Social Anthropology, Addis Ababa University.

Abiy Hailu. 2004. 'Dilemmas of Mass Spontaneous Movement Seeking Government Sponsorship or the Rush for "El Dorado": the Case of the Mana Angetu Internally Displaced Persons', in Pankhurst and Piguet (eds).

Abraham Sewonet. 2004. 'Breaking the Cycle of Conflict in Gambella Region,' in Pankhurst and Piguet (eds).

Abraham Sewonet. 1995. 'The Somali Refugees in Ethiopia, with Particular Emphasis on Camabokar Refugee Camp'. Senior Essay, Department of Sociology and Anthropology, Addis Ababa University.

Abraham Sewonet and François Piguet. 2004a. 'Intra-Regional Resettlement in Ethiopia: Comparing Developments in the First Quarter of 2003', in Pankhurst and Piguet (eds).

Abraham Sewonet and François Piguet. 2004b. 'Intra-Regional Voluntary Resettlement in Amhara Region: A Possible Way out of the Chronic Food Trap?, in Pankhurst and Piguet (eds).

Abraham Workneh. 1996. 'Urban Land Policy: Problems and Prospects, the Case of Addis Ababa. Ministry of Public Works and Urban Development'. Paper presented at Habitat Workshop. Addis Ababa. October.

Addis Ababa Master Plan Project Office. 1984. 'The Metropolitan Development Scheme'. Addis Ababa.

Adelman, H. 2001. 'From Refugees to Forced Migration: The UNHCR and Human Security', *International Migration Review*, 35:7-32.

Adelman, H. 1999. 'Modernity, Globalization, Refugees and Displacement', in A. Ager (ed.), *Refugees: Perspectives on the Experience of Forced Migrants*. London and New York: Pinter.

Adelman, H. and Sorenson, J. (eds). 1994. *African Refugees: Development Aid and Repatriation*. Boulder, CO: Westview Press.

Africa Watch. 1991. *Evil Days: Thirty years of War and Famine In Ethiopia*. New York: Human Rights Watch.

African Parks Foundation. 2007. 'Termination of Management Activities in Nech Sar and Omo National Parks. www.african-parks.org/apffoundation.

African Union. 2008. 'African Union Convention for the Protection and Assistance of Internally Displaced Persons in Africa.' Adopted Draft 1, 11 November.

African Union. 2006. 'Draft African Common Position on Migration and Development.' Addis Ababa: African Union, April.

Agdaw Asfaw and Wolde-Selassie Abbute. 1992. 'Utilization of Horticultural Products in the Beles Valley Resettlement Villages', in Dieci and Viezzoli (eds).

Agneta, F., S. Berterame, M. Capirci, Magni, L. and Tomassoli M. 1993. 'The Dynamics of Social and Economic Adaptation during Resettlement: The Case of Beles Valley in Ethiopia', in M. Cernea and S. Guggenheim (eds), *Anthropological Approaches to Resettlement: Policy, Practice, and Theory*. Boulder, CO: Westview Press.

Ahmed Hassen Omer. 1994, 'A Historical Survey of Ethnic Relations in Yifat and Temmuga Awrajja, Northeast Shawa, 1889-1974'. MA thesis in history, Addis Ababa University.

Ahmed Hassen Omer. 2007. 'Islam, commerce et politique dans l'Ifat (Ethiopie centrale) au XIXème siècle: L'émergence d'une ville carrefour Aleyyu Amba.' PhD thesis, University of Paris I, Sorbonne.

Ahmed Yousuf Farah. 1997. 'From Traditional Nomadic Context to Contemporary Sedentarisation: Past Relations between the Isaq and Gadabursi Clans of Northern Somalia and South-East Ethiopia', in Hogg (ed.).

Akale Kifle. 1997. 'Urban Management in Ethiopia' in *Proceedings of the Workshop on Urban Fields of Ethiopia*. Addis Ababa: Ministry of Public Works and Urban Development.

Alem, A., L. Jacobsson, and M. Araya. 1995. 'Mental Health in Ethiopia', *Ethiopian Journal of Health Development* 9: 47-62.

Alemneh Dejene. 1990. *Environment, Famine and Politics in Ethiopia: A View from the Village*. Boulder, CO: Lynne Rienner.

Ali Said. 1997. 'Resource Use Conflicts in the Middle Awash Valley of Ethiopia: the Crisis of Afar Pastoralism', in Hogg (ed.).

Ali Said. 1992. 'Resource Use Conflicts Between Pastoralism and Irrigation Developments in the Middle Awash Valley of Ethiopia'. MSc thesis, Noragric, Agricultural University of Norway.

Allen, Tim (ed.). 1996. *In Search of Cool Ground: War, Flight and Homecoming in Northeast Africa*. London: James Currey; Trenton, NJ: Africa World Press.

Allen, Tim and David Turton. 1996. 'Introduction: In Search of Cool Ground', in Allen (ed.).

Amaha Wolde-Selassie. 1971. 'The Making of the Imperial Territorial Army in Ethiopia'. BA Senior Essay, Addis Ababa University.

Ambaye Ogato. 2006. 'The Consequences of Urban Development on the Affected People in Addis Ababa: The Case of Gurara'. MA thesis in social anthropology, Addis Ababa University.

Andargatchew Tesfaye. 1992. 'The Social Consequences of Urbanization: the Addis Ababa Experience', *Ethiopian Journal of Development Research* 14:1-41.

Anteneh Feleke. 1996. 'Experiences with the Demobilization and Reintegration of Ex-combatants'. Workshop Report. Addis Ababa.

Antonioli, Paolo. 1992. 'The Cornerstones of Development: Training, Private Cooperatives, Marketing Strategies, and Handing Over', in Dieci and Viezzoli (eds).

Apfel, R. and B. Simon (eds). 1996. *Minefields in their Hearts: The Mental Health of Children in War and Communal Violence*. New Haven, CT: Yale University Press.

Aptekar, Lewis. 2003. 'Cultural Poblems for Western Cunselors Working with Ethiopian Refugees', in F. Bemak, R. Chung, P. Pedersen (eds), *Counselling Refugees: A psychosocial approach to innovative multicultural innovations*. Westport, CT: Greenwood Press.

Aptekar, Lewis and R. Giel. 2002. 'Walks in Kaliti: Life in a Destitute Shelter for the Displaced', in Joop de Jong (ed.), *Trauma, War, and Violence: Public Mental Health in Socio-cultural Context*. New York: Kluwer Academic/Plenum Pub.

Aptekar, Lewis, B. Paardekooper, and J. Kuebli. 2000. 'Adolescence and Youth among Displaced Ethiopians: A Case Study in Kaliti Camp', *International Journal of Group Tensions* 29: 101-135.

Araya, M. and F. Aboud. 1993. 'Mental Illness', in Kloos and Zein (eds).

Areba Abdela. 2005. 'Mass Voluntary Migration: The Resettlement of Arsi and Hararghe Oromo in Bale Zone'. MA thesis in Social Anthropology, Addis Ababa University.

Asfaw Qeno. 2005. 'Socio-Economic Dynamics of Resettlement in Ethiopia with Special Reference to Qeto Resettlement Area, West Wellega Zone, Oromia Region.' MA thesis in Regional and Local Development Studies, Addis Ababa University.

Ashenafi Gossaye. 2001. 'Inner-City Renewal in Addis Ababa. The Impact of Resettlement on the Socio-economic and Housing Situation of Low-Income Residents'. PhD thesis, Norwegian University of Science and Technology, Trondheim.

Asmerom Legesse. 1973. *Gada: Three Approaches to the Study of African Society.* New York: Free Press.

Aspen, Harald. 1994. 'Spirits, Mediums, and Human Worlds: The Amhara Peasants of the North Ethiopian Highlands and their Traditional Knowledge'. Trondheim: University of Trondheim.

Assefa Hailemarian and H. Kloos. 1993. 'Population', in Kloos and Zein (eds).

Assefa Tewodros. 1995. 'The Sedentary Afar of North Eastern Ethiopia: Economy and Relations with Neighbouring Highlanders'. MA thesis in Social Anthropology, Addis Ababa University.

Assefa Tolera. 2002. 'Where Have the Forests Gone? Settlement, Dislocation and Development Discourse in Western Oromia, Ethiopia'. Ph.D. thesis, School of Oriental and African Studies, University of London.

Assefa Tolera. 1999. *Ethnic Integration and Conflict: The Case of Indigenous Oromo and Amhara Settlers in Aaroo Addis Alem, Kiramu Area, Northeastern Wallaga.* Social Anthropology Dissertation Series No. 5. Department of Sociology and Social Administration. Addis Ababa University.

Ayalew Gebre. 2004. 'The Effects of Development Projects on the Metahara Area', in Pankhurst and Piguet (eds).

Ayalew Gebre. 2001. *Pastoralism under Pressure: Land Alienation and Pastoral Transformation among the Karrayu of Eastern Ethiopia, 1941 to the Present.* Maastricht: Shaker Publishing.

Ayalew Gebre. 1995. 'Land Tenure Systems and Their Effects on the Afar', in Seyoum Gebre Selassie (ed.), *Pastoral Land Tenure Systems in the Horn of Africa: A Compendium of Eight Case Studies from Ethiopia, Eritrea, and Sudan.* Addis Ababa: Pastoral and Environmental Network in the Horn of Africa (PENHA).

Ayele Gebre Mariam. 1986. 'Economic Adaptation and Competition for Scarce Resources: The Afar in Northeast Ethiopia'. M.A. thesis, Department of Social Anthropology, University of Bergen.

Ayele Gebre Mariam. 1997. 'Arbore Inter-Tribal Relations: An Historical Account', in Hogg (ed.).

Ayke Asfaw. 2005. 'The Resettlement of Konso Farmers in the Land of the Bodi Agro-Pastoralists, Southwestern Ethiopia'. MA thesis in Social Anthropology, Addis Ababa University.

Bahrin, Tunku Shamsul. 1988. 'Land Settlement in Malaysia: A Case Study of the Federal Land Development Authority Projects', in S. Oberai (ed.), *Land Settlement Policies and Population Distribution in Developing Countries.* New York: Praeger.

Bahru Zewde. 1984. 'Environment and Capital: Notes for a History of the Wonji-Shoa Sugar Estate 1951-1974'. Paper Presented at the Sixth Eastern Africa History Conference, Ambo, 14-21 March.

Bahru Zewde. 1991. *A History of Modern Ethiopia, 1855-1974.* London: James Currey.

Ball, Nicole. 1993. *Development Aid for Military Reform: A Pathway to Peace.* Washington, DC: Overseas Development Council.

Barnard, Alan and J. Spencer (eds). 1996. *Encyclopaedia of Social and Cultural Anthropology.* London: Routledge.

Barth, Frederic. 1996. 'Ethnic Groups and Boundaries', in J. Hutchinson and A. Smith (eds), *Ethnicity.* Oxford: Oxford University Press.

Barutciski, M. 2000. *Addressing Legal Constraints and Improving Outcomes in Development-Induced Resettlement Projects.* Desk Study for Department for International Development (ESCOR). Oxford: Refugee Studies Centre, University of Oxford.

Bassi, Marco. 1997. 'Returnees in Moyale District, Southern Ethiopia: New Means for an Old Inter-Ethnic Game', in Hogg (ed.).

Bauer, Dan. 1973. 'For Want of an Ox…Land, Capital and Social Stratification in Tigre', in H. Marcus (ed.), *Proceedings of the First United States Conference on Ethiopian Studies.* East Lansing, MI: African Studies Centre, Michigan State University.

Baxter, Paul. 1994. 'Pastoralists are People: Why Development for Pastoralists, not the Development of Pastoralism?', *Rural Extension Bulletin* 4: Agricultural Extension and Rural Development Department (AERDD), University of Reading, UK.

Baxter, Paul. 1994b. 'Still Just Time?'. *Rural Extension Bulletin.* 4: 2. AERDD, University of Reading, UK.

Baxter, Paul. 1991. 'Introduction', in P. Baxter (ed.), *When the Grass is Gone: Development Interventions in African Arid Lands.* Uppsala: Scandinavian Institute of African Studies.

Baxter, Paul. 1985. 'From Telling People to Listening to them: Changes in Approaches to the Development and Welfare of Pastoralist Peoples'. Paper presented at International Symposium on the African Horn. Cairo. January.

Baxter, Paul. 1978. 'Boran Age-Sets and Generation-Sets: Gada, a Puzzle or a Maze?' in P. Baxter and U. Almagor (eds), *Age, Generation and Time: Some Features of East African Age Organization.* London: Hurst.

Baxter, Paul. 1975. 'Some Consequences of Sedentarisation for Social Relationships', in T. Monod (ed.), *Pastoralism in Tropical Africa.* London: Oxford University Press.

Baxter, Paul and Richard Hogg. (eds). 1990. *Property, Poverty and People: Changing Rights in Property and the Problem of Pastoral Development.* Manchester: Department of Social Anthropology and the International Development Centre, University of Manchester.

Bayefski, A. and J. Fitzpatrick (eds). 2000. *Human Rights and Forced Displacement.* The Hague/Boston, MA/London: Martinus Nijhoff Publishers.

Beeker, Cohen. 1997. 'Urban Fields in Africa', in *Proceedings of the Workshop on Urban Fields of Ethiopia.* Addis Ababa: Ministry of Public Works and Urban Development.

Behailu Abebe. 2004. 'War Stories, Displacement and Coping Experiences of the Displaced from the Ethio-Eritrean War', in Parkhurst and Piguet (eds).

Behailu Abebe. 2005. 'War, Coping Mechanisms and Cultural Resources in Tigray, Ethiopia: Implications for NGO Psychosocial Programming'. PhD. thesis, Queen Margaret University College, Edinburgh.

Bender, Lionel. 1976. *The Non-Semitic Languages of Ethiopia.* East Lansing, MI: African Studies Centre, Michigan State University.

Bender, M. L. 1971. 'The Languages of Ethiopia: A New Lexicostatistic Classification and Some Problems of Diffusion', *Journal of Anthropological Linguistics* 13 (5): 165-288.

Berhanu Wubeshet. 1989. 'Development and Transformation in the Urban Form of Addis Ababa'. M.Sc thesis, Department of Architecture, Herriot Watt University, Edinburgh.

Berihun Mebratie. 1996. 'Spontaneous Settlement and Inter-Ethnic Relationships in Matakal, North-west Ethiopia'. MA thesis in social anthropology, Addis Ababa University.

Berkes, F. and M. Favar. 1989. 'Introduction', in F. Berkes (ed.), *Common Property Resources.* London: Belhaven Press.

Berterame, Stefano and Loredana Magni. 1992. 'Potters Between Adaptation and Survival in the Beles Resettlement Area, Ethiopia', in Dieci and Viezzoli (eds).

Betru Haile and Wolde-Selassie Abbute. 1995. 'Diagnostic Study on Household Food Security in the Beles Valley.' Addis Ababa: CISP.

Birkie Yami. 1997. 'Urban Morphology in Ethiopia', in *Proceedings of the Workshop on Urban Fields of Ethiopia,* Addis Ababa: Ministry of Public Works and Urban Development.

Birkie Yami. 1992. 'Urban Form and Structure of Addis Ababa: Problems and Prospects'. MA thesis, Faculty of Architecture, Helsinki University of Technology.

Bizuayehu Andarssa. 2004. 'Socio-Economic Impacts of Refugees on Host-Communities: the Case of Somali Refugees in Kebribeyah District, Eastern Ethiopia'. MA thesis in social anthropology, Addis Ababa University.

Black, Richard. 2001. 'Fifty Years of Refugee Studies: From Theory to Policy', *International Migration Review* 35:57-78.

Black, Richard. 1998. *Refugees, Environment and Development.* London: Longman.

Black, Richard and Khalid Khoser. 1999. *The End of the Refugee Cycle? Refugee Repatriation and Reconstruction.* New York: Berghahn.

Blaikie, P. and H. Brookfield. 1987. *Land Degradation and Society.* London: Methuen.

Blain Teketel. 2003. 'Refugees and Environment: A Case Study of the Uduk Refugees in Bonga Refugee Camp, Gambella Regional State, Western Ethiopia'. MA thesis in regional and local development studies. Addis Ababa University.

Blavo, Ebenezer. 1999. *The Problem of Refugees in Africa: Boundaries and Borders.* Aldershot : Ashgate.

Bondestam, Lars. 1974. 'Peoples and Capitalism in the Northeast Lowlands of Ethiopia', *Journal of Modern African Studies,* 12: 428-439.

Boserup, Esther. 1970. *Women's Role in Economic Development.* London: Earthscan.

Bradbury, M., S. Fisher and C. Lane. 1995. *Working with Pastoralists, NGOs and Land Conflict in Tanzania.* A Report on the Workshop in Terrat, Tanzania, 1994. London: International Institute for Environment and Development (IIED).

Brokensha, David and Thayer Scudder. 1968 'Resettlement', in N. Rubin and W. Warren (eds) *The Study of Man-Made Lakes in Africa: an Inter-disciplinary Perspective.* London: Frank Cass.

Bromley, D. 1992. *Making the Commons Work: Theory, Practice and Policy.* San Francisco: ICS.

Bromley, D. and M. Cernea. 1989. *The Management of Common Property Natural Resources: Some Conceptual and Operational Fallacies.* World Bank Discussion Papers No. 57.Washington, DC: World Bank.

Bruce, John *et al.* 1994. *Searching for Land Tenure Security in Africa.* Dubuques, Iowa: Kendall/Hunt.

Bruce, John, Allan Hoben and Dessalegn Rahmato. 1993a. 'After the Derg: An Assessment of Rural Land Tenure Issues in Ethiopia.' Draft report for discussion at Workshop on Rural Land Tenure Issues in Ethiopia, Addis Ababa, 27-29 August.

Bruce, John *et al.* 1993b. 'Tenure in Transition, Tenures in Conflict: Examples from the Zimbabwe Social Forest', *Rural Sociology* 58:4.

Brüne, Stefan. 1990. 'The Agricultural Sector: Structure, Performance and Issues 1974-1988', in S. Pausewang, Fantu Cheru, S. Brüne and Eshetu Chole (eds), *Ethiopia: Rural Development Option.* London: Zed Books.

Buli Edjeta. 2001. 'The Socio-Economic Dimensions of Development-Induced Impoverishment: The Case of the Karrayu Oromo of the Upper Awash Valley'. MA thesis in Social Anthropology, Addis Ababa University.

Butcher, D. 1970. 'The Social Survey", in Chambers (ed.).

Byamukama, Nathan, M. 2000. 'A Critical Analysis of the Demobilization Program in Uganda', in *Proceedings of the Fourth Conference on Democracy and African Conflicts.* Addis Ababa: OSSREA.

Cairns, E. (ed.). 1996. *Children and Political Violence.* Oxford: Blackwell.

Carrithess, M. 1992. *Why Humans Have Cultures: Explaining Anthropology and Social Diversity.* Oxford: Oxford University Press.

Castles, S. and M. Miller. 1993. *The Age of Migration: International Population Movements in the Modern World.* Basingstoke: Macmillan.

Caulk, Richard 1977. 'The Army and Society in Ethiopia', in *Ethiopianist Notes.* 2:17-24.

Central Statistical Authority. 1995a. *The 1994 Population and Housing Census of Ethiopia: Results for Addis Ababa.* Addis Ababa: CSA.

Central Statistical Authority. 1995b. *The 1994 Population and Housing Census of Ethiopia: Results for Tigray Region.* Statistical Report. Addis Ababa: CSA.

Central Statistical Authority. 1998. *The 1994 Population and Housing Census of Ethiopia: Results for the Afar Region.* Addis Ababa: CSA.

Cernea, Michael. 2008a. 'Compensation and Investment in Resettlement: Theory, Practice and Pitfalls and Needed Policy Reform', in M. Cernea and H. Mathur (eds). *Can Compensation Prevent Impoverishment? Reforming Resettlement through Investments and Benefit-Sharing.* Oxford: Oxford University Press.

Cernea, Michael. 2008b. 'Reforming the Foundations of Involuntary Resettlement: Introduction' in M. Cernea and H. Mathur (eds), *Can Compensation Prevent Impoverishment? Reforming Resettlement through Investment and Benefit-sharing.* Oxford: Oxford University Press.

Cernea, Michael. 2005. 'Concept and Method: Applying the IRR Model in Africa to Resettlement and Poverty', in Ohta Haru and Gebre Yostiso (eds).

Cernea, Michael. 2000. 'Risks, Safeguards and Reconstruction: A Model for Population Displacement and Resettlement', in Cernea and McDowell (eds).

Cernea, Michael. 1999. 'Introduction: Mutual Reinforcement: Linking Economic and Social Knowledge about Resettlement', in M. Cernea (ed.). *Putting People First, The Economics of Involuntary Resettlement: Questions and Challenges.* Washington, DC: World Bank.

Cernea, Michael. 1997.'The Risks and Reconstruction Model for Resettling Displaced Populations.' *World Development.* 25 (10): 1569-1587.

Cernea, Michael. 1996a. 'Bridging the Research Divide: Studying Refugees and Development Oustees', in Allen (ed.).

Cernea, Michael. 1996b. *Public Policy Responses to Development-Induced Population Displacements.* Washington, DC: World Bank Reprint Series. No. 479.

Cernea, Michael. 1995. 'Understanding and Preventing Impoverishment from Displacement: Reflections on the State of the Knowledge.' Keynote Address, First International Conference on Development-induced Displacement, Refugee Studies Programme, Queen Elizabeth House, Oxford.

Cernea, Michael. 1993. *The Urban Environment and Population Relocation.* Washington, DC: World Bank, Discussion Paper No. 152.

Cernea, Michael. (ed.). 1991. *Putting People First: Sociological Variables in Rural Development.* 2nd Edition. Washington, DC and Oxford: Oxford University Press for the World Bank.

Cernea, Michael. 1990. 'Internal Refugee Flows and Development-Induced Population Displacement'. *Journal of Refugee Studies* 34:320-349.

Cernea, Michael. 1988. *Involuntary Resettlement in Development Projects: Policy Guidelines in World Bank Assisted Projects.* Washington, DC: World Bank Technical Paper No.80.

Cernea, Michael. 1985. 'Involuntary Resettlement: Social Research, Policy and Planning', in M. Cernea (ed.) *Putting People First. Sociological Variables in Rural Development.* New York: Oxford University Press.

Cernea, Michael and Scott Guggenheim. 1993. 'Anthropological Approaches to Involuntary Displacement and Resettlement', in M. Cernea and S. Guggenheim (eds), *Anthropological Approaches to Resettlement: Policy, Practice, and Theory.* Boulder, CO: Westview Press.

Cernea, Michael and Christopher McDowell (eds). 2000. *Risks and Reconstruction, Experiences of Resettlers and Refugees.* Washington, DC: World Bank.

Chambers, Robert. 1995. 'Poverty and Livelihoods: Whose Reality Counts?', *Environment and Urbanisation,* 7:1.

Chambers, Robert. 1993. *Challenging the Professions: Frontiers for Rural Development.* London: Intermediate Technology Publications.

Chambers, Robert. 1986. 'Hidden losers? The impact of Rural Refugees and Refugee Programs on Poorer Hosts', *International Migration Review* 20 (2): 245-63.

Chambers, Robert. 1983. *Rural Development: Putting the Last First.* Burnt Mills: Longman.

Chambers, Robert. 1982. 'Rural Refugees in Africa: Past Experience, Future Pointers', *Disasters* 6:21-30.

Chambers, Robert. 1970. *The Volta Resettlement Experience.* London: Pall Mall Press.

Chambers, Robert. 1969. *Settlement Schemes in Tropical Africa. A Study of Organizations and Development.* New York: Preager.

Chambers, Robert *et al.* 1987. 'Trees as Saving and Security for the Rural Poor', *World Development,* 17 (3).

Chatty, D. and M. Colchester (eds). 2002. *Conservation and Mobile Indigenous Peoples: Displacement, Forced Settlement and Sustainable Development.* Oxford and New York: Berghahn Books.

Chimni, B. 2000. *International Refugee Law: A Reader.* New Delhi/Thousand Oaks/London: Sage Publications.

Christian Relief and Development Association. 1997. 'NGOs Position Paper on Urban Development'. Draft document. Addis Ababa.

Cilliers, Jakkie. 1995. *Demobilization and Reintegration of Former Combatants in Africa.* Pretoria: the Institute for Defense Policy.

Clark, J. 1991. *Democratising Development: The Role of Voluntary Organisations.* London: Earthscan Publications.

Clarke, John. 1986. *Resettlement and Rehabilitation: Ethiopia's Campaign Against Famine.* London: Harney and Jones.

Clay, Jason and Bonnie Holcomb. 1986. *Politics and the Ethiopian Famine 1984-1985.* Cambridge: Cultural Survival.

Clay, Jason, Bonnie Holcomb and Peter Niggli. 1988. *The Spoils of Famine: Ethiopian Famine Policy and Peasant Agriculture,* Cambridge, MA: Cultural Survival Inc.

Cliffe, Lionel. 2004. 'International and Ethiopian Resettlement Experiences: Lessons fro Planning in Oromia Region', in Pankhurst and Piguet (eds).

Cliffe, Lionel, Philip White, Andualem Taye, Meseret Wondimu and Siraj Kedir. 2002. *Feasibility Study for Voluntary Resettlement Programme: Final Report,* 2 vols, commissioned by UK Department for International Development, University of Leeds. 27 October.

Cohen, R. 2000. 'The Development of International Standards to Protect Internally Displaced Persons', in Bayefski and Fitzpatrick (eds).

Cohen, R. (ed.). 1996. *Protecting the Internally Displaced. World Refugee Survey 1996*. Washington, DC: US Committee for Refugees.

Cohen, R. and F. Deng. 1998. *Masses in Flight: The Global Crisis of Internal Displacement*. Washington, DC: Brookings Institution Press.

Colchester, M. and Virginia Luling. 1987. *Ethiopia's Bitter Medicine: Settling for Disaster. An Evaluation of the Ethiopian Government's Resettlement Programme*. London: Survival International.

Colletta, N. *et al.* 1996. *The Transition from War to Peace in Sub-Saharan Africa*. Washington, DC: World Bank.

Collier, P. 2000. 'Consensus Building, Knowledge, and Conditionality'. In *Annual World Bank Conference on Development Economics*. Washington, DC: World Bank.

Colson, Elizabeth. 1991. 'Coping in Adversity'. Paper presented at the Gwendolen Carter Lectures, Conference on Involuntary Migration and Resettlement in Africa, University of Florida, Gainesville, 21-23 March.

Colson, Elizabeth. 1971. *The Social Consequence of Resettlement. The Impact of Kariba Resettlement Upon the Gwembe Tonga*. Manchester: Manchester University Press.

Commission for the Rehabilitation of Members of the Former Army and Disabled War Veterans (CRMFADWV). 1994. 'Demobilization and Socio-Economic Reintegration of Ex-combatants'. Paper presented at Workshop on Post-conflict Demobilization in Africa'. Kampala, 9-11 November.

Coppock, L. 1994. *The Borana Plateau of Southern Ethiopia: Synthesis of Pastoral Research, Development and Change, 1980-91*. Addis Ababa: International Livestock Center for Africa (ILCA).

Cossins, Noel. 1972. *No Way to Live: A Study of the Afar Clans of the Northeast Rangelands*. Addis Ababa: Livestock and Meat Board.

Crisp, Jeff 2001. 'Closing Remarks'. Biennial Meeting of the International Association for the Study of Forced Migration, Johannesburg.

Crisp, Jeff. 2000. 'Managing Forced Migration: Evolving International Responses to the Refugee Problem'. Paper presented at conference on International Migration and Foreign Policy, Wilton Park, UK.

Damen Hailemariam and Helmut Kloos. 1993. 'Population', in Kloos and Zein (eds).

Daniel Gamechu. 1988. 'Some Aspect of Environment and Crop Macro-Climate in Southwest Ethiopia', in *Proceedings of Workshop on 'Famine Experience and Resettlement in Ethiopia'*. Addis Ababa: Institute of Development Research, Addis Ababa University.

Daniel, V.E. and J.C. Knudsen (eds). 1995. *Mistrusting Refugees*. Berkeley and Los Angeles: University of California Press.

Dawit Wolde-Ghiorgis. 1989. *Red Tears: War, Famine and Revolution in Ethiopia*. Trenton, NJ: Red Sea Press.

De Castro Illera, M. and D. Egre. 2000. 'Successful Involuntary Resettlement: Lessons From Te Urra 1 Project in Colombia', *Hydropower and Dams*, Issue Two: 40-44.

De Waal, Alex. 1991. *Evil Days: Thirty Years of War and Famine in Ethiopia*. New York: Human Rights Watch.

De Wet, Chris. (ed.). 2005. *Development-Induced Displacement: Problems, Policies and People*. New York and Oxford : Berghahn.

De Wet, Chris. 2004. 'Why Do Things So Often Go Wrong in Resettlement Projects?', in Pankhurst and Piguet (eds).

De Wet, Chris. 2001. 'Can Everybody Win? Economic Development and Population Displacement'. *Economic and Political Weekly* (Mumbai) 3650: 4637-4646.

De Wet, Chris. 1998. 'Reconstructing Resettlement: Some Research Suggestions for Developing and Combining Scudder's and Cernea's Approaches to Resettlement', in Cernea and McDowell. (eds).

De Wet, Chris. 1995. *Moving Together, Drifting Apart – Resettlement Planning and Villagisation in a South African Homeland*. Johannesburg: Witwatersrand University Press.

De Wet, Chris. 1993. 'A Spatial Analysis of Involuntary Community Relocation: A South African Case Study', in M. Cernea and S. Guggenheim (eds), *Anthropological Approaches to Resettlement: Policy, Practice, and Theory*. Boulde, COr: Westview Press.

Dechassa Lemessa. 2003a. 'Situation Update SNNPR No 1. 9-15 June'. Addis Ababa: report written for the UN-EUE.

Dechassa Lemessa. 2003b. 'Situation Update SNNPR No. 2 Soddo Walayta Zone'. 26 June. Addis Ababa: report written for the UN-EUE.

Dejene Teshome. 2005. 'The Socio-Economic and Cultural Effects of Urban Development in Addis Ababa: A Case Study of the Belt Highway Project'. MA thesis in Social Anthropology. Addis Ababa University.

Demie Abera. 2007. 'Impacts of Water Reservoir Construction Induced Displacement: A Case Study of Dire Dam', MA thesis in Social Anthropology, Addis Ababa University.

Deng, Francis. 1995. 'Sovereignty, Responsibility and Accountability: A Framework of Protection, Assistance and Development for the Internally Displaced'. Concept Paper for the Brookings Institution/ Refugee Policy Group Project on Internal Displacement, Washington, DC: The Brookings Institution/Refugee Policy Group.

Dercon, Stefan and Daniel Ayalew. 1998. 'Where Have all the Soldiers Gone?: Demobilization and Reintegration in Ethiopia', *World Development* 26 (9):1661-1675.

Dereje Feyissa. 2006a. 'Ethnic Federalism and Conflicting Political Projects: The Case of Anywaa-Nuer Relations in the Gambela Regional State', in S. Uhlig (ed.), *Proceedings of the XVth International Conference of Ethiopian Studies, Hamburg 2003*. Wiesbaden : Harrassowitz Verlag.

Dereje Feyissa. 2006b. 'The Experience of Gambela Regional State', in D. Turton (ed.), *Ethnic Federalism: The Ethiopain Experience in Comparative Perspective.* Oxford: James Currey.

Dereje, Feyissa. 2003. 'Ethnic Groups and Conflict: the Case of Anywaa-Nuer Relations in the Gambella Region'. PhD thesis. Martin Luther University. Halle-Wittenberg.

Dessalegn Rahmato. 2007. *Development Interventions in Wollaita, 1960s-2000s: A Critical Review.* Monograph No. 4. Addis Ababa: Forum for Social Studies.

Dessalegn Rahmato. 2003. *Resettlement in Ethiopia. The Tragedy of Population Relocation in the 1980s.* Discussion Paper No. 11. Addis Ababa: Forum for Social Studies.

Dessalegn Rahmato. 1994. 'Land Tenure and Land Policy in Ethiopia After the Derg', in H. Marcus (ed.), *New Trends in Ethiopian Studies: Papers of the 12th International Conference of Ethiopian Studies.* Vol. II. Trenton, NJ: Red Sea Press.

Dessalegn Rahmato. 1989. 'Rural Resettlement in Post-Revolution Ethiopia: Problems and Prospects.' Paper presented at National Conference on Population Issues in Ethiopia's National Development. Addis Ababa: Office for the National Committee for Central Planning, Population and Development Planning Division.

Dessalegn Rahmato. 1988a. 'Resettlement and the Indigenous People: the Case of Metekel', in *Proceedings of the Workshop on Famine Experience and Resettlement in Ethiopia*. Addis Ababa: Institute of Development Research, Addis Ababa University.

Dessalegn Rahmato. 1988b. 'Settlement and Resettlement in Metekkel, Western Ethiopia', *Africa* (Rome) 63: 14-43.

Dessalegn, Rahmato. 1988c. 'Some Notes on Settlement and Resettlement in Metekel Awraja Gojjam Province', in A. Gromyko (ed.), *Proceedings of the Ninth International Congress of Ethiopian Studies*, Moscow: Nauka Publishers.

Devereux, Stephen. 1996. *Fuzzy Entitlements and Common Property Resources: Struggle over Rights to Communal Land in Botswana*, Working Paper No.44. Brighton: Institute of Development Studies at the University of Sussex.

Devereux, Stephen. 1993. *Theories of Famine.* New York and London: Harvester Wheatsheaf.

DHV Consultants BV. 1994. 'Technical Assistance to the National Parks Rehabilitation in Southern Ethiopia: Technical Proposal'. Addis Ababa: Ministry of Natural Resources and Development and Environmental Protection (Amersfoort/NE).

Diaw, K. and E. Schmidt-Kallert 1990. *Effects of Volta Lake Resettlement in Ghana – A Reappraisal after 25 Years.* Hamburg: Institut für Afrika-Kunde.

Dieci, Paolo and Claudio Viezzoli (eds). 1992. *Resettlement and Rural Development in Ethiopia: Social and Economic Research, Training and Technical Assistance in the Beles Valley*. Milan: Franco Angeli.

Dieci, Paolo and Vittorio Roscio. 1992. 'The Need for a Grass-Root Approach: The CISP Development Project in the Beles Area', in Dieci and Viezzoli (eds).

Dieci, Paolo and Wolde-Selassie Abbute. 1992. 'The Planning of Home Gardening Activities in the Beles Valley Resettlement Villages', in Dieci and Viezzoli (eds).

Dietz, Ton. 1996. *Entitlements to Natural Resources: Contours of Political Environmental Geography.* Utrecht: International Books.

Dietz, Ton. 1993. 'The State, the Market, and the Decline of Pastoralism: Challenging some

Myths, with Evidence from Western Pokot in Kenya/Uganda', in J. Markakis (ed.), *Conflict and the Decline of Pastoralism in the Horn of Africa*. Basingstoke: Macmillan and The Hague: Institute of Social Studies.

Dietz, Ton and M. Mohamed Salih. 1997. *Pastoral Development in Eastern Africa: Policy Review, Options and Alternatives*. Amsterdam and The Hague: Report for I/C Consult, Zeist (for Bilance).

Dinku Lamessa. 2004. 'Socio-Cultural Dimensions of Conflict-Induced Displacement: The Case of Displaced Persons in Addis Ababa', in Pankhurst and Piguet (eds).

Dinku Lamessa. 2003. 'Socio-Economic Dimensions of Conflict-Induced Displacement: The Case of Displaced Persons in Addis Ababa.' MA thesis in Social Anthropology, Addis Ababa University.

Donham, Don. 1986. 'Old Abyssinia and the New Ethiopian Empire: Themes in Social History', in D. Donham and W. James (eds) *The Southern Marches of Imperial Ethiopia: Essays in History and Social Anthropology*. Cambridge: Cambridge University Press.

Doornbos, Martin. 1993, 'Pasture and Polis: The Roots of Political Marginalization of Somali Pastoralism', in J. Markakis (ed.), *Conflict and the Decline of Pastoralism in the Horn of Africa*. Basingstoke: Macmillan; The Hague: Institute of Social Studies.

Downing, Theodore. 1996. 'Mitigating Social Impoverishment When People Are Involuntarily Displaced', in McDowell (ed.).

Driba Dadi. 2005. 'Resettlement in Oromia Region: The Case of Shanaka Resettlement in Agarfa District, Bale Zone'. MA thesis in Geography, Addis Ababa University.

Duffield, M. 1995. 'The Political Economy of Internal War; Asset Transfer, Complex Emergencies, and International Aid', in A. Zwi and J. Macrae (eds) *War and Hunger. Rethinking international responses to complex emergencies*. London: Zed Books/Save the Children.

Dwivedi, R. 2002. 'Models and Methods in Development-Induced Displacement: Review Article', *Development and Change* 334: 709-732.

Dwivedi, R. 1999. 'Displacement, Risks and Resistance: Local Perceptions and Actions in the Sardar Sarovar', *Development and Change* 30: 43-78.

Ege, Svein. 1997. *The Promised Land: The Amhara Land Redistribution of 1997*. Trondheim, Center for Environment and Development: Working Papers on Ethiopian Development No. 12.

Endale, Yonas. 1996. 'Ethiopia's Mental Health Trampled by Armed Conflict', in Allen (ed.).

Ente Nazionale Electrica (ENEL). 1982. '*Gilgel Gibe* Hydroelectric Scheme Feasibility Study.' Addis Ababa.

Engelmann, K. 1968. *Building Cooperative Movements in Developing Countries: The Sociological and Psychological Aspects*. New York: Frederick Praeger.

Environmental Protection Authority. 1997 *Environment Policy*. Addis Ababa.

Ephrem Tesema. 1998. 'Urban Adaptation and Survival Strategies: The Case of Displaced Groups in the Arada Area, Addis Ababa', MA thesis in social anthropology, Department of Sociology, Addis Ababa University.

Ephrem Amare. 1989. 'The History of Metahara Sugar Factory from its Foundation to 1974'. BA thesis, Department of History, Addis Ababa University.

Erlichman, Sarah. 2000. 'Ecohealth and Displacement: A Case Study of Resettlement and Return in Ethiopia'. MA thesis in Environmental Studies, York University, Ontario.

Eshetu Chole and Teshome Mulat. 1988. 'Land Settlement in Ethiopia: A Review of Developments', in A. Oberai (ed.), *Land Settlement Policies and Population Redistribution in Developing Countries*. New York: Praeger.

Ethiopian Investment Authority. 1992. *A Proclamation to Provide for Agricultural Investment*. Addis Ababa.

Ethiopian Herald, Ethiopian News Agency. 2003. 'President Stresses Need to Seek Lasting Solution to Drought,' July 4.

European Commission (EC) Delegation. 1996. *Rehabilitation of the National Parks in Southern Ethiopia Project. 1996*. Addis Ababa.

European Union. 'EC-FSPCO Mission to Metema Woreda, 11-16/3/01'. Addis Ababa.

Ethiopian Valleys Development Studies Authority (EVDSA) 1993. *Omo-Gibe River Basin Development Master Plan Study Reconnaissance Phase Report*. Vol. III. Addis Ababa.

Fahim, H. 1981. *Dams, People and Development: The Aswan High Dam Case*. New York: Pergamon Press.

Fahim, H. 1973. 'Nubian Resettlement in The Sudan', *Ekistics* 212: 42-49.

Falge, Christiane. 1997. 'The Nuer as Refugees: A Study on Social Adaptation.' MA thesis in Social Anthropology, Department of Sociology, Addis Ababa University.

Fauvelle-Aymar, François-Xavier *et al.* 2006. 'Reconnaissance de trois villes musulmanes de l'époque médiévale dans l'Ifat', *Annales d'Ethiopie* 24:135 -175.

Fecadu Gedamu. 1990. 'Pastoral Nomadism and Rural Development', in S. Pausewang *et al.* (eds), *Ethiopia: Options for Rural Development.* London: Zed Books.

Federal Democratic Republic of Ethiopia (FDRE). 2005. 'Proclamation for the Expropriation of Land Holdings for Public Purpose and Payment of Compensation.' *Negarit Gazeta.* July. Addis Ababa.

FDRE 2003. *Resettlement Programme Implementation Manual.* Addis Ababa: Ministry of Rural Development, March.

FDRE. 2002a. *National Food Security Strategy.* Addis Ababa: MoFED.

FDRE. 2002b. *Ethiopia: Sustainable Development and Poverty Reduction Program.* Addis Ababa: Ministry of Finance and Economic Development, July.

FDRE. 2001. 'Ethiopia Development Framework and Plan of Action, 2001-2010.' Addis Ababa: Ministry of Economic Development and Cooperation.

FDRE. 1998. 'A Proclamation to Provide for the Establishment of Cooperative Societies.' *Negarit Gazeta* No. 27 of 1998. Addis Ababa.

FDRE. 1997. *Environmental Policy.* Addis Ababa: Environmental Protection Authority in collaboration with the Ministry of Economic Development and Cooperation. 2 April.

FDRE. 1995. 'Proclamation of the Constitution of the Federal Democratic Republic of Ethiopia'. *Federal Negarit Gazeta*, 1st Year. No 1. Addis Ababa, August.

Feleke Tadele. 2006. *The Impacts of Urban 'Development' on a Peasant Community in Ethiopia.* Social Anthropology Dissertation Series No. 9. Addis Ababa: Department of Sociology and Social Anthropology, Addis Ababa University.

Feleke Tadele. 2004. 'The New Resettlement Programme in Ethiopia: Reflections on the Design and Implementation Approach', in Pankhurst and Piguet (eds).

Feleke Tadele. 2003. 'The Current Resettlement in Ethiopia: A Review of the Design and Implementation Approach.' *Forum for Social Studies Bulletin* 1 (3): 8-12.

Fernandes, W. 2000. 'From Marginalisation to Sharing the Project Benefits', in Cernea and McDowell (eds).

Fernandes, W. 1996. 'Keynote Address: Resettlement Studies and Specific Issues: Sharing in the Benefits of Development', in *Proceedings of Conference on Constructing Livelihoods: Towards New Approaches to Resettlement.* Oxford: Refugees Studies Programme, University of Oxford.

Fernea, R. 1998. 'Including Minorities in Development: The Nubian Case'. Washington, DC: World Bank.

Fernea, E. and R. Fernea. 1991. *Nubian Ethnographies.* Prospect Heights, IL: Waveland Press.

Fernea, R. and J. Kennedy 1966. 'Initial Adaptation to Resettlement: A New Life for Egyptian Nubians', *Current Anthropology* 7: 349-54.

Ferradas, C. 1997. 'From Vegetable Gardens to Flower Gardens: The Symbolic Construction of Social Mobility in a Development Project', *Human Organization* 56 (4): 450-61.

Feseha Tassew. 2006. 'Predicaments, Inducements and Deception in Resettlement: The Case of Kambata Resettlers in Kafa of Southern Ethiopia'. MA thesis in social anthropology, Addis Ababa University.

Fitsum Resome. 2006. 'Development and Risks: Causes, Consequences and Challenges of Inner City Development-Induced Displacement: The Case of Kebele 14 of Arada Sub City in Addis Ababa Metropolitan Area'. MA thesis, Department of Sociology and Social Anthropology, Addis Ababa University.

Flood, Glynn. 1976. 'Nomadism and its Future: the Afar', in Abdul Mejid Hussein (ed.), *Rehab: Drought and Famine in Ethiopia.* London: International African Institute.

Food and Agriculture Organization. 1984. *Ethiopian Highland Reclamation Study.* Addis Ababa: EHRS.

Forsbrooke, H. 1962. 'Foreword', in T. Scudder, *The Ecology of the Gwembe Tonga.* Manchester: Manchester University Press.

Forum for Social Studies (FSS). 2006. 'Understanding the Dynamics of Resettlement in Ethiopia'. *Policy Briefings* No. 4. Addis Ababa: Forum for Social Studies, January.

Fosse, Tonne. 2006. 'Migration and Livelihoods: The Voluntary Resettlement Program in Ethiopia'. MA thesis, Norwegian University of Life Sciences, Department of International Environment and Development Studies.

Fratkin, Eliott. 1991. *Surviving Drought and Development: Ariaal Pastoralists of Northern Kenya*. Boulder, CO: Westview Press.

Freeman, Dena and Elizabeth Watson 1999. 'Regional Variation in the Cultural Systems of Southern Ethiopia'. Workshop report, Oxford.

Gaim Kibreab. 2000. 'Common Property Resources and Resettlement', in Cernea and McDowell (eds).

Gaim Kibreab. 1985. *African Refugees: Reflections on the African Refugee Problem*. Trenton, NJ: Africa World Press.

Galaty, John. 1994. 'Rangeland Tenure and Pastoralism in Africa', in E. Fratkin *et al.* (eds), *African Pastoralist Systems: An Integrated Approach*. Boulder, CO: Lynne Rienner.

Galaty, John, David Aaronson, Paul Salzman, and A. Chouinard. 1986. *The Future of Pastoralists Peoples*. Ottawa: IDR.

Gamaledin Maknun. 1993. 'The Decline of Afar Pastoralism', in J. Markakis (ed.), *Conflicts and the Decline of Pastoralism in the Horn of Africa*. Basingstoke: Macmillan; The Hague: Institute of Social Studies.

Gamaledin Maknun. 1987. 'State Policy and Famine in the Awash Valley of Ethiopia,' in D. Anderson and R. Grove (eds), *Conservation in Africa: People, Policies and Practice*. Cambridge: Cambridge University Press.

Gavian, Sarah and Daniel Gemechu. 1994. 'Commercial Investors and Access to Land', in Dessalegn Rahmato (ed.), *Land Tenure and Land Policy in Ethiopia After the Derg*. Proceedings of Second Workshop of the Land Tenure Project. Working Papers in Ethiopian Development No 8. Trondheim: University of Trondheim Press.

Gebre Yntiso. 2005. 'Promises and Predicaments of Resettlement in Ethiopia', in Ohta Itaru and Gebre Yntiso (eds).

Gebre Yntiso. 2004. 'The Metekel Resettlement in Ethiopia: Why did it Fail?', in Pankhurst and Piguet (eds).

Gebre Yntiso. 2003. 'Resettlement and the Unnoticed Losers: Impoverishment Disasters among the Gumuz Hosts in Ethiopia', *Human Organization* 62 (1):50-61.

Gebre Yntiso. 2002a. 'Contextual Determination of Migration Behaviours: The Ethiopian Resettlement in the Light of Conceptual Constructs', *Journal of Refugee Studies* 15-3: 265-282.

Gebre Yntiso. 2002b. 'Differential Reestablishment of Voluntary and Involuntary Migrants: The Case of Metekel Settlers in Ethiopia', *African Studies Monographs*, 231: 31-46.

Gebre Yntiso. 2001. 'Population Displacement and Food Insecurity in Ethiopia: Resettlement, Settlers, and Hosts'. Ph.D. Dissertation, Department of Anthropology. University of Florida.

Getachew Kassa 2004. 'Settlement Among the Afar Pastoralists of the Awash Valley', in Pankhurst and Piguet (eds).

Getachew Kassa. 2003. 'Crisis, Change and Continuity in some Strategies used by Pastoralists and Agro-pastoralist Groups to Cope with Scarcity, Competition, Conflicts and Other Types of Stresses: Notes from Afar, Issa, Kereyu, Borana, Garri, Degodia and Garrimarro in Northeastern and Southern Ethiopia', in *Proceedings of the 14th International Conference of Ethiopian Studies*. Addis Ababa: Institute of Ethiopian Studies, Addis Ababa University Press.

Getachew Kassa. 2001. *Among the Pastoral Afar in Ethiopia: Tradition, Continuity and Socio-economic Change*. Utrecht: International Books.

Getachew Kassa. 2000. 'An Overview of Government Policy Interventions in Pastoral Areas: Achievements, Constraints and Propsects', in *Proceedings of the National Conference on Pastoral Development in Ethiopia*. Organised by Pastoral Forum Ethiopia. Addis Ababa: Image Enterprise Co.

Getachew Kassa. 1997a. 'Pastoralists in Town: A Case Study of the Afar in the Middle Awash, North East Ethiopia', in K. Fukui, E. Kurimoto and M. Shigeta (eds) *Ethiopia in Broader Perspective. Papers of the 13th International Conference of Ethiopian Studies*. Vol. II. Kyoto: Shokado Books.

Getachew Kassa. 1997b. 'A Note on the Finna (Fimaa) Institution among the Pastoral Afar of the Middle Awash Valley, North Eastern Ethiopia.' *Jouranl of Ethiopian Studies*, XXX (2): 1-26.

Getachew Kassa. 1996a. 'Afar Pastoralism and Society: A Case Study of the Resource Conflicts

Among the Afar, Middle Awash Valley, in North East Ethiopia.' Paper presented at Workshop, 'Resource Conflicts in the Horn of Africa', organized by the Organization for Social Science Research in Eastern Africa, Addis Ababa.

Getachew Kassa. 1996b. 'A Note on the Institution of Fimaa Among the Pastoral Afar of the Middle Awash Valley, North eastern Ethiopia.' Addis Ababa: Institute of Ethiopian Studies (IES), Addis Ababa University.

Getachew Kassa. 1996c. 'The Displacement and Return of Pastoralists in Southern Ethiopia', in Allen (ed.).

Getu Ambaye. 2005. 'Displacement-Induced Resettlement in Jawi, Beles Valley Area of North Western Ethiopia'. MA thesis, Department of Sociology and Social Anthropology, Addis Ababa University.

Giel, R. 1967. 'The Epileptic Outcast', *East African Medical Journal* 45: 27-31.

Giel, R., Y. Gezahegen, and J. van Luuk. 1968. 'Faith-Healing and Spirit-Possession in Ghion, Ethiopia', *Social Science and Medicine.* 2:63-79.

Gilgel Gibe Resettlement Office (GRRO) 2002. 'Post-Resettlement Follow Up Program, Environmental Protection and Use.' Workshop Report, Jimma.

Global IDP Survey/Norwegian Refugee Council. 2002. *Internally Displaced People: A Global Survey:* 2nd Edition. London: Earthscan.

Green, R. 1997. 'Food Security in Refuge and Return: Some Aspects, Entitlements, Markets, and Modalities', in C. McDowell and A. de Haan (eds), *Migration and Sustainable Livelihoods.* IDS Working Paper 65. Brighton: Institute of Development Studies at the University of Sussex.

Grimm, C. 1991. 'Turmoil and Transformation: A Study of Population Relocation at Manantali, Mali'. PhD thesis. Binghamton, NY: State University of New York.

GTZ (Gesellschaft für Technische Zusammenarbeit). 1998. 'Settlement of Demobilized Fighters in Dansha Settlement, Ethiopia'. Report on Project Progress. Eschborn: GTZ.

GTZ. 1996. 'Concepts and Experiences of Demobilization and Reintegration of Ex-Combatants'. A Discussion Paper. Addis Ababa.

GTZ. 1996. 'Experiences with Demobilization and Reintegration of Ex-combatants'. Workshop Report. Addis Ababa.

Guggenheim, Scott. 1994. *Involuntary Resettlement: An Annotated Reference Bibliography for Development Research.* Environmental Working Paper No. 64. Washington, DC: World Bank.

Hacker, Sally. 1989. *Pleasure, Power and Technology: Some Tales of Gender, Engineering, and the Cooperative Workplace.* Boston, MA: Unwin Hyman.

Hadgu Bariagaber. 1995. 'Poverty Assessment in Ethiopia with Reference to Addis Ababa and Institutional Efforts and Coordination for Poverty Alleviation in the City'. Paper presented at Workshop on Urban Poverty in Southern and Eastern Africa, 14-16 March, Nairobi.

Hailemarian Assefa and H. Kloos. 1993. 'Population', in Kloos and Zein (eds).

Hammond, Laura. 2004. 'The Making of a Good Citizen in an Ethiopian Returnee Settlement', in Long and Oxfeld (eds).

Hammond, Laura. 2004. *This Place will become Home: Refugee repatriation to Ethiopia.* Ithaca, NY and London: Cornell University Press.

Hammond, Laura. 2000. 'This Place Will Become Home: Emplacement and Community Formation in a Tigrayan Returnee Settlement, Northwest Ethiopia', PhD. thesis, University of Wisconsin-Madison.

Hammond, Laura. 1999. 'Examining the Discourse of Repatriation: Toward a More Pro-active Theory of Return Migration', in R. Black and K. Koser (eds), *The End of the Refugee Cycle?* Oxford: Berghahn.

Hammond, Laura and Bezaeit Dessalegn. 2004. 'Evaluation of the 2003 pilot resettlement '*safara*' programme', in Pankhurst and Piguet (eds).

Hammond Laura, A. Pankhurst and Bezaeit Dessalegn. 2004. 'Framework for Monitoring and Evaluation of the GFDRE's Voluntary Resettlement Program'. Report submitted to the Multi-Agency Task Force on Resettlement, March.

Hammond, Laura and Bezaeit Dessalegn. 2003. '*Safara:* preliminary assessment of the pilot voluntary resettlement in Ethiopia'. Clark University, commissioned by USAID.

Hampton, J. 1988. *Internally Displaced People: A Global Survey.* Norwegian Refugee Council and Global IDP Survey. London: Earthscan Publications.

Hansen, Art and Anthony Oliver-Smith. 1982. 'Involuntary Migration and Resettlement:

Causes and Contexts', in A. Hansen and A. Oliver-Smith (eds) *Involuntary Migration and Resettlement: The Problems and Responses of Displaced Peoples*. Boulder, CO: Westview Press.

Harbeson, John. 1978. 'Territorial and Development Politics in the Horn of Africa. The Afar of the Awash Valley', *African Affairs* 77: 479-98.

Harbeson, John and Teffera-Worq Beshah. 1974. 'Ethiopian Nomads in Transition: Political and Economic Development in the Awash Valley.' Addis Ababa: Institute of Development Research.

Harrell-Bond, Barbara. 1986. *Imposing Aid: Emergency Relief to Refugees*. Oxford: OUP.

Hathaway, J. 1991. *The Law of Refugee Status*. Toronto: Butterworth.

Helland, Johan. 1997. 'Development Interventions and Pastoral Dynamics in Southern Ethiopia', in Hogg (ed.).

Helland, Johan. 1996. 'The Political Viability of Borana Pastoralism: a Discussion of Some Features of the Political System of the Borana Pastoralists of Southern Ethiopia', in P. Baxter *et al.* (eds), *Being and Becoming Oromo: Historical and Anthropological Enquiries*. Lawrenceville, NJ: Red Sea Press for Nordiska Afrikainstitutet, Sweden.

Helland, Johan. 1980. 'An Analysis of Afar Pastoralism in North-Eastern Rangelands of Ethiopia', in Helland.

Helland, Johan. 1980. *Five Essays on the Study of Pastoralists and the Development of Pastoralism*. Bergen: African Savannah Studies. University of Bergen.

Hobbs, R. and L. Huenneke. 1992. 'Disturbance, Diversity and Invasion: Implications for Conservation', *Conservation Biology* 6: 3240.

Hoben, Allan. 1966. *Land Tenure among the Amhara of Ethiopia: The Dynamics of Cognetic Descent*. Chicago, IL: University of Chicago Press.

Hodes, Richard and M. Azbire. 1993. 'Tuberculosis', in Kloos and Zein (eds).

Hogg, Richard (ed.). 1997a. *Pastoralists, Ethnicity and the State in Ethiopia*. London: Haan Publishing.

Hogg, Richard. 1997b. ' Changing Land Use and Resource Conflict Among Somali Pastoralists in the Haud of South-east Ethiopia', in Hogg (ed.).

Hogg, Richard. 1996. 'Changing Mandates in the Ethiopian Ogaden', in Allen (ed.).

Hogg, Richard. 1989. 'Settlement, Pastoralists and the Commons: the Ideology and Practice of Irrigation Development in Northern Kenya', in D. Anderson and R. Grove (eds), *Conservation in Africa: Peoples, Policies and Practice*. Cambridge: Cambridge University Press.

Homewood, K. and W. Rodgers. 1986. 'Pastoralism, Conservation and the Overgrazing Controversy', in D. Anderson and R. Grove (eds), *Conservation in Africa: Peoples, Policies and Practice*. Cambridge: Cambridge University Press.

Hyden, Goran. 1980. *Beyond Ujamaa in Tanzania*. London: Heinemann.

Hyden, Goran. 1973. *Efficiency versus Distribution in East African Cooperatives: A Case Study in Organizational Conflicts*. Nairobi: East Africa Literature Bureau.

IDS. 1997. *Sustainable Livelihoods Research Program*. IDS Working Paper No. 5. Brighton: Institute of Development Studies at the University of Susses, UK.

Imperial Government of Ethiopia (IGE). 1962. *Charters of the Awash Valley Authority*. General Notice No 299.

Imperial Government of Ethiopia. 1954. 'Charter of the Municipality of Addis Ababa', *Negarit Gazetta*. No 10. Addis Ababa.

Imperial Government of Ethiopia.1945. 'A Proclamation to Provide for the Control of Municipalities and Township', *Negarit Gazetta* No. 7. Addis Ababa.

Imperial Government of Ethiopia. 1942. 'Administration Regulations'. Decree No. 1, *Negarit Gazetta*. No 6. Addis Ababa.

Integrated Regional Information Network (IRIN). 2003. 'Ethiopia: Pitfalls of Resettlement,' *The Addis Tribune*. May 16.

Interafrica Group. 1994. *Demobilization and Reintegration Issues in the Horn of Africa*. Issue Note 2. Addis Ababa: IAG.

Inter-Governmental Authority on Development (IGAD). 2004. 'Eritrea establishes its CEWERU'. *IGAD News*, issue 11. January-February.

IGAD. 2003a. 'Resolving Pastoral Conflicts', *IGAD News*, issue 6. March-April.

IGAD 2003b. 'Develop Policies on Internal Displaced Persons' *IGAD News*, issue 8. July-September.

International Labour Organization (ILO). 1995. *Reintegrating Demobilized Combatants: Experiences from Four African Countries*. Paper prepared for the Expert Meeting on the Design of Guidelines for Training and Employment, Harare, 11-14 July.

International Resource Group on Disarmament and Security in the Horn of Africa and Bonn International Centre for Conversion. 1995. *Report of the Seminar on Donor Response to Demobilization and Reintegration in the Horn of Africa*. Bonn.

Jacobs, Michael and Catherine Schloeder. 1993. *The Awash National Park Management Plan, 1993-1997*. Addis Ababa: The Wildlife Conservation Society International and the Ethiopian Wildlife Conservation Organization.

Jacobsson, L. and R. Giel (eds). 1999. 'Mental Health in Ethiopia.' *Acta Psychiatrica Scandinavia: Supplementum* 397: 100.

James, Wendy. 1996. 'Uduk Resettlement: Dreams and Realities', in Allen (ed.).

James, Wendy. 1986. 'Lifelines: Exchange marriage among the Gumuz', in D. Donham and W. James (eds), *The Southern Marches of Imperial Ethiopia: Essays in History and Social Anthropology*. Cambridge: Cambridge University Press.

Jansson, Kurt. 1990. *The Ethiopian Famine*. Revised and updated edition. London: Zed Books.

Jimma Zone Health Department (ZHD) and Jimma Zone Agricultural Department (JZAD). 2000. 'Gilgel-Gibe Resettlement Assessment of Existing Problems with Suggested Solution.' Jimma.

Kahana, Y. 1985. 'The Zar Spirits, A Category of Magic in the System of Mental Health Care in Ethiopia', *International Journal of Social Psychiatry*, 31: 125-43.

Kassahun Berhanu. 2004. 'The Experience of Returnees' Resettlement in Humera', in Pankhurst and Piguet (eds).

Kassahun Berhanu. 2000. *Returnees, Resettlement and Power Relations: the Making of a Political Constituency in Humera, Ethiopia*. Amsterdam: Free University Press.

Kassahun Kebede. 2001. 'Re-relocation and Dislocation of Communities by Dam Development: the Case of Gilgel Gibe Dam in Southwest Ethiopia'. MA thesis in Social Anthropology, Addis Ababa University.

Kebebew Daka. 1978. *The Cooperative Movement in Ethiopia*. Addis Ababa: Addis Ababa University Press.

Kelieber, R. and D. Brom. 1992. *Coping with Trauma: Theory, Prevention and Treatment*. Amsterdam: Sweta and Zeillinger B.V.

Kelemework Tafere. 2008. 'Social and Economic Impacts of Voluntary Resettlement Programmes in Kafta Humera and Metema *Woredas* of Tigray and Amhara Regional States, Ethiopia'. Report for the Dryland Coordination Group, Mekele.

Keller, E. 1993. 'Government Politics', in T. Ofcansky and B. Laverle (eds), *Ethiopia: A Country Study*/Federal Research Division. Library of Congress. Washington, DC: US Government Printing Office.

Kilowoko, John. 2004. 'Refugees, Repatriation, Resettlement, and Protracted Case-Loads', in Pankhurst and Piguet (eds).

Kingma, Kees. 2000. *Demobilization in Sub-Saharan Africa: The Development and Security Impacts*. Bonn: Bonn International Center for Conversion.

Kingma, Kees and Kiflemariam Gebrewold. 1995. *Demilitarization, Reintegration, and Conflict Prevention in the Horn of Africa*. London: Saferrwoeld and Bonn: Bonn International Center for Conversion.

Kingma, Kees and Vanessa Sayers. 1995. 'Demobilization in the Horn of Africa', in *Proceedings of the IRG (International Resource Group on Disarmament and Security in the Horn of Africa) Workshop, Addis Ababa, 4-7 December 1994*. Brief 4. Bonn: Bonn International Center for Conversion.

Kirsch, O., F. Göricke and J. Wörz. 1989. *Agricultural Revolution and Peasant Emancipation in Ethiopia*. Fort Lauderdale, FL: Verlag Breitenbach Publishers.

Kleinman, A. 1988. *Rethinking Psychiatry*. New York: The Free Press.

Klingebiel, S. *et al.* 1995. *Promoting the Reintegration of Former Female and Male Combatants in Eritrea: Possible Contributions of Development Cooperation to the Reintegration Program*. Berlin: German Cultural Institute.

Kloos, Helmut. 1990. 'Health Aspects of Resettlement in Ethiopia', *Social Science and Medicine*. 30: 643-56.

Kloos, Helmut. 1982. 'Development, Drought and Famine in the Awash Valley of Ethiopia',

African Studies Review, 25 (4): 21-48.

Kloos, Helmut and Ahmed Zein. (eds). 1993. *The Ecology of Health and Disease in Ethiopia*. Boulder, CO: Westview Press.

Kloos, Helmut and Aynalem Adugna. 1988. 'Settler Migration: Causes, Patterns of Movement and Some Demographic Impacts', in: *Proceedings of the Workshop on Famine Experience and Resettlement in Ethiopia. December 29-30*. Addis Ababa: Institute of Development Research, Addis Ababa University.

Knunda, L. 1995. *Women Enterepreneurship in Tanzania: Entry and Performance Barriers*. Dar es Salaam: University of Dar es Salaam.

Koenig, D. 2001. 'Toward Local Development and Mitigating Impoverishment in Development-Induced Displacement and Resettlement.' University of Oxford: Refugee Studies Centre.

Korn, D. 1999. *Exodus Within Borders: An Introduction to the Crisis of Internal Displacement*. Washington, DC: Brookings Institution Press.

Kortman, F. 1988. 'Problems in Practicing Psychiatry in Ethiopia', *Ethiopian Medical Journal*. 26:77-83.

Kortman, F. 1987. 'Popular, Traditional, and Professional Mental Health Care in Ethiopia'. *Transcultural Psychiatric Research Review*. 24: 255-274.

Kuhlman, T. 1994a. *Asylum or Aid? The Economic Integration of Ethiopian and Eritrean Refugees in the Sudan*. Leiden: African Studies Center.

Kuhlman, T. 1994b. 'Organized Versus Spontaneous Settlement', in Adelman and Sorenson (eds).

Kurimoto Eisei. 2005. 'Multidimensional Impact of Refugees and Settlers in Gambela Region, Western Ethiopia', in Ohta Itaru and Gebre Yntiso (eds).

Kurimoto, Eisei. 1997. 'Politicization of Ethnicity in Gambella Region', in K. Fukui, E. Kurimoto and M. Shigeta (eds) *Ethiopia in Broader Perspective. Papers of the 13th International Conference of Ethiopian Studies*. Vol. II. Kyoto: Shokado Books.

Lamouse-Smith, Willie. 1994. *Demilitarizing and Democratizing Africa's Military*. Baltimore, MD: University of Maryland.

Lane, Charles. 1996. *Pasture Lost: Barabaig Economy, Resource Tenure, and the Alienation of their Land in Tanzania*. Nairobi: Initiatives Publishers.

Lane, Charles, Claudia Futterknecht and Liben Jarso. 1993. *Assessment of Land Related Issues in the Awash National Park*. London: Report prepared for CARE Britain.

Lassailly-Jacob, V. 2000. 'Reconstructing Livelihoods Through Land Settlement Schemes: Comparative Reflections on Refugees and Oustees in Africa', in Cernea and McDowell (eds).

Lefever, Ernest. 1970. *Spear and Scepter: Army, Police, and Politics in Tropical Africa*. Washington, DC: The Brookings Institution.

Levine, Donald. 1974. *Greater Ethiopia: The Evolution of the Multiethnic Society*. Chicago: University of Chicago Press.

Levine, Donald. 1968. *The Military in Ethiopian Politics: Capabilities and Constraints*. New York: Russell Sage Foundation.

Levine, Donald. 1965. *Wax and Gold: Tradition and Innovation in Ethiopian Culture*. Chicago: University of Chicago Press.

Lewis, Herbert. 1965. *A Galla Monarchy. Jimma Abba Jiffar, Ethiopia 1830-1932*. Madison, WI and Milwaukee: University of Wisconsin Press.

Lind, Jeremy and Teriessa Jalleta. 2005. *Poverty, Power and Relief Assistance: Meanings and Perceptions of 'Dependency' in Ethiopia*. London: Overseas Development Institute.

Lippitt, Ronald. 1958. *Planned Change: A Comparative Study of Principles and Techniques*. New York: Harcourt.

Lockhart, D. 1984. *The Itinerário of Jerónimo Lobo*. Cambridge: Haklyut Society.

Loescher, Gil. 2000. 'Forced Migration in the Post-Cold War Era: The Need for a Comprehensive Approach', in B. Ghosh (ed.), *Managing Migration: Time for a New International Regime?*. Oxford: Oxford University Press.

Long, L. and E. Oxfeld. 2004. *Coming Home? Refugees, Migrants and Those Who Stayed Behind*. Philadelphia: University of Pennsylvania Press.

Lumsden, D.P. 1975. 'Resettlement and Rehousing: Unintended Consequences Among the Nchumur', in J. Goody (ed.), *Changing Social Structure in Ghana. Essays in the Comparative Sociology of a New State and an Old Tradition*. London: International African Institute.

Lumsden, P. 1973. 'The Volta River Project Village Resettlement and Attempted Rural Animation'. *Canadian Journal Of African Studies* 7 (1): 115-132.

Lundqvist, J. 1981. 'Tanzania: Socialist Ideology, Bureaucratic Reality and Development from Below', in B. Walter and D. Fraser (eds), *Development from Above or Below: The Dialectics of Regional Planning in Developing Countries*. New York: John Wiley and Sons.

Lydall, Jean and Ivo Strecker. 1979. *The Hamar of Southern Ethiopia: Vol. I, Work Journal*. Hohenschäftlarn: Klaus Renner Verlag.

Lynch, M. 2005. 'Lives on Hold: the Human Cost of Statelessness', *Refugees International*, February.

MacDonald, Sir M. 1991. *Amibara Irrigation Project II, Pastoralist and Forestry Development Studies*. Vol. 1. Main Report. Cambridge: UNDP/FAO Report to WRDA.

Mahapatra, L.K. 1999. 'Testing the Risks and Reconstruction Model on India's Resettlement Experiences', in M. Cernia (ed.), *The Economics of Involuntary Resettlement: Questions and challenges*. Washington, DC. World Bank.

Mahapatra, L. K. 1998. 'Good Intentions or Policies are not Enough: Reducing Impoverishment Risks for the Tribal Oustees', in H. Mathur and D. Marsden (eds), *Development Projects and Impoverishment Risks: Resettling Project-Affected People in India*. Delhi: OUP.

Malkki, Liisa. 1995a. *Purity and Exile: Violence, Memory and National Cosmology among Hutu Refugees in Tanzania*. Chicago and London: University of Chicago Press.

Malkki, Lisa. 1995b. 'Refugees and Exile: From Refugee Studies to the National Order of Things', *Annual Review of Anthropology* 24: 495-523.

Malkki, Lisa. 1992. 'National Geographic: The Rooting of Peoples and the Territorialization of National Identity Among Scholars and Refugees', *Cultural Anthropology* 7 (1): 24-44.

Manger, Leif. 2000. 'East African Pastoralism and Underdevelopment: An Introduction', in L. Manger and Abdel Ghaffar M. Ahmed (eds), *Pastoralists and Environment: Experiences from the Greater Horn of Africa*. Addis Ababa: Organisation for Social Science Research in Eastern and Southern Africa (OSSRESA).

Manger, Leif. 1996. 'Human Adaptation in East African Drylands: The Dilemma of Concepts and Approaches', in Abdel Ghaffar Ahmed and Hassen Abdel Ati (eds), *Managing Scarcity: Human Adaptation in East African Drylands*. Addis Ababa: OSSRESA.

Maren, Michael. 1997. *The Road to Hell: The Ravaging Effects of Foreign Aid and International Charity*. New York: The Free Press.

Markakis, John. 1993. 'Introduction,' in J. Markakis (ed.) *Conflict and the Decline of Pastoralism in the Horn of Africa*. Basingstoke: Macmillan; The Hague: Institute of Social Studies.

Maro, P. 1988.'Land Settlement and Redistribution in the United Republic of Tanzania', in A. Oberai (ed.), *Land Development Policies and Population Distribution in Developing Countries*. New York: Praeger.

Marris, Peter. 1961. *Family and Rehousing in an African City*. London: Routledge and Kegan Paul.

Martin, S.F. 2000. *Forced Migration and the Evolving Humanitarian Regime*. Working Paper No. 20, New Issues in Refugee Research. Geneva: UNHCR.

Mathewos Asfaw. 1997. 'A Review of Urban Planning Practices in Addis Ababa with Particular Emphasis on the 1984-1986 Master Plan', in *Workshop on Urban Fields of Ethiopia*. Addis Ababa: Ministry of Public Works and Urban Development, May.

Mathur, Hari (ed.). 1998. 'The Impoverishment Risk Model and its Use as a Planning Tool', in H. Mathur and D. Marsden (eds), *Development Projects and Impoverishment Risks: Resettling Project-Affected People in India*. Delhi: Oxford University Press.

Mathur, Hari. 1995. *Development, Displacement and Resettlement: Focus on Asian Experiences*. New Delhi: Vikas Publishing House.

Matsuda, Hiroshi. 1997. 'How Guns Change the Muguji: Ethnic Identity and Armament', in K. Fukui, E. Kurimoto and M. Shigeta (eds), *Ethiopia in Broader Perspective. Papers of the 13th International Conference of Ethiopian Studies*. Kyoto: Shokado Books.

Mayer, P. and I. Mayer. 1971. *Townsmen Or Tribesmen*. 2nd Edition. Cape Town: OUP.

Mazur, R. 1988. 'Refugees in Africa: The Role of Sociological Analysis and Praxis', *Current Sociology* 36 (2): 43-60.

McAndrew, J.P. 1995. 'Nabacaan No More: Dispersion of Japanese Industrialization Leads to the Forced Relocation of a Philippine Community', in Mathur (ed.).

McCabe, J. Terrence. 1996. 'The Ecological and Cultural Significance of Livestock in the *Enset* Agricultural Complex', in Tsedeke Abate, C. Hiebsch. S. Brandt, and Seifu Gebre Mariam (eds), *Enset-Based Sustainable Agriculture in Ethiopia*. Addis Ababa: Institute of Agricultural Research.

McCann, J. 1995. *People of the Plow: An Agricultural History of Ethiopia, 1800-1990*. Madison, WI: University of Wisconsin Press.

McDowell, C. 2002. 'Involuntary Resettlement, Impoverishment Risks, and Sustainable Livelihoods.' *The Australasian Journal of Disaster and Trauma Studies*, 2: 1-10.

McDowell, Chris (ed.). 1996. *Understanding Impoverishment: The Consequences of Development-Induced Displacement*. Oxford: Berghahn.

McDowell, Chris and Arjan de Haan. 1997. *Migration and Sustainable Livelihoods: A Critical Review of the Literature*. Working Paper No 65. Brighton: Institute of Development Studies at the University of Sussex.

McHenry, D. 1979. *Tanzania's Ujamaa Villages: The Implementation of Rural Development Strategy*. Berkeley, CA: Institute of International Studies.

McMillan, D.E. *et al.* 1998. 'New Land is not Enough: Agricultural Performances of New Land Settlement in West Africa.' *World Development*. 26 (2):187-211.

Mead, Margaret. 1961. *Cooperation and Competition among Primitive Peoples*. Boston, Beacon Press.

Médecins Sans Frontières (MSF). 2003. 'MSF Alarmed at Dramatic Situation at Ethiopia Resettlement Site'. Posted on *reliefweb*. May 12.

Meikle, S. and Y. Zhu. 2000. 'Employment of Displacees', in Cernea and McDowell (eds).

Mekonnen Wube. 2002. 'The Impact of Urban Expansion on the Land Tenure and Livelihood of Rural Households. The Case fo Mekanissa III Housing Project, Addis Ababa, Ethiopia.' MSc thesis, Norwegian University of Science and Technology, Trondheim.

Mekuria Bulcha. 1988. *Flight and Integration: Causes of Mass Exodus from Ethiopia and Problems of Integration in the Sudan*, Uppsala: Scandinavian Institute of African Studies.

Mekuria Bulcha. 1987. 'Historical, Political and Social Causes of Mass-Flight from Ethiopia', in P. Nobel (ed.) *Refugees and Development in Africa*. Seminar Proceedings 19. Uppsala: Scandinavian Institute of African Studies.

Melesse Getu. 2004. ' The Effects of Investment on the Livelihoods of the Tsamako in the Waito Valley' in Pankhurst and Piguet (eds).

Melesse Getu. 2000. 'A Study of Patterns of Productive Resource Control among the Tsamako of Southwest Ethiopia.' Ph.D thesis. Department of Social Anthropology, University of Manchester.

Melesse Getu. 1995. *Tsamako Women's Roles and Status in Agro-Pastoral Production*. Department of Sociology, Anthropology and Social Administration. Social Anthropology Dissertation Series No. 3. Addis Ababa: Addis Ababa University Printing Press.

Mellesse Madda. 2005. 'Promises, Expectations, and Realities of Resettlement: The Dynamics of Intra-Zonal Resettlement in the Walayta of Southern Ethiopia.' MA thesis, Department of Sociology and Social Anthropology, Addis Ababa University.

Meliczek, H. 2000. 'Land Settlement: Experiences and Perspectives'. Eschborn: GTZ.

Mengistu Wube. 2005. *Effects of Resettlement Schemes on the Biophysical and Human Environments: the case of Gambela Region, Ethiopia*. Boca Raton: Universal Publishers.

Mengistu Wube. 1992. 'Southward Dash Northward Resettlement in Ethiopia', in J. Hinnant (ed.) *Proceedings of the Sixth Michigan State University Conference on Northeast Africa*. East Lansing, MI: Michigan State University Press.

Mengistu Wube. 1995. 'An Assessment of Ethiopia's Agricultural Land Resources', in Dejene Aredo and Mulat Demeke (eds), *Ethiopian Agriculture: Problems of Transformation*. Addis Ababa: Addis Ababa University Press.

Mesfin Abebe. 1995. 'Welcome Address' in *Proceedings of Participatory Wildlife Management Workshop*. Addis Ababa, 16-18 May. Addis Ababa: Ministry of National Resources Development and Environmental Protection and Forum Africa.

Mesfin Wolde Mariam. 1991. *Suffering under God's Environment: A Vertical Study of the Predicament of Peasants in North-Central Ethiopia*. Berne: African Mountains Association.

Mesfin Wolde Mariam. 1964. 'The Awash Valley: Trends and Prospects', *Ethiopian Geographical Journal*, 2 (2): 18-27.

Messing, Simon. 1965. 'Group Therapy and Social Status in the Zar Cult of Ethiopia', in F. Torrey (ed.), *An Introduction to Health and Health Education in Ethiopia*. Addis Ababa: Artistic Printers.

Messing, Simon. 1956. 'Group Therapy and social status in the Zar Cult of Ethiopia', *American Anthropologist*, 60: 1120-1126.

Metemma Woreda Office of Agriculture. 2003. 'North Gondar Resettlement Plan: Lasting Solutions to the Problems of Food Security'. Bahr Dar: Amhara Region.

Midgley, J. *et al* (eds). 1986. *Community Participation, Social Development and the State*. London: Methuen.

Ministry of Agriculture and Rural Development (MoARD). 2007. *Food Security Programme: Progress Made in Building Assets of Food Insecure Households*. Addis Ababa: Food Security Coordination Bureau, July.

Ministry of Agriculture and Rural Development (MoARD). 2004. *Food Security Programme Evaluation and Monitoring Plan*. Addis Ababa: Food Security Coordination Bureau, Monitoring and Evaluation Task Force.

Ministry of Agriculture (MOA). 1999. 'Extension System for Pastoral Areas'. Working paper prepared by the Pastoral Extension Team. Addis Ababa.,July.

MoA. 1989. *Gilgel Gibe Catchments Integrated Agricultural Development Project Preparation Report*. Vol. 2. Addis Ababa: Ministry of Agriculture.

Ministry of Finance and Economic Development (MoFED). 2007a. *Ethiopia: Building on Progress: a Plan for Accelerated and Sustained Development to End Poverty (PASDEP) Annual Progress Report 2005/6*. Addis Ababa: Ministry of Finance and Economic Development.

MoFED. 2007b. *Ethiopia: Building on Progress: a Plan for Accelerated and Sustained Development to End Poverty (PASDEP) Annual Report 2006/7*. Addis Ababa.

MoFED. 2006. *Ethiopia: Building in Progress: Plan for Accelerated and Sustained Development to End Poverty (PASDEP)*, Vol. 1. Addis Ababa: MoFED.

MoFED. 2003. *Rural Development Policy and Strategies*. Addis Ababa.

Ministry of Labor and Social Affairs. 1995. 'Survey to Rehabilitate the Displaced Families in Ethiopia'. Addis Ababa: MoLSA.

Ministry of Natural Resources Development and Environmental Protection and FARM Africa. 1995. *Participatory Wildlife Management Workshop Proceedings 16-18 May*. Addis Ababa: MoNREP and FARM Africa.

Ministry of Rural Development, Federal Democratic Republic of Ethiopia. 2003. 'The Food Security Programme'. Paper presented to the Workshop on the Food Security Programme and Intra-Regional Voluntary Settlement, Addis Ababa. June.

Miyawaki, Yukio. 1996. 'Cultivation Strategies and Historical Change of Sorghum Varieties in the Hoor of Southwestern Ethiopia', in S. Sato and E. Kurimoto (eds), *Essays in Northeast African Studies*. Senri Ethnological Studies 43.

Mohammed Hassan. 1990. *The Oromo of Ethiopia: A History 1570-1860*. Cambridge: CUP.

Mohammed Salih. 1999. *Environmental Politics and Liberation in Contemporary Africa*. Dordrecht: Kluwer Academic Publishers.

Monbiot, G. 1994. 'The Real Tragedy of the Commons', *Rural Extension Bulletin*. Reading: University of Reading.

Monod, Theodore (ed.). 1975. *Pastoralism in Tropical Africa*. London: Oxford University Press.

Muderis Abdulahi Mohammed. 1998. 'Resource Deprivation and Socio-Economic Changes among Pastoral Households: The Case of Karayu and Itu Pastoralists in the Middle Awash Valley of Ethiopia'. M.Sc thesis, Agricultural University of Norway.

Mugabe, B. 1997. *Women's Role in the Armed Conflict and their Marginalization in the Governance of Post-Conflict Society: The Case of the Luwero Triangle*. Kampala: Makerere University Press.

Mulugeta Debalkew. 2000. 'Sustainability in Post-War Reconstruction and Development. The Case of TPLF Ex-Fighters in Dansha Agricultural Settlement.' MA thesis in Social Anthropology, Department of Sociology and Social Administration, Addis Ababa University.

Nayak Ranjit. 1998. 'Risks Associated With Landlessness: An Exploration Towards Socially Friendly Displacement and Resettlement', in Cernea and McDowell (eds).

Nazif Abba Macha. 1999. 'Agricultural Situations of the Resettlement Village'. Report of Gilgel Gibe Resettlement Office.

Nebiyu Baye. 2000. 'The Impact of Development-Induced Urban Resettlement Schemes on Relocated Households: The Case of Sheraton Addis Hotel Project, Addis Ababa'. MA thesis in regional and local development studies. Addis Ababa University.

New Coalition for Food Security in Ethiopia (NCFSE). 2003a. *Food Security Programme Proposal*.

Vol. I. Addis Ababa: New Coalition for Food Security in Ethiopia.

NCFSE 2003b. *Voluntary Resettlement Programme (Access to improved land)*. Vol. II. Addis Ababa: New Coalition for Food Security in Ethiopia.

Negaso Gidada. 1984. 'History of the Saayoo Oromoo of Southwestern Wallaga, Ethiopia from about 1730-1886.' PhD dissertation. Frankfurt Institut für Ethnologie, Goethe Universität.

Nelson, Nici, (ed.). 1981. *African Women in the Development Process.* London: Frank Cass.

Newman, Edward and Joanne van Selm (eds). 2003. *Refugees and Forced Displacement: International Security, Human Vulnerability and the State.* Tokyo: United Nations University Press.

Niehoff, Arthur. 1966. *A Casebook of Social Change.* Chicago: Aldine.

Niggli, Peter. 1986. *Ethiopia: Deportations and Forced Labour Camps.* Berlin: Berliner Missionswerk.

Nordstrom, Carolyn and C.G. Robben (eds). 1995. *Fieldwork Under Fire: Contemporary Studies of Violence and Survival.* Los Angeles: University of California Press.

Nwzado. 1986. 'Land Use, Vegetation Types, and Farming Systems of the Middle Beles Pawe Settlement Project'. Bahir Dar: North-Western Zone Agricultural Development Office.

Oberei, A. S. 1988. 'An Overview of Settlement Policies and Programs', in A.S. Oberei (ed.), *Land Settlement Policies and Population Distribution in Developing Countries.* New York: Praeger.

Organization for Economic Co-operation and Development (OECD). 1991. *Guidelines for Aid Agencies on Involuntary Displacement and Resettlement in Development Projects.* Paris: Operations Evaluation Department, Report No 17541.

Oromia Food Security Programme Coordination Office (OFSPCO). 2001. 'Prefeasibility Study on Voluntary Resettlement Programme.' Regional State of Oromia Food Security Programme Coordination Office.

Ohta Itaru and Gebre Yntiso (eds). 2005. *Displacement Risks in Africa: Refugees, Resettlers and their Host Population.* Tokyo: Tokyo University Press; Melbourne: TransPacific Press.

Oliver-Smith, Anthony. 2002. *Displacement, Resistance and the Critique of Development: From the Grass-roots to the Global.* Working Paper 9. Oxford: Refugee Studies Centre, University of Oxford.

Ostrom, E. 1990. *Governing the Commons: The Evolution of Institutions for Collective Action.* Cambridge: Cambridge University Press.

Ostrom, E. and E Schlager. 1996. 'The Formation of Property Rights', in S. Hanna *et al.* (eds), *Rights to Nature: Ecological, Economic and Political Principles of Institutions for the Environment.* Washington, DC: Island Press.

Ottaway, Marina. 1976. *Urbanisation in Ethiopia: A Text with Integrated Readings.* Department of Sociology and Anthropology. Addis Ababa University.

Oxby, Clare. 1975. *Pastoral Nomads and Development.* London: International African Institute.

Paderanga, C. 1988, 'Land Settlement in the Philippines', in A. Oberai (ed.), *Land Settlement Policies and Population Distribution in Developing Countries*, New York: Praeger.

Pankhurst, Alula. 2003a. 'Conflict Management over Contested Natural Resources: A Case Study of Pasture, Forest and Irrigation in South Wello, Ethiopia' in E. Nielsen and P. Castro (eds), *Natural Resource Management Conflict Case Studies.* Rome: FAO, Community Forestry Unit.

Pankhurst, Alula. 2003b. 'Current Status of Knowledge about the 2003 Resettlement. Summary of Findings and Assessment'. Report submitted to Irish Aid. Addis Ababa, December.

Pankhurst, Alula. 2002a. 'Surviving Resettlement in Wollega: The Qeto Experience', in W. James, D. Donham, E. Kurimoto and A. Triulzi (eds), *Remapping Ethiopia: Socialism and After.* Oxford: James Currey.

Pankhurst, Alula. 2002b. 'Social Opportunities and Constraints for Participatory Forest Management' in *Participatory Forest Management Working Group Workshop Proceedings.* Addis Ababa: Ministry of Agriculture with GTZ Advisory Assistance to the Forest Administration, June.

Pankhurst, Alula. 2001a. 'Resource Management Institutions in Post-Conflict Situations: Lessons from Yegof State Forest, South Wello Zone, Amhara Region, Ethiopia', in A. Pankhurst (ed.), *Natural Resource Management in Ethiopia.* Addis Ababa: Forum for Social Studies.

Pankhurst, Alula. 2001b. 'Migration, Resettlement and Return: Hidden Dynamics Between People, Land and NRM', in *Institutions for Natural Resource Management. INFORM Thematic Briefing* No. 3. Addis Ababa: Forum for Social Studies and Brighton: University of Sussex.

Pankhurst, Alula. 2001c. 'Returnees and Natural Resource Management', in *Institutions for Natural Resource Management. INFORM Thematic Briefing* no 4. Addis Ababa: Forum for Social Studies and Brighton: University of Sussex.

Pankhurst, Alula. 1998. 'When the Centre Relocates the Periphery: Resettlement during the Derg', in K. Fukui *et al.* (eds), *Ethiopia in Broader Perspective: Papers of the 13th International Conference of Ethiopian Studies 12-17 December, 1997*. Vol. II. Kyoto: Shokado Books.

Pankhurst, Alula. 1997. 'External Threats to Land Rights and Resource Management: the Case of the Omo-Gibe Valley'. Paper presented to the Workshop on Access to Land and Resource Management in Ethiopia. The Land Tenure Project. Institute of Development Research. Addis Ababa University.

Pankhurst, Alula. 1994a. 'Responses to Resettlement: Household Marriage and Divorce', in C. Lepage (ed.), *Etudes Ethiopiennes. Actes de la Xe Conférence Internationale des Etudes Ethiopiennes, Paris, août 1988*. Paris: Société Française des Etudes Ethiopiennes.

Pankhurst, Alula. 1994b. 'Reflections on Pilgrimages in Ethiopia', in H. Marcus (ed.), *New Trends in Ethiopian Studies*. Lawrenceville, NJ: Red Sea Press.

Pankhurst, Alula. 1992a. *Resettlement and Famine in Ethiopia: the Villagers' Experience*. Manchester: Manchester University Press.

Pankhurst, Alula (ed.) 1992b. 'Urban Poverty in Addis Ababa: A Hundred Case Studies in the Shola Market Area'. Report for Concern, Addis Ababa.

Pankhurst, Alula. 1991. 'People on the Move: The Case of Settlers Leaving Resettlement Areas in Western Ethiopia', *Disasters* 15 (1): 61-7.

Pankhurst, Alula. 1990. 'Resettlement: Policy and Practice', in S. Pausewang, Fantu Cheru, S. Brüne and Eshetu Chole (eds), *Ethiopia: Rural Development Options*. London: Zed Books.

Pankhurst, Alula. 1989a. 'Settling for a New World: People and the State in an Ethiopian Resettlement Village'. PhD thesis, Manchester University.

Pankhurst, Alula. 1989b. 'The Administration of Resettlement in Ethiopia Since the Revolution', in Abebe Zegeye and S. Ishemo (eds), *Forced Labor Migration: Pattern of Movement within Africa*. London: Hans Zell Publisher.

Pankhurst, Alula and François Piguet (eds). 2004a. *People, Space and the State: Migration, Resettlement and Displacement in Ethiopia*. Proceedings of Workshop held by the Ethiopian Society of Sociologists, Social Workers and Anthropologists and the United Nations Emergency Unit for Ethiopia, 28-30 January. Addis Ababa: ESSSWA.

Pankhurst, Alula and François Piguet. 2004b. 'Contextualising Migration, Resettlement and Displacement in Ethiopia', in Pankhurst and Piguet (eds).

Pankhurst, Alula and Getachew Assafa. 2008. *Grass-roots Justice in Ethiopia:. The Contribution of Customary Dispute Resolution*. Etudes éthiopiennes 4. Addis Ababa: Centre Français des Etudes Ethiopiennes.

Pankhurst, Alula and Helmut Kloos. 2000. 'Introduction. HIV/AIDS in Ethiopia, Part I: Risk and preventive behavior, sexuality and opportunistic infections', *Northeast African Studies* 7 (1): 1-12.

Pankhurst, Richard. 1998. *The Ethiopians*. Oxford: Blackwell Publishers.

Pankhurst, Richard. 1997. *The Ethiopian Borderlands: Essays in Regional History from Ancient Times to the End of the 18th Century*. Lawrenceville, NJ: Red Sea Press.

Pankhurst, Richard. 1990. *A Social History of Ethiopia*. Addis Ababa: Institute of Ethiopian Studies.

Pankhurst, Richard. 1987. ' Developments in Addis Ababa during the Italian Fascist Occupation 1936-1941', in Ahmed Zekaria, Bahru Zewde and Taddese Beyene (eds). *Proceedings of the Symposium on the International Centenary of Addis Ababa, November 24-25, 1986*. Addis Ababa.

Pankhurst, Richard. 1968. *Economic History of Ethiopia*. Addis Ababa: Haile Selassie I University Press.

Pankhurst, Richard. 1967. *An Introduction to the History of Ethiopian Army*. Addis Ababa: Imperial Ethiopian Air Force 101st Training Center.

Pankhurst, Richard.1963. 'The Ethiopian Army of Former Times', *Ethiopia Observer* 7 (2).

Pankhurst, Richard and Endrias Eshete. 1958. 'Self-Help in Ethiopia', *Ethiopia Observer* 7 (2).

Pankhurst, Sylvia. 1958. 'Laying the Foundation of the Koka Dam.' Speech of Emperor Haile Selassie I, *Ethiopian Observer* 2 (10).

Partridge, W. L. 1993. 'Successful Involuntary Resettlement: Lessons From the Costa Rican Arenal Hydroelectric Project', in M. Cernea and S. Guggenheim (eds), *Anthropological Approaches to Resettlement: Policy, Practice and Theory*. Boulder, CO: Westview Press.

Paulos, Chanie. 2001. 'The Challenges of the Civil Service Reform in Ethiopia: Initial Observations', *Eastern Africa Social Science Research Review*. 17 : 1.

Perham, Margery. 1947. *The Government of Ethiopia.* London: Faber.

Pettersson, B. 2002. 'Development-Induced Displacement: Internal Affair or International Human Rights Issue?', *Forced Migration Review* 12: 16-19.

Phillipson, David. 1998. *Ancient Ethiopia, Aksum: Its Antecedents and Successors.* London: British Museum Press.

Picciotto, R., W. Van Wicklin and E. Rice (eds). 2001. *Involuntary Resettlement: Comparative Perspectives.* New Brunswick, NJ: Transaction Publishers.

Piguet, François. 2006. 'Mariages interethniques et changement social dans la région Afar de l'Ethiopie'. *Annales d'Ethiopie* 21: 155-75.

Piguet, François. 1998. *Des nomades entre la ville et les sables, La sédentarisation dans la Corne de l'Afrique.* Paris : Karthala.

Piguet, François and Alula Pankhurst. 2004. 'Summary and Conclusion: Migration, Relocation and Coexistence in Ethiopia', in Pankhurst and Piguet (eds).

Piguet, François and Dechassa Lemessa. 2004. 'Review of Voluntary Migration and Resettlement Programmes up to the End of 2001', in Pankhurst and Piguet (eds).

Pimbert, M. and J. Pretty. 1995. *Parks, People and Professionals: Putting 'Participation' into Protected Area Management.* Discussion Paper 57, Geneva: UNRISD.

Pitterman, S. 1984. 'Determinants of Policy in a Functional International Agency: A Comparative Study of UNHCR Assistance in Africa, 1963-1981'. Ph.D dissertation. Evanston, IL: University of Illinois.

Population Reference Bureau. 2003. *Annual Report 2003.* Washington, DC: Population Reference Bureau.

Provisional Military Administrative Council (PMAC). 1979. 'Proclamation No. 173: A Proclamation to Provide for Reorganizing the Relief and Rehabilitation Commission'. *Negarit Gazeta*,. 39th Year, No. 4, Addis Ababa.

PMAC. 1978. 'Proclamation No. 138: A Proclamation to Provide for the Establishment of Cooperative Societies'. *Negarit Gazeta*, 38th year, Addis Ababa.

PMAC. 1976. 'Proclamation No. 78: A Proclamation to Provide for the Establishment of a Settlement Authority'. *Negarit Gazeta*, 35th Year, No. 20, Addis Ababa.

PMAC. 1975a. 'A Proclamation to Provide for the Payment of Pensions to Employees of Undertakings Owned by the Government'. *Negarit Gazeta.* No 43. Addis Ababa.

PMAC. 1975b. 'Proclamation No. 31: Public Ownership of Rural Lands Proclamation.' *Negarit Gazeta.*

Provisional Military Government of Ethiopia (PMGE). 1976. 'Proclamation no.104: A Proclamation to Consolidate Urban Dwellers' Associations and Municipalities'. *Negarit Gazeta* Addis Ababa.

Provisional Military Government of Ethiopia. 1975. 'Proclamation no.47/75: A Proclamation to Provide for Government Ownership of Urban Lands and Extra Houses', *Negarit Gazetta*, Addis Ababa.

Prunier, Gérard. 1994. 'Population Resettlement in Ethiopia: the Financial Aspect', in C. Lepage (ed.), *Etudes Ethiopiennes. Actes de la Xe Conférence Internationale des Etudes Ethiopiennes, Paris, août 1988.* Paris: Société Française des Etudes Ethiopiennes.

Raisin, Joanne. 2003. 'Development with the Poor: The Transitional Asset Protection System TAPS, A Middle Road to Social Protection'. Addis Ababa. March.

Region 14 (Addis Ababa City) Administration. 1997. *Five Years Strategic Plan.* Addis Ababa.

Region 14 (Addis Ababa City) Administration. 1994. 'Regulation to Provide for the Lease Holding of Urban Lands', *Negarit Gazetta* no. 3/94.

Regional State of Oromia (RSO). 2002. *Feasibility Study for Voluntary Resettlement Programme: Final Report.* 2 vols. Environment and Development Group. School of Geography, University of Leeds.

Relief and Rehabilitation Commission (RRC). 1988. '*Settlement activities an agricultural development in Resettlement Farms*, Addis Ababa: RRC [in Amharic].

RRC. 1985. Special Report to Donors Meeting', Addis Ababa, April.

RRC. 1982. *Report on settlement farms in the Awash Valley.* Addis Ababa: RRC Report [in Amharic].

Rew, A., E. Fisher and B. Pandey. 2000. *Addressing Policy Constraints and Improving Outcomes in Development-Induced Displacement and Resettlement Projects.* Oxford: Refugee Studies Centre. University of Oxford.

Robertson, A.F. 1984. *People and the State. An Anthropology of Planned Development.* Cambridge: Cambridge University Press.

Robinson, Courtland. W. 2003. *Risks and Rights: The Causes, Consequences, and Challenges of Development-Induced Displacement.* Washington, DC: Brookings Institution SAIS Project on Internal Displacement.

Robinson, J. 2002. *Development and Displacement.* Oxford : The Open University.

Roder, W. 1994. *Human Adjustments. The Kainji Reservoir in Nigeria.* New York and London: University Press of America.

Rogge, John. 1994. 'Repatriation of refugees', in T. Allen and H. Morsink (eds), *When Refugees Go Home.* Geneva: United Nations Research Institute for Social Development and London: James Currey.

Rogge, John. 1981, 'Africa's Resettlement Strategies', *International Migration Review* 15(1): 195-212.

Roy, A. 1999 *The Cost of Living.* New York: The Modern Library.

Salem-Murdock, Muneera. 1993. 'Involuntary Resettlement: A Plea for the Host Population', in M. Cernea and S. Guggenheim (eds), *Anthropological Approaches to Resettlement: Policy, Practice, and Theory.* Boulder, CO: Westview Press.

Salini Costruttori. 1989. *The Tana-Beles Project Ethiopia.* Rome: Salini Costruttori.

Salome Gabre Egziabher. 1969. 'The Ethiopian Patriots, 1936-41', *Ethiopia Observer,* 12 (2).

Salzman, Philip and John Galaty (eds). 1990. *Nomads in a Changing World.* Naples: Istituto Universitario Orientale.

Schlee, Gunther. 1990. 'Holy grounds', in Baxter and Hogg (eds).

Scoones, Ian. 1998. *Sustainable Rural Livelihoods. A Framework for Analysis.* Brighton: IDS Working Paper No. 72.

Scoones, Ian *et al.* 1996. *Hazards and Opportunities: Farming Livelihoods in Dryland Africa: Lessons from Zimbabwe.* London: Zed Books.

Scott, James. 1998. *Seeing Like a State: How Certain Schemes to Improve the Human Condition Have Failed.* New Haven, CT and London: Yale University Press.

Scudder, Thayer. 1999. 'The Emerging Global Crisis and Development Anthropology: Can We Have an Impact?', *Human Organization.* 58 (4): 351-364.

Scudder, Thayer. 1997. 'Resettlement', in A. Biswas (ed.), *Water Resources: Environmental Planning, Management and Development.* New York: MacGraw Hill.

Scudder, Thayer. 1996. 'Development-Induced Impoverishment: Resistance and River Basin Development', in McDowell (ed.).

Scudder, Thayer. 1993. 'Development-Induced Relocation and Refugee Studies: 37 Years of Change and Continuity among Zambia's Gwembe Tonga', *Journal of Refugee Studies,* 6(2): 123-152.

Scudder, Thayer. 1990. *Evaluation of the Gwembe Valley Agricultural Mission – Harvest Help, Zambia.* Binghamton, NY: Institute for Development Anthropology.

Scudder, Thayer. 1985. 'A Sociological Framework for the Analysis of New Land Settlements', in M. Cernea (ed.), *Putting People First: Sociological Variables in Rural Development.* Oxford: Oxford University Press.

Scudder, Thayer. 1969. 'Relocation, Agricultural Intensification and Anthropological Research', in D. Brokensha and M. Pearsall (eds), *The Anthropology of Development in Sub-Sahara Africa.* Lexington, KY: University of Kentucky Press.

Scudder, Thayer and Elizabeth Colson. 1982. 'From Welfare to Development: A Conceptual Analysis of Dislocated People', in A. Hansen and A. Oliver-Smith (eds), *Involuntary Migration and Resettlement. The Problems and Responses of Displaced People.* Boulder, CO: Westview Press.

Sen, Amartya. 1981. *Poverty and Famine.* Oxford: Clarendon Press.

Seyoum Gebre Selassie. 2004. 'Salient Points on the Utility of Population Resettlement Programmes in the Amhara Regional State: Report on the Workshop held in Bahr Dar', in Pankhurst and Piguet (eds).

Seyoum Gebre Selassie. 1995. 'Pastoralism and Land Tenure Systems in the Horn of Africa: A Comparative Overview', in Seyoum Gebre Selassie (ed.), *Pastoral Land Tenure Systems in the Horn of Africa: A Compendium of Eight Case Studies from Ethiopia, Eritrea and Sudan.* Addis Ababa: Pastoral and Environmental Network in the Horn of Africa.

Shacknove, A. 1985. 'Who is a Refugee?', *Ethics* 95: 274-84.

Sharp, J. 1987. 'Relocation, Labor Migration, and the Domestic Predicament: Qwaqwa in the 1980s', in J. Eades (ed.), *Migrant Workers and the Social Order*. London: Tavistock Publications.

Sharp, J. and A. Spiegel. 1985. 'Vulnerability to Impoverishment in South African Rural Areas. The Erosion of Kinship and Neighborhood as Social Resources', *Africa*. 552: 133-151.

Singh, N. and V. Titi (eds). 1997. *Empowerment: Towards Sustainable Development*. Ottawa: International Institute for Sustainable Development.

Singleton, B. 1996. 'A Clinical Phenomenology of Spirit Possession Beliefs and Practices in the Evangelical Churches of Addis Ababa, Ethiopia'. PhD dissertation, School of Professional Psychology, Sacremento, CA.

Sivini, G. 1986. 'Famine and Resettlement Program in Ethiopia', *Africa (*Rome) 41: 211-242.

Soguk, N. 1999. *States and Strangers: Refugees and Displacements of Statecraft*. Minneapolis, MN: University of Minnesota Press.

Solomon Debebe. 2005. 'Resettlement and Cultural Dynamics: The Case of Qwara Resettlement Site in North Gondar Zone, Amhara Region'. MA thesis in social anthropology, Department of Sociology and Social Anthropology, Addis Ababa University.

Solomon Eshete. 1996. 'Nech Sar National Park Proposed Resettlement Programme'. Addis Ababa.

Solomon Gebre. 1994. 'Profile of Poverty in Addis Ababa: A Social Problem Ignored'. Addis Ababa: Institute of Development Research, Addis Ababa University.

Sorensen, B. 1998. 'Self-help Activities Among Internally Displaced People', in W. Davies (ed.), *Rights Have No Borders: Internal Displacement Worldwide*. Norwegian Refugee Council and Global IDP Survey. London: Earthscan.

Spencer, Sarah (ed.). 2003. *The Politics of Migration. Managing Opportunity, Conflict and Change*. Oxford: Blackwell Publishing.

Stein, Judith. (ed.). 1984. *Women's Views of the Political World of Men*. New York: Transactional Publishers.

Stockwell, Edward and Karen Laidlaw. 1981. *Third World Development: Problems and Prospects*. Chicago: Nelson-Hall.

Summerfield, D. 1998. 'The Social Experience of War and Some Issues for the Humanitarian Field', in P. Bracken and C Petty (eds) *Rethinking the Trauma of War*. London: Free Association Books.

Sutcliffe, Peter. 1992. 'Peoples and Natural Resources in the North and South Omo and Kefa Administrative Regions of Southwestern Ethiopia. A Case Study in Strategic Natural Resource Planning'. Addis Ababa: Ministry of Planning and Economic Development, National Conservation Strategy Secretariat.

Taddesse Berisso. 1995. 'Agricultural and Rural Development Policies in Ethiopia. A Case Study of Villagization Policy Among the Guji-Oromo of Jam-Jam Awraja'. Ph.D dissertation, East Lansing, MI: Michigan State University.

Tadesse Djote 2006. 'Development-Induced Displacement of Peasants along the Kaliti-Debrezeit Road'. MA thesis in social anthropology, Addis Ababa University.

Tafesse Mesfin and Bereket Tarekegn. 2004. 'Conflict and Peace-Making in South Omo: Lessons from Current Initiatives', in Pankhurst and Piguet (eds).

Teferi Abate. 2000. 'Government Intervention and Socio-Economic Change in a Northeastern Ethiopian Community: An Anthropological Study'. PhD dissertation in Social Anthropology, Boston University.

Tegegne Gebre Egziabher. 1989. 'Land Settlement Practices and their Implication for Regional Planning: An Independent Study'. Addis Ababa.

Tegegne Teka. 1988. 'The Evolution of Settlement and Resettlement Organization in Ethiopia', in *Proceedings of the Workshop on Famine Experience and Resettlement in Ethiopia*. Addis Ababa: Institute of Development Research.

Tekeste Negash and Kjetil Tronvoll. 2000. *Brothers at War: Making Sense of the Eritrean-Ethiopian War.* Oxford: James Currey; Athens, OH: Ohio University Press.

Teklegiorgis Goitom. 1973. 'Reconnaissance Report of Hydroelectric Possibility on Little Gibe River'. Addis Ababa.

Tenassie, Nichola. 1988. 'Resettlement in the Ten-Year Perspective Plan', in *Proceedings of the Workshop on Famine Experience and Resettlement in Ethiopia*'. Addis Ababa: Institute of Development Research.

Tesfaye Tafesse. 2007. *The Migration Environment and Conflict Nexus in Ethiopia. A Case Study of Amhara Migrant Settlers in East Wollega Zone*. Addis Ababa: OSSREA.

Teshome Emana. 2007. 'Urbanization, Cultural and Socioeconomic Dynamics, and the Strains on the Local People in Sebeta Area', MA thesis in Social Anthropology, Addis Ababa University.

Thiele, G. 1986. 'The Tanzanian Villagisation Programme: Its Impact on Household Production in Dodoma', *Canadian Journal of African Studies*, 20 (2) : 243-258.

Thiele, G. 1985. 'Villagers As Economic Agents: The Accident of Social Reproduction', in R. Abrahams (ed.), *Villagers, Villages and the State in Modern Tanzania*. Cambridge African Monographs No 4. Cambridge: African Studies Centre, University of Cambridge.

Thompson, Larry for Refugees International. 2005. 'Ethiopia: Local People Burned out of Homes to Make Way for National Park.' Communications and Media (http:/www.interaction.org/newswire/detail.php?id=3940)

Tibebe Alemayehu. 1997. 'Park versus Pastoralists: Conflict in the Awash Valley of Ethiopia.' M.Sc thesis, Agricultural University of Norway.

Tibebe Eshete. 1994. 'The *Sedqo* institution of the Amhara and the Somali: ethnic partnership and discordance', in H. Marcus (ed.), *New Trends in Ethiopian Studies. Proceedings of the 12th International Conference of Ethiopian Studies*. Lawrenceville, NJ: Red Sea Press.

Timberlake, L. 1986. *Africa in Crisis: The Causes, the Cures of Environmental Bankruptcy*. Philadelphia: Earthscan.

Tranquilli, Roberta. 2004. 'Resettlement in Amhara and Southern Regions: a comparative assessment of the 2003 Programmes', in Pankhurst and Piguet (eds).

Travers, L. and Y. Kimura. 1993. *China: Involuntary Resettlement*. Washington, DC: World Bank.

Triulzi, Alessandro. 1081. *Salt, Gold and Legitimacy. Prelude to the History of a No-Man's Land Bela Shangul, Wallagga, Ethiopia (ca. 1800-1898)*. Naples: Istituto Uniiversitario Orientale.

Tronvoll, Kjetil. 2000. *Ethiopia: A New Start*. London: Minority Rights Group International.

Tronvoll, Kjetil. 1996. 'Mai Weini, A Study of the People, their Livelihood and Land Tenure during Times of Turbulence', PhD dissertation, University of Oslo.

Tsegaye Berhe. 1999. *The Tigrean Women in the Liberation Struggle and its Aftermath, 1975-1996*. Addis Ababa: Addis Ababa University.

Tsehay Berhane Sellassie. 1980. 'Women Guerilla Fighters'. *North East African Studies*, 1(3).

Tuffa, D. 1995. 'Urban Development of Addis Ababa: Plans and Realities'. MSc thesis, Faculty of Architecture, Helsinki University of Technology.

Turton, David. 2005. 'Who is a Forced Migrant?', in De Wet (ed.).

Turton, David. 2002a. 'Forced Displacement and the Nation-State', in Robinson (ed.).

Turton, David. 2002b. 'The Mursi and the Elephant Question', in Chatty and Colchester (eds).

Turton, David. 1996. 'Migrants and Refugees: a Mursi Case study', in Allen (ed.).

Turton, David. 1995. 'The Mursi and the Elephant Question', in *Proceedings of Participatory Wildlife Management Workshop*, Addis Ababa, 16-18 May.

United Nations Development Program/Relief and Rehabilitation Commission (UNDP/RRC). 1986. *The Nomadic Areas of Ethiopia*. Addis Ababa: UNDP/RRC.

UNDP/RRC. 1984. *The Nomadic Areas of Ethiopia*. Study Report No. 2, Addis Ababa.

UNDP/UNCHS Habitat/ World Bank. 1995. *Urban Management and Poverty: Policy Program Options for Urban Poverty Reduction: A Framework for Action at Municipal Government Level*. Washington, DC: World Bank.

United Nations High Commissioner for Refugees. 2003. *Refugees by Numbers*. Geneva: UNHCR.

UNHCR. 2002. *Refugees by Numbers*. Geneva: UNHCR.

UNHCR. 1996. '*Focus: The Internally Displaced*', No. 103. Geneva: UNHCR.

UNHCR. various years. *Statistical Yearbook*. Geneva: UNHCR.

United Nations Regional Information Networks. *Fire razes home in displaced* camp, May 27, 2003.

USAID. 2002 'Exploring New Opportunities to Address the Needs of the Predictable Food Insecure Caseload: TAPS and the R2D Pilot,' December.

Van Heer, N. 1998. *New Diasporas: The Mass Exodus, Dispersal and Regrouping of Migrant Communities*. London: UCL Press.

Van Uffelen, Gerrit-Jan. 2006. 'Return After Flight: Exploring the Decision-Making Theory of Reasoned Action.' PhD thesis, Wageningen University. CIP-DATA Koningklijke Bibliotheek. The Hague, The Netherlands.

Vecchiato, Norberto. 1993a. 'Illness, Therapy, and Change in Ethiopian Possession Cults', *Journal of International African Institute* 632: 176-195.

Vecchiato, N. 1993b. 'Traditional Medicine', in Kloos and Zein (eds).

Viezzoli, Claudio. 1992 'Scenarios of Economic Development in the Beles Valley,' in Dieci and Viezzoli (eds).

Vivero, J.L. and F. Beernaert. 2001. 'Report on the Assessment Mission to Metemma Woreda (North Gondar). Fact Finding Trip to the Potential Host Areas for the Planned Resettlement Scheme.' Delegation of the European Commission to Ethiopia.

Voelkner, H.E. 1974. *The Social Feasibility of Settling Semi Nomadic Afar on Irrigated Agriculture in the Awash Valley, Ethiopia*, UNDP/FAO/ETH 721006, No. 23, Rome.

Voutira, Eftihia and Barbara Harrell-Bond. 2000. 'Successful Refugee Settlements: Are Past Experiences Relevant?', in Cernea and McDowell (eds).

Walta Information Centre. 2001. *Internet Responses to the Ethio-Eritrean War*. Addis Ababa: Berhanena Selam Printing Press.

Water Resource Development Authority of Ethiopia (WRDAE). 1986. 'Gilgel Gibe Hydroelectric Power Project: Public and Environmental Health Implications'. Water Resource Development Authority, Ethiopia. UNDP/WHO.

Webb, Patrick and Joachim Von Braun. 1994. *Famine and Food Security in Ethiopia: Lessons for Africa*. Chichester: John Wiley.

Weidner, Edward. 1968. 'Developmental Change and the Social Sciences', in A. Gallarher (ed.) *Perspectives in Developmental Change*. Lexington, KY: University of Kentucky Press.

Westermeyer, J. 1984. 'Economic Loss Associated with Chronic Mental Disorder in Developing Countries', *British Journal of Psychiatry* 144: 475-481.

Western, J. 1981. *Outcast Cape Town*. Minneapolis: University of Minnesota Press.

Whisson, M. 1976. 'The Significance of Kinship in a Cape Peninsula Township', *African Studies*, 35 (3/4): 253-271.

Wijbrandi, J. B. 1986. *Organized and Spontaneous Settlements in Eastern Sudan: Two Case Studies on Integration of Rural Refugees*. Amsterdam: Department of Development Studies, Faculty of Economics, Free University of Amsterdam.

Windstrand, Carl (ed.). 1972. *African Cooperatives and Efficiency*. Uppsala: Scandinavian Institute of African Studies.

Wolde-Selassie Abbute. 2003. 'Resettlement as a Response to Food Insecurity: The Case of Southern Nations, Nationalities, and Peoples' Region SNNPR'. Assessment Mission: 12 May – 2 June. Addis Ababa: report written for the UN-EUE.

Wolde-Selassie Abbute. 2002. 'Gumuz and Highland Settlers: Differing Strategies of Livelihood and Ethnic Relations in Metekel, Northwestern Ethiopia.' Ph.D dissertation, Faculty of Social Sciences, University of Göttingen.

Wolde-Selassie Abbute. 2000. 'Social Re-Articulation after Resettlement: Observing the Beles Valley Scheme in Ethiopia', in Cernea and McDowell (eds).

Wolde-Selassie Abbute. 1998. *The Dynamics of Socio-Economic Differentiation and Livelihood Strategies: The Case of Relocated Peasants in the Beles Valley, North-Western Ethiopia*. Discussion Paper No. 26. Göttingen: Institute of Rural Development, University of Göttingen.

Wolde-Selassie Abbute. 1997. 'The Dynamics of Socio-Economic Differentiation and Change in the Beles-Valley/Pawe Resettlement Area, North Western Ethiopia'. MA thesis in Social Anthropology, Addis Ababa University.

Wolf, Eric. 1966. *Peasants*. Englewood Cliffs, NJ: Prentice Hall.

Women's Affairs Office, FDRE and the World Bank. 1998. *Implementing the Ethiopian National Policy for Women: Institutional and Regulatory Issues*. Washington, DC: World Bank,

Wood, Adrian. 1985. 'Population Redistribution and Agricultural Settlement Schemes in Ethiopia 1958-80', in J. Clarke *et al.* (eds), *Population and Development Projects in Africa*. Cambridge: Cambridge University Press.

Wood, Adrian. 1982. 'Spontaneous Agricultural Resettlement in Ethiopia', in J. Carke and L. Kosinski (eds), *Redistribution of Population in Africa*. London: Heinemann.

Wood, Adrian. 1977. 'Resettlement in Illubabor Province, Ethiopia.' PhD dissertation. University of Liverpool.

World Bank. 2007. *Environmental Health and Safety Guidelines*. Washington, DC: World Bank.

World Bank. 2002. *World Development Report 2002: Building Institutions for Markets*. Washington, DC:

World Bank.

World Bank. 1998a. *Recent Experiences With Involuntary Resettlement: Thailand –Pak Mun*. Washington, DC: World Bank.

World Bank. 1998b. *Recent Experience With Involuntary Resettlement: Togo-Nangbeto*. Washington, DC: World Bank, Operations Evaluation Department, Report No. 17543.

World Bank. 1997. 'Project Appraisal Document. Federal Democratic Republic of Ethiopia'. Energy II Project Report No. 1717o-ET.

World Bank. 1995. 'From Emergency to Development: The Demobilization and Reintegration of Ex-Combatants in Ethiopia.' Draft Paper.

World Bank. 1994. *Resettlement and Development: The Bankwide Review of Projects Involving Involuntary Resettlement*. Washington, DC: World Bank.

World Bank. 1993. *Demobilization and Reintegration of Military Personnel in Africa: The Evidence from Seven Country Case Studies*. Washington, DC: Africa Regional Office, World Bank.

World Bank. 1988. *Involuntary Resettlement in Development Projects: Policy Guidelines in World Bank – Financed Projects*. Technical Paper No. 80. Washington, DC: World Bank.

World Commission on Dams (WCD). 2000a. *Dams and Development: A New Framework for Decision-Making*. London: Earthscan Publications.

WCD. 2000b. *Wcd Case Study: The Pak Mun Dam and Mekong River Basin, Thailand*. Final Draft, May.

World Health Organization. 1995. *World Mental Health: Problems and Priorities in Low-income Countries*. Geneva: World Health Organization.

Wubshet Dagne. 1997. 'An Assessment of the Life of Internally Displaced Person in Addis Ababa'. Senior Essay. Sociology and Anthropology Department. Addis Ababa University.

Yacob, Arsano.2000. 'Pastoralism in Ethiopia: The Issue of Viability', in *Proceedings of the National Conference on Pastoral Development in Ethiopia*. Addis Ababa, February.

Yacob Arsano. 1995. 'Development of Land Tenure Policies in Ethiopia with an Illustrative Case of the Ogaden' in Seyoum Gebre Sellassie (ed.), *Pastoral Land Tenure Systems in the Horn of Africa: A Compendium of Eight Case Studies from Ethiopia, Eritrea, and Sudan*. Addis Ababa: Pastoral and Environmental Network in the Horn of Africa (PENHA).

Yeneneh Tesfaye. 2005. 'Socio-Economic and Psychological Dimensions of Conflict, Displacement, and Post-war Reconstruction: The case of Zalanbasa town in Northeastern Tigray.' MA thesis in Social Anthropology, Addis Ababa University.

Yeraswork Admassie. 2000. *Twenty Years to Nowhere: Property Rights, Land Management and Conservation in Ethiopia*. Lawrenceville, NJ: Red Sea Press.

Yeraswork Admassie. 1995. *Twenty Years to Nowhere: Property Rights, Land Management and Conservation in Ethiopia*. Uppsala: University of Uppsala.

Yigremew Adal. 1997. 'Rural Land Holdings Readjustment in West Gojam, Amhara Region', *Ethiopian Journal of Development Research* 19 (2): 57-89.

Yisak Tafere. 2002. 'Socio-Economic Reintegration of Ex-Soldiers: A Case of Two Cooperatives: One Male and One Female in Addis Ababa.' MA thesis in Social Anthropology, Addis Ababa University.

Zelalem Abera. 2005. 'Resettlement and Environment in Peripheral Areas of North-Western Ethiopia: The case of Metemma, 1980s-2004.' MA thesis in Social Anthropology, Addis Ababa University.

Zenaw Assefa. 2007. 'Squatter Settlements, Urban Development Policies and Strategies, and the Struggle of the Peripheral Inhabitants of the Yeka Sub-city of Addis Ababa.' MA thesis in Social Anthropology, Addis Ababa University.

Zerihun Mohammed. 2007. 'Natural Resource Competition and Inter-Ethnic Conflict – The Case of Arsi Oromo and Sidama in South-Central Ethiopia.' PhD thesis. Department of Geography, University of Cambridge.

Zetter, R. 1995. 'Shelter Provision and Settlement Policies for Refugees', in *Studies on Emergencies and Disaster Relief*. Vol. 2. Uppsala: The Nordic Africa Institute.

Zolberg, A.A.R. and P.M. Benda (eds). 2001. *Global Migrants, Global Refugees, Present Solutions*. New York: Berghahn.

Zolberg, Aristide, Astri Suhrke, and S. Aguayo. 1989. *Escape from Violence: Conflict and Refugee Crises in the Developing World*. New York: Oxford University Press.

Index

EASTERN AFRICAN STUDIES

These titles published in the United States and Canada by Ohio University Press

Revealing Prophets
Edited by DAVID M. ANDERSON & DOUGLAS H. JOHNSON

East African Expressions of Christianity
Edited by THOMAS SPEAR & ISARIA N. KIMAMBO

The Poor Are Not Us
Edited by DAVID M. ANDERSON & VIGDIS BROCH-DUE

Potent Brews
JUSTIN WILLIS

Swahili Origins
JAMES DE VERE ALLEN

Being Maasai
Edited by THOMAS SPEAR & RICHARD WALLER

Jua Kali Kenya
KENNETH KING

Control & Crisis in Colonial Kenya
BRUCE BERMAN

Unhappy Valley
Book One: State & Class
Book Two: Violence & Ethnicity
BRUCE BERMAN & JOHN LONSDALE

Mau Mau from Below
GREET KERSHAW

The Mau Mau War in Perspective
FRANK FUREDI

Squatters & the Roots of Mau Mau 1905–63
TABITHA KANOGO

Economic & Social Origins of Mau Mau 1945–53
DAVID W. THROUP

Multi-Party Politics in Kenya
DAVID W. THROUP & CHARLES HORNSBY

Empire State-Building
JOANNA LEWIS

Decolonization & Independence in Kenya 1940–93
Edited by B.A. OGOT & WILLIAM R. OCHIENG'

Eroding the Commons
DAVID ANDERSON

Penetration & Protest in Tanzania
ISARIA N. KIMAMBO

Custodians of the Land
Edited by GREGORY MADDOX, JAMES L. GIBLIN & ISARIA N. KIMAMBO

Education in the Development of Tanzania 1919–1990
LENE BUCHERT

The Second Economy in Tanzania
T.L. MALIYAMKONO & M.S.D. BAGACHWA

Ecology Control & Economic Development in East African History
HELGE KJEKSHUS

Siaya
DAVID WILLIAM COHEN & E.S. ATIENO ODHIAMBO

Uganda Now • Changing Uganda
Developing Uganda • From Chaos to Order
Religion & Politics in East Africa
Edited by HOLGER BERNT HANSEN & MICHAEL TWADDLE

Kakungulu & the Creation of Uganda 1868–1928
MICHAEL TWADDLE

Controlling Anger
SUZETTE HEALD

Kampala Women Getting By
SANDRA WALLMAN

Political Power in Pre-Colonial Buganda
RICHARD J. REID

Alice Lakwena & the Holy Spirits
HEIKE BEHREND

Slaves, Spices & Ivory in Zanzibar
ABDUL SHERIFF

Zanzibar Under Colonial Rule
Edited by ABDUL SHERIFF & ED FERGUSON

The History & Conservation of Zanzibar Stone Town
Edited by ABDUL SHERIFF

Pastimes & Politics
LAURA FAIR

Ethnicity & Conflict in the Horn of Africa
Edited by KATSUYOSHI FUKUI & JOHN MARKAKIS

Conflict, Age & Power in North East Africa
Edited by EISEI KURIMOTO & SIMON SIMONSE

Property Rights & Political Development in Ethiopia & Eritrea
SANDRA FULLERTON JOIREMAN

Revolution & Religion in Ethiopia
ØYVIND M. EIDE

Brothers at War
TEKESTE NEGASH & KJETIL TRONVOLL

From Guerrillas to Government
DAVID POOL

Mau Mau & Nationhood
Edited by E.S. ATIENO ODHIAMBO & JOHN LONSDALE

A History of Modern Ethiopia, 1855–1991 (2nd edn)
BAHRU ZEWDE

Pioneers of Change in Ethiopia
BAHRU ZEWDE

Remapping Ethiopia
Edited by W. JAMES, D. DONHAM, E. KURIMOTO & A. TRIULZI

Southern Marches of Imperial Ethiopia
Edited by DONALD L. DONHAM & WENDY JAMES

A Modern History of the Somali (4th edn)
I.M. LEWIS

Islands of Intensive Agriculture in East Africa
Edited by MATS WIDGREN & JOHN E.G. SUTTON

Leaf of Allah
EZEKIEL GEBISSA

Dhows & the Colonial Economy of Zanzibar 1860–1970
ERIK GILBERT

African Womanhood in Colonial Kenya
TABITHA KANOGO

African Underclass
ANDREW BURTON

In Search of a Nation
Edited by GREGORY H. MADDOX & JAMES L. GIBLIN

A History of the Excluded
JAMES L. GIBLIN

Black Poachers, White Hunters
EDWARD I. STEINHART

Ethnic Federalism
DAVID TURTON

Crisis & Decline in Bunyoro
SHANE DOYLE

Emancipation without Abolition in German East Africa
JAN-GEORG DEUTSCH

Women, Work & Domestic Virtue in Uganda 1900–2003
GRACE BANTEBYA KYOMUHENDO & MARJORIE KENISTON McINTOSH

Cultivating Success in Uganda
GRACE CARSWELL

War in Pre-Colonial Eastern Africa
RICHARD REID

Slavery in the Great Lakes Region of East Africa
Edited by HENRI MÉDARD & SHANE DOYLE

The Benefits of Famine
DAVID KEEN